Webmastering For Dummies, 2nd Edition

Cheat Sheet

A Webmaster's Bookma...

Professional Organizations

The Association of Internet Professionals:
www.association.org
An organization for Web site pros of all types

The International Webmaster's Association:
www.iwanet.org
Establishes professional standards and certification guidelines

Webgrrls and SFWoW: www.webgrrls.com
and www.sfwow.org
Women Webworkers (and some guys) share resources

Management

The Industry Standard:
www.theindustrystandard.com
Offers Internet industry news, analysis, and opinion

Red Herring: www.redherring.com
Covers the business and investing side of technology

Fast Company: www.fastcompany.com
Chronicles new business practices

IDG.net: www.idg.net
A portal to industry magazines, research, and more

E-Commerce Management Center:
www.tauberkienan.com/ecommerce
Nuts-and-bolts e-commerce advice and tools

SmartAge: www.smartage.com
Running small business e-commerce Web sites

Tech Development

Developer Shed: www.devshed.com
Practical tech information and tools; free code

BrowserWatch: www.browserwatch.com
Keep track of news in the world of Web browsers

Server Watch: serverwatch.iworld.com
Feature-by-feature comparison of Web servers

Website Garage:
websitegarage.netscape.com
Services and tools for improving your site

Design and ...

UseIt.com: www...
Leading autho...

Builder.com: www.builder.com
Beginners' tutorials, advanced tips, product reviews

Webmonkey.com: www.webmonkey.com
A learning center for design and HTML writing

Web Pages That Suck:
www.webpagesthatsuck.com
Learn good design by looking at bad design

Lynda Weinman: www.lynda.com
Design tips and the browser-safe palette

HTML Master's Reference:
www.htmlreference.com
Easy reference to all the HTML 4 tags, style sheet attributes, and browser-specifc extensions

DreamInk: www.dreamlink.com
Tutorials galore: design, navigation, more

W3C's XML Information: www.w3c.org/XML
Defines XML and how to use it

Weblint: www.weblint.com
An installable error-checking tool

Backward Compatibility Viewer: www.delorie.com/Web/wpbcv.html
How your page will look in various browsers

Style Guides

The Yale C/AIM Web Style Guide:
info.med.yale.edu/caim/manual/index.html
It's a manual, it's a tutorial, it's a great place to learn about HTML style

Band-Aid AP Stylebook:
web.missouri.edu/%7Ejschool/missourian/style
A quick reference to editorial style

Webmastering For Dummies, 2nd Edition

A Webmaster's Bookmarks (continued)

Content

Poynter Institute: www.poynter.org
Research and advice on content, especially online journalism

Content Exchange:
www.contentexchange.com
Resources for content professionals

The Slot: www.theslot.com
A copy editor's take on good and bad English usage

Screaming Media and iSyndicate:
www.screamingmedia.com and
www.isyndicate.com
Services for the exchange of licensed content

Community

Virtual Communities:
virtualcommunities.start4all.com
A community-builder's portal

Liszt: www.liszt.com
Lists of online discussion groups

eGroups: www.egroups.com
Lets you start an e-mail discussion group

Zaplets: www.zaplets.com
Offers options for launching communities

TalkCity: www.talkcity.com
A high-end, big volume community hosting service

Commerce

RSA Data Security: www.rsa.com
"The Most Trusted Name in Cryptography"

CyberSource: www.cybersource.com
Valuable information about online transactions

CommerceNet: www.commercenet.com
An association promoting and serving e-commerce

Legalese

FindLaw: www.findlaw.com
A portal to law resources online

The Nolo Press Self-Help Law Center:
www.nolo.com
Covers all aspects of law, including intellectual property

To Market, to Market

Iconocast: www.iconocast.com
Marketing facts, analyses, and "insider" tips

ClickZ: www.clickz.com
Information, viewpoints, and tales from the trenches

Search Engine Watch:
www.searchenginewatch.com
Understanding search engines; optimizing for ranking

Awards

The Webbys: www.webbyawards.com
See the winners to see what's cutting edge

Cool Site of the Day: cool.infi.net
Another award you'd be proud to get

Employment and Contracting

CraigsList: www.craigslist.com
Ads and notices related to the Net industry

Design Firms: www.designfirms.com
Searchable directory of design firms

Proven Resumes: www.provenresumes.com
How to write effective resumes in digital formats

Salary.com: www.salary.com
Standard job descriptions; salary comparison tool

Hungry Minds™

For Dummies®: Bestselling Book Series for Beginners

TM

BESTSELLING BOOK SERIES

References for the Rest of Us!®

Are you intimidated and confused by computers? Do you find that traditional manuals are overloaded with technical details you'll never use? Do your friends and family always call you to fix simple problems on their PCs? Then the ...For Dummies® computer book series from Hungry Minds, Inc. is for you.

...For Dummies books are written for those frustrated computer users who know they aren't really dumb but find that PC hardware, software, and indeed the unique vocabulary of computing make them feel helpless. ...For Dummies books use a lighthearted approach, a down-to-earth style, and even cartoons and humorous icons to dispel computer novices' fears and build their confidence. Lighthearted but not lightweight, these books are a perfect survival guide for anyone forced to use a computer.

> *"I like my copy so much I told friends; now they bought copies."*
> — Irene C., Orwell, Ohio

> *"Quick, concise, nontechnical, and humorous."*
> — Jay A., Elburn, Illinois

> *"Thanks, I needed this book. Now I can sleep at night."*
> — Robin F., British Columbia, Canada

Already, millions of satisfied readers agree. They have made ...For Dummies books the #1 introductory level computer book series and have written asking for more. So, if you're looking for the most fun and easy way to learn about computers, look to ...For Dummies books to give you a helping hand.

Hungry Minds™

Webmastering
FOR
DUMMIES®
2ND EDITION

by Daniel A. Tauber and Brenda Kienan

Hungry Minds™

HUNGRY MINDS, INC.

New York, NY ◆ Cleveland, OH ◆ Indianapolis, IN
Chicago, IL ◆ Foster City, CA ◆ San Francisco, CA

Webmastering For Dummies,® 2nd Edition

Published by
Hungry Minds, Inc.
909 Third Avenue
New York, NY 10022
www.hungryminds.com
www.dummies.com (Dummies Press Web site)

Library of Congress Control Number: 00-108202

ISBN: 0-7645-0777-X

Printed in the United States of America

10 9 8 7 6 5 4 3 2

2O/QT/QS/QR/IN

Distributed in the United States by Hungry Minds, Inc.

Distributed by CDG Books Canada Inc. for Canada; by Transworld Publishers Limited in the United Kingdom; by IDG Norge Books for Norway; by IDG Sweden Books for Sweden; by IDG Books Australia Publishing Corporation Pty. Ltd. for Australia and New Zealand; by TransQuest Publishers Pte Ltd. for Singapore, Malaysia, Thailand, Indonesia, and Hong Kong; by Gotop Information Inc. for Taiwan; by ICG Muse, Inc. for Japan; by Intersoft for South Africa; by Eyrolles for France; by International Thomson Publishing for Germany, Austria and Switzerland; by Distribuidora Cuspide for Argentina; by LR International for Brazil; by Galileo Libros for Chile; by Ediciones ZETA S.C.R. Ltda. for Peru; by WS Computer Publishing Corporation, Inc., for the Philippines; by Contemporanea de Ediciones for Venezuela; by Express Computer Distributors for the Caribbean and West Indies; by Micronesia Media Distributor, Inc. for Micronesia; by Chips Computadoras S.A. de C.V. for Mexico; by Editorial Norma de Panama S.A. for Panama; by American Bookshops for Finland.

For general information on Hungry Minds' products and services please contact our Customer Care Department within the U.S. at 800-762-2974, outside the U.S. at 317-572-3993 or fax 317-572-4002.

For sales inquiries and reseller information, including discounts, premium and bulk quantity sales, and foreign-language translations, please contact our Customer Care Department at 800-434-3422, fax 317-572-4002, or write to Hungry Minds, Inc., Attn: Customer Care Department, 10475 Crosspoint Boulevard, Indianapolis, IN 46256.

For information on licensing foreign or domestic rights, please contact our Sub-Rights Customer Care Department at 650-653-7098.

For authorization to photocopy items for corporate, personal, or educational use, please contact Copyright Clearance Center, 222 Rosewood Drive, Danvers, MA 01923, or fax 978-750-4470.

For information on using Hungry Minds' products and services in the classroom or for ordering examination copies, please contact our Educational Sales Department at 800-434-2086 or fax 317-572-4005.

Please contact our Public Relations Department at 212-884-5163 for press review copies or 212-884-5000 for author interviews and other publicity information or fax 212-884-5400.

Hungry Minds™ is a trademark of Hungry Minds, Inc.

About the Authors

Daniel A. Tauber and **Brenda Kienan** met as employees of a computer book publishing company and immediately recognized each other as obsessive and highly geeky. Within a very short time, they set out to write books together, and in the course of that, Dan introduced Brenda to the Internet (well, newsgroups, really, because the Web and Web browsers were just glints in the eyes of their inventors at the time). They did much of the research for their early books on the Internet, and thus Dan made Brenda into the Internet junkie she became. Not too long after that, the Web debuted, Webmastering beckoned, and they both changed jobs.

Things got very interesting very quickly. You see, while these two had always enjoyed a good adventure, they didn't fully realize that being pioneers meant walking across the continent behind a wagon, dodging oxen poop. What's more, no one told them that no maps were yet available. They, along with a small army of other Internet pioneers, learned a lot of lessons the hard way, which maybe isn't so bad — after all, this book is the result of that experience.

Dan, by the way, is now an e-commerce technology executive. He has a degree in computer science, and in the course of his career as an Internet professional has led technical development of Web sites for Fortune 500 companies and the publishing industry.

Brenda has produced, directed, and acquired content for the e-commerce, publishing, and search engine industries, and has managed teams ranging from two to 46 people. She shares her knowledge by teaching and speaking on e-commerce management and content strategy at a variety of venues.

Daniel A. Tauber and Brenda Kienan have written twelve books. They're married now (to each other) and they have a daughter who will never know what the world was like before the Internet changed it.

You can visit their Web site at www.tauberkienan.com.

Dedication

To Lori, Jacob, Jessi, Kevin, and Sarah, with bright hopes for their futures.

Authors' Acknowledgments

This one was another dash to the finish. For their efforts and support we'd like to thank the many people who made it possible.

At IDG, thanks to Steve Hayes for signing us up; to Michael McCue for reviewing the legal chapter; to Shirley Jones for shepherding us through development with kindness and wisdom; to Kim Darosett, Rebecca Huehls, Amy Pettinella, and Jill Mazurczyk for buffing the manuscript to a sparkle; to Allen Wyatt for checking details; and to Amanda Foxworth, Maridee Ennis and all the production crew for forging edited manuscript into printed matter; also to all the Dummies groups for their gung-ho enthusiasm.

Thanks to Savitha Varadan, who drafted several chapters, and Maureen Nelson, who researched several more. Kim Albee, Grace Allison, Barbara Bruxvoort, Diane Rowett Castro, Debra Goldentyer, Tamra Heathershaw-Hart, Barbara Holmes, Carolyn Lamont, Claudia L'Amoreaux, Marcy Lyon, Bob McLean, Mitch Levy, Ann Marie Michaels, Ann Navarro, Kim Nies, Melissa Rach, Valerie Singer, Michael Stein, Akemi Tazaki, J. Tarin Towers, and C. J. Yem all contributed thoughts or influence. Our thanks to each of those fine people, as well as to Brenda's students, who ask all the right questions. From the Association of Internet Professionals, Cybernauts, Bay Area Editors' Forum, Webgrrls, and San Francisco Women on the Web, we receive valuable insights daily; our ongoing thanks to everyone there.

Dave and Sherry Rogelberg at Studio B are just the best. Thanks to them for all they do.

Our family and friends have our constant gratitude if not our constant attention. Thanks as always to Joani and Jessica Buehrle; Sharon Crawford and Charlie Russel; Kevin, Caitlin, and the little Cunninghams; Rion Dugan; Fred Frumberg; Jessica, Martin, and the wee Grants; Caroline Heller; Mai Le Bazner, Katri Foster, and Peter Bazner; the McArdle and Undercoffer families; Carolyn Miller; Lonnie Moseley and Cordell Sloan; Wynn Moseley and her family; Margaret Tauber; Ron and Frances Tauber; Judy Tauber; and Robert E. Williams III. Many thanks to Claire Elizabeth Tauber, both for "copperating" and for making it clear where our priorities lie.

Thanks also to John and Aida Bjorklund, Nina Duhl, Kent Gerard, Jill Goldreyer, Ana Ortiz, and Charlie Wright, who kept heart, health, and hearth pasted together during the writing blitz. And finally, thanks to the best auntie-godmother a little girl ever had for being there so often and so well. We couldn't have done it without you.

Publisher's Acknowledgments

WWe're proud of this book; please send us your comments through our Online Registration Form located at www.dummies.com.

Some of the people who helped bring this book to market include the following:

Acquisitions, Editorial, and Media Development

Project Editor: Shirley A. Jones

Acquisitions Editor: Steven H. Hayes

Copy Editors: Kim Darosett, Rebecca Huehls, Amy Pettinella

Proof Editor: Jill Mazurczyk

Technical Editors: Allen Wyatt, Michael McCue

Editorial Manager: Leah P. Cameron

Editorial Assistant: Seth Kerney

Production

Project Coordinator: Maridee Ennis

Layout and Graphics: Karl Brandt, Beth Brooks, LeAndra Johnson, Jacque Schneider, Brian Torwelle, Jeremey Unger

Proofreaders: Laura Albert, Corey Bowen, Vickie Broyles, Joel Draper, Carl Pierce, York Production Services, Inc.

Indexer: York Production Services, Inc.

Special Help
Diana R. Conover, Curtis Miller, Rebecca Senninger

General and Administrative

Hungry Minds, Inc.: John Kilcullen, CEO; Bill Barry, President and COO; John Ball, Executive VP, Operations & Administration; John Harris, CFO

Hungry Minds Technology Publishing Group: Richard Swadley, Senior Vice President and Publisher; Mary Bednarek, Vice President and Publisher, Networking and Certification; Walter R. Bruce III, Vice President and Publisher, General User and Design Professional; Joseph Wikert, Vice President and Publisher, Programming; Mary C. Corder, Editorial Director, Branded Technology Editorial; Andy Cummings, Publishing Director, General User and Design Professional; Barry Pruett, Publishing Director, Visual

Hungry Minds Manufacturing: Ivor Parker, Vice President, Manufacturing

Hungry Minds Marketing: John Helmus, Assistant Vice President, Director of Marketing

Hungry Minds Online Management: Brenda McLaughlin, Executive Vice President, Chief Internet Officer

Hungry Minds Production for Branded Press: Debbie Stailey, Production Director

Hungry Minds Sales: Roland Elgey, Senior Vice President, Sales and Marketing; Michael Violano, Vice President, International Sales and Sub Rights

◆

The publisher would like to give special thanks to Patrick J. McGovern, without whom this book would not have been possible.

◆

Contents at a Glance

Cartoons at a Glance

By Rich Tennant

page 373

page 7

page 293

page 153

page 357

Fax: 978-546-7747
E-mail: richtennant@the5thwave.com
World Wide Web: www.the5thwave.com

Table of Contents

Part 1V: Working: Get Credentials, Get Hired, Hire Others *357*

Introduction

· ·

A few years ago, when we left our more traditional jobs and ventured into the world of Web work, we said we wanted to be pioneers. This was our chance to zip off toward the frontier, and we couldn't have been more optimistic. We sent out a few résumés, got new jobs, and headed bravely into the unknown. Sheesh. Someone might have told us that being a pioneer means walking across the continent behind a wagon, dodging oxen poop all the while, and feeling never quite sure you're headed in the right direction.

This is the book we wish we'd had when we started out. It's packed with the sum of our experience on the wildest adventure we might have imagined. It's also packed with tips and tidbits we picked up from a lot of other smart people who headed into an adventure with bright shining eyes but no idea what they were getting into.

Who You Are and What You Already Know

You may come from any of several backgrounds. Not all Webmasters are programmers or system administrators; some are content people, designers, production folk, even managers. Truth be told, when we set out to be Internet professionals, we thought one of us was a Webmaster but one of us was not. One of us, a techie, had gotten it in mind way back when the Web was being born that he wanted to put together a Web server, and he spent evenings and weekends doing just that, right under his company's nose, without them knowing. That's how lots of Webmasters came into being in those days, and it was clear to both of us that he (Dan) was a Webmaster. His path started with that first server and led to technical development of very big Web sites.

Meanwhile, the other of us (Brenda) went about the business of creating and developing content, without knowing for a long time exactly what to call herself professionally. Content manager? Online publisher? Producer? Not a programmer and no system developer, she was never inclined to call herself a Webmaster, but felt confident in her skills as a content creator, developer, and strategist, and as a Web team manager. She had no trouble finding work in an industry that for a good while didn't even have an agreed upon title for her.

Finding the Webmasters' Guild definition of a Webmaster (quoted at the beginning of Chapter 1) was a great revelation to us — at last a clear, comprehensive description of what a Webmaster is and does. Voilà — we were *both* Webmasters. (There's nothing like a little external validation in life.) Later, the Webmasters' Guild folded itself into the Association of Internet Professionals, and more clear definitions of the various roles that team members could play in building and running a Web site were developed. (Dan now acts as a technology executive and Brenda as an executive producer and content strategist.)

You may have opted for being an Internet pro because you thought it would be a lot of fun (it is), or you may have had contributing to or running the Web site thrust upon you as part of your job. In either case, this book is for you. It's also for those who manage and hire Internet people, and even those who are investigating Web strategies to see what's best for their company. You may be an executive, a hiring manager, a system administrator, a designer, a marketeer, a "usability analyst," or an HTML jockey. Whatever your position in the scheme of things, we think this book will provide you with strategies you can use in creating and implementing your Web endeavor from budget through concept, staffing, implementation, and maintenance. We even cover promoting your site and measuring your success.

We do assume that you have knowledge of the Internet and its tools and that you're comfortable talking the talk of browsers, ftp, servers, and clients. You needn't be a programmer, nor need you aspire to becoming a programmer. You don't even have to know HTML, though you do know what HTML is.

What This Book Covers

From soup to nuts, this book covers Webmastering — all sorts of Webmastering, including content development, design, production, tech stuff, and management. Above all, this book is about how to create a strategy, how to follow it through successfully, and how to know you have succeeded. Sure, we talk about how to create a smashing site, but we also talk about hiring a team, jobbing out to front-end firms and back-end developers, creating a budget, legal pitfalls, selling on the Web (as well as other sorts of e-commerce), promoting your site, and more.

Part 1: Who You Are and Where You Start

Logically enough, we start with what Internet professionals do, what roles they play, how they interact on a team, and where Internet pros can meet each other to trade tips and technologies. We also cover setting goals for your site, because that's the foundation on which a winning Web site is based. We introduce the notorious three Cs — content, community, and commerce — and describe how each can fit into your overall strategy. Of course we also delve into selling on the Web so you can determine whether that's a worthy goal for your site. Then we finish off with the one-two combination of budgeting and some legal bugaboos you should watch out for. This is all basic stuff you need to know about to get your site strategy in place and get going.

Part II: Building: Organize, Implement, Deploy, Launch

Planning and creating a site is a big job. We cover these topics from beginning to end, telling you about the all-important process of organizing content, creating a site map and storyboard, working out specs and creating a request for proposal, and so on. We also walk you through HTML and the stuff that jazzes up plain Web pages, as well as snappy newer options like XML. Then we cruise you through the ins and outs of working with design shops, front-end firms, and back-end developers both big and small, offering scads of tips gleaned from working in the industry.

This is no server administrator's book (there are plenty of those around), but every Internet pro should know enough about the tech end to be able to make sound judgments. And so we peek behind stage to have a look at various tech delights: Web servers, types of connections, databases, and transaction systems. We also cover dealing with ISPs, hosting companies, and database developers (who sometimes seem to speak a different language than the rest of us).

Part III: Winning: Promote Your Site and Assess Its Success

After you've created a winning Web site, you'll want to let others know about it. In Part III, we cover how to mix online promotion and offline promotion, and the ins and outs of each. We go into listing your site with online indexes and search engines (Yahoo!, Google, AltaVista, and the like). We tell you how to find out how many backlinks lead from other sites to yours. We also introduce promoting your site in a variety of creative ways ranging from using traditional print media to . . . well, you'll see. And finally, we cover the various ways you can measure success in an industry that just a year ago offered few standards and even fewer means of measuring. All in all, we tell you how to win and how to know you have won.

Part IV: Working: Get Credentials, Get Hired, Hire Others

Whether you're looking for work or looking for workers, you need to know what makes a Webmaster qualified and where Internet pros get their credentials. Part IV follows up on topics introduced back in Chapter 1 and touched on throughout the book. It covers what makes a Webmaster a Webmaster — what fresh and transferrable skills an Internet pro should have and where Webmasters get their training.

In Chapter 18, we describe for those doing the hiring what to look for in job candidates. We also offer to job seekers some tips from the pros about what to do to get a foot in the right door. Perhaps best of all, in Chapter 19 we offer you who are new to the field some questions you may want to ask prospective employers and yourself before you take that oh-so-promising job with an Internet start-up company!

Part V: The Part of Tens

As an added bonus, we offer several chapters at the end of this book that are filled with quick tips, tricks, and ideas you can put into play right away. We describe ten techniques for managing projects like the pro you are; ten indications that it's time to redesign your site; and ten methods for managing content, keeping it fresh, and assuring yourself as well as your site's users that yours is the high quality content they seek and enjoy.

How to Use This Book

You needn't read this book cover to cover. Simply flip to the sections that interest you as you face one challenge or another. Or, if you want to get a complete overview of the craft of running a Web site, go ahead and read the whole thing — we're not stopping you!

Icons Used in This Book

This book is dotted with nifty icons marking text that's of special interest. Here's what all those nifty icons mean:

This one points out important bits of information you won't want to forget.

Shortcuts, tricks, winning tactics — they're all marked with this icon. To save yourself time and cut straight to winning strategies, look here.

The world won't end if you fail to heed advice marked by this icon, but you probably ought to listen up anyway. You'll save yourself a lot of grief if you do.

You probably already know that the Web is teeming with information — this icon flags URLs that will help you in your Webmastering endeavors. You'll want to bookmark many of these sites.

To find out what others who've gone before you have to say, look for this icon. It marks quotes from experienced Internet folk, anecdotes based on our own experience in the field, and stories from the real world of Webmastering.

Contacting the Authors

If you'd like to drop us a line, send kudos, straighten us out on something, or pass along a tip, send e-mail to webmastering@tauberkienan.com. If you'd like to see what we've been up to or look into other resources we offer, visit our Web site at www.tauberkienan.com.

Off You Go

This book is meant to act as your guide to the wonderful world of Webmastering. Just because we ventured into the frontier unprepared doesn't mean you have to. It's still a brave new world out there, and you're headed for a big adventure. Keep this book beside you and, as you go, flip to the section you need. Have fun!

Part I
Who You Are and Where You Start

The 5th Wave   By Rich Tennant

"Just how accurately should my Web site reflect my place of business?"

In this part . . .

Some people are born Webmasters (well, not many), some become Webmasters, and some have Webmastering thrust upon them. Whichever description fits you and whatever your focus (content, tech, design and production, marketing, business, or management), you need a firm foundation in what you do and where to start. That's what this part is all about.

In Part I, we tell you all about different types of Internet professionals, what they actually do, and how they work together as teams. We also walk you through setting goals for your online enterprise or project; understanding content, community, and commerce; creating a budget; and the legal bugaboos you ought to be familiar with before you get rolling.

Chapter 1

What Webmasters Really, Really Do

In This Chapter

▶ Definition of a Webmaster

▶ The many roles of today's Webmasters

▶ The types: tech, content, design and production, marketing and business, executive

*1*t's the hippest, coolest job anyone could have, isn't it? Now, *what is it you do, exactly?* Ask any ten people in the industry what a Webmaster is or does, and they'll offer a variety of answers. Guess what. They're probably all correct. Basically, a Webmaster is the person who runs or manages a Web site. That's simple enough, and most folks in the industry can agree up to that point. But beyond that — at the point where you start talking about what skills, credentials, and qualities a Webmaster should have — opinions take off in every direction. Depending on who's doing the talking, a Webmaster may be a fresh-faced, entry-level programmer; a senior programmer with database skills; or a marketing manager with years of experience. The Webmasters' Guild (now folded into the Association of Internet Professionals `www.association.org`), created this definition:

> "The goal of a Webmaster is to design, implement, and maintain an effective Web site. To achieve this, a Webmaster must possess knowledge of fields as diverse as network configuration, interface and graphic design, software development, business strategy, writing, and project management. Because the function of a Webmaster encompasses so many areas, the position is often not held by a single person but by a team of individuals."

Historically, the first person who stood up in a company and advocated having a Web site became the Webmaster by default. That's not so bad — evangelizing is actually an important part of running a Web site. First, there is the evangelizing that leads to getting a green light from top management to create a site and then the evangelizing of the site to the world at large. But skills of persuasion alone don't make a Webmaster. Especially (but not solely) when one person holds responsibility for the Web site, he or she must also have a keen understanding of the company's core business, knowledge of the Internet and its technologies, solid marketing savvy (especially if the site's purpose is marketing), the ability to put himself or herself in the user's shoes, and so on. Perhaps the most important quality a Webmaster can show is vision — you *are* inventing the future, after all — combined with hard-nosed practicality and a dash of deep curiosity.

There are Webmasters and there are *Webmasters.* Some are the technical sort, who administer servers, and some are more responsible for the site's content, its look, or perhaps its overall management. In this book, when we refer to a Webmaster (or site manager), we're talking about the person who "owns" a Web site — the guy or gal who has overall responsibility for running the show. In cases where the job is done by a cast of two or even thousands, we're still going to call that collective group the Webmaster (except when we call it the *Web team* or when we refer to one specific job that might be held by a team member or the site manager). Now, what is it that the Webmaster does again?

Webmaster Roles and Reasons for Being

When the Web was very, very young (say, in 1994), there were maybe a handful of people who called themselves *Webmasters,* and they were mainly tech folks who, for one reason or another, figured they should put together a Web server. In those days, the Webmaster may have set up the server and maintained it, may have done all the programming or HTML coding, and then may have whipped up a nifty design (well, at least it was nifty to that person's eye). The self-appointed Webmaster probably also wrote every speck of copy for the site. Web sites were simple back then. Henry Ford once said you could have a Model T in any color as long as it was *black;* similarly, in the "old" days of Webmastering, the constraints of HTML were such that you could create a Web site in any color, as long as it was gray, with simple black text and blue links.

Ah, but those days are long gone. One day someone in the company caught on to the technical whiz's secret hobby — it may have been about the time the Internet became a familiar phrase on television. Suddenly the Web site became *important.* Today, creating a company Web site is more often a high-profile activity that involves an entire team. That team may include someone to plan and manage the site, someone to write or edit the content, a marketeer, a designer, a tech wizard, and more. Even in a small one-person operation, where a single soul is charged with creating a Web site, the roles and responsibilities of that person are increasingly diverse.

Tim Berners-Lee may easily be considered the original Webmaster. His home page (`www.w3.org/People/Berners-Lee/`) even says something to the effect that he invented the World Wide Web — which he did.

The Webmaster as visionary

Unfortunately, many folks cling to the familiar. Adventurous as the human spirit may be, human beings also fear what they don't know, so the relationship of our species to change is ambivalent at best. We do explore — we head for new continents, new planets, new ideas, new technologies. Then, when we get there, we try to make whatever we discover into what we already know. We settle new lands by re-creating our home culture, and we interpret new ideas by comparing them to the familiar — sometimes by even failing to comprehend the new idea just because it is unfamiliar and other times by turning what's new into the familiar! It takes people a while to willingly embrace and weave into their lives the new and the different.

A Webmaster must be able not only to see into the future but also to invent it. A Webmaster — even a Webmaster working in solitude on a small site — must be able to envision the site and how it will look, work, and fulfill its promise. A great Webmaster can embrace new technologies and apply them as appropriate to fulfill the Web initiative's goals. What's more, a Webmaster should be able to describe that vision of the future in such clear terms that he or she can win others over to it.

The Webmaster as evangelist

Powers of persuasion come in very handy for the Webmaster. In the course of events, he or she may find it necessary to first sell a specific Web initiative to the company and then sell the idea that the project is a worthy cause. After the first rush of excitement the Web inspired, many companies began to realize that a Web site was not a free ride. For much of 1996 and again in 2000 (when Internet stocks took a dramatic tumble), *retrenchment* was the watchword. Did the site make money? Where were the riches everyone expected to roll in so easily? Luckily, people got a better grip in 1997, and since 2000, the industry has shaken itself down again into companies that have the strong business models required to succeed and companies that don't and won't.

A Webmaster's role may include assessing the company's strategy and persuading the powers that be that the described Web initiative is the way to go, but that role may also involve reeling in expectations and focusing on what the Web site can realistically do for the company. Evangelizing the site to the outside world — marketing the site itself — is the subject of Chapters 15 and 16.

The Webmaster, who has presumably embraced an evolving, dynamic world filled with change, must also help foster in others some level of comfort with change. On the Internet, things change very quickly. It may not be clear to a company's decision makers that new tools are needed every few months to keep up with the dynamic rate of movement on the Web. The Webmaster may have to work at convincing certain executives that the request for a Sun workstation or a T1 line is not frivolous but is indeed well thought through.

To get and keep confidence that the site is worthwhile and that investing in new tools is not throwing good money after bad, the Webmaster must continue to evangelize the online opportunity, the site, and the ability of the Web site to fulfill the company's business goals. (See Chapter 2 to look into setting goals for the site that align with company goals.)

The Webmaster as business strategist

A company's Web site shouldn't be just a company hobby. Like everything else the company does, the Web site — to be successful and to be seen as successful — should further the company's overall ambitions. A company Web site should operate based on a business plan that's geared toward making and keeping the Web initiative effective and manageable. In this case, the Webmaster acts as a business strategist, defining and prioritizing goals for the Web site and generally managing the fulfillment of the site's mission. The site's goals, of course, should be based on those of the company.

At first, a Webmaster may find that keeping a tight rein aimed at a focused goal is the way to go. As with any business initiative, early successes can lead to the kind of recognition that brings bigger budgets and the resources needed for more ambitious projects. When dealing with a Web endeavor, striking out toward a bold result can also lead to bigger budgets. Whether that or the narrow-focus strategy is best in a given company is one of the many business judgments a Webmaster may make.

The intrepid Webmaster, fulfilling the role of business strategist, often finds that various departments in the company have differing — or even conflicting — wishes for the way the Web site strategy should go. Here, again, is an opportunity for the Webmaster to act as a business strategist, in this case judging which is the best direction from an overall business perspective. Forget going in all possible directions — trying everything and seeing what works is never a good idea.

Keep in mind that most business endeavors succeed if they have less than three key objectives. Prioritizing those objectives up front is also usually a wise move. Chapter 2 is geared toward helping you focus on your goals.

It's up to the Webmaster to help the company see the opportunities available in the Web site enterprise and to exploit them fully. By their very nature and because the medium is still in its youth, Web site initiatives are a risky business. A Webmaster may be called on in the most conservative of blue-suited companies to propose a venture and predict its success without the long-term, hard data normally required to back up the plan. A clear sense of business judgment and confidence in assessing the suitability of the venture can really come in handy. Skill at adapting to frequent, large-scale change is an asset, as is an ability to help the company and its people to adapt similarly on the fly.

The goal of the site is *always* to advance the goals of the company. This means that, while the Webmaster may yearn deeply to be first on the block to implement a shiny new technology, he or she has to consider the business implications of every aspect of the site, including the relative wisdom of implementing something that's exciting but untested in the marketplace.

A Web site's success from a business viewpoint can be hard to measure. The online industry is still young; mileposts, metrics, and benchmarks are in development but not yet universally accepted. It often falls to the Webmaster to guide the company in developing its expectations of the online initiative and then manage the company's expectations as things change. Chapter 17 covers measuring success as it is currently seen.

The Webmaster as manager of expectations

Someone has to see to it that everyone whose opinion counts in a company understands what can and can't be done on, through, and to the company Web site. Historically, the first barrier to implementing a Web site has often been that people didn't understand what could be done; they had no specific expectations of the site because they didn't know what to expect.

In a subsequent phase — the enthusiasm phase — people often get very excited and want to post everything within reach on the company Web site. They may imagine that millions are going to flock to the site just because it's been launched or that millions are going to buy the company's wonderwidgets just because they're shown on the Web site. Expectations in this phase have risen to an unreasonable level, making the likelihood that the site is going to be *seen* as successful very slim, even if it actually *is* successful.

The Webmaster's task is to guide the company in clearly setting and understanding realistic goals for the site and in assessing what resources are needed to meet those goals. Both actual costs and opportunity costs have to be considered: If we post x on the site, we are spending our resources and can't do y — is that the right business choice? The Webmaster must lay out a thoughtful plan, manage expectations as they arise, and manage the perception of results. (You may think of the Webmaster as sometimes slipping into the role of spin doctor!) Measuring success, again, is the topic of Chapter 17.

The Webmaster as creative implementer

With all the roles a Webmaster has — acting as visionary, evangelist, business strategist, and manager of expectations — at the end of the day, the Webmaster must have implemented a winning site that runs reliably 24 hours a day, 7 days a week. To make that so, he or she must engage in a long list of ordinary activities, which range from server and database maintenance through checking links and logs and ending, perhaps, in creatively implementing content.

For many Webmasters, the tasks involved in maintaining the site are a joy. Many Webmasters love doing server maintenance — somehow it seems like polishing or tinkering with a fine car. There is surprising room for creativity in everyday tasks, and for the Webmaster, devising a better system for checking the error logs may be one of the special, warm-hearted moments of Webmastering.

What's more, because the site's basic purpose is to further the goals of the company, the Webmaster sometimes has to simply implement content or methodology that someone else sees as urgent. In those moments, it's the Webmaster's task to bring forward the best in that content, making it as easy to navigate and as dynamic and useful as any of his or her own pet content. The Webmaster's responsibilities are to the user, to the site, and to fulfilling the site's mission.

The Five Types of Webmasters

It's the rare Webmaster today who has sole, overall responsibility for a large company Web site; often various team members are given specific assignments and roles. The team may include one or more people who handle technical development or administration; several who do design and production; others who create, edit, or acquire content; and still more who establish and manage business relationships between the Web endeavor and outside partners. Someone called a producer, who is responsible for making the project come alive, may manage the site and those members of the team responsible for making the site happen. And yet more, higher-up executives may be responsible for the overall Internet enterprise. Note that among all these people, many will never lay eyes on the server itself. In the sections that follow, we discuss the various jobs a "Webmaster" (meaning an Internet professional who is an involved member of a Web team) may have.

There are five basic types of Webmasters. However, in some cases, a single Webmaster takes on all the jobs described in the following sections in a one-person-band approach. This is certainly the case in a small company, or in an organization where the Web site is not mission critical or where the online initiative's budget is small. If that's the case where you are, it's still important to know and understand the various roles a Webmaster may have and how these roles interact.

You may be tempted to save a few bucks by assigning responsibility for your company Web site to someone in a seemingly related department — for example, marketing — as something to do in his or her spare time. Remember that fulfilling such a responsibility is a very low priority to that person. If your site is important enough to create, it's probably important enough to assign to someone who knows what he or she is doing. Chapter 18 describes hiring qualified Internet professionals.

If your Web site "team" is really a one-person band, find someone who can strategize, organize, edit, and control documents as well as manage projects (including hiring and overseeing outside contractors). This person should be able to code HTML, but you can contract out the real technology and design. You should also send the text out to a freelance editor for quality assurance. All that won't be terribly difficult if you have a good site manager on your side. Again, to know what roles you're asking your site manager (or Webmaster) to do or to manage, read on.

The tech Webmaster

In a first-things-first world, the one, true Webmaster is the person who keeps the technical underpinnings of the site shiny and running smoothly. This person may be responsible for overseeing the server (or maybe even *servers* if the site is a very big one), for keeping the connection going, for seeing to it that any database back ends are nicely integrated into the site systems, and for reading the log files and responding to any problems that may occur.

The tech-type Webmaster may also be called on to do programming, coding, scripting, database development, and search-engine configuration, or to spec and buy hardware and software or get bids from vendors. (Whew!)

A typical tech team working on a large Web site may consist of a CTO (chief technical officer) and/or a technical lead (or director of technology or some such) supervising some combination of the following:

- **A system architect:** Responsible for the overall technical strategy for the Web site
- **Database administrators (also known as DBAs):** Design, manage, and monitor the database
- **A system administrator or network administrator:** Keeps the servers and networking running
- **Developers or programmers:** Write programs in Java, C++, Perl, or some other appropriate language
- **HTML coders:** Usually *hard code* (write code manaully rather than with authoring software such as Microsoft FrontPage) to create Web pages

Note that these definitions aren't strict — the HTML coders can and do often write some Perl or Java, for example, and sometimes the system administrator, programmer, coder, and system architect are all rolled into one.

Webmastering as a team effort

Bob Maclean, a director of technology managing a team responsible for eight Web sites, says, "Most large-scale commercial sites have a diverse group of technical people working on them. Their skills range from system administration to software development to project management. This is in addition, of course, to the content, design, production, and other people. It's crucial for all these people to understand and respect each other's roles. Everyone must be working toward a common goal that's aligned with the company's business plan, and the project's endgame has to be clear to the whole team."

It's not strictly necessary for any tech Webmaster to have a degree in computer science — a solid background in the skills is more important. Someone who has been responsible for keeping a LAN or a big database running or who has been actively engaged in software development has the basic skills needed for these jobs. Knowledge of TCP/IP is a big plus — a requirement for the system administrator and a help in the other jobs. Programming skills in Java, C++, or Perl are a plus for any of these positions and a requirement for programmers and architects.

Tech Webmasters absolutely must have a fundamental curiosity about the tools of their jobs, because they have to stay on top of technological trends. If you're hiring a tech Webmaster, you need to find someone with plenty of enthusiasm and some intellectual adventure. On the other hand, the system administrator, for example, also has to be diligent enough to read log files regularly and disciplined enough to stay on top of what those log files reveal.

The technical positions are obviously very important — without the server, there is no Web site. What's more, the techie is doing his or her job best when the effects of the work are invisible to others. Think about this: If the server is running well and the connection never goes down, it's easy for the clueless to start wondering what the techie is doing with his or her time. We've seen cases where the techie looks like a hero for repairing systems that crash all the time. Keep in mind that the truly heroic tech Webmaster is the one who maintains a stable, smooth-running, trouble-free system.

It's also *very* important for other members of the Web site team to consult the tech people before forging ahead with plans to alter the site; all too often, some piece of the technical underpinnings may be at stake. For example, marketing folks may think it's a fine idea to add personalization on every page in the site. But if they were to consult with the technical people, they may find that implementing such extensive personalization on this particular site would trip up the server's successful handling of online transactions.

The bottom line is that, while the techie's job, when done successfully, is often seemingly invisible, the techie's presence in matters of creating and implementing what goes online should be very high profile. It is a bad idea to simply expect this person to find a way to put in place whatever the rest of the team thinks should be done. When anyone on the Web site team has a scheme for implementing just about anything that doesn't already exist on the site, the first step should always be to consult with the technical team.

The content Webmaster

It's pretty unlikely for one person to have the hard-core technical skills of a tech Webmaster *and* be well versed in handling content. If you're putting together a team but can hire only two people, these two people should be a techie and a content professional. The content Webmaster is typically responsible for, well, creating and managing content. That can mean as little as writing, editing, and posting static Web pages or as much as driving strategy for a bigger Web site that uses state-of-the-art technologies for managing and delivering content.

The content Webmaster may be charged with selecting or acquiring content, determining how the site's offerings will be presented, establishing the style of writing, and overseeing fulfillment of the site's *branding* (its recognizable identity) down to the details of which phrases will act as links. (See Chapter 3.) In some cases, the content pro will also deal with standards for look and feel, for how the interface works, or even for the whole shebang of what the site is actually like. In those cases, this person is perhaps acting as the site's *producer.* (The producer title has evolved from the multimedia field that preceded Web development by a few years; see the sidebar "What I really want to do is produce.")

What's a Webmaster to you?

Akemi Tazaki, who frequents the Webgrrls mailing list, answered from the tech viewpoint, "A Webmaster is a system administrator with Internet technology knowledge and skills — a computer (professional) with multimedia/Internet computing and good hardware knowledge. He or she knows several programming languages, like C++ and Java, *and* knows how to document and manage a software program.

(An applet or a CGI script is actually a small software program.)" She also suggests that a Webmaster needs a BS degree with on-site training or significant experience in and tremendous curiosity about high-tech matters. "Basically," she says, "you need to get turned on deeply by the technology and have really *good* reading skills so you can make yourself an expert."

What I really want to do is *produce*

In the movies, the person who calls the shots (pun intended) is called a *director*. In television, that person is called a *producer*. (In movies, the producer is more of a business type who gets the financing and puts deals together but does not usually direct the content.) In the multimedia milieu, the shot-caller is again called a *producer,* as in television. That language has carried over to professional Web site teams, where the person who calls the shots and carries forth the site's mission is often called a producer rather than a Webmaster. Producers, however, typically have pretty good technical knowledge. If they don't actually do scripting and HTML production work, they can at least carry on an intelligent conversation in those areas. At best, they can press themselves into service doing a bit of coding to keep a project on track.

If you're really strapped and can hire only one person for your Web team, find a good producer. Why? Because you can job out a lot of site maintenance to your Internet service provider and job out design to a design firm. But someone has to make decisions and manage people or vendors. That person must be familiar with your company's products, strategy, and positioning among competitors. The person should also be familiar enough with Internet technologies to be able to talk intelligently with techies and your ISP or hosting company, and he or she should have enough grasp of current and future technologies to envision and imagine ways to create and expand the message you want your site to deliver. In short, it's the producer's job to act creatively to manage the site and ensure that it achieves its purpose.

In a company that specializes in creating Web sites (a *Web shop*), the producer is often the person who has the most contact with the client. In that case, this person may be called on to help the client focus on goals and concepts, define the site and maintain the schedule and budget, and report to both the client and the Web shop on progress. (Chapter 10 covers working with Web shops.)

It has often been said that on the Web, content is king. Yet, oddly enough, many companies think first about hiring a tech Webmaster when they search for someone to be on staff. Then they seem to expect this person to be a programmer, writer, editor, designer, and marketing strategist all rolled into one. Don't fall for that. If you do, you'll end up with a site with possibly strong underpinnings but probably weak content. Think about it — how many people visit a Web site to admire its robust server and elegant scripting?

In a best-case scenario, the online content professional will have writing and editorial skills along with some HTML ability, and a better than basic understanding of Web page layout and site navigation.

What separates a *content editor* from a *content developer* is that the editor handles only text and perhaps images, whereas the developer has more Web site savvy. Knowing HTML, usability, site architecture, and so on helps the content developer make decisions about or have influence on the overall direction of the site or the areas of the site he or she is charged with. Similarly, a *content strategist* has more experience and skill than the content developer, brings to bear additional business and marketing savvy, and often has executive-level influence on the Web site.

Although people with experience as editors and writers in print media are often well qualified with language and have transferable skills, they should add to their skill base if they want to pursue an online content job. Taking classes in HTML and Web site management (as well as a class in writing and editing for Web sites) will augment a print editor's understanding of how content can and does work online. Similarly, anyone who is responsible for editing content should be trained in professional copy editing as well as legal issues such as copyright. Chapter 3 discusses content, while Chapter 7 introduces some basic legal issues that affect Web sites.

The design and production Webmaster

In the world of Web sites, production often means design, and design often means page layout. Some companies do manage to hire a designer, an illustrator, a couple of HTML production people, and a creative director to set the design direction and keep everyone on track. But others simply hire one person who falls somewhere in that continuum and then expect that person to fill all those roles. So what else is new in business?

A few years ago, there was such a shortage of people with specialized Web site design skills that anyone with the slightest design experience could easily get Web site work. We still see job postings every day for Web site designers, but those doing the hiring now have higher expectations — not just any designer who can use a Web browser can get the big bucks. Designers are expected to be familiar with HTML, electronic typography, Adobe Photoshop, Adobe Illustrator, compression software, the 216-color "browser-safe" palette, and even site architecture, Java, Flash, and more. Luckily, universities and design schools are seeing this need. Many now have entire programs for training people to do Web site design. Many more offer individual classes in Web site design, tools, and technologies.

 A design or production Webmaster may be a Jack or Jill of all trades. He or she may handle everything from overall site design through spot illustrations that go on the pages, creation of page templates that make production simpler, HTML production itself, scanning art, and maintaining HTML tags that specify certain types of links. In smaller organizations, this person also tracks the work flow and hires out art jobs as needed. For tips on outsourcing Web site design or other production work, turn to Chapter 10. The main things to remember about the design personnel you hire are as follows:

 ✔ They should have a style compatible with your site.

 ✔ They should have the special technical skills that a Web site requires.

✔ They should be able to understand and visually interpret the goals of your site. For example, if your site is primarily a source of functional information, the designer should make navigation easy. However, if your site sells fine furniture, you probably need a more designerly look that is compatible with the style of the furniture itself.

The marketing or business Webmaster

As e-commerce booms, more and more Web site teams are adding to their ranks one or more people who focus on promoting the Web site itself or on forming and nurturing strategic relationships with other companies. The typical marketing pro on a Web site team engages in any or all of the activities described in Chapters 15 and 16 for promoting a site. He or she should have professional marketing experience; a keen understanding of what works online is at least as important as a degree in marketing.

On the business side, a company Web site team generally relies on the company's finance, human resources, and other departments to fulfill those functions. Of course, a stand-alone dot com will need those services and many others. In either case, these folks (whose jobs are certainly important) aren't, strictly speaking, part of the team that creates and runs the site.

Someone may be assigned to do business development for the Web site; generally, this person establishes and maintains strategic alliances or otherwise extends the company's business reach. If the Web site gains revenue by selling advertising, ad sales may be a business development function. Web site teams large enough to have a marketing pro but not large enough to further segment the jobs often assign business development responsibilities to marketing.

FIELD NOTES

What one Web wizard does

Web diva Tamra Heathershaw-Hart says, "Yes, you do have to be a designer and an engineer and a marketer if you're a one-person-band Web shop . . . I have to know how to make beautiful art work at 216 colors, how to do animated GIFs, how to lay out sites using table codes (and still make them readable to older browsers), how to make server-side includes work on an NT server, how to create database-driven sites, how to hook up secure ordering, how to set up mailing list software, how to write proposals, and how to market my clients' sites so they get visitors. And don't forget knowing how to install chat software!"

The executive Webmaster

Simply speaking, the executive Webmaster is the boss. The boss may come from the tech world, the content world, or the production world. Or, he or she may just come from upper management with a background in marketing, editorial, or even operations; this person may in fact have no Web site experience, though this is not the wisest way to go. Although many non-Web-world skills — such as managing a local area network (LAN), editing print media, or managing a company — are highly transferable to Web sites, trying to direct a Web site team with no background in Web sites at all is a big handicap.

If you're in a position to hire the boss of a Web site team, it's important to find someone who has experience overseeing complex projects and preferably has experience managing the technical, content, or production side of a Web site. Even having a little experience in any of those areas combined with a solid management and business background can work out well. If you're a manager who finds yourself thrust into the role of running a Web site team and you have no Web site experience, consider jobbing out a great deal of the work and calling in consultants until you're up to speed with the technology and issues.

The person who is charged with directing a Web site team is often called an executive producer, but sometimes called an Internet group director, a vice president of interactivity, or any of a number of other creatively-worded titles. All roughly correspond in print media to the title of editor-in-chief (head honcho in charge of content) or publisher (head honcho in charge of business).

The executive Webmaster's role often includes making and tracking the overall budget, and overseeing the creation of strategic partnerships or the making of business alliances. This is a business role, and traditional business and management skills are transferable here. Increasingly, universities and professional development programs are offering specialized degrees and certificates for e-commerce executives and managers. We can only think that as the people at the top become increasingly Internet savvy, the industry as a whole will benefit.

In the early days of Web site management, the overall running of the site often fell to the person who first got the idea and the impetus to set up a fledgling site. As the industry matures, this job is more often assigned to an actual site manager. If the Web site initiative's mission is to market a company, service, or product, the Web site team boss may be a marketing manager. If the site is to publish strong content, a content type may be a far better bet. If it's supposed to be offering the company or the public whiz-bang technology, a tech type — maybe someone with innovative vision about the technology — may be the chosen one.

In Chapters 18 and 19, we talk more about hiring and being hired. To know what your site is up to, though, as well who's the right kind of Webmaster to run the Web site, you need to establish what the site's goals and mission will be. That's also where you start the process of planning your Web site. These topics are covered next.

Chapter 2

Your Site's Goals Define Everything Else

● ●

In This Chapter

▶ Defining your site's goals

▶ Examining the eight basic purposes of a Web site

▶ Identifying your audience

▶ Creating value and establishing branding

▶ Exploring revenue models and other resource issues

▶ Considering measurements of success

▶ Writing a mission statement

● ●

*B*efore you build your Web site, you must plan it. But before you plan your Web site, you must have a pretty clear idea of what you intend the site to accomplish. This is only logical, right? For example, no one builds a house without a plan. To build a house, most folks hire an architect who comes up with a plan, taking into consideration the purpose of the building, the budget, the sort of look the client is hoping for, and so on. To build anything, you must start with defining the goal for that thing. So whether you job out the fine-tuning of your plan and the building or you simply appoint yourself architect of your own site, it's up to you to determine your site's mission and goals.

Although it's always wise to be flexible, you don't want to have to undo today's work in order to implement something new six months from now. When you define your goals, think about them in terms of what you want to accomplish in the short term *and* the long term. But keep in mind that on the Web, the short term is pretty immediate, whereas the long term is maybe a year or two from now. (This way of thinking differs from the traditional corporate world, where making five-year plans is the norm.)

Keeping Your Eyes on the Prize

Internet years, it is said, are just three or four months long. Things move so fast that you may be tempted to zip past the planning stage and move directly into building your Web site. This is a big mistake. Trust us — you'll only wind up spending that same time unknotting all the problems that arise daily from having done things so much on the fly. If we make one point repeatedly in this book, it's this: Like a finely trained athlete, you, the wonder Webmaster, need to stay light on your feet but keep your eyes fixed firmly on the prize.

It's true that unlike other forms of media — print, for example, where you must dot every *i* and cross every *t* before you go to print — the Web lends itself to incremental development. You can put up the home page today, expand a certain area tomorrow, and introduce entirely new subject matter and technologies any time you like. And although anyone with a word processor and an Internet-access account can start building a Web site in the next half hour, that level of "flexibility" inspires a lot of people to put slapdash Web sites up before they're ready.

What happens when you lose focus

One of the worst things that can happen to a Web site is what we call *Winchester Mystery House syndrome.* You see, smack dab in the middle of Silicon Valley, in San Jose, California, is the Winchester Mystery House. It was built by a dotty heiress to the Winchester gun fortune, who believed that if she ever stopped building the house, she would die and be haunted. So the house contains rooms upon rooms, and they go willy-nilly in every direction. This irrational maze of a house is very amusing to the present-day tourists who visit it, but do you want your Web site to resemble a dotty Victorian fun house or to achieve a true purpose?

Now imagine Winchester Mystery House syndrome applied to your budget, your staffing, or your site's concept. The mind just boggles, eh?

What you gain by setting goals and planning

Okay, it's true that coming up with a clear plan costs you time and maybe even money in the short run. You may think that planning means that oh-so-important Web site will take longer to launch, but here we offer you a money-back guarantee. In the long term, we guarantee you that focusing on your goals before you plan your site can save you both time and money.

Remember, your purpose is not to go to launch with a complete site that includes every bell, whistle, and piece of brilliant content you envision for your site. You don't have to have every single content area or useful gizmo in place at the start. In fact, if you wait for your site to be "finished," you may never launch. Your goal is to launch with a focused site that supports your vision. To do that, you need to create a plan that makes the site you launch a building block — not a roadblock — to the site you've envisioned for the future. You can then add areas and features to the site in phases over the course of a specified length of time.

One more thing: Over time, your plans for your site will change. Change is bound to happen — it's just the nature of the Web. As new technologies and opportunities arise, your company will have new and different ideas and so will you. Don't worry — be happy. Change is a good thing.

Take a look at Figure 2-1, which shows the general stages of planning and building a Web site. (Not every company or Web site team goes about planning and building exactly the same way; this illustration is intended only to give you a point of departure.) In the rest of this chapter and throughout the next few, we introduce you to the various issues that you need to consider as you work through the defining and strategizing stage.

Figure 2-1:
Your mileage may vary, but these are the usual activities of building a Web site.

Define and Strategize	Organize and Design	Build and Implement	Deploy and Launch
Analyze situation	Spec content, tech, design	Write, edit content	Build "Beta"
Develop business models	Develop content assets	Track assets (ongoing)	Test for quality assurance
Determine ROI	Develop visual vocabulary	Design interface	Fix bugs (may be final)
Analyze competition	Establish tech benchmarks	Build prototype ("Alpha")	Revise content (may be final)
Test market	Create site map	Test alpha with users	Get executive approvals
Develop strategies	Test concepts, user tasks	Revise based on tests	Deploy to server
	Revise based on tests		LAUNCH
	Design navigation		
	Design page elements		

© 2000 Tauber Kienan Associates
www.tauberkienan.com
info@tauberkienan.com

What Exactly Are You Doing Here?

Before you start planning your Web site, ask yourself — and whoever is footing the bill — a few questions. Here's where you put on your marketeer and business-strategist hats. (We get to content strategy in the next chapter.) Here are the basic questions to answer now:

- ✔ What is your purpose?
- ✔ Who are you trying to reach (and what do they want)?
- ✔ Who are your competitors?

After you've considered these questions, you're in a good spot to start planning your site. You can then follow up with a few more questions, such as these:

- ✔ How will you establish a specific identity that differentiates you from your competitors and makes your site (or product, or service, or company) immediately recognizable to your audience?

- ✔ What will you offer that will attract your target audience, fulfill their expectations, and inspire them to keep coming back to the site in the future?

And then you can consider these more hard-core business realities:

- ✔ What business model will work for you?
- ✔ What resources do you have?
- ✔ What expectations of success do you have?
- ✔ How will you measure success?

In some cases, the company for which you're creating that nifty Web site already has clearly set, company-wide goals. It probably sells or provides a product or service — most organizations do. In that case, the overriding goals of the site may well parallel those of the company. However, online audiences don't always match offline customer bases, and in some cases, companies may want their Web sites to promote their products but not sell them (because, perhaps, selling is taking place more favorably through traditional, nonvirtual resellers).

It's generally best to specify no more than three important goals for a Web site and to prioritize them clearly. For example, your site may have as its goals (a) promoting the company's image and products, (b) supporting customers or clients in using the products well, and (c) selling the product or service directly via the Web site.

The Basic Purposes of Web Sites

At their most basic, Web sites usually serve some combination of eight basic purposes. Some sites serve several of these purposes, whereas others are focused more purely on a single intention. But in general, most sites attempt to accomplish one or more of these goals:

- ✔ **Entertain:** Sites that entertain may have entertainment as their sole purpose, or they may enhance an entertainment product or event that occurs in the "real" world. And some companies find that using entertainment as a vehicle for promoting a product, service, or event draws in just the right audience. Providing an entertaining Web site one that's focused on an amusement or a game often pulls in a younger audience, and using an entertaining theme (like a fun story line) can work well when the product is geared toward adults and the theme is tied in with a broadcast or print promotion campaign. Including entertainment on your site can also enable you to inform, educate, sell, or attain any of the other goals mentioned in this list.

✔ **Inform:** Sites that are *content-driven* (meaning that the text, listings, or data on the sites are the sites' main reason for being) provide an audience with information — for example, news or feature articles, sports information, weather data, stock quotes, or parenting advice. And some sites inform customers about how to use a product, inform people about a philosophy or belief, or inform businesses about another business's services.

✔ **Sell:** Sites that sell run the gamut. Most are obvious business-to-consumer retail sales sites and business-to-business wholesale sites. But some sales sites, called *purchase-support* sites, provide potential customers only with the information (and persuasion) needed to make a buying decision sans the actual opportunity to make the purchase online. (The purchase might take place at an offline, "real-world" store or dealer, for example.) And still other sites are intended to generate sales leads that in-person sales reps follow up on.

✔ **Promote:** Promotion sites provide a persuasive message that puts the company, product, service, viewpoint, person, or opportunity being promoted in the best possible light. In a real sense, they are selling, though the selling is less direct than on a sales site. And in another sense, they inform, though the content of a site that promotes is not objectively informative. A corporate image site is a promotional site, as is a political candidate's site (although in that case, the site may strive to appear to have an informative style rather than a blatantly promotional style).

✔ **Distribute:** Sites that distribute products digitally include those that offer software, images, sound, video, and other stuff for download or as streaming media. Some sites distribute images or content, for example, for a licensing fee, whereas others offer free software or code but also allow users to download new versions of software they've purchased (or perhaps patches or drivers for that software). Anything that can be digitized can be distributed over the Net. Online software distribution makes sense, because it eliminates the middle person (and all the packaging) and delivers the software directly to the computer that will run it.

✔ **Research and report:** Research sites elicit information *from* users (either a general population of users or a targeted group or segment of a group). This method for gathering information can be a real boon to marketers, researchers, and informants alike — it can be faster and less expensive than conducting surveys by phone or in person. In some cases, after a site gathers data via a questionnaire or form on a Web site, the raw data is then compiled to create information that is then fed back to the site's visitors either on the site's pages or via a downloadable report that may be free or for sale.

Some sites conduct research automatically, without the necessity of users filling out a survey. Software and server logs (see Chapter 17) can track, for example, a wide range of information about the technologies site visitors are using and report on that. *Data mining* (automatically tracking the usage and buying habits of users) enables companies to target their offerings more appropriately and provides them with an asset they can sell. (Users are less inclined to object to companies sharing pooled information about trends in group buying habits than they are to object to companies sharing information about individual users.)

✔ **Foster or serve community:** Community sites create, build, or serve some group of people who share interests and experience a bond (however fleeting) with the group. These sites can offer e-mail interaction, online discussions, chat, or other electronic interaction, but some community sites simply serve a real-world community (a church, for example, or perhaps a parenting group) without offering online or e-mail interaction. (See Chapter 4 to find out more about what drives and serves communities.) Auction sites, in a sense, are community sites, in that they enable groups of people with a common interest (in buying and selling) to interact.

✔ **Facilitate workflow:** These sites enable workgroups to be more productive or to work together despite the barriers of time and distance. Publicly available sites that offer calendaring, file sharing, group interaction, and other workgroup tools fall into this category, as do private intranets and extranets that are used to make work among colleagues or collaborators, well, work.

Your mission, then, is to determine which of these purposes (or which combination of purposes) is most suitable for your site. Keep in mind that a site can have more than one purpose. Many sites have a main purpose and a secondary or even third-level purpose. If your company sells music CDs, for example, your Web site can provide content that enhances the user's experience (and draws traffic and supports sales) as well as selling the CDs directly to the public. Of course, along the way, the site can also promote the company's image.

If your company is a manufacturer rather than a retailer, its Web site may be geared toward bringing in the right audience for that product, providing those folks with information about the product's sterling virtues, offering them a community of product users who can share tips with each other or get online help, and then providing links to where to buy the products or a zip code database that lets users find a nearby retailer. Think for a moment about a movie studio's Web site. It can offer film clips, audio or video interviews with stars, behind-the-scenes glimpses at the making of the film (notice that these are all purchase-support items!), and screening schedules (which is a lot like pointing to a retailer near you).

The notorious "three Cs" (or is it four?)

A lot has been made of the so-called "three Cs" of the Internet: *content, community,* and *commerce.* In the early years of the Internet, content was king, and many smart people interpreted that to mean that Web sites needed a lot of text, or special contests, or even gimmicky story lines with perhaps live actors on Webcams acting out the narrative. We know of one early search engine that financed (and almost launched) an online soap opera to lure in traffic, and a car company that bought an abused gorilla from a shopping mall, set it up in a deluxe compound, and then created a Web site about the gorilla. So how exactly does a soap opera enhance a search engine? And what is it about a gorilla Web site that helps sell cars? Both efforts, though well executed, flopped in that they didn't achieve their intended business goals.

Later, when a few sites that offered chat or discussion groups did well, many other sites did, too. It was generally believed that community was the way to go. And then, when it became apparent that Web sites were expensive to launch and maintain (see Chapter 6), a general expectation arose that the sites should rake in revenue, and many people thought that meant the sites would have to sell products online. (Hey, that sounds like commerce!) But community technologies like chat and discussion groups didn't fly on every Web site (see Chapter 4), and it turned out that not all companies were best served by selling their products online (see Chapter 5).

Eventually, people started talking about a fourth C, but to some that C was *convergence* (the combining of the other three Cs) and to others it was *context,* though the meaning of *context* wasn't completely clear to everyone. Chapter 3 discusses the three or four (or is it five?) "CS" of customer service further.

As you consider goals, note that your Web site should not be just a billboard, brochure, or calling card. Users will come to your site only if it provides value. That value — the utility, convenience, or entertainment factor — can take many different forms, but it must be there. Something entertaining can be of as much value as something that informs or facilitates workflow. This isn't all that surprising — would you watch television if it didn't illuminate or entertain you? Even TV commercials generally have some content — some cute story line or seemingly informative pitch.

Defining the Opportunity

To come up with a thoughtful and viable strategic plan, you must first clearly outline the opportunity before you. To get a grasp on the opportunity, you must know all about your audience (or *target market*), what they want, how you can reach them, and what competitors are after the same market. You can reach your audience and fend off your rivals only if you're very, very clear about who's who and what's what.

Identifying your audience

To define your audience, find out about its demographics — for example, the age range, gender mix, and income and education levels of people in your audience, and how they access the Internet. The basic question you want to answer is this: "Who wants what I'm offering?" Follow-up questions may be "Where are these people?" and "How do I get to them?" You'll also want to know what your audience generally believes (or is put off by) as well as their desire for accessibility and ease versus sophistication. The basic question here is "What drives people to choose products like mine?" This and other "psychographic" information define your audience's thinking. You need to know about demographics and psychographics for two reasons: This information can help you know your audience and focus on your goals, and it can bolster your proposals.

In the course of your career as an Internet pro, you may write a lot of proposals both long and short. You may propose buying a new server, redesigning the site, and maybe even creating the site to begin with. Take note: Demographic and psychographic information make a proposal a lot stronger. What's more, demographic and psychographic information can tell you about your site, what offerings and features should work, and why one thing works and another doesn't.

Brick-and-mortar companies (companies that have their main presence in the so-called real world as opposed to only online) generally have a good idea who their customers are and what facts and attitudes describe those customers. And start-up companies generally need to know who their customers are before hanging out their shingles. But for both brick-or mortar companies and start-ups, it's important to remember that the online audience or market may differ from the brick-and-mortar market. The online audience may have a different skew in any number of ways — gender, age group, income level, and education level, for example. The online audience may also be driven by different needs or attitudes than the brick-and-mortar audience. Find out who you're talking to online — who makes up the target audience for your Web site?

After you get your site launched, you can use a variety of methods — tracking log files, using site-statistics software (see Chapter 15), gathering data via registration forms and surveys, and so on — to find out more about your site's visitors. In the meantime, you can compile data about your intended audience by gleaning stats from trade associations, from research reports available for purchase online or in print, from articles in the news or business journals that quote such sources, or (if you have a big budget) by hiring a research firm to do a study for you.

Only by knowing your audience well can you know what they want. They may be compelled by convenience, utility, or interest in a topic, depending on a lot of factors. In truth, a product (whether it's an actual product, a company, a service, a public figure, or a Web site) must always serve some driving need or solve some problem or offer some special value to a targeted market just to be of value at all. Marketing types, in defining a product, first identify the audience (the target market), then create a product, and then delve into *positioning* — creating a personality for the product to make it attractive to the audience. The same process works for creating a Web site.

To focus your efforts on identifying your audience and creating a quality experience for those folks, you can start by addressing the questions posed in the questionnaires titled "Identifying Your Audience" and "Creating Quality of Experience" in the E-Commerce Management Center at www.tauberkienan.com.

Considering international and regional audiences

The Internet is . . . dare we say it . . . *international*. As of this writing, American Internet users outnumber those in any other country, but evidence is mounting that this statistic will shift within a few short years. This trend begs the question about whether you need to accommodate international users.

If your product or service is international in scope, you can provide multilingual versions of your site or offer stand-alone sites for your international compadres. (Be sure to take into account cultural differences as well as language differences.) If not, you have no reason to worry about this point — just focus on your target audience. Do, however, politely indicate on your site what region of the world you are focusing on. (See Chapter 3 for pointers on content development issues such as this.)

On the other hand, if your product or service is priced differently for different regions within your own country, or in your country and another country (say the United States and a European country), you may want to provide different information to people in those areas. Unfortunately (or fortunately), you can't prevent people in one region from accessing information that you put on the Web. If you're in a situation like this, you may want to consider not putting the questionable information online. Just skip it. Or, you may want to offer two paths (leading to separate subsites for distinct geographic regions) from your home page. On each subsite, you can tailor the information for the specific audience.

Some folks may think that if the Web is global, it isn't an appropriate venue for local companies. If you run a small restaurant, what's the point of putting up information about your restaurant so that people from around the world can access it? Okay, maybe you'd catch a few tourists swinging through town, but is a Web site worth the trouble?

Just because seemingly everyone is on the Web, you don't have to include everyone in your audience — just focus on your target audience and ignore everyone else. We've created sites for nonprofit agencies serving only the San Francisco Bay Area. Is it a problem that people all over the world can access those sites? Not at all — anyone is welcome to visit, and if he or she finds something of interest there, it's all well and good. But the audience is primarily local, and we made that clear on the first page and in the areas devoted to services offered and to fundraising.

Taking a look at the competition

One definition of *positioning* (a commonly used marketing term) may be "how your product is focused against the marketplace and its competitors." To know how to position your site — how to put the right spin on the site's purpose(s) and know which goals are best to pursue in the course of the Web initiative — you must know what your competitors are up to. Identifying your competitors' strategies may be easier if you're creating a site for an existing company that has existing competitors than if you're creating a site based on a new idea. If your competitors are known and have an online presence, you can certainly investigate their sites and create a list of their offerings and features as compared to yours. (A formal study of this is known as a *competitive analysis*.) You can also project or imagine what they may do in the future, given their corporate personalities. But you can't know exactly what they're planning (it's almost certainly a guarded secret). So make your strategic decisions based primarily on what you know about your audience rather than on reactions to what your competitors are doing.

If you're creating a site that is so original that it has no competitors, don't imagine that it never will. A newly launched idea on the Web — if it's successful — has about a 15-minute chance of being the only one of its type, and that's only if no one knew a thing about it two weeks ago. We've seen cases where one site announced a batch of nifty new features literally two weeks before its launch, and a competitor beat that site to the punch. The Internet is a fast, fast business. To stay on top, you need to anticipate what your competitors will be doing (even if you don't limit your efforts to reacting to them by copying whatever they do).

What's more, you may find that the competition takes the form of people's preconceived notions. ("Oh! You're an auction site." "No, we're not an auction site, we're . . . something else.") Or the competition may be even more nebulous. It may be that your idea is so new and original people have never heard of anything like it.

You must differentiate your site from your competitors' sites, and you must create a clearly defined personality for your site that identifies to visitors what makes the site and its offerings unique. To do this, you must study your competition. Do it now, as you plan your site, and make it your habit to surf the sites of competitors every day or two *especially* after you've launched your site. If you're a freelancer or you work for a Web shop, ask your clients right away who their main competitors are. Look closely at the content and organization of those companies' sites. If the company's competitors don't yet have a Web presence, question your client closely about its competitors' images, your client's products, and what differentiates your client from its competitors.

Promises, promises

Promises are easy to make and even easier to break. Promising Web site visitors that you'll be adding future enhancements to your site is one way to make them want to come back and see what you've added. The crucial mistake that Webmasters make, however, is promising content that's never delivered — or is delivered too late. In the following example, provided by author and Internet pro J. Tarin Towers, substitute the topic of *your* Web site for the words *pickled cabbage*.

"Suppose I visit your site, which you've proclaimed is 'soon to be the premier Internet resource for pickled cabbage!' Okay, I say to myself. There aren't too many sites about pickled cabbage right now, so we'll see what they do. The first time I visit, your site (pickledcabbage.com) is about a month old. Much of it is under construction, with 'Coming Soon' plastered across about half the proposed sections. Now, if I'm really a dedicated pickled cabbage fan, I *may* deign to revisit the site a month or two later and find out what's cooking. What I want to see is what you promised me when I first found your site: the premier Internet resource for pickled cabbage lovers. Unless you've filled in all the blanks, you won't get a third visit from me, much less a link on my site or a glowing recommendation to my friends who also adore pickled cabbage. If you have filled in all the blanks, congratulations. I'm your fan, and I'm going to keep my eye on your page. But bear in mind what I'm going to expect to see. Pickled Cabbage News, for instance, just better have *new* news from the world of pickled cabbage, while Pickled Cabbage Link of the Moment should certainly be a different link from the last time I visited. In surfing the Net for sites about some of my own interests, such as comic books, computer games, and Web page design, I can't tell you how often I've had my high hopes for a new site dashed on the rocks of neglect. Make me a promise you can actually fulfill, and then follow through, and I'll be your fan. Promise me the stars, then give me a couple of asterisks, and I'll grumble about you to all the other pickled cabbage lovers I know."

Branding: Creating a Recognizable Identity

Creating branding simply means creating an immediately recognizable identity for a company, product, or service. Almost any American can hear "Tide" and "Cheer," and immediate pictures of the packaging of those two products pop into mind — that's branding. The first result of branding is *mind share,* and as any marketing pro will tell you, mind share leads to *market share.* In study after study, research has shown that branding works. In one study, 82 percent of buyers said that recognizing brand was the deciding factor in their purchase decisions.

Yet branding is a concept that's bandied about without adequate understanding. Branding isn't just about packaging. If branded products didn't work, no amount of packaging and advertising would sell them. Just as a person's identity includes his or her name, appearance, and reputation (including whether he or she functions reliably), a company, product, or service's branding does, too. The branding of a Web site includes its look and feel, features, offerings, the style of language used on it, and the overall experience users have of navigation, usability, and functionality.

To create branding, you must be creative, consistent, and aggressive. You must be creative in the sense that you find clever ways to differentiate and position the product (whether it is laundry detergent, a Web site, or a political candidate), consistent in the sense that you don't, for example, use irreverent language on a site with a pinstriped look that's aimed at a conservative audience, and aggressive in the sense that you use every opportunity to fulfill the branding and extend it to the target audience. Even the site's overall integrity, its domain name, its *palette* (the range of colors used), its navigation, and the way its links are phrased contribute to its branding.

For that reason, in this book, we stress repeatedly the importance of creativity and consistency. Without those qualities, what you will be promoting is a site that lacks the integrity that drives a fine user experience. And you will find that going back later and fixing that — rebuilding and relaunching a good site after your users have come to recognize yours as a flawed or weak site — will leave you rowing upstream against the tide of a very difficult competitor: the preconceived notion that your site isn't so great. *Remember:* Mind share is a terrible thing to waste.

To get a grip on some key issue in establishing your branding, see "Branding Questions" in the E-Commerce Management Center at www.tauberkienan.com.

Defining the Business Model

You also must consider whether your site is going to be a *revenue producer* (meaning that it brings in money but is not yet expected to be profitable), a *profit center* (meaning that it is expected to be profitable), or a *cost center* (meaning that it is not intended to produce revenue or profit, and costs more money than it directly produces). A promotional or marketing site is one example of a cost center — it may well contribute to the effort of selling products, but it doesn't directly produce revenue. A nonprofit site, by the way, is one that is run by an official nonprofit designation that has a special tax status. A nonprofit site may be engaged in fundraising, in which case the site is intended to produce at least revenue and probably a profit (at least in the sense that it should take in revenue that exceeds the cost of maintaining the site), although the organization itself is not for profit.

Revenue models we know and love

You need to know the source of your site's funding. You must know who holds the purse strings and whether the funding is coming from an existing source, anticipated revenue, or anticipated investment. This information is very important. It tells you a lot about where the Web initiative is positioned in importance, how stable the endeavor's financial foundation will be, and how far you can go in building a site and a team to run it. Then you need to know what people and equipment resources are budgeted. Some sites make money, some save money, and some are just for fun.

Advertising and subscriptions

You may think that your paid subscription to a magazine funds the magazine's publication and that all those ads are just gravy for the publisher. In fact, subscriptions are usually a relatively small piece of the revenue pie, and ads are what count big time. Individual publications are either *circulation driven,* meaning that most of the revenue comes from paid subscriptions, or *ad driven,* meaning that most of the revenue comes from ads. The "circ-driven" publications have relatively few ads and a high percentage of editorial content — they also have relatively few subscribers and often charge a great deal for subscriptions.

For a while, people thought that applying subscription/advertising models to Web sites was a no-brainer. But to have strong circulation for your publication — be it print or Web — you need whiz-bang editorial content, which isn't cheap. To get high ad rates, you need big traffic. To get big traffic, you need great content. You also need time to ramp up your traffic, and money to promote the site. Any fledgling publication is expected to bleed money for three to five years before it starts to turn a profit, if it ever does. (Not all survive.) Content-driven sites that produce a profit are, as of this writing, still rare.

Content-driven sites often do offer basic content for free and premium content for a fee. Some sites have also had success requiring users to register (by providing valuable demographic data via a form) in order to get access to premium content. But paid subscriptions haven't yet taken their place as the success story many people anticipated.

Licensing content to others

Some content sites have done well by licensing content to others. Here's how this works: You create the content, and it's very popular. Then companies with deep pockets but no content to speak of pay for the privilege of using your content on their site, sometimes in a co-branded situation that shows users that you created the content. This takes a lot of attention to the licensing deals. Perhaps you'd need a rep on staff to make the deals, negotiate favorable contracts, and tend your relationships with co-branding partners, or you'd need a syndication or licensing service to take you on as a client. Licensing also brings up many intellectual property issues (see Chapter 7).

Sponsorship

Sponsorship takes two forms: (a) corporate or organizational sponsorship, where a company or group pays costs and is visibly recognized as the sponsor and (b) individual sponsorship, where interested parties send in donations to keep things going. (Note that this second method is somewhat like the model of software that's distributed as shareware — if you like it, you voluntarily pay for it.) Corporate or organizational sponsorship is discussed in Chapter 15.

Paid placement

So you're sitting there watching some big Hollywood movie, and there in the scene, the characters are quietly (or not so quietly) using products like soft drinks or books — and you recognize the brand name. Is this a lucky accident for the companies whose products are shown? No! They went to a lot of trouble — and usually some expense — to get that stuff up there on the screen in front of you and millions like you. This is known as *paid placement*. In the Web world, paid placement occurs when a company ponies up to have its logo placed strategically on a site — perhaps in an image or animation. If you use paid placements on the sites of others, make sure the use supports the overall theme of your own site.

Commissions and affiliate fees

Auction sites take a commission on a transaction that occurs between two parties; this model is also used by other sites that offer consumer-to-consumer, business-to-consumer, or business-to-business buying and selling. Keeping traffic (and sales) up and the credibility of the site (which is affected by the trustworthiness of those buying and selling) high boosts use of such a site. Revenue is likely to follow. Keeping the infrastructure overhead down boosts profit.

Affiliate fees result from referrals. The affiliate site or page contains a link sending traffic or sales to a site that runs an affiliate program, and the referring site gets a bounty or fee for the referral. This can be win-win, in the sense that the referrer gets paid and the site that's getting the sales or traffic has maximized doorways leading to it via a simple kind of "franchise" program.

Reduction of costs

Anything that can be digitized can be distributed over the Internet. Costs that were traditionally associated with packaging, shipping, and distributing via retailers are then outright nixed — only the pure product is delivered. And in a real coup, it gets to market a *lot* faster.

Reduction of costs also takes place when information is delivered efficiently. When human resources information is delivered to employees via an intranet rather than thousand of bound and printed handbooks, or when product information is made available to sales reps or buyers via an extranet rather than printed catalogs, the cost savings can be great (and so can the improved processes).

Yet another cost savings occurs when online tools are used for file sharing, scheduling, production management, and other workflow processes. Here, the savings include those associated with distributing information, but also with improved productivity and getting the product or project done more quickly, which provides a competitive edge in the market and can result in more revenue because of better sales.

Budgeting people and equipment

Let's face it: If you're setting up an IS department, a restaurant, or an office-supply store, you can rely on past experience and perhaps even books on the topic to point you on your way. But specifying what you need to set up your Web initiative can be dicey business. Sure, you can say that you need this sort of server and that sort of connection. The big challenge is in anticipating the workloads of various team members and in specifying how many people you need to get the job done. It's especially tough to anticipate what it will take to keep the site fresh — what it will take to create a new site is a lot easier to plot. And as any manager can tell you, managing the workload and the cost of labor to accomplish that workload is a big part of keeping things in line.

Frankly, you're in trouble if your resources consist of borrowed time from various people in various departments. In that case, the Web initiative often falls to the bottom of those people's priority lists, in favor of the most urgent tasks that are involved in the company's core, profit-making business (that is, unless the core, profit-making business *is* the Web initiative).

In a best-case scenario, you can point out to those who approve the checks that for *x* dollars, they can accomplish *x* goals, staying within the budget. Or you can put on your evangelist hat and persuade them that in order to accomplish the higher goals that you've set for the Web endeavor you need a more generous budget. To sort through what resources you may need, read the rest of this book; to look into writing a budget, turn to Chapter 6. When you propose a budget for consideration, the more concrete information you have, the more credible your request is.

Establishing the Meaning of Success

When it comes to expectations of success, you may well encounter two extremes. Some people in your company may not have a clear picture of success, because they don't know what to expect, and some people may have unabashed visions of sudden wealth and wild, widespread fame. But it is a rare CEO or investor who springs for a budget and resources for a Web initiative (or any other project) without a realistic vision of success.

Part of your role as Webmaster is to manage expectations. You need a clear picture of what success means in your company in general — for example, is success measured by numbers or by the meeting of goals? Then, you need to know what the vision of success for the Web site is. With those items in mind, you are in a position to help guide or shape that vision of success. You can help guide expectations by researching what has happened for sites like yours over the past year or so, but again, because you are in a pioneering field, you may find yourself the first to wander down the path you're on.

You may be tempted — because, for example, it may seem appropriate in order to get the big budget — to suggest very high expectations for your site. You may want to believe that within minutes of launch, you'll be selling millions of wonderwidgets, or that you can end world hunger. Maybe you just think you are going to get a million visitors per month. Here's your dilemma: Although high expectations can inspire bigger budgets, you may be setting up your Web endeavor for a big fall if you inflate expectations to unreasonable levels or fail to manage any overly high expectations in others. When considering what the site can do — what will signify its success — it's generally best to err on the conservative side. Then you (and the site) can look brilliant when you do succeed.

Make sure that the measurements of success established for your site are in line with the site's goals and are attainable. Chapter 17 goes into detail about measuring success; before you take another step review that material so you have a full grounding in appropriate measurements and how the actual quantifying can occur.

Writing a Mission Statement

As a quick exercise for focusing on your site's purpose, write a brief mission statement. Don't slave over this task — it's mainly just to get you going. It's not meant to have historical significance. Start by jotting down a few pieces of information:

- ✔ Exactly what product or service does your company provide?

- ✔ Name three to five important goals your company hopes to achieve. Some of these goals may be as simple as selling *x* product. Some may address promoting a certain image or reaching a certain group of people. If you aren't sure of your company's goals, a quick conversation with the marketing honchos or a check of the corporate values may help.

- ✔ What three words describe your company's corporate image?

- ✔ Who is your target customer or audience?

- ✔ How can the Web initiative help to achieve the company's goals or reach the audience?

- ✔ What types of content or technology are available, especially within the limitations of your budget? (Don't dwell on this — just brainstorm very briefly.)

- ✔ What does the success of your Web initiative look like to your company, given the nature of your site's goals and the company's core values?

Keep your mission statement simple. Just string together all the pieces of information into sentences. If one goal seems to conflict with another, look for priorities and consider dropping the less-important goals. If one piece of information appears out of whack with others — for example, if the corporate image is fun, fresh, and sassy but the audience is comfort-craving and quiet — seek clarification from the marketing department. Now tack your mission statement up where you can see it, and file a copy of it for handy reference. You can refer to it when you've forgotten your primary purpose, and you can place it in some edited form into important documents like proposals and reports. You can also change it as needed — make it a living document that truly expresses your current mission, not a marker on the tomb of your past ambitions.

Chapter 3

Creating Content of Consequence

- -

In This Chapter

▶ Understanding the nature of content

▶ Considering how content can drive traffic (and sales)

▶ Setting your content strategy

▶ Developing high-quality content

▶ Building easy maintenance into the content plan

▶ Producing content for international users

▶ Creating effective wireless content and broadband content

- -

*A*ll too often, people who hear the maxim that "content is king" interpret that to mean that their Web sites must be chock full of reading material in order to be attractive to users. Content is important, that's for sure. Without something that's of interest to users, a Web site is nothing. All Web sites have content, every one of them. And in the process of planning your site, you must address these big questions up-front: What is the actual content, what is the most effective content given the site's strategic purpose, and how can you shape and present the content to achieve the site's purpose. This chapter is about approaching content strategically and then translating strategy into practical guidelines for hands-on content development.

What the Heck Is Content?

REMEMBER

Not all Web sites are content-driven, but all Web sites have content. A Web site's content is, simply, whatever is contained and presented on the Web site.

On a content-driven site — one that offers "editorial" content such as text, images, or media that a user can peruse as its main purpose — the content is the text, images, or media. On a site that distributes downloadable software, the downloadable software is the site's main content, although any text, images, and other elements that support the download process are also content. Even the error messages contain content; small pieces of content such as the text in an error message are often called *microcontent*.

Stickiness and the competitive edge

A Web site that is *sticky* is generally known to be one that keeps its users "sticking around." Stickiness is that quality in a Web site that keeps users there *and keeps them coming back*. But a common misconception among those creating or managing Web sites is that stickiness is attained only by giving users plenty to read, do, and experience on the site. These people think lots of text, along with quizzes, doo-dads, and gee-whiz wonders will make the site stickier. Well, not all food should be coated in caramel sauce, and not all Web sites need to be sticky. At least not sticky in ways that distract users from the site's purpose. Too much text and too much wizardry can make your site resemble a cross between the Library of Congress and a carnival. Perhaps more importantly, do you invariably want users browsing around all the live long day? If yours is a site that sells, for example, do you want them browsing or do you want them buying? Stickiness is not always created by inspiring browsability.

To create stickiness, know what your users want at your site. Focus on that, and do what you do well. If you manufacture ice cream, pouring more caramel sauce, nuts, whipped cream, and cherries on it won't persuade people that yours is the best ice cream. Stick to the ice cream. Make it the best. Make it easy to find and enjoy.

Use your knowledge of your audience to select what you offer them with care and to make your site highly usable. The stickiest sites are not just those that don't keep users trapped inside, they're also those that users go back to again and again and tell their friends about. If your site possesses a fine-tuned usability and a well executed combination of charisma, credibility, and consequence, then users immediately imagine your site and no other when they think about the site's topic or purpose. Give your site that kind of stickiness, and you'll have a competitive edge that's hard to beat.

Both *data* and *listings* are also content. Many e-commerce sites include some sort of data or listings. *Commodity data* can take the form of information about products in a catalog, for example. Stock quotes are another example of data. *Listings* provide information in a list (surprisingly enough), usually with some sort of organization that helps people make good use of the information. Examples include entertainment schedules or a portal's listing of links to other Web sites.

What content you choose for your site and how you present it has a profound impact on the experience users have of the site (and thus your company, product, service, or message). One philosophy says that a Web site is like a casino, in that it ought to have plenty of entrances, lots to do while you're there, and not a lot of obvious exits. The content is the "lots to do while you're there." Choosing and shaping a Web site's entrances, exits, and content is the foundation of such disciplines as content strategy and content development.

Designing Content to Achieve Goals

In a Forrester survey of 8,600 Web-enabled households (see Figure 3-1), a whopping 75 percent of the respondents cited "high-quality content" as the factor that most compelled them to revisit their favorite sites. Other studies have shown repeatedly that content drives user interest in Web sites — and that, friends, means that content drives traffic.

And yet, traffic is not the ultimate goal of all Web sites. (We go over this in Chapter 2.) For example, the purpose of content for a sales site must be to draw in traffic as well as to support the conversion of visits by users to purchases by users. Ultimately, in fact, the goal of content on a sales site may be to inspire and retain customer loyalty. (See Figure 3-2.) Similarly, the goal of any site's content should be to further the overall purpose and business goals of the Web site.

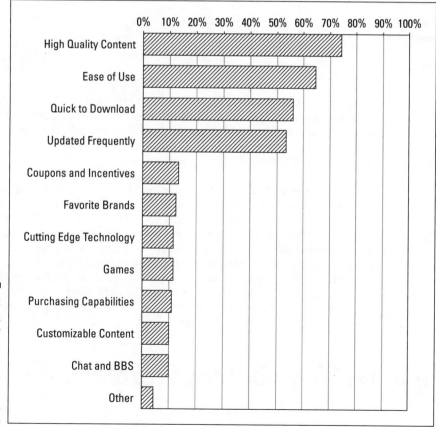

Figure 3-1:
Users rank high-quality content as the top factor in attracting traffic.

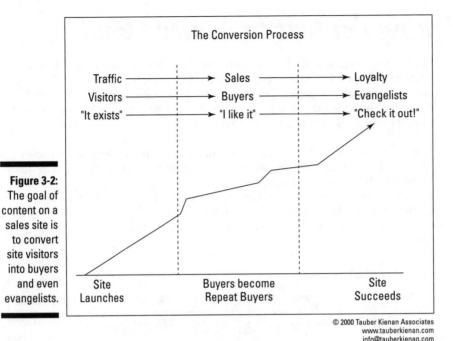

Figure 3-2:
The goal of content on a sales site is to convert site visitors into buyers and even evangelists.

What sort of content you have and how interactive it will be (as well as how it will be managed) also determines what technology you need to deliver the site's message or to fulfill its goals. With all this, you must determine what content is best for your site before you proceed to organizing your site plan, choosing technologies, designing, and building.

After you implement the site, the equation flips over. At that point (and thereafter), the technology choices you made while building will affect your future abilities and strategies. For example, if you can't afford a sophisticated database and content management system now, your options for creating thousands of frequently updated pages in the future may be limited. All the questions you must address as you design and build your site start with one question that is deceptively simple: What is your content strategy? Before you build, you must address what content you will offer when your site launches, what personality the content will have, and how you plan to expand and maintain your offerings down the road.

Approaching Content Strategically

To approach content strategically means, quite plainly, to start the content plan by defining the audience, the opportunity, and the business model and to build a set of guiding principles that drive the selection and development of content. Ask yourself

✔ What uniquely distinguishes your company, product, service, or Web site? What strengths and weaknesses can you identify?

✔ What distinguishes your competitors, and what are their strengths and weaknesses?

✔ Where is your audience located? Will your reach be local, regional, national, or international?

✔ What main purpose does your Web site aim to achieve? Do you have a second or third purpose? What are they?

✔ What business model supports the site?

✔ What main message do you intend to convey? Is there another one that would be detrimental?

✔ What image do you want to convey? Choose just a few among these or other words: able, aggressive, casual, credible, confident, conservative, corporate, creative, dramatic, earthy, educational, elegant, energetic, formal, fun, hip, innovative, irreverent, modern, personal, retro, rural, serious, sporty, sympathetic, technical, understated, urban, warm, witty.

✔ If your site were music, would it be classical, jazz, rock, easy listening, hip hop, or what?

✔ What three to five keywords describe the site's subject or topic? (For example, for a site about Shakespeare's poetry, the keywords may be *Shakespeare, bard, poem, poet, sonnet.*)

✔ What photographs, illustrations, or art convey the site's identity or message? What types of images should you avoid?

✔ Does including the company's history, philosophy, or a general background support the site's purpose? What about executive credentials or biographies?

✔ Do white papers, case studies, research results, or testimonials bolster the intended message or identity?

✔ Should you minimize maintenance? Do you have the people power to make frequent updates? How often will updates occur, and what will be refreshed?

✔ Must the site echo the look of your brick-and-mortar location, your print or broadcast media, or your other Web sites?

Think deeply on these matters. Then consider closely the nature of any risks your endeavor may run up against. For example, if you reach for a teenage audience, you may not retain the adult audience that you already have. Consider business risks (such as the possibility that funding may run out before profitability is achieved) and legal issues (such as how you can be sure that you have the proper rights to use any content you license) as well. (See Chapter 7 for the lowdown on legal matters.)

Content, community, commerce: The three Cs

Plenty of folks believe that the famous three Cs (content, community, commerce) are the cornerstones of success for any Web site. Unfortunately, many people also interpret the adage that you need content, community, and commerce much too literally. They think it means that every Web site must have articles (or other written text), chat (or other forums for interaction), and shopping (or some other method of exchanging funds). Please, please, don't be so dogmatic.

Yes, a Web site that integrates content, community, and commerce into its offerings works well. But understanding what constitutes content, what inspires community, and what drives commerce is absolutely crucial. When you approach content at its highest levels, you must *take into account the content, community, and commerce aspects of each kind of content you offer.* That includes

- **The site's text and images.** This means all of the text (yes, every bit) that's about anything whatsoever, including the text users see as they traverse the transaction system. And it means every image, too, including photos that show products or a community gathering.

- **Any community-oriented offerings.** These may be schedules of events, minutes from meetings, or other Web page content that supports a community just as much as newsletters, discussion groups, chat, and other technologies that allow the community to interact online.

- **Anything that has a commerce purpose.** This includes, but is not limited to, the content that serves a shopping, promotional, or marketing purpose.

In other words, as you develop content, consider how content, community, and commerce fit into each piece of the puzzle. Rather than simply divvying up the site into separate areas for content, community, and commerce, consider how each area and each page can include all three. Amazon.com does an excellent job of this. On its product pages (those pages that offer individual books for sale, for example) all of the data a customer needs to make a purchase decision is clear and obvious (the price, page count, and so on are right there). That's obviously *commerce.* Along with the facts appear supporting *content* (reviews and comments) as well as opportunities for users to comment on the product, read the comments of others, and even vote on how useful they find the comments. (Hmm. Don't those last bits sound like *community?*) Within any single page, in that case, commerce, content, and community are interwoven to support the sites' purpose, which is to sell.

Think about how the users or customers visiting your site will experience any specific piece of content (including text, articles, sales pages, and more);

how you can further community through the commerce aspects of the site; how each page of content, community, and commerce adds to the company's bottom line; and so on. Chapter 4 discusses the specifics of community and Chapter 5 offers hard-won wisdom about e-commerce.

As you choose and develop content, consider both your company's viewpoint (in terms of how the content will achieve the site's intended purpose), and the user's viewpoint (in terms of how the site will work and appeal to its intended audience). Note that you can and you must create a context for content that facilitates usability and furthers the site's overall message and personality. In fact, *context* is known far and wide as the fourth C.

Context: The fourth C

Context is the atmosphere or environment in which you understand or experience something. It's the total picture that informs each piece of the picture. When it comes to your Web site, the context that you create through various choices you make regarding navigation, text, and other factors will affect the message you deliver and how effectively it will be understood by your audience. Consider how out of place hip-hop slang would seem on a Web site that has a conservative look (or vice-versa), and you'll get the picture about context.

On any Web site, creating context for experience includes issues of usability. It includes how the navigation, look and feel, download times, text, art, transaction system, community interaction, and other components of the site hang together and affect each other. The most skilled content strategists and developers consider both how content affects the context and how context affects the content. For that reason, it is sometimes said that if content is king, usability is queen. And that, friends, means that content people think deeply about usability. Usability people think about content, too.

Consequence: A new C for a new decade

We propose a new C to add to the growing list: Consequence. The basic question about a site's consequence is *Does the site do something that matters to its audience?* The novelty of Web surfing has worn off, you see, and just surfing isn't compelling anymore. Browsing has instead become purposeful. Most people, when they venture onto the Web, are now seeking something specific. They often start at search engines or simply type whatever they think the URL or domain name for what they seek might be into their browser's address box. This suggests an increasing need for addressing real user needs on Web sites.

If you focus primarily on the flashy coolness factor of your Web site's offerings, yours is likely to be a flash-in-the-pan site at best. Focus on offering what your audience truly needs, and you are far more likely to win over your audience now and in the long run. Ask yourself ruthlessly about your site's total concept and each piece of what makes up the site: Does your content meet the needs of your audience? That's the basis of strategy.

Creating a strategic foundation

A Web site, whatever its purpose, is at least *like* a product in that it must have utility, packaging, and promotion to make a go of appealing to people. Some Web sites are products in and of themselves. Portals and news sites are products in and of themselves, as are pretty much any sites that exist for their own sake rather than to promote, sell, or distribute another product (or a company or service). No matter what a site's purpose is, in fact, one can argue that the site itself is as much the product as the site's offerings. This isn't so different from retail sales — in that case, the store is as much the product as are the products within the store.

Unlike some other products (laundry detergent, for example), a Web site's packaging and utility are combined and include a lot more text and other elements than most marketers normally have to handle. Although it's often said that a Web site should be more interactive and full featured than a brochure, simply slapping a little interactivity on what is essentially a brochure isn't enough. The best sites are strategically planned to provide users with an overall experience.

 To create a strategic foundation for your site, determine what the site's branding (its personality or identity) will be and what its offerings will be. Also determine (and document) which are the important areas of the site. Then consider which area is really the heart of the site. For example, if your site informs and sells, is the information more important or the shopping cart? After you identify the heart of your site, determine which areas support that more central offering.

Use what you know of the site's audience and goals to establish guidelines and conventions that lead the writers, designers, and other creative implementers as they further plan and finally create the site. Figure what purpose each area of content has, what priorities the company and the users have in each area, and what path users can best take from there. Ask yourself repeatedly, "Who are the users for this area and this page?" "What drives them?" Break your answers down not just into demographics and psychographics (as described in Chapter 2), but also according to what each segment of users is doing. For each area and page, ask yourself

- What product, service, message, or other utility will you offer here?
- What promise or value proposition is made directly or implied?

✔ How will this area or page deliver on the promise?

✔ What will users want to do, learn, or get here?

✔ Where will users go from here, what will compel them to go there, and what will they do, learn, or get there?

Chapter 8 describes a set of methods for translating these choices into a concrete site plan. Here, we stick to thinking through the ideas.

Creating branding via content

Branding is creating an immediately recognizable identity that is clearly differentiated from that of all competitors. Branding works because it establishes in the minds of the largest number of people possible an identity to which they mentally hop in a heartbeat. Remember that *first impressions last.* When a user opens up a Web page, in the first second of glimpsing at it, he or she has an immediate impression of the page's usability, readability, scannability, and personality. Some words or phrases (such as headings, links, and text that's emphasized in any other way) leap off the page and into immediate view. Some images also jump off the page. A skilled content developer selects these words, phrases, and images, and shapes them carefully to create the right impression based on the site's goals.

From planning to process to reality

Content architect Kim Nies works with clients on "a combination of content strategy and content management." She says, "I work with clients and our internal team to determine client content needs and the process to fulfill those needs. Once we've completed the needs analysis, I help build and manage the project." In Kim's perfect world, clients would know at the outset of a project that "the Web is not voodoo . . . and it's not any other kind of magic. The Web can do many things and can really help businesses, but there must be clear thinking and planning for a site to work. It's almost always more complicated than clients think it will be. Sometimes they have to totally change their way of thinking."

She goes on to recommend that clients have "realistic expectations and sample content" in hand when they approach a Web shop. "Content is one category where clients usually think they've got it together. They say they've got content for this section and that, but when we actually receive it, the content is unusable or needs much work before it's ready to go online." Kim's advice is to plan content thoughtfully and in detail: "Realizations about content can have implications for the entire concept and structure of the site, so it's essential to find out what you're really working with at the beginning."

All content is brandable. All content can be created and shaped to have personality. Even pure editorial content (such as news articles), commodity data (such as product information or specs), and listings (such as a portal's index of links) can gain identity, or, in other words, branding. Editorial *voice* (tone and word choices) and *standards* (rules for consistency) contribute as much to branding as look and feel do. Tone of language and word choices give the text personality just as color choices give the design personality. And language, usability, and look all affect the site's overall identity.

Being creative, consistent, and aggressive in putting forth the brand message extends to the content strategy and its implementation, as well as to sentence phrasing, linking, and even some punctuation. After you (or your team) set standards for your Web site, you must ruthlessly hunt down "violations" of branding (for example, sudden uses of the wrong typeface, poorly positioned comments about a product, or just misuses of a word) and correct them. Applying branding to content or language doesn't mean being cute at the expense of usability, however. When content strategy, branding, and the content development that follows them are all done correctly, navigation should be clear, and important phrases such as headings (or headlines) should be understandable. For more about the overall branding of your site, see Chapter 2.

Even pure editorial content has branding

When editorial content is the offering, the watchword is *purity*—that is, the editorial content must be *pure*. To be credible to readers (or users), it has to be untainted by suspicion on the part of its audience that anything as crass or dubious as the wishes of advertisers or other business partners drove the choice of subject or the text. If a site is promotional or *advertorial* (which means that its editorial content is actually advertising in disguise), the editorial content isn't so pure. When a site is sales-driven or ad-sales-driven, the pressure is on between those people selling the products or ads (which brings in the bucks) and those creating the editorial content (which brings in the audience,

without whom there'd be no one to see the products or ads).

With all that, you may think that sites that offer pure editorial content are above the less pure concept of branding. But think about it. If we mention *The New York Times*, doesn't a recognizable identity pop into your head? *The Wall Street Journal? National Enquirer?* Yes, even pure editorial content has branding. Consider Salon.com, The Onion.com, and CNN.com. Each has a distinct look and feel, a distinct take on what it addresses, and a distinct *editorial voice* (which is the sum of its tone, word choices, sentence structures, and so on).

Developing Content

Content development is the process of following through on a strategic plan by creatively implementing it. The goals of strong, effective content development include assuring readability and usability, carrying out the branding (establishing and enhancing the site's personality), creating a context (an appropriate environment for experience), delivering information, compelling users to click through to the site, and ultimately (again), meeting the site's defined business goals. Well-developed content

✔ Reaches a specified audience

✔ Deepens and fulfills the site's branding opportunities

✔ Increases the credibility of the company, service, products, information, or other offerings the site presents

✔ Assures the user a quality experience and on e-commerce sites, expedites service and customer care

✔ Streamlines processes on all sites

Thoughtful, competent content development starts with an understanding of the big-picture plan and adds to that plan by interpreting it appropriately. A skillful content developer takes into account the business factors and the audience needs that drive the content strategy. He or she also makes many tactical decisions about what goes on which page, how text is worded, how linking is used and linked phrases are shaped, and so on. As you consider the audience for your site, break down what you know into a series of assumptions about what users want to know or accomplish at each page, as well as where they'll go from that page. Remember that, even on a sales site, the goal of the user is not always simply to buy. Clarify for yourself what that means more specifically. On a sales site, a wide variety of buyers may show up, including

✔ **Casual surfers,** who are drawn in by the site's content or by following a link on another site

✔ **Comparison shoppers,** who are looking at the contrasts among brands, products, features, prices, and so on

✔ **Previous purchasers,** who are back looking into what's fresh and who may be seeking another product, an upgrade, or support with what they already have

✔ **Buyers,** who may arrive ready to buy as either first-time customers or repeat customers

As you develop your content, think about the site features that will help each of these groups. The point is not to make separate pages and paths for people with varying motivations or needs. But do take them all into account as you develop content. To continue with our sales site example, make sure that first-time buyers have access to adequate information about your purchase system, what credit cards you accept, and your return policy; also make sure that repeat customers don't have to wade through endless detail about how to make a purchase. Give repeat buyers suggestions for upgrades and complementary products without confusing the comparison shoppers with items that aren't within the range that they're investigating.

Whatever your site's purpose and whatever its content, during the content development process, you (or your minions, if you have them) have to go through the site page by page, ironing out details. You can do this on the fly while you're building the site — as so many others do — or in preproduction planning. We recommend planning. You can find out about more things to consider as you develop your overall strategy in Chapters 4 through 7. Chapter 8 describes tools that you can use to plan and build your site's organization. Here, we stick with understanding the key issues you need to address in developing any kind of content for any kind of Web site.

Each page on any kind of site is likely to include *primary content,* which is the most important content for users to see, read, or experience. On a content-driven or informational page, the primary content may be an article; on a page in a product catalog, it may be the product description and data (the price, size, and so on).

Many pages also have *secondary content,* which is often the content that fulfills the apparently secondary purpose of the page. For example, on a site that offers new parents information about bringing home baby for the first time, an article on that topic may be the primary content, and a secondary content area on the page may offer products related to safety (like car seats) for sale. In yet a third (or *tertiary*) content area, a testimonial or a link to related sites or articles on infant safety might be offered. We are not talking about so-called second-level content here; *second-level content* is a term people use to describe content that is on the second level down in a site map (see Chapter 8). We are talking about bits of primary and secondary content within a given page, rather than looking at levels of the site as a whole.

The purposes of secondary and tertiary content on a Web page often include

- ✔ **Cross-selling:** Offering a product or service that's related to the primary offering on the page. As an example, on a sales site's page that describes one automotive book, suggesting other books with related themes or accessories for the same type of car is a cross-sell.

- ✔ **Upselling:** Offering an upgraded version of the product or service that's featured in the primary content on the page. For example, a sales page for a product may offer a discount for a volume purchase of the product, or a higher-priced package that includes that product bundled with others. A page selling a subscription might offer a longer-term subscription at a discount.

✔ **Promoting:** Offering some special promotion like a contest, rebate, or discount; or offering a snippet pointing out the best thing about the product; or, on a community page that lists discussion groups, showing users a juicy tidbit from one discussion to encourage them to participate.

✔ **Harmonizing:** Offering a smidgen of content, an image, or some other feature that acts as a counterpoint to the main content.

✔ **Commenting:** Offering some remark, such as a testimonial, an editorial or interpretive comment, or a quote.

✔ **Guidance:** Offering links that lead to some special, related area of the site. (Note that this should not typically take the place of the nav bar; it should be more similar to harmonizing.)

Presenting alphas, betas, and staging servers

One does not wave one's hands or even a magic wand and — poof! — there's a Web site, all set to launch. Building a site takes time and involves moving through a number of stages. You must develop your site and test it before you make it public, and to do so, you have to put it somewhere where the public can't get to it but your team and the testers can. The first and second rounds of site development are known as the *alpha* and *beta* stages. Pages on an alpha site can be in any state of development — from nonexistent to fully tested and ready to deploy. That's up to you. If you're contracting out your site's building, the Web shop folks building it are probably going to host the alpha site on their server — the one where they do their work. (This is also known sometimes as the *production* server.) They probably don't want you to make changes directly on the alpha site (because they need to know what changes are made), and they may even restrict your ability to look at it, for fear that you may see something that's not done and express undue anxiety.

At a later stage, the site can be placed on the *beta* server. Again, what marks this stage is up for negotiation. Usually, all the content and graphics are done. The links should all work. Beyond that, who knows. At the beta stage, you open the site to a wider range of testing, although you probably don't make it available to the public. Beta sites are usually housed on a different server (or at least a different part of the server) than the alpha site.

All this talk of multiple servers may sound intimidating, but it's not so bad. You can quite reasonably run your alpha, beta, and even your publicly accessible Web server all on the same physical machine. (See Chapter 11.) The point is to keep these three versions of your site separate.

When your site is operational, you'll presumably keep freshening up and adding to its content. You then need a *staging* server to act as the beta server for new material. A staging server provides you with a place to work and try out new things without making them public. (Just imagine what it would look like if some hapless user started accessing a page while you were working on it.) In a sense, your alpha and beta sites are actually on staging servers; the point here, though, is that you need a staging server on a continual basis as long as you have a site.

You must enforce security on the staging server so that access to it is limited to only those who need it. You don't want the public looking around your staging server. You also don't want just anyone inside your company to look at it.

Making Content More Usable

One famous truism about online content is that people don't like to read online. But the results of a four-year joint study by Stanford University and the Poynter Institute (www.poynter.org) show that users do read online content, they simply read differently online. The study showed that online readers skim headlines, summaries, images, and captions, reading "shallow but wide," and then pursue their interest in some specific topics in depth. Usability studies by Jakob Nielsen (www.useit.com) and others also point to patterns in how users experience online content. And professional content producers, strategists, developers, and editors have learned a thing or two about what works. At last, a picture of the best way to present users with online content has emerged.

Keep it short, chunk it up

First, be brief and to the point. Stick to one idea per paragraph and one point per sentence. Use short sentences. Just as importantly, create short pages. Break longer text into shorter chunks. Asking users to read 500 words on one page is about the max; 250 or less is much better. But don't just arbitrarily break wordy text into shorter pages ending with <u>Read On</u> or <u>Continued</u> links. Brief phrasing is easier for users to read than blocks of narrative text. Make text scannable by following these tips:

- Write 50 percent less text than you might normally
- Keep paragraphs short
- Use bulleted lists wherever possible
- Use headings (as many as three levels) to facilitate finding information on the page
- Make headings more meaningful than clever; cleverness at the expense of understanding makes finding what users seek on a page more difficult

Now notice how much easier you found reading and grasping the info in the bulleted list above than in the narrative text that follows:

> You should write 50 percent less text than you might normally. Keep paragraphs short. Use headings (as many as three levels) to facilitate finding information on the page, and use bulleted lists wherever possible. Make headings more meaningful than clever; cleverness at the expense of understanding makes finding what users seek on a page more difficult.

You can use bold text or highlighting to emphasize important words or phrasing, but don't overdo it. When too many things are emphasized on a page, they all lose their impact. Also, instead of using *continued* links, put in place a meaningful phrase that will compel users to click forward. (See "Leveraging Linking" and "Writing for Web sites" later in this chapter.)

Assign on-screen real estate wisely

The portion of a Web page that's on-screen and immediately visible without scrolling is known as *above the fold.* That term is borrowed from newspapers, where the most important headlines and images appear literally above the fold in the newspaper. On a Web page, the most important content also appears in the area above the fold. People don't scroll down below the fold unless they have good reason. In your site planning and maintenance, consider which material is the most important (from all the material you want to present) and put it above the fold.

Use summaries and the inverted pyramid model

Strong leads spark interest. (*Leads* are opening sentences.) It's no accident that journalists and other writers slave over the opening lines in their work. You have a little over one second to snatch your reader's attention. The first sentence of any writing has to do that, while subsequent sentences must compel readers to keep going.

In high school English composition classes, teachers instruct their students to present a premise in the first sentence of a piece of writing and then to address that premise in subsequent sentences that lead to some conclusion. In journalism school, writers are taught the opposite: The conclusion comes first, followed by the information that led to the conclusion. This structure is known as the *inverted pyramid model.* The main point, or freshest news (the conclusion of the story) is at the base (or top, really) of the upside-down pyramid, with older information and detail below. Generally, the inverted pyramid model works best for Web sites because users get the point right away and then read more deeply if they're interested.

Using the inverted pyramid model also allows you to present summaries or opening blurbs on major pages (such as the home page) more easily. You can, if the material is written properly, simply use the ever-so-brief opening paragraph as your front-page summary with a link leading to the full story or more information on another page. Users will get your point, even if they don't read on, and if they do read on, they'll get more of your point. See news sites (such as CNN.com) for examples, but also notice how other sites use this method. Retail sites have a link leading to the product page in the catalog, and portals have a link leading to the featured site or story. For an excellent discussion of using the inverted pyramid model on Web sites, see www.useit.com.

Leveraging Linking

When a user opens up a Web page, in that first crucial second of glancing at the page, certain items jump into the user's perceptions. The headings, images, and boldface text are among those items, but so are the links. By virtue of being a different color and often underlined, all links are highlighted. You can use that highlighting both to aid navigation and to underscore (excuse the pun) your site's benefits and branding.

To leverage linking as a navigational and branding opportunity, determine what payoff or benefit the user gets from following the link. Link not on click here (what does that tell the user about what he or she gets for following the link?), but on some more compelling phrase. Choose the right phrase (you may have to rewrite entire sentences to do this), and you telegraph to users who are scanning the page both where they can go and what they can get there. That makes your site (even in its depths) seem at first glance as unique and wonderful as it is. Note how much more interesting this seems: "Read Stephen King's new novel" than this does: "To read Stephen King's new novel, click here."

Link enough but not too much. Not all sites should encourage browsing; think strategically to determine if your site should have many links (to spike interest in hopping around from page to page) or a few links that lead the user down a subtly prescribed path. If yours is a sales site, for example, your policy for site development may say that all roads lead to the sale. In that case, most links on the site lead to the catalog or product info. From there, the main route is through the purchase path. Users should be able to go back and make changes to their orders (or keep shopping), but links that act as distractions from buying simply won't exist.

Whatever the nature of your site, consider linking policy questions such as these:

- ✔ How many links are allowable in a paragraph or on a page? (Remember that more links means more exit points.)

- ✔ What information should you include for links to downloads, large graphics, or special media? For example, users may need to know about the format and size of the files.

- ✔ Is linking outside of the site okay? Do those links open a new browser window?

- ✔ When and how should links be in the form of buttons instead of text? (Remember that changing buttons requires having an artist design and produce the button; changing text is easier. But graphical buttons are usually more noticeable on a page than text links.)

- ✔ Which important links go on the nav bars or in the footer (the text at the bottom of every page)?

Keeping Content Fresh

Users enjoy not just high-quality content, but also content that's *updated frequently*. Look again at Figure 3-1, which cites a Forrester survey of 8,600 Web-enabled households, if you have any doubt. Note, however, that the survey asked what drove *repeat traffic*. Also note that *high-quality content* (75 percent) beat out *updated frequently* (66 percent) by a significant margin, and consider this: How often must a site that offers stable, carefully researched reference material be updated? Must every page of every site be updated frequently? Like many other rules of Web site design and development, people can take the one about frequent updates too literally. And updating content costs time, money, and attention to detail. The real trick in making your site tick is to apply updates where needed and when needed and to minimize the need for them wherever possible.

Decide which content must be evergreen

Producers of online content have borrowed the concept known as *evergreen* from broadcast and print publications. Evergreen content is content that remains fresh on and on into not-quite-eternity because it contains few indicators of changing eras. In broadcast, to keep content evergreen, the announcer or characters are dressed in more timeless styles, they avoid slang and references to current events, and they focus on topics that will interest people for some duration.

You can keep your online content evergreen most easily by avoiding language that dates the content. In addition to actual dates, terms like *now, soon, yesterday, last month, recent, current,* and *next* place the text in a certain time slot. If you simply avoid using those words (and phrases like *current catalog, next version,* and *this season*), you won't have to keep up with their implications.

Avoid other things that change, too. Let's face it: People get promoted, change companies, and (unfortunately) get hit by buses. How stable is a list of employees? Because executives tend to stay with the company — and because

who they are has influence on investors, job candidates, and others —
including executives' names and titles on the site is fine. And because the
media insists on having a contact name and number on every press release,
you must include that information in your online press room. But because
growing companies often experience turnover, move staff from office to office,
or upgrade their phone systems (resulting in a shuffling of direct lines), it's
often best not to post most specific information about staff and how to contact them. Don't list staff names and titles. Stick to just the main phone number
and one or two other key phone numbers, such as the customer service
number.

You can and should target some content for frequent or at least periodic
updates. Again, make strategic decisions about which content areas, types,
or pages are the most high-profile ones. Comb content that changes less frequently for markers of changing times, and make that material evergreen. But
apply your content resources wherever you can to get the most impact for
making updates. You can automate processes to maximize your resources
(see Chapters 13 and 22). You can measure the effect of your content on your
audience (see Chapter 17). But before you start building your site (or even
writing your content), decide where you are willing to put your efforts and
where your efforts will best pay off. Make the rest evergreen.

Avoid the generic and overused

Some words and phrases are so overused on the Web that they've lost their
impact. Some others have always been so vague that they weren't very
helpful. We recommend avoiding the following cliched or overly generic
words and phrases:

- ✔ **Click here:** This term does not tell users what they will get or where they
  are going. Find phrasing for your links that describes what the benefit or
  payoff is if users follow the link's path. *That* will inspire them to click.

- ✔ **Check out:** This may have become as common as it is because programmers with little writing experience created so many early Web sites. You
  have many options for replacing *check out*. Try these terms: see, look
  into, investigate, explore, try, experience, enjoy, consider, delve into, or
  take a gander at. Avoid excessive embellishment, but among these
  phrases and others, choose those that are most suitable for your site's
  audience.

- ✔ **What's new:** In the early days of the Web, before people got a clue, many
  sites had What's New areas. Users had to drill down to and through those
  areas to find what was fresh and interesting. Now everyone knows that a
  Web site is all about what's new, and that what's new should be obvious,
  right? Labeling the obvious (like writing *pipe* on a pipe) is unnecessary
  and silly, and on a Web site, it dilutes the power of the site's message.

✔ **"Welcome to . . .":** Like the stereotypical diner waitress, many Web sites start their content by saying "Welcome to" whatever. You can *be welcoming* without saying it literally. (Conversely, you can say it and not seem welcoming at all.) Carefully choosing the words that appear on your pages is crucial. Pages must be short, which means that each word counts. Perhaps more importantly, search engines weigh how often significant words (assumed to be keywords) appear as compared to the number of other words on the page, so having words that are beside the point dilutes your content as well as your standing in search engine rankings.

✔ **Under construction:** You simply shouldn't post anything that is under construction. Launch new pages, areas, or sites when they are ready. You have no excuse for showing users your unreadiness, and apologizing for it doesn't help.

✔ **Hot, cool, or neat:** Again perhaps because people who are not professional writers create so many sites (it's incredible how many people undervalue good writing), all too many wonderful things on Web sites are described as hot, cool, or neat. Yawn. Just exactly what is so hot, cool, or neat about those things? Get past the generic and tell users what is special rather than your opinion that something is special. These alternatives aren't so commonly used: terrific, wonderful, unique, well-crafted, clever, surprising, lovely, beautiful, charming, quaint, slick, handsome, or modern. Intrigue your users by painting a clear picture (in words) of what you want them to appreciate.

✔ **And more:** Way too much marketing and sales copy consists of a quick list of attributes or benefits ending in *. . . and more!* If there's more, perhaps you need another bullet point to list more.

✔ **The buzz:** This word seems to be buzzing around everywhere lately. Everyone and all of his or her siblings, cousins, and acquaintances have named either the Web site's e-mail newsletter or the thinly disguised What's New area of the site *The Buzz.* The buzz sounded fresh, cute, and zippy until it was swarming all around us and became annoying. Find a fresher take on your news.

Note, however, that some words and phrases serve their purposes best by being standardized. Just as everyone in the United States understands what an *Exit* sign means, everyone on the Web recognizes basic conventions such as, *Contact Us, Help,* and *About the Company.* How do *click here, what's new,* and *welcome to* differ? Well, they generally are intended to lead to something that's terrific, wonderful, or fresh, not something that's fairly standard. To focus a user's attention on the terrific, wonderful, or fresh and get them to go there, make that something seem as special as it is and more special than the standard stuff.

When to break the rules

Knowing when to bend or break the rules is a real skill in the management of anything, including Web sites. If posting the names, titles, and contributions of specific employees is going to boost morale at a key time, you may want to bend your keep-it-evergreen policy. And if your site promotes an eatery where at every table all the wait people say, "Welcome to Pearl's Oysters," then by all means, ditch our advice to not use that "Welcome to" phrase on your Web site. It's your call. After all, our overarching advice is to think strategically and make your content appropriate to your audience, business model, and overall goals.

Planning ahead for content maintenance

Decide how much maintenance the site as a whole will get and how much each area or page will get. Be realistic. Compare and contrast the level of maintenance that would be optimal for your users with the level of maintenance that you can actually do. Consider your staffing levels, your priorities, and (if you are a one-person band) your energy and how much stamina you have for upkeep. How often will you rotate new content in and out? How often will you update products, prices, dates, people's names, and other information that seems to change frequently?

As you develop your site plan, make notes for each page or type of content. Note whether it is necessary to make the entire site, an area, or any given page evergreen. If you plan to change or update the content at some point, make notes regarding your plan for maintaining, archiving, or eventually axing that material. How often will you do it, and what types of changes will you make?

Using the Right Media for the Occasion

Use bells and whistles (and doo-dads, gadgets, and gee-gaws) only when they further the true cause. Knowing what to use when is a challenge. Here are a few pointers:

✔ Use animation to show change or transition, to help users visualize something that's 3-D, or to enrich a user experience — but not just as a cheap and flashy attention getter. (Unless, of course, yours is a circus or carnival site.)

✔ Use audio and video to promote entertainment events and use audio as background for video clips that really need it (like dance). But remember not to rely on sound for sites geared toward low-bandwidth, hearing impaired, or international users who may not get the benefit of audio. Also, remember that a downloadable transcript will arrive on the user's computer much more quickly than streaming media or downloadable media. Sometimes a transcript is better.

✔ Use 3-D effects when they're truly needed, for example, to facilitate planning or workflow. Often, 3-D visual modeling can aid processes of engineering, space planning, biotechnology, and other disciplines. However, remember that the software users need for 3-D effects is still buggy, and because navigation isn't standard, you need to make the effort to show users how it works.

✔ Use PDF (Adobe Acrobat) files when you need to retain the page layout that was created for print, for example, when you want users to download, print, and fill out a form (such as the IRS's tax forms) that must be processed in the physical world. The files (especially if they include lots of art or color) can be big, bigger, and bigger still, and they take a while to download. True repurposing of print content for online use involves chunking it up, making it interactive, and otherwise converting it into Web pages.

Going overboard with gratuitous special media is easy. Think about why you want to use any given media and what best serves the user experience. Also, make sure you've secured the right permissions for reusing content; just because you have the rights to use a piece of text or art in print doesn't mean you can use that stuff freely online. (See Chapter 7.)

Writing for Web Sites

Write for the people in your audience. Know what kind of language will reach them and use that language. We're talking about tone and word choices here — not English, French, or Swahili. Travel and food writing, for example, uses lots of adjectives and descriptive phrasing; the goal is to evoke an experience for the reader. How-to writing (like this book) uses lots of action verbs because the text is about *doing something.* To get a sense of how writing differs from one topic to another, get a newspaper and browse through the sports, home, business, and travel sections. Then, to get a sense of how writing varies from one publication to another, compare three magazines on the same topic. Then notice the word choices and tone that distinguish various well-known publications such as *The New York Times, The Wall Street Journal, People,* and *Martha Stewart Living* from each other. Try the same exercises with online publications and see how similar or different they sound from one another. The ground rules you set and follow for the use of language can solidify or dilute your content's personality. (See the section titled "Creating branding via content" in this chapter.)

Keep it plain, Jane

Avoid excessive embellishment in the language of your site as well as in its design and gadgetry. Stick to basic sentence structures. Keep sentences, as well as paragraphs, short. Go with just one idea per paragraph and one point per sentence. Say what you have to say to make your point, but say no more than that. Use plain language — ordinary words like *use* win out over words like *utilize.* Plain English is simple, honest, and without hype. It doesn't let cleverness obscure meaning. Be unambiguous. Use words exactly as they are really, truly defined and use any given word to mean the same thing every time you use it.

Of course, times may arise when your branding requires humor, slang, or cute twists on phrasing — hey, the book you hold in your hands uses a dash of humor here and there! But as you surely know by now, people scan what they read online. They read more slowly online (25 percent more slowly, according to research), and anything you do that requires them to read even slightly more deeply to get your drift is likely to snow them under. So for the most part, keep it simple.

Use lists for scannability

Use bulleted and numbered lists to make text scannable, but use them appropriately. Bulleted lists are best used when the order of the items listed doesn't have to be consecutive:

- Apples

- Oranges

- Bananas

When the order does have to be consecutive (as in a list of steps to be completed one after another), use numbered lists:

1. Peel the apple.

2. Slice the apple.

3. Eat the apple.

As you write bulleted lists, make your list at least two items but no more than seven. (Between three and five is actually optimal.) Break longer lists into several shorter lists as necessary. Use the same sentence structure for all the bulleted items within one list; for example, if some start with verbs, they should all start with verbs. Similarly, avoid mixing incomplete sentences (fragments, in other words) with complete sentences in the same list. This aids readability and is analogous to making the navigation of links on your site easy and intuitive. For more on writing bulleted lists and other writing tips, see the excellent articles on Ron Scheer's Web site at www.ronscheer.com.

Write sales copy that sells

Good sales content closes the sale. It's not intended to encourage browsing. Okay, in some cases (for example, bookstores), browsing online recreates the store experience, and that can be a good thing. But in general, sales *copy* (or text) gets to the point and sticks to it. And the point is that this is a terrific product that the user should buy now.

To make good sales content, first put goods out in the open. Let people see what they're buying (what's that they say about one picture and a thousand words?) and give them all the info they need to make a purchase decision. Keep the writing short but make the benefits of having this product or service clear. In your lead (your opening sentence), launch right into this. Tell people that this product is hand-crafted, indestructible, or whatever it actually is. If you say the product is full-featured, then name those features! Tell people what the product can do for them: It can make them slim, happy, or healthy; it can solve all their business problems (name them); it can inspire small songbirds to hover around them if they simply *buy this product now.* (Notice the call to action at the end.) Don't tell people what isn't true or make false claims (cite the songbirds only if they'll really show up), but do place everything in the most positive light possible. A little house isn't cramped, it's cozy. A low-cost product isn't cheap, it's inexpensive or (better yet) a good value.

Don't place barriers in the way of a sale. Don't require users to register before seeing the products (or at any point before registration is actually necessary to complete the sale). Don't force users to click around to get all the information they need. Make the purchase path clean, clear, and as easy to complete in as few steps as possible. Chapters 5 and 14 offer more tips for setting up online sales.

Watch out for adjacency

When two pieces of content are adjacent to each other and have conflicting messages, they unintentionally comment on each other. The classic example of how this can be a problem is when a newspaper article about a famine appears next to the grocery store ad for the Thanksgiving turkeys. On Web sites, the problem of adjacency arises similarly, and banner ads that appear in rotation bring up the problem. For example, a banner ad for an airline probably shouldn't pop up on a page that talks about plane crashes.

Another problem can occur when a site has a linking policy that sets up an adjacency issue. For example, we were once reading online content about satellite images, and illustrating the article was a photo showing (according to the caption) a satellite image of Atlanta, Georgia. Cool! Reading along again in the text, we learned that, in addition to Atlanta, Georgia, satellite images of Chicago; Portland, Oregon; and Shenshen, China, were also available. So we clicked the <u>Portland, Oregon</u> link. A map showing the location of Portland, Oregon, appeared. No satellite image. We clicked <u>Atlanta, Georgia</u>. Same thing. Clicking around the site further, we came to realize that this site had a policy of linking all location names to maps showing users where that place was. The policy was great for the site's other content, but because in this case the links appeared next to the satellite image of a city, we had been set up to expect to see more satellite images when we clicked on the other location links. When you set your policies, friends, take into account how adjacency can rear its head in unexpected ways.

Work those keywords

Many, many articles and books tell you to optimize your site for better search engine indexing by including strategically chosen keywords in the page's title, META tags (special HTML code that allows you to insert keywords and a description), and the first few paragraphs of text.

What most people do, though, is create their content, build their sites, and then go back to do the keyword chore. Okay, so really, many people never do. It's just too daunting. But they know they should. How, they may wonder, does a person figure out how to get the keywords into the text when the text is already on the page and rewriting it is so much like wrestling a big, toothy bear?

Here, friends, is our tip of the day: Write the keywords first, before you create the content. Make choosing the keywords part of your strategy phase and then require the person who actually writes the copy to work in the keywords. To do this, simply select four or five words that are clearly and closely the topic words for the page. For a page about fly fishing for bass on a specific river, the keywords (or phrases, in this case) may be *fish, fly fishing, bass,* and the name of the river. At the planning stage, you just need to jot down the keywords. Chapters 8 and 16 show you what to do with them to max your chances with the search engines. Clue your writers (or yourself) into how to use keywords before they become an afterthought.

Attend to the microcontent

Give those page titles, error messages, footers, e-mail subject lines, and other small pieces of text some attention, too. Itty-bitty bits of text add up to big impact on users. When an error message appears on-screen, the user's eyeballs are on it, and if the user doesn't understand the error message, that affects the user's experience of your site's usability. Similarly, when you send e-mail newsletters or announcements, the subject line is either going to draw people in or it isn't. Use the basic principles of keeping content short, to the point, and easily understandable as you shape your microcontent as well as the bigger bits of text.

Going International

International sites are those that are targeted to users in various countries, while *localized sites* are those that are targeted especially to users in a given country or region. If you are conducting online sales, you must take into account a variety of issues that have to do with taxation, fulfillment, and shipping when you venture abroad. And if you are creating either an international site or a localized site, you have to take into account differences in language, culture, and custom.

Obviously, you ought to avoid specific cultural references (for example, references to specific sports, celebrities, holidays, and so on). Remember that people in other countries probably know as little of your culture as you do of theirs. Avoid visual or language puns as well as most humor. Humor, at its essence, tickles our assumptions, and many of our assumptions are based on what we have learned in our culture.

Consider how to handle dates and times. The European system goes day/month/year while the American system goes month/day/year. Using Greenwich mean time (and saying that you are doing so) is probably safest. Also, determine how to handle currencies. (Hmmm . . . will you list all of them? And how can you handle the shifting exchange rates?)

Get actual international users to test international sites (not just Americans who speak Spanish, Russian, Japanese, or Farsi). Native speakers understand cultural nuances in language and customs to which non-native speakers probably won't be attuned. Beware of offering gifts or incentives to international testers; gift-giving customs (and laws) vary from culture to culture.

If your site is created in English but meant to address English-speaking people in non-English-speaking countries, use basic sentence structures. (That's *basic,* not infantile.) Using internationally recognized symbols, such as flags or icons, is fine, but again, don't speak down to your users. They're smart people. After all, they speak multiple languages.

A Word on Wireless

More and more, wireless devices (handheld computers, PDAs, cell phones) are delivering online content. As you develop your wireless content, remember that, just as print content does not translate to the Web without significant reshaping, Web site content is not going to convert neatly to wireless. You must willfully cut, edit, and shorten the material to make it right for wireless.

The most obvious issue is that the screen real estate that's available on handheld devices is miniscule compared to a Web page. Perhaps the best way to present material on the smaller screen is to offer users a short list of carefully chosen big-picture categories or headings. (Keep the headings themselves short!) A news site may have categories like International, National, Local, Business, Sports, and Weather, for example. After the user selects one of the categories, subcategories or a short list of headings (five or six at most) that describe the exact content within may appear.

Next, you may offer the user the actual content or the option to choose between a one-paragraph summary and the ruthlessly-shortened-but-still-longer-than-a-summary version. A niftier idea is to offer those on cell phones an audio version of the content. An even jazzier application of wireless content is to have the cell phone actually ring to alert users of something of interest to them — say, an unfavorable traffic report on their morning commute route or important changes in stock quotes. The wireless medium generally lends itself to more audio. Movie and music reviews can include sound clips, and people can hear jokes with a stand-up comic's voice and timing or access personal coaching via a directory that rings up the coach for consultation.

Where the medium is going is still before us as we write this book. In 2000, researchers said that 3 percent of the market had online access via wireless devices, but that some time in 2001, that number would explode to 78 percent. AvantGo (www.avantgo.com) is currently a market leader in offering wireless content. We look forward to seeing how AvantGo and others leverage the medium.

You must certainly select what goes out via wireless carefully. But you'd be well advised also to take advantage of the unique opportunities presented by wireless. *Remember:* Wireless means on the go. Good wireless content contains whatever people want on the spot, such as new car reviews while they're test driving cars, access to real estate listings as they come out, or quick tips for using Excel as the boss hands out assignments. But elevating wireless to its best potential may mean, for example, connecting people with like interests by cell phone or PDA as they near each other. It may mean using voice, sound, or the wireless device itself to ping users to call home at a certain time. It will certainly mean finding services and offering content that's fresh and different and uses the medium well.

The Big Deal about Broadband

Bandwidth-gobbling content is still rare as of this writing, but according to Forrester Research, by 2003, 27 million users will have broadband access. Broadband enables plenty of easily imaginable opportunities for streaming audio and video, video shopping, games, movies, and live entertainment events. But it also opens a world of possibilities for demonstrating surgical procedures and many business, medical, education, engineering, and research applications. You can see some b2c (business-to-consumer) and b2b (business-to-business) uses of broadband by starting your explorations at OnBroadband.com (www.onbroadband.com), a broadband portal.

As always, we admonish you to think carefully and strategically when you consider broadband. Your broadband content should fulfill well-defined goals for your site. It's the rare site that has its purpose simply wowing the public. Broadly speaking, the use of broadband should be for a reason, not just to inspire a gee-whiz reaction among users.

In general, the novelty of simply browsing Web sites has worn off. Most users today are on the Web seeking something that is of use to them. Whether (and why) users will sit at their computers watching a feature film when they could be comfortably munching popcorn while watching TV from a living room easy chair remains to be seen. But broadband, like other twists on the online medium, has many potential applications that can be of true use. Among those may be many community-oriented applications. Community is the subject of our next chapter.

Chapter 4

Building Community for Fun and Profit

*T*he term *community* was bandied about quite recklessly in the online world for a while. It showed up in all sorts of business and project plans with little true regard for what it really meant. Generally, the uninitiated thought that by opening up a chat room you were launching "community" on your site and that millions would flock to the chat room to participate simply because it was there. Little did they realize that merely throwing open your door did not a party make. These days, community is recognized as a key element in the dynamics and success of many Web sites. To know whether community is right for you as well as how to launch, grow, and leverage community, you have to know what makes communities tick.

What Community Truly Is

Community is not technology. Community is not chat, online conferencing, newsletters, discussion groups, or message boards. Community is a feeling, in a sense — it's a bond. A community is basically a group of people who share an *affinity*. That affinity might be the result of common interests, experiences, goals, or something else. Whether you're a collector of pink Royal Lace depression glass, a newly minted stay-at-home dad, or an up and coming Wall Street whiz kid, you probably feel kinship with others like you.

For a community to form and grow, its members must *interact* with each other. If you haven't spoken to anyone from your high school class for years, you probably don't consider yourself part of the community of the Class of . . . well, never mind. Also, to be members of a community, people must actually identify themselves as such. Sally may write stories and poems by the dozen, but if she doesn't think of herself as a writer, she will not think of herself as part of the writing community.

Members of the community begin to feel a *bond* with each other as they interact. They trade information, and in a best case scenario, a kind of *reciprocity* grows — an exchange of favors, quips, and interest that furthers the bond and the community spirit. Affinity, interaction, bonding, and reciprocity knit themselves into more affinity, interaction, bonding, and reciprocity. As long as things are humming along, they all feed each other.

To build a thriving online community, you must first target a specific group of people and their affinities. Then you must figure out what they want and need, and deliver it to them.

In some cases, the people in your target group will want to interact online. Sites that offer that include iVillage (`www.ivillage.com`) and TalkCity (`www.talkcity.com`). In some cases, they'll want information that serves their real-world community; an example of this is the Redland Baptist Church Web site (`www.redlandbaptist.org`). The LinuxWorld Web site (`www.linuxworld.com`) offers both interaction and information to the Linux developer community. And sites such as eBay (`www.ebay.com`) and ChemConnect (`www.chemconnect.com`) add a twist to the idea of community — they bring together a community of buyers and sellers by offering those people a forum for acting on their interest in buying and selling. (For a terrific portal offering vast information about online communities, see `virtualcommunities.start4all.com/`.)

When we talk about community in this chapter, we focus on interactive community, but keep in mind that much of what we say also applies to sites that serve a community without offering interactivity, as well as sites that offer communities of buyers and sellers a forum for their activities.

When we talk about community, we are, in fact, implicitly describing *interaction*. For a community to form, interaction has to occur, whether that is the interaction of ashram members at their places of meditation, of teenagers in a chat room, or of buyers and sellers online or at a real-world auction house.

For your online community to thrive, its users must not only visit your site regularly, but also interact with the site (its tools and functionality), with you (or whomever handles user relations), and with each other. Additionally, users ought to have a vested interest in the site and the community it represents; they should feel that the site *reflects them* as well as being *for them*.

If you can achieve all of these things, you have an ace community in the works. This chapter shows you how to get started.

What Community Can Do for You

Before you launch community, you must establish the goals you want it to achieve. That will enable and define the success you expect. Here are some typical goals for online community efforts:

- Increase overall site traffic so you can sell ad space, content, services, or products to advertisers, sponsors, or partners.

- Create a *destination Web site* — one whose main attraction is the particular community itself, the interactive tools it offers, or its selection of community-oriented links.

- Enable users of a product to support each other in using the product, optimizing it, and providing the product's manufacturers with valuable user feedback.

- Incorporate users' voices into a Web site by soliciting community input.

- Form an audience for your organization's or a person's opinions and philosophies.

- Amass user demographic information (gleaned from registered user data) that can be sold to other companies. (Note that selling aggregated data is very different from selling the names and e-mail addresses of individual users. *Aggregated* data describes trends but cannot be used to target or contact individual users, so selling it does not inspire the same panic as selling information about individual users.)

Obviously, your community goals are related to your overall site goals (see Chapter 2). Community for the sake of community can be the goal, and if yours is an altruistic effort, that's dandy. But if you are creating community for business reasons or you want revenue of some sort that at least sustains the community effort, go to Chapter 2 for a more detailed discussion about setting goals, read about budgeting in Chapter 6, write up a quick business or project plan, and make sure you're going to achieve what you hope to achieve.

Technologies and Techniques for Community

To contact and convert users into active community members, allow community members to interact with each other, and turn the community's voice into visible, living parts of your Web site's content, you have to understand and choose among several options for community technologies, including

- **E-Mail Newsletters:** Based on a *mailing list* (a list of subscribers' e-mail addresses), an e-mail newsletter goes out from one source (usually the "list owner") to many recipients and is often used to announce news, provide tips or information, or broadcast messages from the owner of the list (new features! special deals!). In a variation, messages can be routed through a central location from one member to all other members (garage sale! job available! does anyone know a good dentist?) rather than directly and solely from the list owner. When the message goes from the owner of the list and its goal is to encourage users to visit the Web site for more information or to reap benefits, the e-mail newsletter is a highly effective method for upping traffic numbers. See Chapter 15 for more information about increasing traffic. Newsletters usually focus on topics of interest to their subscribers and can be formatted to be very attractive. (Chapter 15 shows some examples.) E-mail newsletters can be as short as one paragraph or considerably longer, but they must offer subscribers value of some kind or else they are perceived simply as junk mail.

- **E-Mail Discussion Groups:** Again based on a mailing list of subscribers, an e-mail discussion occurs among numerous participants. Each message goes from one person (who is as likely to be any member of the list as it is to be the "owner" of the list) to everyone on the list. This allows any user who subscribes to the list to make comments, ask questions, and send news that's of interest to the group. Again, each user's e-mail goes to everyone who's on the list; each response also goes to everyone.

- **Message Boards:** Message boards are electronic forums that appear directly on Web pages. Here, the users don't have to subscribe; they can simply join in by posting messages to the discussion (using their Web browsers). Threaded discussions on a message board organize all messages according to an initially posted subject with the responses to that subject indexed below it, while serial discussions show all the messages, whatever their subject, in a single, unindexed list.

- **Chat Areas:** In chat areas, sessions, or rooms, users can see, follow, and respond to a discussion that's occurring in real time. They use chat software to read and particiapte in the discussion, typing their own comments and seeing them along with those of other participants on screens as all the comments are typed. Many users can chat in one session simultaneously. Chat areas work well when a session has a *big draw,* such as a celebrity guest, or when the site already has a *lot* of foot traffic.

We discuss these technologies further in the sections that follow; we also introduce snazzy emerging technologies such as online conferencing and wireless- and broadband-based communities. Then, in later sections of this chapter, we talk about how to create, manage, and serve online communities.

E-mail mailing lists: Newsletters and discussions

Through the no-hassle power of e-mail, you can provide a forum through which users can actually talk to each other. You can also use e-mail to remind users of the existence of your site, motivate them to return to it, and encourage them to be active, enthusiastic members of a community. To do either, you need to develop a mailing list of users' e-mail addresses. You can collect this information by offering users a chance to *opt in* (elect to receive mailings or participate in discussions). Assuming that they want in and including them all but offering them the choice to unsubscribe is known as letting them *opt out*. For the best success, let users opt in and position opting-in as an opportunity to enjoy a special, value-added service. Make the option to join very visible on your home page, or make it an option on your registration pages if you request that users become registered members of your Web site. See an example of an opt-in sign-up box in Figure 4-1.

Figure 4-1:
A sign-up box like this encourages users to subscribe.

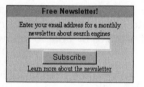

In newsletter and discussion group scenarios, the e-mail message has to pass through an e-mail server before the message goes to the distribution list. If the server is fast and capable, delivery can be quick, but the interaction doesn't occur in real time, as it does in chat.

Managing your mailing list can be accomplished via various tools (offered at www.topica.com, www.egroups.com, www.listbot.com, www.zaplets.com, www.onelist.com, www.lyris.com, and www.skylist.net, among others) that provide Web-based administration. Some are free, but others base their fees on the number of subscribers. More expensive options also allow more customization and tech support. If you anticipate sending many messages, you'll need more robust servers behind the scenes; don't expect the free or cheap tools or services to handle thousands of messages per day. And if you're headed toward millions of messages per day (good for you!), you need to get the help of a highly skilled and professional outsourced service to handle the whole business.

Message boards: Web-based discussions

Another kind of online discussion takes place in an electronic forum displayed on a Web page rather than via e-mail. This sort is called a *message board* or *discussion forum*. Users generally don't have to subscribe per se to a message board in order to participate. You can, if you must, require them to register as a user of your site or your message board before they join the fracas, but beware that user participation plummets when you make people jump through hoops on the way in. Message boards are not real-time discussion (as is chat). Rather, users post comments, read responses, and respond to other users' messages day or night, whenever they want. (In a chat, everyone has to be sitting there typing at the same time.) Sometimes, the discussion occurs peer-to-peer, and sometimes it centers around some expert or authority (say, an instructor in a distance learning setting) leading or guiding the discussion or answering questions. Two models exist for message board displays:

- ✔ **Threaded discussions:** A message appears, and all the responses related to it are grouped under it. The user sees just the message headings and can click on one to actually read it. Threading makes following a conversation easier and is especially preferable if the discussion is about something utilitarian or practical in nature. For example, if the message board is about do-it-yourself home repair and a user posts a question about laying a tile roof, you want interested users to be able to follow all the responses.

- ✔ **Serial discussions:** The messages are not grouped or indexed in any way. They simply appear in a single list in the order they are posted. While this is not as easy for a user to follow, it can be okay for discussions that are meant, for example, to encourage socializing among members.

You can either purchase software and run a message board on your site yourself or outsource the job. Owning the software may provide you with more control over the technology, but it will open cans of worms having to do with your time, your expertise with and access to the server, and so on. Outsourcing options range from free services (see www.everyone.net) to highly professional firms that specialize in community applications (TalkCity, at www.talkcity.com is an example). As usual, the more traffic you expect and the more mission critical your discussion group is, the more service you want and the more you'll probably pay.

Can we chat?

Live chat is, in many ways, the ultimate in community interaction. Here, dozens, hundreds, or even thousands of people engage in lively, interesting, useful, and friendly real-time conversations with others they might never have the chance to meet face-to-face under ordinary circumstances. At least, that's the ideal. The reality of live chat can fall short of that rosy image. Chat sessions, like discussion groups, can sometimes deteriorate into hostile flame wars and pointless non sequiturs, or chat can simply falter for lack of steam or sufficient participants.

To make chat work takes a bit of exertion. As you reach for community interaction and involvement, remember that human nature is on your side: People love to talk, and live online chat is popular. But like any event, a chat has to be set up well and announced. If you plan to run a chat room, here are some questions to consider

- ✔ What's the best setting and biggest draw for your audience? This may be a celebrity interview, a Web simulcast of a live event, an industry expert who can offer advice or answers to specific questions, or a chance to talk to others without barriers or formalities.

- ✔ Should you have a hosted chat, with a moderator or leader, or an unhosted chat, in which users can say whatever's on their mind to anyone who happens to be in the chat room?

- ✔ Can you spur conversation by setting a theme or topic for discussion each week in your chat area?

- ✔ Should you provide private chat rooms linked off the main, "public" room so that people can enter in one-on-one chats?

- ✔ Will children or teenagers be in your audience? If so, what special issues might you need to watch out for in your chat area?

- ✔ What kind of guidelines should you post for using your chat room? And, in case people don't abide by your guidelines, what kind of terms and conditions should you notify your users of in advance, to mitigate your liability for any objectionable chat room content?

Implementing Web chat

You can buy proprietary chat servers and implement them, or you can sign up for the services of an outsourced chat provider (such as TalkCity, at www. talkcity.com). Most of the popular proprietary chat servers are based on HTML or Java and allow you to offer graphics- and voice-enabled chat in addition to simple, text-based chat. User and administration features vary widely among the different programs; do careful comparison shopping in advance. Chat server software generally costs between a few hundred dollars and a few thousand, though programs are available free for a limited number of users (such as Virtual Places; see www.vplaces.com). Several large community Web sites have used ichat (www.ichat.com) successfully. The Palace server and client (www.thepalace.com) are popular with consumer sites that want to offer a fun graphical environment and customizable, animated 3-D *avatars* (icons that represent individual users in the chat room).

Pulling people in

Forrester Research has reported that without the draw of a celebrity host or an extraordinarily hot (and especially underserved) topic, to sustain a successful chat area a Web site needs "foot traffic" of at least 25,000 unique daily users to the Web site hosting the chat. (Sustaining a message board requires 2,500 unique daily users.) A general-interest site like Yahoo!, which has far more than the minimum daily visitors, draws enormous numbers of users to its chat areas; it has enough people passing through to siphon off a few and sustain traffic levels in its chats. For smaller, niche sites, the challenge is bigger. Knowing your audience well enough to provide chats about highly compelling topics can work. But remember — if you are not Macromedia, it's unlikely that users will think to go to your site to talk about Macromedia products. (They'll go to Macromedia.) And while having an expert or celebrity to "star" in your chats can work, that person has to be a true celebrity for his or her name to attract enough people.

A focused topic that has a big, underserved audience can also work — we once saw a chat on birdwatching get very lively indeed with no celebrity expert on hand and just a little publicity. (Birdwatchers seem to care intensely about their hobby and have little opportunity to talk with each other about it.)

If you intend to launch community on your site, just remember that any kind of community technology (e-mail discussions, message boards, or chat) must be supported by existing high levels of traffic to your site, or they must have a strong draw to pull people in, or both. Nothing is more deadening to interaction, bonding, and reciprocity than walking into an empty, lifeless party. Make sure that a real reason for people to gather is at the center of your community effort.

Keep in mind that in addition to the cost of a chat server (and, in some cases, a client), you do have to consider how the additional load on your system could affect processing time. You also have to employ someone to spend time administering the server (to install software, configure the chat rooms, and so on). If you have a moderator who is tech-savvy, this person could also serve as the administrator.

If you sign up with a service, the service does the back-end work for you, for example, running the server and configuring the chat rooms. The service may also promote the chat on its site, which will have already attracted many chat fans, and even toss in a moderator. As always, you must clarify what you'll receive for your buck-ohs.

One issue you must deal with when implementing chat is the privacy and comfort of your users. What if some unscrupulous user starts harassing other users by e-mailing them directly or attacking them online? You can minimize this hazard by requiring users to register as members on your site (free of charge), and then log in before participating in chat. This protects users'

privacy because actual e-mail addresses won't be visible, just the login names. Also, requiring registration and log-in ensures that you can contact users who post inappropriate comments, remind them of your guidelines, and, if necessary, bar them from accessing the chat room and perhaps other community areas in the future.

Hosting a special-event chat

Host a live chat revolving around a special event — say, a celebrity interview — publicize it well, and watch traffic soar. The bigger the celebrity, the bigger the draw. (But booking a celebrity can be costly, so be sure the expense is worthwhile and choose a celebrity of major interest to your audience.) You can have an interviewer ask questions of the celebrity while the community simply reads the exchange, or you can allow users to pose questions directly.

Be aware that direct questions from users can make the interview hard to follow, because users are likely to toss many questions at your guest and the questions appear in random order. Also awkward moments can occur if a user asks a guest to defend himself or herself against some charge (for example, if a musical or literary guest is accused of plagiarizing someone else's work). Of course, this could also be interpreted as a "juicy" moment, as the "shock jocks" of broadcasting have shown. But be careful, because letting users attack your guests can compromise your professional reputation. If you do decide to let users speak directly to a high-profile personality, we recommend having a moderator monitor the chat; don't leave your guest to fend for himself or herself.

Web simulcasts of real-world events are also popular. Form a strategic partnership with a media outlet such as a radio or TV station, and if it hosts a broadcast interview or event that resonates with your audience, you can arrange a live Web simulcast, along with chat rooms where users can converse about the event as it unfolds.

Live "parties," or online gatherings, have also proven to be well-liked. Arrange a gathering focusing on some timely event, such as a holiday or other day that is special to your audience, and invite your users to mingle with each other in celebration of the event. When a lifestyle Web site for baby boomers invited its sizable community to a virtual holiday party in a chat room that it had set up especially for that purpose, "party guests" arrived at the appointed hour (though some were "fashionably late," as can be expected). They chatted with fellow users they had not seen online in a while, met new friends, met staff members, and (virtually) toasted with eggnog.

To get your users together to enjoy special occasions together as a community via a chat session, reach past the mundane. You can offer party favors in the form of downloadable screen savers commemorating the occasion. Give away door prizes by mailing them to randomly selected winners. Be creative. Entice your users to participate.

Publicize your special event to newcomers by announcing it to appropriate media outlets (as discussed in Chapter 15) and to other Web sites. Also be sure to let your own users know when and where your special event will be. A few days in advance, signpost the upcoming event with a link on your home page and other high-visibility pages. Give simple online instructions for logging on, tell what kind of event it will be and how best to participate, and specify any guidelines for chatting. Also, provide links to any software users may need well in advance of the event, so people won't be scrambling at the last minute.

Running an open chat space

An *open chat space* is one that's available to anyone at anytime. Chat spaces like this generally require more technical maintenance and more server space but can be lively and worthwhile in cases where users are beating down doors to interact with each other. A chat space that's open 24 hours a day but going unpopulated ends up showcasing the fact that community is not thriving at this location. Who needs that?

Open chat spaces frequently inspire or allow . . . shall we say, a social or flirtatious overtone. Whatever the initial topic was, users in open chats often end up merely socializing and segueing into at least sexually suggestive conversation. In its place, that might be fine, but this sort of chat may require moderation, especially if children can access the chat space or if you're trying to project a professional image and focus on your industry, company, service, or product.

To keep an open chat space more focused on a topic, instead of 24-hour open chats, you might run weekly scheduled chats on specified topics. A general interest site, for example, might have a Saturday-morning home repair discussion and a Sunday-afternoon mystery for users to solve online in the allotted time, while saving romance for the regular Friday-evening singles club.

Online conferencing, wireless, and broadband

As the online medium grows to include wireless access via handheld computers, PDAs, and cell phones, and as broadband access becomes more accessible, the nature of online community will change. Wider availability of broadband is likely to bring about more online conferencing, for example. Participants who can see and hear each other are likely to behave differently from those in the more "traditional" communities accessed by chat, e-mail, and message boards. (The Online Community Report, at www.onlinecommunityreport.com, reports on . . . guess what . . . online community news.)

Broadband, with its sophisticated and almost film-like look, allows for more realistic avatars as well as smoother movement through virtual rooms or game environments. In a prime example of a useful application of broadband, Microsoft's Virtual World Research Group and the Fred Hutchinson Cancer Research Center has produced a 3-D virtual community to support people with cancer. Participants in this group are hospitalized patients; through their online avatars they communicate with each other and with their care-givers. The online community delivers caring, sensitive information and advice to people who might otherwise feel far more isolated.

As wireless becomes more important, online communities will also adapt to the wireless environment. Some who could not participate in online communities before will be enabled. Those who have not had access to PCs for financial reasons, for example, may have easier access to cell phones and handheld devices such as PDAs. The audience may grow, but their level of technical expertise may dwindle. How online communities are configured and managed will surely change in response.

The types of services that can be offered will change as well. As of this writing, in Japan, one wireless operator offers a service known as Cupid. Cupid matches up people with similar interests, but more importantly, when two Cupid customers are geographically near each other and their interest are aligned, Cupid alerts them via their cell phones. They can then arrange to meet each other at a mutually convenient spot. Businesses will surely develop new methods for staying in communication with the community of their customers via wireless. Just as e-mail, discussion groups, and chat opened new doors for serving customers, the opportunity for real-time communications via wireless will change the business-customer relationship. Chapter 3 discusses wireless online content and describes various call-back features that might be used in business or by harried commuters.

Online conferencing, broadband, and wireless access are all, as of this writing, in their infancy. Within a very short time, they will show their true merit as online community platforms. As you consider these platforms for your community efforts, remember that the gee-whiz factor has to be balanced by real return on investment.

Getting Return on Your Community Investment

For a Web site that will serve or develop community, stimulating interaction and communication between the site's users and operators is vital. The rewards of asking your people (the foundation of your community) their opinions and desires are manifold:

- ✔ You get insight into how satisfying the user experience is and what you can do to the site to continually improve it.

- ✔ Users feel greater loyalty and affinity with the site and with fellow users because they see that their collective feedback has impact on the site.

- ✔ You gain a way of adding community-driven content to your site by posting your users' feedback, stories, and other submissions online in strategic spots.

Start by soliciting user comments and feedback on the site, on current issues surrounding the topic or industry your site covers, or on a position your site has taken about its content. You might ask for user reviews of products you sell or have reviewed online or for stories about users' experiences. You can post these online in a special user-submitted content section or pepper snippets throughout your site.

To elicit user-submitted content, try a contest. For example, if you run a site selling scuba diving equipment, you can generate community involvement by running a contest for the best diving story or underwater photo. (Have your legal counsel review your terms and conditions for any contests, especially if the contests require skill, which is a highly subjective area.) You can also run a regular column featuring a different user essay or story each time. A column like this requires minimal editing and production time on your end, but could, with careful promotion, become a robust and highly anticipated community-driven feature.

Be sure that users are aware that you may publish their words or photos on your site. On Web pages or online forms where you solicit user feedback, comments, stories, photos, and so on, include a note stating that by making a submission, users agree to let you publish the submission online at your discretion. State further that you retain the right to edit user comments for length or grammar. If you don't make these matters clear up-front, you have to get users' permission later before publication and you have to run edited comments by the users to get their approval.

Crediting a user for his or her comments or photos by name is always best. This not only helps you avoid legal trouble (see Chapter 7), but also increases your community's sense of participation in and ownership of the site. Crediting users also encourages other users to send in content, promotes dialogue among users, and underscores the affinity that already exists within the community.

A word to the wise about editing: Don't edit user-submitted content too much. You don't want to lose the tone and spirit of the community member who sent it in; the content is supposed to be community-driven, after all. Also, user-created content is meant to save you some time and effort; don't spend all the time you've saved by rewriting the content. Of course, any egregious spelling errors can be corrected "silently," without getting advance approval.

Once you've posted an item of user-submitted content online, has the opportunity played itself out? Not at all. You can still leverage the content by archiving it in a linked Web page (or pages) and directing people to the archive. That way, it can remain useful as background info or related history for many months to come. Say you publish user reviews of the latest consumer electronic gadgets. Letting newcomers see what your users said about older models can be helpful. They can then get a context for the reviews and a sense of how stringent or easygoing they are.

Do display the original publication date on archived material, so that users don't mistake it for current material. You don't want to look like you are offering outdated content. (Psst! Put the newest stuff at the top of the list, where it's most visible.)

By the way, the usefulness of archiving applies to all forms of community, not only to content that the community consciously sends in. For example, after you've distributed an e-mail newsletter to your mailing list, you can post it online for interested readers in an archive called "Back Issues." Or, you may decide to pull comments older than three months off your active message boards, but continue to archive old comments in case new users would like to see how the discussions have evolved over time. If you run a live chat on an important topic, such as alternative treatments for breast cancer, you'll be doing your users a service if you archive the transcript of the chat and continue to allow your audience access to this content.

Large amounts of archived content are more useful when they are searchable. One simple method for implementing content searchability is to provide a search engine on your site that allows users to search your content. (Google, at www.google.com, and Atomz, at www.atomz.com, both offer credible options.) Or you can use a tool such as Microsoft FrontPage or any of several other tools to add a full-text search function that allows users to search each page of content on the site, including archived content. More sophisticated options are also available, of course. If you use ListBot to manage your discussion groups, for example, the program creates automatic archives of all messages posted and then points users to the archive, where they can perform a search.

If you have the resources to develop a more sophisticated archiving system still, create a database where archived content resides, along with a front end that allows users to search the database. (If you set up a database-backed delivery system for your entire content overall, this will be a relatively small addition to your plans. See Chapter 13 for more about databases.)

Issuing the Invitation

To invite folks to join in the community you offer, provide entry via your home page. A simple sign-up button, dialog box, or link will do. Be sure to signpost the benefits of membership right there, in a few concise, clear words. Tell people whether the benefit is a free e-mail newsletter full of tips or unlimited access to all community tools such as discussion groups, live chat, match-making, e-postcards, expert advice, or whatever else you offer.

If you've acquired a list of user names and e-mail addresses from a partner or other source, you can extend your invitation by e-mail, but *only if those users have agreed to receive such messages.* Send unsolicited e-mail without permission, and you will simply antagonize and alienate the very people you hoped to attract.

You might also run banner ads *in-house* (on your own site) or on other key sites that complement your own, promoting your community tools and linking to a sign-up area. See Chapter 15 for more information on banner ad campaigns.

A Warm and Hearty Welcome

Make your community members feel welcome and appreciated. You needn't say something as literal as "Welcome! I'm your community host tonight, how may I serve you?" but you should be welcoming in whatever manner is right for your crowd. As soon as users join, send an e-mail greeting them (even if it's only an automatically generated message). In the e-mail

✔ Remind users of the benefits of joining and participating in your community.

✔ Notify users of any important community guidelines.

✔ Refer users to any particularly useful community tools.

✔ Describe your privacy and security policies. Most users prefer to know if their info is shared and with what kinds of companies it may be shared. (eTrust.com, at www.etrust.com, can help you write an appropriate privacy policy.)

✔ Tell new community members who to contact in case of problems, service issues, or the unfortunate that need to cancel their membership. Obviously, you don't want to accentuate the negative, but offering this information reassures users that they can exit your community gracefully when the time is right and that helps them feel comfortable about becoming a member.

As your community gets involved in your site, look for ways to leverage the contributions of the most vocal members. Take note: In discussion groups only about 10 to 15 percent of participants actively contribute, 2 to 5 percent predominate, and 85 to 90 percent of users simply *lurk* (read messages but refrain from sending any of their own). Don't fret over the majority that is not posting messages; that's just life. Instead, reward the 2 to 5 percent who make up the core of the conversation. These folks are involved, enthusiastic, offer productive commentary, and make the discussion group a lively and entertaining forum for all concerned. To keep them participating at this level, you can offer them the chance to be a moderator (with a title) or give them logo merchandise or a discount on your products or services. Many companies have done this and found that it increases user loyalty.

In time, you may notice that your community has grown in size and has, in fact, started to generate new subcommunities. Some Web sites respond to this by trying to reign in their community and direct it back to the original focus. However, the growth and development of multiple communities can be a good thing. Creating spin-off satellite communities or partitioning your original site for these new communities can expand your site and your audience, too.

Whatever you do, don't simply ignore the burgeoning of subcommunities. If your users get bored or burned out, they'll turn to other sites. Community is organic — don't just let it grow, *help* it grow. Tailor your community offerings to subcommunities. If you continue to give your users lots of ways to communicate and interact with each other meaningfully, they'll reward you with loyalty and the good word of mouth that results in more traffic.

Providing Value and Security

A community that is not getting value for the time it invests is not going to gel, and a community that does not feel secure in the community environment is not going to stick around. Value has to do with the quality of interaction that occurs, as we've discussed throughout this chapter, but it's also affected by the overall user experience (how easy getting in and out of community forums is, for example), as well as the quality of any other content or service that's offered on the Web site. Security has to do with the stability of the community (bonding with fly-by-night operations or individuals is difficult at best) and the certainty that any communication delivered to the community is actually seen. (Messages meant to appear in a community forum that vanish instead are a disappointment; again, bonding is unlikely if you don't feel you are being heard.)

In a case where your goals do not include forums of people talking with each other, you can focus on online events. A consumer health site, for instance, could offer a guided meditation through a chat room. And even in the case of e-commerce outreach or customer care, you can inject value into newsletters, discussion groups, message boards, and chat if you use them to deliver product training, customer service, news, or analyses of issues in your industry.

You can also differentiate your site by offering fresh, original content that isn't the run-of-the-mill stuff that's found all over the Web. Investigate what content and tools your competitors offer, both to see if you can adapt any of their techniques and to avoid simply repeating the content they have. The key is to differentiate your offerings and tailor them to your goals and your audience. (See Chapters 2 and 3.)

Can advertisements and classifieds in community areas be considered acceptable? Yes, if they are tailored to the community appropriately. (If not, they intrude on the atmosphere and undermine people's comfort levels.) If you operate an automotive information site for car buyers, car ads may be fine; if you offer a lifestyle site for divorced people, ads for matchmaking services may be good; and if you run a home-buying site, real estate ads may be appropriate.

Ensuring the security of the online environment is crucial. Keep your Web site and community stable and secure by choosing reliable and scalable technology and Web-hosting services (see Chapter 12). Know the policies of any potential vendor regarding keeping member information private. (After all, to your members, your vendor is an extension of your company; their mistakes are your mistakes.) Verify that whomever you hire maintains firewalls that strictly restrict access to their servers and generally take security seriously. (Make sure members' passwords will be secure. Start by setting up a policy that passwords must include a mix of lowercase and uppercase letters along with numbers or punctuation.) And in your vendor contract, state explicitly that member information will be your property not the vendor's.

Remember, too, that major changes in even the look, feel, and functionality can be disruptive to a community; you'll risk losing members if you make big changes to the front end or the back end without notifying and reassuring them in advance. To select a reliable and robust community software product, research the options thoroughly. Check descriptions of products on sites such as CNET's Builder.com, join discussion groups for online community managers to get informed opinions, and ask users and Webmasters of other community-rich sites.

If and when you must make any changes, announce this fact to your members in advance via e-mail and with an online notice. Tell them what to expect, apologize for any inconvenience, assure them that you value their participation, and let them know how the change benefits them.

Treat the interactions of your community like the vital asset it is. Choose a community software package that can make back ups of the interactions on your community tools. Make back ups regularly (daily is a good idea) and let your users know somewhere in the community guidelines that their interactions are protected in case of software crashes. This can only inspire extra confidence in your site and in the notion of joining your community.

To Moderate or Not?

Any online community can be moderated or free-form. In a moderated discussion, a specific, trusted person (or group of people) guides the interaction, responding to questions and reminding people of the proper uses of the list. A moderator can be someone who works for you, or, if your community following is strong, you can ask an active member of your community to take on the role.

You may or may not want your community forums moderated. On the upside, higher quality information often appears in a moderated discussion, but on the downside, the process of moderating can be time consuming. In a business setting, moderation will keep the community on track and in line with your business goals.

If your community forum is meant to include minor children, you really must have a moderator to avoid liability for any objectionable content or situations the children might otherwise be exposed to. (If your community forum is not meant for children, you might be able to mitigate your liability by clearly indicating that only those over 18 or 21 are allowed to enter the discussion area; check with your legal counsel for applicable laws.)

In a business setting — a situation where the interaction is meant to stay focused around a targeted topic, for example — a moderator is the key to achieving business goals. In cases where the goals are more organic, liability is not at stake, the interaction is among adults, and those adults can and will take responsibility for themselves and any misunderstandings that arise, moderation might not be necessary. As always, the decision belongs to you, the "owner" of the community setting.

Whether you moderate discussions or not, put a disclaimer on their entry pages stating that you are not responsible for the content or accuracy of user posts and that you are simply providing a forum in which users can exchange comments and information. Adding a <u>Read our terms and conditions</u> link to the disclaimer at the bottom of every page of your community forum is also a good idea.

In some cases, the moderator actually reads each post before it gets put online, and weeds out any spam, flames, slander, obscenities, or whatever violates the community ground rules. In other cases, the moderator steps in only when necessary. A competent moderator of either type can help to keep discussions on track and generally foster a cohesive user experience. But when moderating is bungled it can badly dampen the spontaneity and "flow" of a discussion.

A good moderator should be skilled in communication and diplomacy. As with all group interactions, online community dynamics are complex. In the flush of familiarity, one person says something to another who takes it the wrong way or is offended by it. The second person makes a clever but insulting crack, others join one side or the other, and boom — a flame war has broken out. Personalities can easily be misunderstood or rub each other roughly, and because face-to-face accountability doesn't exist online, some people say things they may not otherwise. The moderator must be able to stay calm, be fair, and smooth ruffled feathers, preferably without alienating anyone.

Moderators usually have the power to kick out any unrepentant and unruly members, though they often deliver a warning or reprimand before taking that final step. (Note that the troublemaker can easily rejoin the group under a pseudonym or with a fresh e-mail address.) To inform all community members and potential members about the ground rules up front, moderators also maintain the site's community guidelines, which should be posted online in the community area and perhaps e-mailed to community members as often as once a month as a reminder.

The moderator's job is not all about playing bad cop; moderators also send out notices about upcoming special events, new discussion groups, and new topics for regularly scheduled chats. They can take the lead when interviewing special guests and nudge a discussion along by asking questions, raising overlooked issues, and so forth. Moderators also troubleshoot user problems — they can unsubscribe users who've misunderstood the instructions for changing e-mail addresses, help with difficulty signing in to a discussion group, and act as a go-between with the people who handle the servers.

Managing Community Tools

As with most of your Web site, you can host and manage your community areas either by hiring someone or doing it yourself in-house. Unless you have a large company with the hefty resources required to host and develop your own community tools, outsourcing the job is easier and nets you more expertise. Working with a community hosting service that builds and runs the community tools for you saves time and effort and can deliver quality results. You'll of course have to pay for the service, figure out the details of the contract, and manage the ongoing relationship once it's in place (see Chapter 10). You'll also have to decide whether to moderate or not, who will do that, and perhaps handle some other management as well.

Hosting services generally charge monthly fees and, sometimes, set-up fees. Some hosting services are free, but free services generally offer limited functionality and might not offer any technical or management support. They also often offer limited ability to change their look (to match your own), and they may paste intrusive ads into the community interactions. If community is going to be a small play on your site, a free service might be acceptable. But if you plan to offer multiple community tools, even if that's going to occur a few months down the road, starting with a robust community hosting service is better, because changing services can be disruptive (see the section "Providing Value and Security" earlier in this chapter). In addition to functionality, check to see if the service has a user-friendly interface.

Look at working with a community hosting service as an important investment in your Web site. While you must fully grok that a community is not technology, you must also get the operational underpinnings of your community in place before you can turn it into the solid, committed, flourishing online element you want it to be.

Chapter 5

E-Commerce in All Its Forms

*W*ay back in the nether years of the Internet, lots of people thought e-commerce meant plain and simply *businesses selling online* (to consumers). But that was before the world wide *imagination* kicked in. These days, business-to-business (b2b) Web sites are as common as business-to-consumer (b2c) sites, and a staggering array of business activities take place online, ranging from the small to the mighty, and from sales to collaborative product development and more.

E-Commerce Is Business Conducted Online

Commerce is business, and *e* stands for electronic, so *e-commerce,* friends, is business conducted electronically. All business. (Or should we say all *kinds* of business.) E-commerce includes creating, managing, conducting, and extending commercial relationships by using the Internet as a vehicle.

Of course selling is one e-commerce activity, but even selling via the Internet can take many forms, including

- ✔ **Selling directly to consumers:** Selling via a Web site with a transaction system

- ✔ **Providing purchase support:** Offering (on the Web site) all the relevant information necessary to make a buying decision, along with a method for finding a brick-and-mortar location where customers can actually buy the product

> ✔ **Generating leads:** Providing product info and enabling customers to contact a sales rep
>
> ✔ **Offering aggregate buying:** Allowing groups of customers to pool their orders to get volume discounts from the seller

Additionally, consumers (or businesses) can sell to each other in an auction model. This is known as customer-to-customer, or c2c selling. In other twists, businesses sometimes sell to other business as well as to consumers, which is known as b2bc selling, or businesses sell to businesses that then sell to consumers, which is b2b2c. It's a virtual certainty that other variations on selling will have been developed and implemented by the time you read this. But as we said, e-commerce isn't limited to just selling. In the sections that follow, we introduce some other applications of e-commerce.

B2C in action

Beyond simple and not-so-simple sales scenarios, b2c e-commerce can take many forms. Think back to our big-picture list of potential purposes a Web site can fulfill — sell, educate, inform, promote, entertain, research and report, build or serve community, facilitate collaboration, you know the drill. Consumer-targeted Web sites can offer b2c interpretations such as these:

> ✔ **Distance learning** through online courses offered by existing educational institutions or by purely digital education companies
>
> ✔ **Consumer information** offered on a knowledge-on-demand basis to inform the public about products, safety, recalls, recommendations, and so on
>
> ✔ **Promotion** of a product, service, company, event, or even a belief or viewpoint
>
> ✔ **Online events** created as pure entertainment; also entertainment Web sites that augment broadcast or other media with deeper information, easy reference, or the option to discuss an entertainment event with fans and participants
>
> ✔ **Surveys** conducted to poll people via Web sites; the survey's results may then be published online as well

Governments can provide citizens with easy online access to records, as well as enable them to get permits and pay taxes. Businesses can offer technical or product support around the clock (at a substantial savings over running a 24-hour call center). Doctors or medical institutions can offer online reference about immunizations, first aid, and other matters to their patients.

Aren't these *all* descriptions of commercial activities that can take place via Web sites?

B2B in action

It's been said that b2b is where it's at. As of this writing, researchers and pundits alike have predicted an explosion of b2b activity. Like b2c Web sites, b2b sites can run the gamut. They can sell, educate, inform, promote, entertain, research and report, build or serve community, or facilitate collaboration and work flow. Consider these examples:

- ✔ **Corporate training** delivered via online learning venues
- ✔ **Product data and technical support** provided by a manufacturer to its resellers
- ✔ **Conferencing and collaboration** conducted online among partner companies
- ✔ **Receipt and processing of requests for proposals** via a secure Web site
- ✔ **Nonprofit fundraising and sponsorship** solicited from corporate sources through a Web site that describes the nonprofit organization's work and the benefits of giving

Printers can accept files from designers via the Internet; projects of all sorts can be tracked as they progress; trade associations can keep member companies informed; social service agencies can conduct outreach to schools, juvenile facilities, and other agencies; engineers and scientists can collaborate; and medical schools can model surgical procedures for viewing by other medical groups. These are all examples of business applications that can take place on Web sites.

New business models for a new century

To their users, Web sites can fulfill a variety of functions (selling, educating, informing, promoting, and so on). But to the companies that build, maintain, and staff those Web sites, the picture looks a bit different. Businesses usually expect their Web sites to fulfill the function of bringing in cash directly, saving cash, making it easier to make cash, or some other clearly defined economic goal. Some typical business goals often expected of Web sites include

- ✔ **Generating revenue:** A Web site can generate revenue through sales of products, services, or subscriptions; through sales of ad space or sponsorships; through the licensing or syndication of content; through commissions taken when, for example, a sale occurs on an auction site; or through *product placement* (which is the paid-for appearance of a product in, for example, a film clip or some other entertainment event).
- ✔ **Reducing expenses:** A Web site can enable a company to reduce expenses through the digital distribution of a product (such as software, music, imagery, or text) that was previously delivered via print or CD-ROM or

as a packaged product; through faster, better online communications with sales reps; or through optimized management and workflow processes (such as those that take place when work groups collaborate using an intranet, Web conferencing, or an e-mail discussion group).

✔ **Enhancing customer relations:** A Web site can enhance customer relations by offering faster, easier access to information about your company, product, or service, and by offering quick access to the company itself (or its people). The Web site also enables the company to track customer preferences and customize solutions, content, or products presented.

✔ **Supporting the business:** A Web site can support a business by making it easy for potential investors, partners, job seekers, the press, and others to get information or contact your company; by forming strategic partnerships; by sharing resources with partners; or by providing the information your sales reps need to make their lives easier and speed up the sales process.

In general, e-commerce can drastically reduce the time it takes to get a product or service to market. It can also improve customer relations, which leads to more revenue, lower costs, or both. And the benefits of e-commerce aren't mutually exclusive; they build on one another. A well-constructed customer care area or FAQ on your site, for example, will reduce expenses (fewer calls to your service center), enhance customer relations (faster, easier answers), and support your business (isn't that obvious?), all leading to more revenue!

The traditional sales model

In the model that's been in place among humankind for thousands of years, customers go to a business seeking a product or service. (See Figure 5-1.) They approach the store with some idea of what they want (even if what they want is just to look around to see what's there). Many aspects of e-commerce revolve around the traditional sales model, with a lone store existing online to attract customers to buy its wares.

Businesses cooperating: Aggregators, portals, and malls

Somewhere along the way, someone thought up malls, where many businesses exist under one roof. Customers visit malls either to shop among the many stores there or to stop in at one particular store (in which case they might drift into others, too). In the physical world, strip malls and office parks work on a similar model (see Figure 5-2). In the virtual world, some Web sites act as aggregators or portals to other sites that offer related or complementary products, services, or information; others act as malls, combining many online stores into one point of entry.

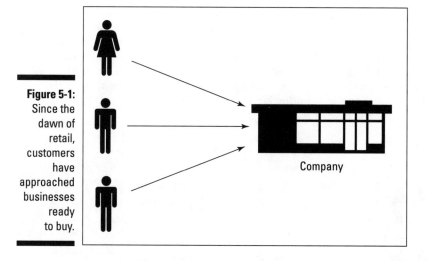

Figure 5-1:
Since the dawn of retail, customers have approached businesses ready to buy.

Company

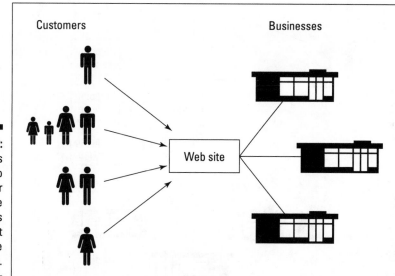

Customers

Businesses

Figure 5-2:
Businesses can clump together to share resources and attract more customers.

Web site

Businesses forming strategic partnerships

E-commerce enables many new models to exist. One such model is known as *extended partnerships*. In the extended partnerships model, a Web site might offer content, community, commerce, and *fulfillment* (delivery of the ordered goods), all of which are supplied by various partners. For example (see Figure 5-3), a Web site that focuses on weddings might offer wedding-related content licensed from a content provider; honeymoon travel, lodging, and packages supplied through partnerships with major airlines, hotels, resorts, and cruise operators; and dresses and wedding accessories supplied by various retail partners (with shipping provided by major carriers that are also partners). Perhaps then the central offering of the wedding Web site is its pulling together of partners along with the e-mail discussion group for brides-to-be and the nifty honeymoon registry, which lets guests skip the purchase of yet another fondue set and instead make contributions to the happy couple's cruise to Majorca.

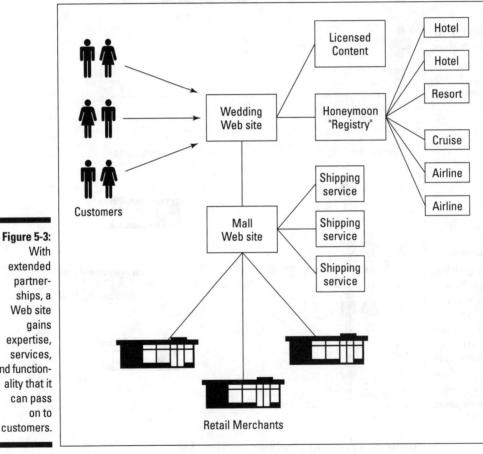

Figure 5-3:
With extended partner-ships, a Web site gains expertise, services, and function-ality that it can pass on to customers.

The e-commerce winning formula

Be first, be different, be best — that's the e-commerce mantra. You have to be first to get your stake into the ground. You have to be different to capture the imagination of your target market or audience. But if you are first and not best, you'll have pointed out to competitors a fine opportunity that they can move in on. If your competitors do what you do but do it better, they can take over a market that you defined. They'll differentiate themselves by improving on your grand idea, and you'll be history.

In this chapter, until now, we've been talking about e-commerce as a big, broad topic. But let's face it; a lot of what's going on in e-commerce is actually selling of one sort or another, and focusing on selling is a handy model for discussing the ins and outs of dealing with customers.

Selling Online: What Works

To succeed in any business, you must know who your key market is and why they want to do business with you. You also need to size up your competition and identify what strengths and weaknesses they bring to the game. You'll have to set goals and know what *metrics* (items of measurement) will indicate your success. And you'll have to know what people in your audience in particular, but also customers in general, perceive as creating and supporting a trust-worthy image. This is no joke — your business will depend on it. These are the basics.

Know your customers inside out

Know what makes your target market tick. In Chapter 2, we talked about some things you can focus on to get acquainted with your site's users. We discussed demographics (what facts define the audience), psychographics (what the audience believes or is motivated by), geographic location (where the audience is physically located), and technology (how users access your site).

After your site is up and running, you'll know much more about its users. They aren't always the same bunch as customers in your brick-and-mortar business. Although they may be a subset (those among your customers who have online access), they may also be a group of people with a very different angle on what you offer.

A classic example is that general interest online bookstores sell many, many more technology books (compared to books on other topics) than do the same bookstores' brick-and-mortar stores. We've worked on Web sites for companies selling a variety of products, and often those companies have found their online audiences wanting entirely new products, utterly different from what the brick-and-mortar stores sold.

The customers for your existing business may be local or regional, but the Web is international. Will you serve an international market with your Web site? If so, will you translate your content into various languages presented on a group of international sites or expect the French to read it in English? (They don't like that, you know.) Will you accept assorted currencies? How will you handle VAT and other taxes? And how will you handle the costs of shipping to various countries? If you're going to remain local, regional, or even national, clearly spell that out at least in the sections of your site that address purchasing and shipping options. (If you're very local — say, if you're a steakhouse in Chicago or an insurance broker licensed only in Nevada — you may want to say so on your home page to avoid getting inquiries from misguided residents of Tampa or Toledo.)

You can find out more than you ever imagined about your site's users; see Chapter 17 for more on finding out what's up with them after launching your site. And before you build your Web site, be sure to build systems into your e-commerce plan for finding out what you want to know about your customers.

Always keep one eye on the competition

You're pedaling hard to reach that target audience, and guess what? If you glance back, right behind you, coming on strong, you see a pack of others, pedaling just as hard and maybe gaining on you.

You have to be better and different as well as first, remember? To keep your number one spot, you need to conduct an occasional *competitive analysis.* That's just research into who's doing what and how, all categorized into a format that enables you to compare the different competitors. A nice spreadsheet will do, with the names of your competitors down the left side and column headings having to do with what they offer, how they price it, what strengths and weaknesses are apparent, what markets they've landed, and so on. (Keep in mind that what you focus on depends on your product and industry.)

Because e-commerce is new, and because it is such a hotbed of innovation, sometimes preconceived ideas or the lack of them become the competition. It's like this: Once we were reading this wonderful (and old) book in which programmers were being interviewed about what they were working on. One, Jaron Lanier, was being interviewed about a new idea he had. This was a fun read for us, because Jaron Lanier was describing something the interviewer had no clue about. Pulling out every descriptive phrase he could, the programmer tried to describe his idea to the interviewer. But it was a brand new idea. The interviewer, who could draw on no experience he'd ever had to place the concept in an understandable context, was stumped. But we, because we were reading the interview years after the fact, knew exactly what Jaron was describing. Jaron Lanier, you see, was trying to paint a picture of what he was about to invent — virtual reality.

Since our first foray into the professional online world, we've often had the experience of earnest people pitching products and ideas to us that when we saw the demo turned out to be quite different from what we thought we understood. (And, with all due humility, we're not stupid. Or at least our families say we're not. . . .)

To describe your product or service to others, you must come up with a brief "elevator pitch" (a one-sentence summary that nails the idea immediately). That's not so easy when you must not only convey your idea but also educate the hearer about something for which he or she has no frame of reference based on past experience. If you find yourself having to create a competitive analysis where the competitor is actually a preconceived idea or the lack of one, your elevator pitch will become all the more challenging and all the more important.

A couple of special notes on innovative ideas: Protect your ideas by getting anyone you approach with your pitch to sign a *nondisclosure agreement* (NDA). (Chapter 7 talks about this process in more detail.) And exercise care in announcing your innovative enterprise, because timing is everything. Announce too soon, and you'll alert any potential competitors that the race is on. They might even beat you to launch. Announce too late, and you might find that your competition has snatched all the glory before either of you launch. (Who said this was going to be easy?)

Set realistic goals and benchmarks

In most industries, it takes a while to make a profit. What made people think that e-commerce was going to pay off in a heartbeat is beyond us. Most new businesses bleed money for three to five years before they turn a profit, and most new businesses are starting up in industries where people have some clue what success actually looks like and how to get there!

First, you need to know that your e-commerce venture may take a while to reach maturity. Along the way, you may change your plan several times over, and you may unearth opportunities you don't see at this very moment. Nonetheless, you have to start out with some sense of what success will look like. Before you write your business plan or project plan, make sure you read Chapter 17 of this book, where we lay out the various types of success that various types of sites can expect.

Establish benchmarks that match your goals. For example, you may determine that the best measures of your sales site's success will be volume of sales (revenue generated) as well as

✔ **Conversion:** The percentage of site visitors who make a purchase, converting those visitors to buyers

✔ **Repeat sales:** The number of buyers who come back and buy again

✔ **Market penetration:** The number of *potential* customers who actually do purchase your product at your Web site

You need to make projections for each of these metrics. Make your projections real, based on real research. Chapter 6 discusses budgets and getting a clear picture of what *return on investment* (ROI) you expect. Profit, as you probably know, is created when revenue exceeds cost. The most preferred return on investment occurs at the magical moment when profit is about to be achieved.

Short of profitability (and leading up to it), perhaps among the most intended goals are that traffic will convert to sales, buyers will become repeat buyers, and that loyalty to your product and site will convert users into evangelists. (See Figure 3-2 in Chapter 3.) That sort of success builds on itself and (along with careful marshalling of resources to keep costs down) is likely to lead to ROI and profitability.

Keep in mind as you're assessing your goals that an abstract but quite important cost associated with any enterprise is the *opportunity cost.* That's the cost of doing one thing when you could be doing another. The online world is full of opportunities, but you really can't do everything. (Well, at least most people can't.) You have to choose one or two opportunities at the cost of forgoing others. A key business decision is determining which of the opportunities that lie before you is most likely to result in success, and which is also attractive but perhaps less doable.

Setting realistic goals and benchmarks, assessing opportunity costs, and projecting ROI will help you align your resources with your goals. These tasks, along with keeping your eye on your budget is what ultimately (along with wit, fine weather, and a dash of good luck) leads to business success. The foundation of sales, though, is trust. Selling is about trust — about getting it and keeping it.

Build trust and then keep it

So you walk into a sporting goods shop, a restaurant, or a big department store, and what do you want to know before you lay down your hard-earned moolah? You want to know that you are buying a good product, that you are going to get what you pay for, that it will be delivered in good condition, and that, if something goes wrong, someone will make it right. Much of the evaluation you do before making a purchase involves answering these questions, and if you're over 9 years old (you are, aren't you?), you probably know the importance of being a savvy consumer. You also want to know — though you may not consciously think about it — that the seller is not going to abuse the trust that you place in your (however brief) business relationship.

Every day, millions of consumers fork over their credit cards to waiters, gas station attendants, phone order clerks, and sales reps. We all blithely write our credit card numbers on magazine subscription forms, too. Any one of those folks that you've given your credit card number to could take, use, and even distribute it to whomever they bump into on the street, for fun or for profit. But we go ahead, calmly handing over our credit cards and letting total strangers simply walk out of sight with them for minutes at a time. Why do we do that? We do it because we trust the system. On the whole, we believe that the gas station, store, or restaurant looks okay and does not sanction abuse of customers by its employees, and that the vendor we are dealing with and the credit card company itself will cooperate with each other and with us to resolve any problems. We feel a sense of . . . *security.*

In e-commerce, security is a technology issue (see Chapter 14, where we talk about transaction systems), but it's also a credibility issue.

Nobody wants to buy from a huckster. Instill in your online customers a deep sense of security in your operation, and they'll be a lot more comfortable doing business with you. Take a look at the real-world successes of catalog and mail-order companies like Lands' End (`www.landsend.com`) and Harry & David (`www.harryanddavid.com`), and so on. Their Web sites are extensions of long successful catalog sales models. And those models are as close as a non-Internet model can get to what works online. People buy from these companies because mail order is convenient but also because the companies are known to provide good merchandise and fast delivery in a trustworthy manner. They follow these simple guidelines that you, too, can use:

- ✔ **Look credible.** Project a professional and trustworthy image, whatever that means in your industry. Selling CDs for garage bands, for example, means something different than selling the services of an investment firm. Your Web site is your storefront — it may be the only representation of your business a customer ever sees — and a customer's first visit to it forms an overall impression of your credibility. You don't necessarily need to make the site overly designerly — unless you're selling design services or fashion accessories — but you must at least make it attractive and easy to navigate. (Accessibility to products is crucial.)

- ✔ **Leverage the familiar.** If your company is well known and has spent bundles creating a corporate identity, you're in. But if your company is a more fledgling outfit, you may consider partnering with established companies to make yourself seem credible, touting that famous client that you snagged, or even getting testimonial quotes from well-known backers or supporters. At the very least, use recognized, credible systems for payment and for your underlying technology. Even just saying that your transaction system is powered by a secure server from a well-known technology company makes you seem more credible than if you use an obscure payment scheme and a homemade security system.

- ✔ **Give customers all the information they need to make a purchase decision now.** Don't go overboard, though — one picture of that super-duper ergonomic chair along with a list of available colors and special features is enough. There's no need for slow-to-download 3D animation showing the chair flipping and rotating in all nine color choices.

✔ **Make placing an order easy.** Place a simple Buy button where it is most visible without pushing it in your customer's face. Also, remove all barriers to placing an order, including the barrier of not understanding something. Confused customers often don't ask for help; they frequently just leave the store. Make sure that your forms are simple but complete, and that your ordering system walks people through the steps without making them hop through so many hoops that they tucker out and take off. (A purchase should require as few Web pages as possible; five or six well-defined steps are about the max. Being able to make the purchase in fewer clicks is better.)

✔ **Provide understandable, familiar ways for the customer to pay.** Use a shopping-cart system that features a secure server and a reliable, trusted payment method, for example, the standard credit cards. Also, offer information about why your system is safe. In addition, you may want to offer alternative ways to pay so that if a secure shopping-cart system seems just too avant-garde to some customers, they can call in (or even fax) their orders the old-fashioned way.

✔ **Make the point at which the transaction is actually going through crystal clear.** Don't leave people wondering whether their attempt to buy actually worked. Offer them a chance to review their purchases and the option to add to their purchase or even put things back. As they approach the moment of actual payment, let them know it's occurring, and afterward, acknowledge their purchase, tell them when to expect delivery, and *thank them*. Your confirmation can come to customers in the form of a Web page or via e-mail, but make it snappy. It should arrive quickly, and it should have the same friendly, sincere, professional, formal, hip (or whatever) tone as your site. Among the confirmation information, give people an order number they can use to track the purchase should they wonder what's up later.

✔ **Explain your system for delivering what you sell.** A simple link to a "How This Shopping System Works" page can go a long way toward building customer confidence.

✔ **Back up your products with assurances that you will make things right if something goes wrong.** Make sure you've posted your return policy; this is law in some places but good business everywhere. Again, it's a matter of inspiring customer confidence. Also, keep in mind the power of the unlimited money-back guarantee. Not many people send the merchandise back for silly reasons, but many people buy based on the idea that they have a guarantee. (For a peek at an eye-openingly generous return policy, take a gander at the policy that Lands' End offers.)

✔ **Treat your customers with respect.** Don't reuse information you get from your customers without their permission. If they gave you their e-mail address as part of a transaction, don't decide off the cuff to use it to spam them with announcements. No one likes getting junk mail. And above all, don't *ever* sell or otherwise provide your customer list to another company or person without offering your customers an option out of that (and telling them up front you may be planning to do it). You may not get off the Internet alive if you do.

What sells online

Some people think of the Internet as the great business leveler, where a couple of Joes with a good idea can hang out a virtual shingle and make a million, or where a mom-and-pop shop has the same chance of success as a giant multi-national corporation. Don't kid yourself. It's true that some products — like software — can be distributed via Web sites at tremendous savings in packaging, promotion, and distribution. But launching and running a big-league Web site is not for the faint of heart. Nor is it cheap. (See Chapter 6 for more about what Web sites cost.)

No selling-regulations bureau exists on the Web to stop you from trying to sell whatever you want. If you want to get out there and push smoke shifters, gumballs, or snail traps, you can give it a whirl. No one is going to stop you. The big question is, will people buy what you have to offer? Underlying that question are more basic questions regarding why some things sell and some don't. We make no claims to be the final word on these topics. We can report what we've seen, but the Web is such a wonder that no one knows what's going to come up tomorrow or next week.

As of this writing, we can report the success to varying degrees of Web sites selling the following items:

- ✔ Hard deliverables (physical objects that are easily understood and easily shipped), like books, computers, car parts, flowers, wine, CDs, and cigars

- ✔ Software, music, stock photography, and other stuff that can be digitized and delivered via download

- ✔ Services, like those offering package shipping, travel packages, investment brokerage, or the best price on new or used cars

- ✔ Information, like news from a reliable journalistic source, reports from research giants, and reference materials from credible publishers

Remember purchase support

Companies that deliver big-ticket items, such as capital equipment, do in fact conduct online commerce. Although many do not (yet) actually sell the big pricey stuff directly via a Web site (how would you test drive that backhoe?), they often provide *purchase support* — all the info that you need to support your decision to buy their products. Does this work? You bet it does. Twenty-four hours a day, seven days a week via their Web sites, companies pump out information about models, features, options, nearby dealers, and so on. They also let users see the equipment of interest in a range of choices, make financing options clear, and do whatever they can to make their products appealing online. This plethora of information can lead to increased sales that can be documented.

It's no wonder that hard deliverables sell — these are many of the same items available through catalogs, by fax, and by mail order. The attractions? For one thing, you as the user/customer generally know what you're going to get. You can see pictures of the merchandise, or maybe you already know the products or the company's reputation. The stuff is real, solid, and tangible, and you have a reasonable expectation of it arriving on your doorstep in one piece. The convenience of catalog shopping is strong motivation. Many folks think that buying through catalogs is fast, easy, and convenient and offers free parking to boot. All of those qualities transfer directly to an online environment, assuming that the online shopping system is orderly (so to speak), understandable, and secure.

Note that it's tough to make money selling items that cost less than about $10 online, because *microtransactions* (sales involving as little as pennies), long promised and technically feasible, have not caught on. On the other hand, e-commerce enables multiple buyers to pool their orders and conduct *aggregate buying*, which allows them to get volume discounts. As e-commerce develops, new models for buying and selling appear frequently.

The attraction of digital distribution revolves around faster time to market (on the seller's end) and convenience (on the buyer's end). The makers of software, for example, no longer have to create packaging, cut millions of CDs, print documentation, or maintain warehouses and a third-party distribution system. The expenses of manufacturing and distribution go way, way down. What's more, the software company, which had been paying large percentages of the purchase price to distributors and retailers as their cut, no longer has to share. So it's possible for the manufacturer's profit margins to grow even if users pay less for the software. And users can buy digital goods online any time of the day or night, so that at midnight when you need a piece of software (or just have to hear a certain tune), you can download it *now*.

Service is by its very nature virtual — no goods are delivered by service companies. Services sell online, but the trick here is that the service has to be as good as or better than nonvirtual services of the same type that are offered in the real world. In some cases, an online setting allows a company to offer a special service that it can provide its customers only through a Web site. FedEx (www.fedex.com), for example, offers something online that could never have worked otherwise: instant package shipping and tracking. The FedEx site leverages brand recognition and plenty of visibility in print and TV advertising — FedEx is no penny-ante operation — but the real kicker is the online service itself, a work that defines the term *value added*.

Why information is challenging

The Web has been touted by many as one of the most important developments in information delivery since . . . television! The telephone! The *printing press!* (No one seems to go quite so far as to say that it's as important as the development of written language.) And yet, online publishing — a thriving idea — did not immediately pay off in big bucks the way many thought it would. Perhaps that's because the founding tradition on the Net was to offer information for free. Or perhaps it's because people thought they were paying for the paper rather than what was printed on the paper.

A model of distribution and selling

Taking a quick look at one model of distribution can help to focus your efforts. Here, as usual, we encourage you to use several tactics in implementing your overall strategy. For example, to sell shareware online, you may consider the approach of creating a tightly focused site like WinZip's and then getting your product listed at CNET's highly successful Shareware.com site (www.shareware.com). While you're at it, hit all the computer-book Web sites, where whole areas of the sites are often devoted to downloadable software. Use the create-a-nifty-logo-icon idea (see the section of this chapter on downloadable software) to encourage Web-masters everywhere to make your product's presence known. The point here is to maximize your visibility. Then, at your site, make downloading a breeze and offer two or three simple payment systems: perhaps a phone/fax/mail order system with a simple form provided and, if you're up to it, a form-based secure server system. (A shopping cart seems like overkill here.) As always, the key is maximum visibility followed by easy access to both the product and payment. That strategy works for many products, not just shareware.

Oddly, users who were perfectly happy in the past to pay for their newspaper subscriptions balked at paying for the same news from the same journalists when the content was published in online versions. For a while, it seemed as though in an online context, publishers had to add value to the basic information they published and charge for the value added rather than just for the delivery of information. But that approach made the already expensive venture of publishing even more so.

E-books have held promise, but in their early iterations, they required users to buy separate handheld devices to read them. Users found that added expense and inconvenience unattractive. Some large reference databases and archives of articles and other content have found that users will pay for the search and information delivery service they offer. In that case, quick access to the information was convenient and satisfied a user need. And some content-driven daily e-mail newsletters have done well with advertising sales. The ads, inserted between bits of content in the newsletter, don't bother the users, who want the content.

For publishers, as for any business, the venture has to be cost-effective (and preferably profitable!). One publisher who delivers information only online reports these opportunities for turning content into profit

 ✔ **Advertising;** however, traffic has to be mighty high to attract big-money advertisers

 ✔ **Product sales,** with products related to the content matter, for example, sold via the Web site

 ✔ **Subscriptions,** which can be sold to an e-mail newsletter or to premium Web site content, for example, or to an offline, traditional print publication (a magazine or print newsletter associated with or repurposing content from the Web site)

 ✔ **Syndication,** or the licensing of the right to reproduce the content to others

Another option is to run highly profitable conferences on topics related to the Web site's topic (in which case the conference is actually supporting the Web site and you have to ask yourself, Which is the real product?). Similarly, if the profit comes from a print publication associated with the Web site's topic, what is the real product?

The answer is that the product is *content.* And the lesson is that the Web site, is, after all, just another delivery vehicle. In business, you have to find ways to maximize revenue (and profits). And the smart money — whether you're in the information business or any other — is on finding and leveraging as many revenue streams as possible. As always, the trick in e-commerce is to use the medium to deliver to customers what they want, in the way that attracts them, while maximizing revenue and minimizing costs.

Save a Bundle: Provide Customer Care

In e-commerce as in traditional commerce, your customers are your business. They are your reason for being, and just as you must get to know them and keep up with their changing needs, you must also provide them with ongoing care during (and sometimes after) your business relationship. Great customer care (before and during the sale) avoids the headache and expense of customer service (solving problems after the sale). The goals of providing top-notch customer care are to

- ✔ Achieve, expand, and retain loyalty
- ✔ Jack up profits (get costs down and sales up)
- ✔ Minimize time-to-market
- ✔ Improve the products and services you offer
- ✔ And ultimately, to serve the customers — to make them satisfied, happy campers

Why online customer care matters

It's very simple: To your online customers, you are your Web site. The impression that you create through your Web site will be, to the many people you intend to have as your customers, the only impression they have of your business. When customers open up your home page for the first time, they'll have either the impression of an easy-to-use, credible Web site offering fine products and services, or not.

Everyone knows that first impressions are lasting. It's also true that *poor impressions fade slowly.* Make a misstep in caring for your online customers, and they'll remember it for a long time. No amount of free pizza coupons made up for the time we were poorly treated by a delivery pizza company some years ago — in fact, we immediately dumped the coupons and never ordered that company's pizza again. (Yes, the experience was that bad.)

Because the e-commerce industry is new, when it comes to creating an overall impression of the industry, everyone in e-commerce is rowing up stream. If the industry gets a bad rep (or doesn't establish a good one), business as a whole will be bad. As an industry, you must work hard to establish marketplace credibility. An overall impression of your industry as one that delivers and does it well and quickly benefits everyone.

What's more, "making up for it later" gets very expensive. A single phone call to a company's customer service center can cost the company an average of ten dollars. Taking returns or sending out compensation adds costs on top of that. Wouldn't it be easier to get it right before you have to do damage control?

According to a study by the National Association of Consumer Agency Administrators, here are the top complaints that e-commerce customers had in one year:

- ✔ Did not receive goods or services ordered
- ✔ Received damaged merchandise
- ✔ Experienced problems obtaining refunds on returned goods
- ✔ Was overcharged
- ✔ Believed advertising was false or misleading

And in a post-holiday customer service test conducted by Jupiter Communications, 42 percent of the studied e-commerce sites failed in these ways:

- ✔ Never responded to customer inquiries concerning returns
- ✔ Took more than five days to reply
- ✔ Didn't offer to respond via e-mail to reported problems

This is not the stuff of a good impression. Luckily, customer service has been on an upswing since then. The industry has learned form its mistakes and is focused more on positive customer care.

The best in customer care

First and foremost, providing the best customer care means knowing who your customers are and providing them with the best possible product or service. It also means building a robust, secure, thoughtful, *working* Web site. Both before your site is built (while you're testing concepts and working models) and after your site is launched (while you're gathering feedback and site statistics), you'll want to focus on some key issues. Get a base of information about who your users are, but also look into whether they're happy. Are you offering them what they want and need? What else might they want? Offer surveys and quick feedback forms to make inquiries. Offer easy e-mail links to give your customers fast communications paths. Taking these simple steps goes a long way toward building loyalty and showing customers that they matter.

Communicate!

Make yourself (okay, your minions will do) easy to reach. Your Contact Us page and your online store should include e-mail links that lead to the correct person or to a forwarding service, an 800 number for those who'd rather call than send e-mail, and a surface mail address (perhaps this one's for those who'd feel better just knowing where you are). When you get communications, respond immediately. People want quick answers, especially to e-mail. Generally people expect some kind of immediate answer (even if it's just automated), and if they don't get a real answer within 45 minutes or so, they start grousing.

In your responses, you should address the actual issue the sender has raised. You also, however, have a unique opportunity, in that you have the customer's attention. You can offer other products or additional services if you do it diplomatically (so it sounds like a service or aid rather than like a sales pitch). "Oh! You say your 10-year-old PC isn't up to the latest in software? I'm afraid an upgrade to your PC isn't going to be cost effective for you — can I help you find a new computer in your price range?"

Always offer options to customers for resolving their issues. They'll feel more in control if they can choose among several possibilities rather than being told they must take a single path or else. (Funny, this is what works with our 2-year-old, too. Must be human nature.)

You can deliver online help or customer service via e-mail, user-driven or employee-moderated discussion groups, and even through live chats. Chat for this purpose is kind of expensive, though — having an on-call support person at the ready for chat is as pricey as having that person at a phone call center. Focusing your help efforts on less expensive options like e-mail can cost 60 to 70 percent less than call centers, on the other hand.

Perhaps the least expensive option should be your frontline defense. An easy-to-find, intuitively organized, up-to-date FAQ or customer service page empowers users to find answers to their questions in a jiffy without (ahem) bothering anybody who has to be paid for the interaction. A good, working customer service page should answer the right questions and answer them well. It doesn't need to be formatted in the standard question-and-answer style of a typical FAQ, but it must anticipate what people might wonder about most often and give them up-front answers. (Do choose whether you're going with the question-and-answer format; switching back and forth is confusing to people.) A good FAQ (let's just call it that, for simplicity) is easy to find and access, and its organization is immediately obvious.

Here are a few more pointers for creating a good FAQ:

- ✔ Organize the information intuitively, with a short, linked list of topics or questions at the top of the page leading to the answers below. Also, organize topics or questions in the order they might occur to people or in the order of frequency or some other clearly recognizable system.

- ✔ Write the material from the viewpoint of the customer, not the marketing department, programmer, or product manager.

- ✔ Make entries brief and to the point, be clear and complete, and link from one item to another (or to other Web pages) as necessary.

A good FAQ also is updated frequently, but only with truly frequently asked questions and their answers. ***Remember:*** Keep it short. Keep the questions short, the answers short, and the page as a whole as short as can be while still addressing the relevant issues.

Communicate positively

Because so much of what happens online is in writing, having good writing skills has put a new twist in the customer care job description. Grammar isn't just a matter of technicality, it actually exists (surprise!) to help people understand each other. More and more companies that provide customer care via e-mail are giving potential employees grammar and spelling tests, and are retraining existing employees to boost their writing skills.

It's also important to phrase communications positively in order to send customers the message that you care and that you're on top of things. We don't mean "lie to spare their feelings," and we don't mean "lie to protect the company." We do mean that it's quite possible to find phrasing that communicates clearly, completely, and positively. Think for a moment about the differing impressions these communications make:

Discouraging	Upbeat and Helpful
"That item isn't in."	"We'll have it next week."
"The cut of that jacket isn't for you."	"This style may be very flattering."
"We don't accept fax orders."	"We offer easy, secure credit card transactions."

When a problem occurs, make good

Okay, so life being what it is, things go wrong. Even the most customer-conscious company sometimes has a problem to solve (or a customer who is seemingly impossible to please). You must have systems in place not for just taking down complaints and addressing them, but also for tracking and documenting solutions. Having such a process in place makes it easier to implement the same solutions in the future. It also prevents three customers who turn out to be friends or cousins from comparing notes with each other and discovering that you treated one differently than the others. In other words, having systems in place saves time, money, and complications.

You can also convert some of what you discover into entries on your FAQ. After all, FAQ lists are compilations of frequently asked questions (and answers).

Making returns easy makes friends all the time. Often, the mere option to return things inspires confidence but does not always inspire returns. But when returns are warranted, customers don't want to be forced through hoops to send the items back. Again, for an example of an extraordinary returns policy, take a look at Lands' End. Its no-hassle returns policy asks only the questions the company needs to ask to improve its service. Some items aren't worth the cost (to the product's producer or reseller) of returning. Why take returns of melted chocolate? In some cases, your no-hassle easy return policy will boil down to taking the customer's word that the chocolates were mush and sending out a new package as quick as can be.

Remember that your goal is to turn a problem into an opportunity. With talented customer care representatives, you can usually transform a customer's experience of a bungled transaction into a sense that all is right in the world and your company made it so.

Chapter 6

Budgeting Tips and Tactics

- -

In This Chapter

▶ Budgeting cycles in the brick-and-mortar world and the dot-com worlds

▶ Approaching the budgeting process

▶ Looking at and creating a Web site budget spreadsheet

▶ Investigating expenses and activities that inspire budget categories

▶ Meeting ROI (return on investment)

- -

*S*omewhere in the world there are probably people who think budgeting is a barrel of fun. To many, budgeting is a terrible chore. But, to build and run a sterling Web site, you've got to face budgeting squarely and make it your friend. A good budget will help you make solid business decisions and keep costs in line. It's also a necessity when you outsource some or all of a Web-site project. A budget is a good tool for projecting and assessing the *return on investment* (ROI) your initiative enjoys. Finally, you pretty much can't get funding without budgetary approval, so you've got to have a budget, if only to provide something to your boss or investors to sign off on. Basically, you need a budget and you must build one.

Yes, that's right, *you* must do it. Don't let a budget be suggested by a firm you hire to build your site or imposed on you by someone who knows little of online matters. A contractor cannot know your business dealings. It may be tough enough for you to put together a budget — after all, you are still in a start-up endeavor in a start-up industry even if you've been at it since the birth of browsers. But you must do it, and in the end, you'll be glad you did. (Hmm. We're starting to sound like our mothers.)

 Your company may already have a budget process in place. If it does, you should have an easier time because you can get guidance in putting together your budget. If you know nothing of budgeting, we recommend *Managing For Dummies,* by Bob Nelson and Peter Economy (IDG Books Worldwide, Inc.), which includes an excellent chapter on the basics of budgeting.

In this chapter (in this book), we clue you in to some general budgeting tips and then the specific budget categories you need to consider in creating an overall budget for your online endeavor.

How Often to Budget

Most traditional, brick-and-mortar companies have an annual budgeting process, but things change a lot faster than that in the online world. You may well find that the budget you create early in the year has less to do with reality come the middle of that fiscal year than you (or your CFO) would like. Given the fast pace of the Internet industry, you may have to create interim budgets and adjust your budgetary thinking throughout the year. You'll certainly have to write project budgets now and again. Nonetheless, an annual budget is the way to go for planning purposes and to fit in with your company's overall systems.

Remember that a budget is an important management tool, whether you are on a tight rein or have unlimited funds. Either way, producing a budget helps you to understand what to spend money on and in which areas you should concentrate your fiscal management efforts.

Tips for Approaching the Budgeting Process

In most budgeting processes, the new budget is based on the old budget, although with a bit of shifting from this category to that and some rounding up for some items and down for others. The adjustments are usually based on last year's experience, your overall judgment, and projections regarding how next year will go. But you, luckily or unluckily, work in a new field (and possibly in a start-up). You may not have history to fall back on. In fact, the odds are that you'll wind up building your budget from scratch. Here's a quick game plan you can use to get started:

✔ **Look into your company's budgeting processes.** Start by finding out what documents, if any, your company provides to managers to guide them in the budgeting process. Read these guidelines thoroughly, and follow them. Your budget may not be approved if it is not understandable to the accountants and execs, and following their guidelines is always a good idea. (If you're working in a start-up, get guidelines from your CFO [chief financial officer] or consult with an accountant. Be sure to take into consideration what format and information investors or VCs [venture capitalists] will want to see.)

✔ **Do research and meet with the people involved.** Get models wherever you can. Look into what other departments have done, and call around for estimates and price quotes. Meet with your Web team if you already have one, and get their input. Meet with other departments as needed to find out how they imagine your online endeavor could fulfill their needs, so you can determine what that will cost.

✔ **Develop an overall strategy for your Web endeavor.** Based on your findings and meetings, project what the Web endeavor might involve in the coming year. Think about whether you'll need a redesign (you probably will), where your database and server stand and whether they'll support the growth you anticipate, and what it's going to take to revisit or revamp your site's goals. Also, consider what's needed to maintain and expand the site.

✔ **Exercise judgment.** While budgets are supposed to be about facts and numbers, the building of budgets requires a healthy dash of judgment. Look through all the information you've gathered and consider the options. You may need to sort through your expectations and those of others, then revamp your strategies several times over.

✔ **Play with the numbers.** In the course of your thinking and planning, create a spreadsheet. (We cover this in upcoming sections.) Attach specific numbers you've gathered through your research into specific items, tally things up, and see what you see.

✔ **Think it all through yet again.** Don't think that your first pass at making a budget will be your last. Go back, examine your assumptions, adjust your strategy, consider dropping unnecessary expenses, and then see what happens. Now do it again. You'll find as you do this that different considerations occur to you each time. This is good. This allows you to strategize more thoroughly. This is budgeting.

Take it from us, there are tried-and-true tricks for making your budget fly and keeping it in line. Here are some quick tips learned in the trenches:

✔ **Pad a few things.** Selectively padding an item here and there gives you a bit of room to maneuver. Remember, nobody looks smart by going over budget, but coming in under budget makes you a genius.

✔ **Consider the company values as you create your budget.** If your company places a premium on quality, tie a special budget request to improving quality in your Web site. If your company is in a consolidating mode, tie requests to savings. You get the picture, right?

✔ **Create an item or two that are specifically meant to be expendable.** You're a team player, right? And you sure don't expect to have the whole of your first budget proposal approved. You may want to add a couple of items to it that can easily be axed without harming your overall endeavor. Pop in something you know won't pass, and think of it as the sacrifice that saves another item that's important, but perhaps less understood. Do this cautiously, though — if your budget seems like fiction, the whole thing might get the ax (and so might you!).

✔ **Tie big expenditures to equal-value payoffs or consequences.** When you make big requests, be sure to note what the payoff is and when it's expected. The payoff does not always have to occur within the fiscal year, but it should not be so far off that it becomes unimaginable. Try something like, *if we purchase this Sun Sparc workstation, we'll be able to* *handle the projected increase in traffic for the next two years. That will bring in at least a 300 percent increase in ad space revenues.* Alternatively, you can indicate what dire consequences will occur if your proposed expenditure doesn't happen. *If we don't buy a new database server and spread the Web server load over three machines, when traffic increases as projected, the site's downtime will also increase; we will see as much as 27 percent downtime during peak traffic hours.*

✔ **Make the budget modular.** Write your budget to clearly show that a given project or goal is going to cost X amount; provide supporting documentation that shows the basis for your estimates. Then if you don't get budgetary approval for those items, you can address the implication that the specific projects or goals have not been funded. And if you do get budgetary approval, it underscores to everyone the importance of specific initiatives within the company's overall plan.

What Budgets Look Like

In a nutshell, every cost associated with your site should be represented as a line item somewhere on your budget. Some budgets are long and complex (hey, when the federal government budget is printed it goes to *volumes*), some go into projecting future requirements and expenses, and some are much, much simpler. You don't have to write the federal budget to account for what you're going to do with your Web site. All you have to do is whip up a few good spreadsheets.

A sample spreadsheet is available from the E-Commerce Management Center at www.tauberkienan.com for you to download and use. It contains a budget for building a mid-sized Web site. It does not include the ongoing expenses associated with maintenance and keeping an in-house team on staff. Take a look at that sample spreadsheet, and you'll see fairly standard organization for a budget. One line exists for each item of expense, and the amount of the projected expense is indicated. No big deal.

To take things a step further, items are grouped into general categories, and each category is summed up. At the bottom of the spreadsheet, the whole shebang is summed up, so anyone can see what the endeavor is going to cost.

One special category, however, does not fit into the final sum shown, and that is *ongoing expenses.* In budgeting tradition, these are regular expenses you'll encounter from year-to-year; for example, staff salaries, travel expenses, continuing education, staff bonuses, rent and other overhead, and so on. If you want to expand out your budget to create line items for these expenses, simply follow the pattern shown of setting up categories, columns, and rows.

The Spreadsheet User Group, at www.sheet.com, publishes a print magazine about spreadsheets. The Excel Tutorial (www.usd.edu/trio/tut/excel) includes everything you ever wanted to know about spreadsheets — and a quiz.

Elements of the Spreadsheet Columns and Rows

As you probably know or have noticed, a spreadsheet (available from the E-Commerce Management Center at `www.tauberkienan.com`), consists of columns and rows. Look at our downloadable sample spreadsheet, and you'll see that we have included these column headings:

- ✔ **Item** for a column of short words to describe each item in the budget. As you read this chapter we'll suggest some line items that are commonly placed in a Web site budget.

- ✔ **Notes** for a column that allows one to describe the items in further detail. The Notes column may be a good place to indicate the vendor name if you're outsourcing, or what exactly is included in the scope of the listed item.

- ✔ **Hours** for a column that describes the number of hours worked by in-house people. Here you can indicate the estimated number of hours in-house people will spend working on a given item. You can also use this column to show the estimated hours a contract person will take to do a given job, if you're paying them hourly. If you're outsourcing some part or all of the work of building your site (see Chapter 10), leave the item under this heading blank and enter the estimated costs in the Fixed Cost column instead.

- ✔ **$/Hour** for a column that shows the estimated hourly cost of your in-house people on this item. This is not the same as the Hours column, which shows the number of hours — this column shows the money involved. You may want to go with a general estimate and keep it the same for all items that in-house people will work on, or you may want to enter more realistic numbers that are based on the type of work involved. For example, someone doing scripting will usually be paid more per hour than someone writing editorial copy.

- ✔ **Fixed Cost** for a column showing the nonvariable cost of an item. This may be the cost of physical stuff, like computers, or it may be an item such as work you plan to contract out to an outsider. Basically, if you think you'll pay a fixed amount for someone's work instead of an hourly rate, show that amount here. Sometimes you'll have both an hourly and fixed cost associated with an item. That's no problem — just indicate both and sum them up in the next column, *total cost.*

- ✔ **Total Cost** for a column showing the (you guessed it) total cost for the item. It is the sum of the hourly cost and the fixed cost. This is the number you look at to see what the item actually is going to cost (or at least what you hope the item will cost).

Excel resources at your service

Microsoft Excel is the product of choice for many spreadsheet number crunchers. To delve into Excel and what you can do with it, you may want to consider these handy online resources:

The official Microsoft Excel home page at www.microsoft.com/office/excel offers an overview, as well as tutorials, links, and tips. Microsoft Excel Support is at www.microsoft.

com/office/support.htm. At CNET's Help.com site (www.help.com), do a quick search on Excel and you'll find pages packed with Excel information as well as the opportunity to sign up for a newsletter packed with Excel tips. John Lacher, CPA, offers tutorials as well as sample macros and applications via his Excel Help Pages (www.lacher.com).

The spreadsheet's rows show the categories of expense involved in putting together a Web site. In the sample spreadsheet provided in our E-Commerce Management Center, the categories shown are

- ✔ Planning
- ✔ Design
- ✔ Development (content and technical)
- ✔ Deployment
- ✔ Promotion
- ✔ Maintenance

We talk in more detail about the activities that inspire these categories throughout the rest of this chapter.

General Types of Expenses

In putting together a budget for your Internet endeavor, you obviously have to consider the types of expenses you'll encounter. This, of course, is true of every budget for every endeavor, but it's a trickier matter in this case, because the industry is still young. In the sections that follow, we offer pointers for categories to consider. You may find that your needs are quite different, and you'll almost certainly find that your needs will evolve with time, but this discussion should provide you with a starting point. In the broadest sense, you can split your costs into three general categories: infrastructure, production, and ongoing support, each of which represents a distinct part of building and running your site.

Infrastructure

In this book, when we talk about infrastructure, we are simply talking about what you need in place to do business and run a Web site. Depending on the size of your site and how much of your site you plan to outsource, your "infrastructure" may be limited to one person, a computer, DSL access, and an account at an Internet service provider, or it may be a 70-person group with workstations and multiple T1 lines. Infrastructure is all the stuff you need to do your job. This might include office space, the Internet connection, general telephone service, network servers, the depreciation or rental of computers, and more.

Infrastructure costs are often difficult to pin down; the good news is that sometimes this aspect of your budget is included in your company's overall budget and (if your Web team is part of a larger company) it may not be your problem. Or you may find that you have to consider some parts of it but not all of it. For example, if your company has an IS department that runs the company's Internet connection, it's likely that the cost of that connection appears in the IS department's budget. It need not also appear in yours — you can simply ax that item from your budget. Likewise, if every employee in your company is provided with a computer automatically, you won't have to budget that basic piece of equipment for your team, because it is accounted for elsewhere in the company's budget.

 How infrastructure costs fit into your budget varies tremendously from one company to another. Some companies split these costs across all projects over the course of a year. Other companies ignore these when putting together a specific project's budget. Just follow the norms for your company.

Production

Production as we are defining it in this moment is all about producing the site. Production in this sense may include everything from conceptualizing and planning through design, technical implementation, HTML production, and all that's involved in actually launching. Production does not include ongoing support. (Further, the term "production" is used differently elsewhere in this book, to indicate the process of building the actual pages after they've been designed. These two definitions follow industry-standard lingo.)

Ongoing support

The cost of running your site day-to-day after its launch is easy to overlook. Don't forget that you must keep content fresh, maintain servers and databases, and generally keep things humming. Depending on the size of your site and your plans for updating content, ongoing support may consist of a room full of content producers, designers, developers, and others forging ideas into Web pages that are dynamically generated through the use of scripts. Also, a few full-time people working away on developing zippy new content, coding it, and posting it; or a single person spending a few hours a week reviewing your server's log files. Whatever the size of your site and your ambitions for it, you'll need to provide appropriate ongoing support. Remember to account for that in your budget.

Specific Activities that Inspire Budget Categories

Getting all the budget categories correct is trick one in setting up a budget. It's treacherously easy to overlook entire categories when figuring how much a project will cost. This gets compounded by the newness of online media and the speed at which the industry evolves. What's more, things change from one Web site to another. Here are some categories for your consideration; think of these as a starting point as you develop your own, more specific set.

Planning

Planning costs time, and time, as we all know, is money. In many cases, planning also costs in outsourced services such as running focus groups or otherwise testing the assumptions that go into planning, or in hiring consultants to coach executives or the team in assessing needs. Planning involves these key activities:

- ✔ Defining the target audience
- ✔ Analyzing the competition
- ✔ Testing concepts and assumptions
- ✔ Assessing needs, including personnel, hardware, software, and connectivity

Don't forget to account for project management in your planning budget. Project management can include all of the other planning we've mentioned, but it's also an expense that goes on through the length of the project. Typically, project management can eat up as much as 20-25 percent of your overall project budget (excluding infrastructure). To keep project management costs from bloating the budget, hire good management or excel at management yourself. Much of this book is about just that.

Content development and editorial

Content was king in the early days of the Web, and now it is again. (Was there really ever any doubt?) You'll have to devote some funding to developing your site's content. (As we said in Chapter 3, *all* sites have content, and all content is ripe for branding.) How much funding you'll need depends on what sort of content you plan, how much of it involves hands-on creation rather than repurposing or licensing, and how much of it is editorial content as opposed to other sorts. "Content development" as an activity may mean, for example, chunking up existing material and optimizing it for interactivity; writing page after page of new copy and creating new graphics; or organizing the site's architecture and navigation, choosing the site's offerings, determining how they'll best be presented, shaping the copy, and reviewing pages after they've been coded. Consider which of the following areas are relevant to your endeavor:

- Concept development (see Chapters 2 through 5)
- Editorial development, copy editing (checking accuracy, clarity of meaning, and other details), and content review (see Chapters 3 and 22)

Architecture, storyboarding, and creating navigational maps

One of the more challenging aspects of putting together a good Web site is setting up easy navigation — how people move around the site. You may need to budget for

- Creating a site map and storyboards (see Chapter 8)
- Determining the navigational scheme (again, see Chapter 8)

You may also have to budget for the services of a professional information architect, or you may find that this entire activity is folded into the costs associated with designing your site. (Some front-end companies include information architecture in the scope of design and development.)

Design

The cost of design can vary widely depending on the type of firm you choose (see Chapter 10). If your company has an established corporate image and a design department with Web savvy, you may want in-house designers to do the work. If not, or if you want a branding firm or ad agency to create design consistent with other media the company puts out, outsourcing may be the way to go. In the design section of your budget, consider these activities:

✔ Creating "roughs" of each *type* of page

✔ Creating templates of key pages

✔ Creating repeated design elements (like logos, buttons, and visual branding elements) to be used throughout the site

✔ Creating or procuring any pictures or other artwork used in the site (see Chapter 7 to find out about buying and licensing art)

Technical development

Building the back end may be part of the package when you hire a Web shop; alternatively, it may be the work of a specialized company. If you're building a highend transaction system, you'll probably want to work with a company that has substantial experience building robust databases and smoothly functional, secure transaction systems. Often the back-end developers and the front-end designers will be two different companies. Even if the back-end development is done by your in-house development team, you'll have to budget for their time (and any consultants they may need). Typical activities in this area include

✔ Writing technical specs and flowcharting the site's functionality (see Chapter 8)

✔ Developing the database and integrating it with the transaction system (see Chapters 13 and 14)

✔ Writing any custom scripts, including CGI or ASP scripts, JavaScript, and any custom applets (see Chapter 9)

Production

Production is highly visible work, but having in place the proper funding for activities that occur before production — like planning and design — can reduce the time and cost involved in production by a large margin. What is actually involved in producing a Web site varies depending on the type of content included. Some typical categories to account for here are

✔ Turning graphics and other media into appropriate formats for the Web (see Chapter 9)

✔ Creating all HTML pages based on the roughs, final designs, and story-boards (see Chapter 9)

Reviewing and site testing

This category is too often overlooked. When you create your budget, include a line item for review processes and site testing. Budget time you can devote to an in-house testing procedure that may be as simple as a few folks taking a day to pound on the site to see if it works or as complex as a review team looking at every page and another testing all functionality. You may even hire a professional testing lab to test concepts, usability, and functionality. Let us just say here that more testing is always better. Chapter 22 of this book covers testing issues and review processes. In budgeting, consider these site-testing categories:

- ✔ Usability testing, including getting users, a focus group, or a professional testing lab to test concepts before building, then testing the site in its alpha and beta stages, and perhaps even testing the site immediately after launch
- ✔ Reviewing design roughs and templates
- ✔ Reviewing HTML as it's produced
- ✔ Testing navigational elements of the site during the building process
- ✔ Verifying links
- ✔ Verifying that the site works in the beta stage, before launch, and after going live

Deployment

Generally speaking, your site will be created on a staging server. (See Chapters 2, 8, and 11.) It will have to be moved from the staging server to its true home on your Web server before launch. You must budget time to have someone move files from the staging server to your live server. Then you can launch. Here are some tasks to be done and budgeted for:

- ✔ Making any changes to configuration files on the server as required by the new site content
- ✔ Uploading the site files to the final, live server
- ✔ Verifying that content is working and correct on the final server before launch

Changing your mind is never cheap

Unlike print, where you have to settle all the details of text and design before you actually go to press, the Web is a medium of incremental change, which is one of its advantages but also a bit of a booby trap. Because you can change almost anything on your Web site any time, it is often a temptation to never make up your mind. You may think, for example, that once you have hired a design firm you can revamp your concept and design several times over, both before and after launch, without a "deadline." Watch yourself — Web endeavors are highly prone to *feature creep*, a condition in which people get all kinds of brilliant thoughts about what can be done without thinking about whether those ideas are cost-effective.

Further, if you never settle on visual and editorial standards (see Chapter 22), or if you don't create and stick to a workable directory structure (see Chapter 8), your staff may wind up reinventing the wheel daily, because they simply don't know that one decision or another has been made. Exercising creativity is a fine thing, but to keep your budget in line, you (meaning either you the site manager or the collective you, if a group is making decisions) simply must make up your mind and then help others to know and apply what you've decided. Otherwise, you are wasting time, and as we all know, time spells money.

Marketing the site

To make your site a success, you'll need to promote it. In Chapter 15, we cover a variety of methods for marketing and promoting your site. You need not spend a fortune on this, but you ought to consider any expenses involved as you create your budget proposal. This is a great place to tie in specific references both to the site's goals (Chapter 2) and future payoffs. Marketing your site can include registering it with search engines and directories like Yahoo!, establishing back links from related sites, placing banner ads, and using more traditional print and broadcast promotional efforts. Sending out e-mail newsletters is highly effective. Of course, marketing is a very creative process, and you'll probably think up whole new ways to market your site.

Here are some marketing activities you may need to consider in building your budget:

- ✔ Registering your URL with search engines and indexes
- ✔ Building a mailing list of interested users and sending out e-mail newsletters
- ✔ Tying your site in to print and television/radio advertisements
- ✔ Creating relationships with the press; announcing key developments including the launch of your Web site

✔ Establishing strategic partnerships

✔ Running banner ads on highly targeted sites

Remember that notoriety is self perpetuating. If you get some name recognition through advertising, for example, that will inspire more interest on the part of the press when you reach for media coverage. Leveraging attention into more attention is a great way to get more bang for your buck.

Maintenance

Web site projects often start with a high degree of enthusiasm. During the planning, designing, building, and deployment phases, everyone is focused on the launch. After launch, the champagne flows, confetti is tossed, and various team members fly away for tropical vacations. Oops. Who's going to maintain the site? And did you budget for that?

After your site is launched and marketed, it will have to be maintained. You'll need to create, acquire, and add new content, freshen up what's there, fidget with navigation to improve it, write and edit new pages, implement new technologies as appropriate, and more. You'll also have to maintain the server(s) and database(s) (see Chapters 11 through 14), monitor log files, and track your success (see Chapter 17). Remember to budget for these activities:

✔ Updating content and building out popular or strategic areas of the site

✔ Implementing bug fixes and addressing link rot

✔ Managing the hosting relationship (and perhaps relationships with outsourced content producers, designers, developers, and so on)

✔ Administering the servers

✔ Managing customer service (and fulfillment if the site sells products)

What's It Really Going to Cost

To determine the real projected cost of your endeavor, you have to get actual bids. To get actual bids that you can compare to each other, apples-to-apples, you need to define the project and give the same definition (usually in the form of a request for proposal, or RFP) to prospective vendors, such as front-end design firms or back-end developers. However, it helps to have some sense of what's possible for various types of budgets before you get your hopes up, so here is a quick snapshot of what you can do for how much. (You can get a more detailed picture of the average cost of specific types of Web sites from the netB2B Web Price Index at www.netb2b.com.)

To build

Building your Web site can cost anywhere from $1,000 to $500,000 or even more. Where you fall in that very wide range is a function of, well, your intentions and what you have in your pocket to back up your intentions.

- ✔ Starting at the high end, $500,000 or so will buy you a slick, robust site that is competitive in its appearance and functionality. You can hire a branding consultant to work with your design firm, or a leading edge agency that does branding, usability testing, design, and production. A separate back-end development firm might handle the database, transaction system, and programming, but you can and should expect them to know security like it's their best friend. You can also expect the systems they develop to handle millions of users per month. You can expect to hire writers, artists, and editors to contribute their talents to your site, and in the end, you ought to have a humdinger of a Web site.

- ✔ An investment of around $50,000, on the other hand, will buy you the services of professional designers but not branding consultants. You can build a back end, but it won't handle as much traffic or as many transactions (say, a few hundred thousand users per month instead of millions), and it will probably be less customized.

- ✔ In the $10,000 range, you'll have access to professional designers (though not the highend firms) and they will probably create a few templates for you or some hired coders to implement. You can also afford a programmer to create some forms, or perhaps a simple database that serves content and may be integrated with a simple transaction system. Your database and transaction system will not be customized beyond adding a few graphic elements to the interface (for example, your logo).

- ✔ At the $5,000 level, you can create a simple site with no database or transaction system. If you hire a newbie designer, he or she might throw in coding; alternatively, you can have a freelance designer create a few templates and you can hire a coder or do your own coding. Expect to wind up with no more than approximately 20 pages; sticking to text and a few images (rather than anything like forms or nifty navigation tricks that require programming) will allow you to maximize your page count while keeping costs down.

If yours is a very small operation, you might wonder what you can do for even less. To create a small site on a shoestring, consider hiring a designer to do one template and then plan on a site of no more than five pages, or create the site yourself using an authoring program such as FrontPage (*FrontPage For Dummies,* by Asha Dornfest (IDG Books Worldwide, Inc.), is an excellent introduction). Or you can use one of the many services that offer the option to choose among design options and insert your on content — these services usually also include hosting and even a transaction system and are very economical. Yahoo! (store.yahoo.com), SmartAge (www.smartage.com), and bCentral (www.bcentral.com) all offer such services.

To maintain

Remember that Web site that cost $500,000 to build? It's going to have to be promoted and maintained. A budget of $5 million per year isn't unreasonable for a company site or a start-up dot-com's site that cost $500,000 to build. You'll have to buckle down and determine in advance what your site is going to cost to freshen up and support. Remember to account for in-house staff time, adding and deleting catalog items, revamping navigation and making incremental design changes as needed, server administration and the management of hosting services, keeping an eye on stats as they roll out, and any promotional activities you engage in.

 To minimize maintenance costs, start at the level of planning your site. Clarify your site's goals (as discussed in earlier chapters). Include in the site only features that support those goals and that you are actually going to be able to maintain. Keep in mind that jazzier effects require programming, and that you can minimize expense by sticking with simple text and images rather than more flashy media. Keep your staffing costs down, and get bids by the project or page rather than by the hour. And finally, always remember that feature creep will bloat a budget faster than oats swell in a pig's belly.

ROI Meets Management Buy-In

 It's very important to remember that ROI (*return on investment*) is what managers and executives want to see. It's a poor business that shows no profit, and while one can consider that a Web site is succeeding based on any of a number of criteria, the bottom line is, after all, the bottom line. You must, must, must keep your finger on the pulse of how your site's success is showing return on the investment made in it. This is crucial to getting management buy-in for expanded endeavors in the future, and it's often even more crucial to keeping your job!

According to one International Data Corporation group report, an intranet site can easily show an astounding 1,000 percent ROI. This means that for every $100 you spend on an internal Web site, you can expect to get a $1,000 return on the investment.

But calculating ROI in the case of Web sites does not always have such optimistic results. As of this writing, many sites are not profitable. Some produce revenue, but they cost more than they take in. Others are rightfully seen as loss leaders (which are expected to bring in business but by losing money up front) or as cost centers (which are seen as an ongoing expense of doing business).

To calculate the return on investment for any business venture involves comparing hard costs (dollars spent) and soft costs (time spent, for example) to gains. To find the percentage of return you expect for a given project or venture, add up what you expect to get and divide it by what it's going to cost to get that, then multiply times 100 to get a percentage. Use this basic formula:

```
(Net revenue + hard savings + soft savings — total
          investment)/(Total investment) x 100 = ROI
```

Again, the result of the formula (ROI) will appear as a percentage.

In a budget or business plan, provide explanation of the source of revenue and where the savings will occur as well as your budget for the investment (essentially, the costs, which will appear in a spreadsheet as described earlier in this chapter).

You can also show various options or plans, with the ROI you expect for each of them. For example:

Option	Total Investment	Total Revenue + Savings	Return on Investment
Plan A	$114,346	$156,000	136%
Plan B	$153,597	$156,000	102%

When you provide options, be sure to describe what makes each option more or less attractive. For example, Plan A might involve using more in-house people with less innovative skills, which would keep costs down but not necessarily jack the project into the highest reaches of coolness, and which would take the in-house staff away from other things they might be doing. Plan B might be more expensive because it involves outsourcing, but that might buy innovation and expertise you don't have.

In the end, remember that while everyone wants to see ROI, the anticipated return on investment is not always the deciding factor in whether to proceed or how to proceed. A lot of Web sites wouldn't exist today, for example, if people expected them to be turning a profit. Intranets seem to get high return, mainly because they save a bundle. All that stuff that used to be distributed on paper and in tidy binders can now be accessed by employees via the intranet, and does not have to be distributed via HR personnel assembling it, walking it around, and handing it out. But public Web sites (including e-commerce sites) are expensive to launch and run, and as of this writing the industry is still casting about for tried-and-true profit models.

FIELD NOTES

Watching the bottom line

Lonnie Moseley, president of a technical solutions company, points out that "Keeping costs in line matters as much as how much business walks through the door. Yours can be the busiest shop on the block, but if you don't keep your eye on profit and ROI, all you have is a hobby."

Nonetheless, you must calculate ROI for both large and small endeavors to get management buy-in, to satisfy investors that you are capable of eventually turning a profit, and to reassure yourself that you are making sound judgments about how and where to spend your hard-earned budget.

Chapter 7

Legal Bugaboos for the Lay Webmaster

● ●

In This Chapter

▶ Who owns what on the Web

▶ Respecting intellectual property and protecting your own

▶ Understanding the public domain and fair use

▶ Looking into licensing,™ and ®, and trade dress (look and feel)

▶ Knowing which art you can and can't use

▶ Considering the law on linking

▶ Avoiding libel and slander

● ●

A few short years ago, the Internet seemed as lawless as the Old West, and many people liked it that way. But as overall popularity and commercial development grew, it became increasingly clear that the laws that apply to and protect other media (print, television, film, music, and so on) also apply to the Internet. In most cases, this has been a good thing, resulting in better protection for all. But some laws or legal precedents seem to some people to have made life more complicated for those running Web sites. As they say, the jury is still out, and Internet law will continue evolving far beyond its current early stage.

In the meantime, you, as an Internet pro, should know and observe the law of the online land. This can prevent you from, for example, copying and using material that was created by others as if it were your own, and it can help you know how to discourage others from doing the same to you. In most cases, the laws that protect us all are pretty sensible, and your best protection is to understand the basic issues. This chapter introduces you to the concepts behind intellectual property as it pertains to the Internet.

We are not attorneys, and nothing written here is meant to be legal advice. To get the lowdown on your specific legal situation, the person to see is an actual attorney who specializes in Internet or e-commerce law. For general legal information online, try FindLaw at www.findlaw.com. But keep in mind that Internet law is a rapidly changing field, the Internet is global, laws vary by jurisdiction, and no one is quite sure how a lot of key Internet law issues will play out in the courts. It's best to consult an attorney for the most up-to-date information and for advice about specific situations.

One more thing: This chapter may worry you. Keep in mind that as the Internet pro managing a Web site, you must take into account business risks of all sorts, including legal risks. It's up to you to determine how to assess any potential risks and how to handle them.

Intellectual Property and Web Real Estate

Say you launch your browser and open a Web page. It includes text, perhaps graphics or video snippets, a sound file or two, a bit of Java, and certainly a bunch of code lurking behind the page. To you, as a user, the Web page looks like a single thing, and if it has a copyright notice on it (and if you happen to read that copyright notice), you may think that the entire page belongs to Wilma Webwanderer, who created it. But this is not necessarily so. True, the page is Wilma's, but that video may be licensed, and rights to use that sound byte may be assigned. And if Wilma used an outside development firm to create the page, the code itself or perhaps the Java may belong to the development firm and not Wilma.

Similarly, regardless of who actually creates your Web site, you need to know what components you can or cannot use legally and whether you have to pay for their usage. Otherwise, you risk the possibility of getting a cease-and-desist letter from a lawyer, demanding that you dismantle your site and/or pay for your unknowing use of material that belongs to someone else. You also risk being sued.

Intellectual property laws

This brings us to the topic of *intellectual property,* which refers to copyrights, trademarks, patents, and trade secrets. Intellectual property is, essentially, something that is owned (at least initially) by someone who thought it up and created it. Intellectual property can include, for example, the elements of a Web page (such as the HTML code, images, sound, and other content), domain names, product names, computer software, Internet business methods, and even the look and feel of a Web site.

Although the creator of a piece of text, code, and so on is presumed to be its owner, he or she can transfer ownership of it to others, either entirely or in limited ways. You may have acquired some of the content, features, or functionality of your site by licensing it from someone else; or, conversely, you may be granting licenses to your own intellectual property to someone else.

Clearly, intellectual property is a business asset. But unlike more three-dimensional property, such as your office building, inventory, or equipment, intellectual property is not usually something you can touch. Intellectual property does take a tangible shape when you document it, reproduce it, or capture it in a physical form. In fact, a hallmark of intellectual property is that, unlike tangible property, it can be reproduced and used an infinite number of times. Intellectual property has lots of applications on and implications for the Internet. From the content that's presented on your Web site and the ideas expressed, to the way the site appears and the code that ensures the functioning of the back-end systems, everything that forms part of your site is owned by someone. But there are often several different owners, and exactly who owns what isn't always clear. Contracts are typically used to address this. In contracts, a creation that is intellectual property is referred to as *the work* (usually with a capital *W*). For the rest of this chapter, we use the term *work* with this connotation.

The major categories of intellectual property laws in the United States that are important for Webmasters to know and consider include

- ✔ **Trademark law:** Protects words, names, and symbols used by businesses to identify the source or origin of their goods and services in commerce. Trademark law includes a subcategory known as trade dress law.

- ✔ **Trade dress law:** Protects the packaging, presentation, or general look of a product. In the case of Web sites, the trade dress may be the distinctive look of the site itself.

- ✔ **Trade secret law:** Protects valuable information that is not widely known and has been consciously kept secret by its owner, such as the exact recipe for Krispy Kremes.

- ✔ **Copyright law:** Protects original works created by an author or artist, including written material, illustrations, music, and videos. (Licensing is discussed later in this chapter.)

- ✔ **Patent law:** Protects new, useful, and nonobvious inventions and processes.

Of these, copyright law is often the most relevant for a Webmaster; it's also one that's among the toughest to pin down in some ways. Copyright protects the expression of an idea, not the idea itself. When it comes to the expression of ideas, a Web site is no different from a magazine, a book, or even a CD-ROM. They all contain some combination of text, graphics, video, and audio, which someone created.

Use of materials on a Web site does involve some unique issues. For example, because of the borderless nature of the Internet, any licenses that you may obtain for using material that was created by others on your site should specify worldwide rights. We discuss this topic further in upcoming sections. First, we look at who might own what on a Web site.

Who owns what on a Web site

Who "owns" intellectual property is a question that gets at the heart of the information age. As previously mentioned, a Web page often consists of diverse elements: coding, graphics, text, design, and more. Who created which part has a great deal to do with who owns what — remember, the author of the work usually owns the work, at least at first. There may be multiple creators involved as well as copyright, trademark, trade dress, and licensing concerns.

It's best to start with the basic assumption that someone owns everything. You must not assume that anything on the Internet is in the *public domain* (which refers to material that is not protected by copyright and therefore free to use by anyone without permissions). It's best for now — unless you don't care who owns what or who may sue you — to err on the side of caution. In general, it's safest to assume that, if you want to use something that you find on the Internet in your own Web site, you must at least get permission and perhaps even sign a licensing contract or similar document.

Be aware that whether you hire an individual or agency to create your site or do it yourself, you are still responsible for knowing the details of your site's various components (its text, images, code, tools, and so on), including whether you have legal rights to use or reuse the components. Consult an attorney for professional review of any contracts you want to sign with developers, designers, writers, content providers, and others.

Ownership of ideas

As noted previously, in general, you cannot legally own an idea. Only the way an idea is expressed can be owned and protected. For example, you cannot legally claim as your own the idea of a story about a poor, downtrodden young woman who hooks up with a wealthy, handsome man and lives happily ever after. However, you can legally protect a claim to a specific and uniquely expressed novel, film, or other work based on a rags-to-riches theme. Similarly, you cannot claim ownership of the fact that Central Park lies between the East and West sides of Manhattan; but you can protect ownership of your own unique and particular map, drawing, or other rendering of this specific geography.

It is the tangible form, expression, or implementation of an idea, then, that can be owned and protected under copyright laws — not the idea itself. Even in the case of patents for inventions, it is not the idea that is protected by the patent; rather, it is the application of the idea that is patented. To get the patent, you have to show that you have a written specification. The spec must show the specific invention that will make real the idea. In the case of copyrights, too, you have to show that you have expressed an idea in some tangible form that is distinct from how anyone else has expressed it.

Ownership of content

Content on a Web site includes text, images, video, and sound, but it also includes the way ideas are expressed or communicated through these elements. Note that the ideas themselves are not owned; it is the expression of the ideas that can be owned, and they are ownable commodities the moment they become fixed in some tangible form. (See the section "The Large and Small of Copyright Law," later in this chapter, for details.)

So, an artist, a musician, or a writer — the "author" — owns any original work that she or he creates. In fact, any individual who writes an ordinary sentence (even if it's only in an e-mail) owns his or her "work" — the sentence, provided that it's sufficiently original. (However, if an employee writes an e-mail at work, the terms of his or her employment agreement might stipulate that the e-mail is the property of the company, as are all other works the employee creates.) In traditional media, including books, poetry, screenplays, music, song lyrics, maps, illustrations, written instructions, and more, a work is generally owned by its creator (or author). Although the author initially owns the work, the author may assign or license the copyrights in the work to another person or entity. In some competitive industries, workers are required to assign rights to all works created during the term of their job contracts, even if the works are not created on company time. Similarly, some publishing contracts stipulate that the publisher be assigned rights to the book, article, or other written work being created.

Ownership of trade dress

The distinctive design of a product and its packaging may be protectable as intellectual property, whether the product is a health-food line, a cookbook series, or even a Web site. *The design,* in this context, is called trade dress.

Offline examples of protected trade dress include the interior look of theme restaurants such as the Hard Rock Cafe and the look of the cover of this book. In the online world, the specific attributes of a site's design (such as colors, graphics, navigational tools, layout, typeface, and anything else that is distinct about the site's visual appearance) are commonly protected as trade dress. The look and feel of a Web site is an important part of a company's overall branding (see Chapter 2). In addition, the "look and feel" of a Web site may be protectable under copyright law, if it is sufficiently original.

Why is trade dress important intellectual property? Think, for example, about the design of a business news site and how it would differ from that of a spa travel site: The former intends to convey timeliness, authority, insider smarts, and knowledge across many industries; the latter intends to convey wellness, pampering, rejuvenation, and fun. Each set of attributes forms part of the branding for the corresponding site. Both of these sites would, presumably, select colors, graphics, and so forth to encapsulate the intended experience for the user. Each site would also probably invest all kinds of resources to extending its branding to its offline materials, and neither would look favorably at any other site simply helping itself to the trade dress it has so carefully crafted and promoted.

Ownership of back-end systems

As you may know, the term *back end* describes generally the technical workings of a Web site. A back-end system can be as simple as a set of *scripts* (simple programs) that allow a user to fill out a form to add her or his name to a mailing list; or it can be as complex as a database-driven catalog and transaction system that permits credit-card purchases.

If you hire an individual programmer or a back-end development firm to create or update your back end for you, you must find out if they incorporate pieces of proprietary code or tools (*proprietary* means owned by them or by someone else). The code or tools may be protected under copyright or patent laws. Make sure up front that you know who owns what. Has the programmer or back-end firm developed and licensed some pieces of code to you? Have they licensed any tools from someone else on your behalf? What are the terms of any such licenses — for example, for what purpose and what length of time are they licensed? Find out about this during your initial interview with the programmer or developer, before the contract gets written and signed. After you understand all the terms, be sure they are spelled out in the contract. (Refer to Chapters 10 and 13 for more information about working with programmers and developers, and the kinds of questions you need to ask them.)

If you use a ready-made back-end program, you actually are licensing the technology. The manufacturer still owns the program; by purchasing a copy, you have paid for the right to use it (within defined limits).

Online legal resources for you and me

To look into the basic legal issues described in this chapter, start with these online resources:

✔ FindLaw (www.findlaw.com) is a comprehensive, searchable index of legal resources.

✔ Attorney Ivan Hoffman posts useful articles about Internet law and publishing, based on his professional legal experience, at www.ivanhoffman.com.

✔ Nolo Press (www.findlaw.com) is a rich resource for all sorts of legal information.

✔ Quirk & Tratos, an intellectual property and Internet law firm, posts articles on trademarks, copyrights, patents, trade secrets and, Internet law on its Web site at www.quirkandtratos.com.

We describe more online legal resources throughout this chapter.

The Large and Small of Copyright Law

Copyright (and patent) law first sprang up in Europe to encourage the evolution of tools. It all started when a king granted to owners of early printing presses the *right* to make *copies*. Practically speaking, artisans of the day (writers, mapmakers, and printing press operators, for example) needed to believe that they would gain something from their efforts and that their work would be protected — otherwise, what was the point? Because others believed that protecting the work of artisans would benefit the public, copyright law was born.

In the United States, copyrights are governed by federal law. In the United States, the copyright to a work is initially owned by the author, as soon as he or she fixes a work in *any* tangible form — printed or otherwise. For example, a written work can be created in a word-processing program and saved on a hard disk, fixing it in digital form, and that is considered "fixed in tangible form." Likewise, art or music that is distributed digitally over the Internet (and exists *only* in digital form) is also considered fixed in tangible form and is owned by someone. (Obviously, however, you cannot simply compose a piece of writing or music in your head or imagine a visual image and then claim ownership of it; you must fix it in some tangible form.)

Given all this, you've perhaps begun to realize that while you may not have thought of yourself as a publisher before, you are — you publish a Web site. Copyright law does indeed affect you and your Web site. Whatever the purpose of your Web site (whether your site is a business site or purely for personal expression), you need to know some basic facts to protect yourself from having portions of your site "pagejacked" and to protect yourself from *infringing on* (violating) the rights of others.

Copyright laws protect the tangible, original expression of what is contained in your Web site: the content, the code, and the look and feel of the site. As mentioned previously, to hold copyright, you must be the author, or you must have been assigned rights by the author. As you acquire, create, and license components of your Web site, it's important to understand what copyright is, what you are protecting when you own copyrights, and how the law protects a work. You also want to know how to assess whether you are acquiring a work from the true copyright holder.

The Copyright Web Site, at `www.benedict.com`, is an all-around guide to copyright law that anyone can use, and it pays special attention to Internet issues.

What is a copyright?

Copyright is an intellectual property right that confers (for a limited time) certain exclusive rights to authors of original works that are fixed in tangible form. In the United States, copyright law is federal law with both civil and criminal provisions. Most copyright lawsuits, however, are civil suits. They generally involve one party suing another rather than any sort of criminal indictment. Criminal charges usually only occur over cases of commercial counterfeiting, such as fraudulent reproduction of CDs or videos.

Copyright law protects any original material that's fixed in a tangible form beginning the moment it's fixed (for instance, e-mail is considered copyrighted the moment you type it). It does not cover ideas, factual information, blank forms, systems, or specific words, titles, or names — just *the expression of an idea* in an original work. It also doesn't extend into any previously existing material that an author may incorporate into the work.

A key word here is *originality*. However, the standard by which originality is judged is pretty generous. *How To Play Golf in Ten Seconds* needn't be utterly different from the thousands of how-to golf books that preceded it; it need only have minimal creativity and be solely the work of the stated author.

As we point out earlier in this chapter, Web pages can be comprised of a number of separate elements (text, images, code) that can each be viewed as individual works themselves. So, can such a Web page be considered an original work? To further complicate things, a Web page can change in appearance depending on what browser it is viewed in. In that case, can a Web page be considered a creation that is fixed in tangible form? The answer to both questions in courts of law has been *yes*. The logic is that a Web page is an original construction of elements arranged and rendered by a creator in a fixed and tangible form (which is digital and is distributed over the Internet). So like printed works, Web sites and individual pages are subject to copyright laws.

Note that a work need not be officially registered to be protected under copyright law (although registering the work is valuable if you ever have to drag someone into court), nor does the work have to include a copyright notice. If you own it, you own it. By the same token, simply placing a copyright notice on a work does not necessarily mean you own the work. You cannot assert rights to something you don't actually own. First, you must own the work; the copyright notice simply indicates your assertion of ownership (and warns off infringers). Copyright law recognizes a bundle of rights, including

- The right to reproduce the work by any means and in all media
- The right to prepare derivative works based on the copyrighted work
- The right to distribute copies of the work
- The right to perform or display the work in public

How copyright law works

Outside the United States, copyright law is governed by the Berne Convention; in the United States, it's governed by federal law. According to United States laws, works created on or after January 1, 1978, are protected by copyright for the life of the author plus 70 years, whether or not they carry a copyright notice. For works created or published before January 1, 1978, the rules are different; check with the U.S. Copyright Office or a copyright attorney for specifics.

Any or all of the bundle of rights that make up copyright can be transferred by the owner of the copyright to others. For example, the owner of a photograph's copyright can transfer to the owner of a Web site the right to copy and distribute the photo online, then transfer to someone else the rights to display the photo in a brick-and-mortar public place. Depending on how the transfer was defined, the photo's owner may retain the right to license uses of the work to others for other purposes, and can, for example, create other new works based on the original photo. Transfers of rights such as these examples must be agreed upon in writing, and the agreement has to be signed by the copyright owner. When a copyright is transferred, sold, licensed, or assigned, the terms must be carefully laid out. But first everyone must be clear who holds the copyright. Does a copyright notice prove ownership? Read on.

Posting a copyright notice

Although a copyright notice is no longer required in order to assert ownership over a work, marking your Web site and pages with a copyright notice in the standard format does provide some benefits. First, it may deter some would-be or unwitting infringers from heisting your property. Additionally, if your material is properly marked with a copyright notice and then someone nabs something, it may be easier to prove "willfulness" on that person's part. (It's more difficult for infringers to claim naiveté when the Web page they nabbed had a copyright notice on it.) Because users of your site can enter it through any page on the site, placing a copyright notice on every page may be your best bet in notifying visitors of your ownership.

The conventional form to use for your notice is *Copyright © [date] by [owner's name]*. Note, however, that at this time, a standard HTML code for that © symbol does not exist — at least not for all browsers. You can use the code #169; or &copy to produce the symbol in most browsers. But because not all browsers will display the symbol, even if you use the symbol, you ought to use the word *copyright*. The phrase *All rights reserved* isn't required in the United States as of this writing; however, certain countries require it for copyright protection there, and, in any case, it never hurts to use it. Additional legal language may be suggested by your attorney, depending on your circumstances and the degree of protection that you need.

You can view the source, but don't take it

When you set out to design and publish a Web page, you come up against a boggling array of issues to consider, even as you scribble ideas on a napkin. Like most people setting out to author an original, creative piece, you probably find yourself trekking out to see what others have done.

Many Web browsers let you view "the source" — the code behind a given Web page. (You can see the code underlying the page, though not the code that drives the back-end system.) Being able to see the source code is really handy in that you can peek into what makes up a successful Web page. Lucky you — this is like being a newly minted architect and getting to see blueprints of the Coliseum or I.M. Pei's glass pyramid. It's very cool and even a big convenience. But a serious issue lurks in this convenience.

Because accessing the process behind the design is so easy, it seems harmless to many to cut and paste that code, perhaps modifying it or perhaps just telling yourself that you're "borrowing" the tools to make your site. You may have even been told by an unwitting instructor or colleague that this is acceptable. However, this is both unethical and illegal. Even if the owner of the site has not marked it saying that you may not take anything, everything there is intellectual property — even the code — and you may not legally snag that code for your own purposes.

You can use someone else's code if (and only if) there is a notice on his or her Web site explicitly granting permission to others to use the code. (This is often known as an "open source" arrangement.) If you take advantage of such a scenario, print out the notice and keep it in your records. It might also be a good idea to have your legal counsel review the notice before you proceed.

Registration with the U.S. Copyright Office (www.lcweb.loc.gov/copyright), part of the Library of Congress, is optional but does provide additional evidence to support your claim that you are the creator of a work. Note that you do have to register a copyright before you can file an infringement suit, and registering may also grant you certain additional benefits, which you can read about at the U.S. Copyright Office site.

Infringement myths and realities

Many urban myths float around in the online world, along with an unfortunate naiveté surrounding copyrights. Here are some common questions and misunderstandings:

> ✔ **Shouldn't the author of a work simply be flattered that I showcase the work on my site?** Most are not. At the very least, they almost certainly want you to get permission. They may prefer that you pay a licensing fee, and if you don't, they may sue you.

✔ **I credited the author when I posted his or her work on my site; isn't that enough?** Unless you get explicit permission (or "public domain" or "fair use" apply, as described in upcoming sections), you are infringing. By crediting the owner of the work, you've only saved yourself from being a plagiarist (someone who illegally passes off the work of others as his or her own). You're still an infringer.

✔ **I changed the work a bit before I posted it on my site, so now it's okay, right?** No. Don't expect to evade liability by altering a work that you've illegally copied. If you do so, you've violated several rights: the right to copy the work, the right to publicly display the work, the right to distribute the work, *and* the right to prepare new works based on the original.

Ignorance or lack of intention isn't much of a defense. Think of the infringement case revolving around George Harrison's song "My Sweet Lord." His company, Harrisongs Music, was found to have infringed on the copyright of Bright Tunes Music Corporation, the folks who owned the song "He's So Fine" (recorded by the Chiffons). The court found that Harrison's song lifted copyrighted harmonies from the earlier song; its ruling was based on unintentional infringement.

Also, don't make the mistake of thinking no one will notice if you use someone else's material. People often search the Web for their names (some people actually "ego surf" just for fun!). Copyright owners sometimes search for tiles or distinctive phrases from their works, and if they find unauthorized use of their works, they are entitled to take action.

The relative newness of the Internet means that some applications of existing copyright law and some newer laws specific to the Internet are currently being tested and refined in the courts. For example, the Digital Millennium Copyright Act (or "safe harbor" act) passed in the United States in 1998 established that if a company or individual claimed that a site infringed on their copyright, the ISP hosting the site could avoid liability in part by removing the unauthorized material or the entire site immediately (thus finding a "safe harbor" from claims of infringement). This action by ISPs has frustrated those who feel that their sites have been shut down without any proof against them. In order to get their sites reinstated, the site owners have to indicate willingness to defend their sites in a court of law — thus hitting the ball back into the court of the company or individual claiming infringement. But for some sites, this is not feasible, because a legal defense is beyond their budgets. How this safe harbor act stands up to legal challenges remains to be seen.

Having your site yanked or incurring other penalties can be costly and time consuming. It's far better to be safe than sorry, so if you want to use someone else's work, send out a quick e-mail and get permission in advance. Obtain written permission to protect yourself in the event that the copyright owner or some subsequent owner accuses you of infringement and denies having given you a license or permission.

There are a few occasions when it can be acceptable to use someone else's work without getting permission. We discuss these cases next.

Public Domain and the Fair-Use Follies

Some works exist in what's called the *public domain.* A work that is in the public domain can be used by anyone for any purpose without prior permission. Works can become part of the public domain in any of many ways, including

- ✔ The copyright expired and was not transferred to heirs or sold
- ✔ The copyright was not proper according to the laws in effect at the time the work was published (for example, the work may have been published prior to 1978 and the copyright owner failed to put a copyright notice on it)

The specific rules of public domain are beyond the scope of this book; they're very complex and vary from country to country. Suffice it to say that the Bible, the plays of William Shakespeare, and other very old stuff are in the public domain; the works of Ernest Hemingway and Marilyn Monroe's diary, for example, are not. Publications belonging to the U.S. government are in the public domain, but only because the U.S. government agreed to make them so; this is not true of the publications of all countries.

In fact, laws governing the public domain vary from country to country and can be complicated. If you're conducting international business or using sites in other countries as resources, it's best to get qualified legal advice from a copyright attorney.

When you're in the thick of trying to track down copyright owners and get their permission, it can be tempting to happily deceive yourself into thinking that something is in the public domain just because it's on the Net. This is not true. We've seen cases where otherwise conscientious people have picked up images and writings from Web sites (some of which claimed to be, for example, clip-art sites offering work that anyone could use for free), assuming that the stuff is in the public domain. A quick glance at the material with a practiced eye revealed that this photo was from *Sports Illustrated,* and that piece of writing was lifted from a well-known book — this is bad news for everyone involved.

The *fair use* rule was created to allow people to quote or reproduce portions of a work in reporting events, reviewing the work, creating educational materials, and creating parodies. Under this doctrine, an author or an Internet pro may make limited use of a work that was created by another without permission, but only for limited purposes and only in limited amounts. Fair use is a privilege, not a right. And the qualifying word *limited* is of paramount importance in applying the idea of fair use. It's pretty tough to know when the use of a piece is actually fair use, so it's best to be very conservative — the only way to prove fair use is in court, and many authors are quite willing to let a judge or jury decide. Get to know the rules, ask experts, and use good judgment and common sense.

One important aspect of fair use is that the use should not deprive a copyright holder of income. For example, if a teacher makes five copies of a newspaper article for educational purposes, that may be fair use (assuming that the class is not a profit-making venture). However, if a teacher photocopies an entire book for her class so students can save money, that is not fair use; the author has a right to earn money for his or her work. Other uses that *may* be deemed fair use include

✔ A short passage or quote appearing in an article or news report

✔ A short passage or quote appearing in a parody of the original work

✔ A short passage or quote appearing in a criticism, commentary, or review of the work to illustrate a point or give a flavor of the work

✔ A short passage or quote appearing in a scholarly, scientific, or academic work for illustration, clarification, or footnote purposes

Modern technology unfortunately makes copyright infringement easy. One can retrieve whole works in digital form with no trouble and attach them to an e-mail message that can then be spread within seconds to hundreds or thousands of people. Because of this, fair use on the Internet actually lacks clear parameters. In most cases, copying of a work or a portion of a work online is not considered fair use and is considered a violation of copyright law.

Again, courts usually consider a clear case of infringement to have occurred when the user's motive is for monetary or commercial gain. As an illustration of this point, consider a case involving *The Nation* magazine, which obtained President Ford's memoirs before their publication. In an article of 200,000 words, the magazine quoted a few hundred words verbatim from the memoirs. Was it fair use? It was a small amount of the memoir, after all, in an article. The case went to the U.S. Supreme Court, which ruled that this was not fair use. The reasoning was that in this case the *amount* of the material did not matter. The quoted material dealing with the pardon of President Nixon was found by the court to be at the very core of the book. It was seen as "the most interesting and moving aspect of the entire manuscript," which, having now been published in a national magazine, reduced the book's commercial value and impaired the ability of both the book's author and its publisher to gain income from the book. The use of the material in the magazine was also seen as having been used to further the magazine's commercial appeal.

As is true of so much of copyright law, the question of fair use is one of context and other subtle matters. Four factors are considered in determining whether a use is "fair." They include the purpose and character of the use, the nature of the copyrighted work, the amount and substantiality of the portion used, and the effect of the use on the market for the copyrighted work. As always, our advice is to consult professionals regarding specific cases and to learn the law so that you can exercise good judgment.

As a general rule, most of what appears on Web sites is copyrighted material. If you want to use something you find on someone's site, simply assume that the stuff is not in the public domain and that your use would not fall under the doctrine of fair use; *get permission*. Having considered all this, you say that you've decided to be a moral and upright Netizen and now want to know your options?

A Licensing Lowdown

You have two choices when it comes to securing the rights to use material that others own: You can request permission, which is usually a relatively simple matter of asking for it and being granted it. Or, you can seek a license, which may carry with it special restrictions or may require paying a fee. Permissions don't have to take special form, although your legal department (or the other party's) may prefer that you follow a certain format.

Obtaining a license to use copyrighted work is something like renting a house or a part of it. The owner of a copyright can grant as many licenses as he or she wants, even at the risk that one renter's use may overlap another's (unless there is an "exclusivity" provision that restricts the copyright owner from doing so). Licenses can either be exclusive or non-exclusive.

- ✔ **Exclusive licenses** contain some range of restrictions on the copyright owner's right to license to other parties. Exclusivity can be restricted or limited, to a certain period of time, to a particular geographic area, or for specific uses. (These are just examples.)

- ✔ **Non-exclusive licenses** allow the copyright owner to grant similar licenses to other parties. For example, a photograph may be licensed for six months of use in a particular blue jeans ad in a specified national magazine to one licensee, and licensed for a year's use in a corporate brochure to another licensee.

Assignment of copyright is not a licensing arrangement. Rather, it is a transfer of rights by the copyright owner, typically for a lump-sum payment, royalty payments, a portion of the income produced by the work, or some other consideration. For example, a graphic artist may license an image to a Webmaster in return for money and/or a promise that the Webmaster will market the graphic and direct more work toward the designer. Any purchaser of an assigned right may, in turn, sell that right unless doing so is specifically prohibited in writing.

For the copyright owner, licensing provides a way to earn money from the copyrighted work and allow others to use the work without giving up ownership of it. For the licensee, it offers the chance to use the work without having to pay a huge amount of money to buy the copyright outright. Licensing is cheaper than outright acquisition of a copyright. Think of all the pop songs you hear as background to commercials for cars, dishwashing liquid, and even Web sites; licensing agreements are what got them there.

Work for Hire and What It Means

As we describe earlier, copyright can be transferred via assignment or licensing. Copyright can also be transferred through *work-for-hire (WFH)* agreements. Basically, in a WFH scenario, party A hires or commissions party B to create a work, and the question then is who will own it.

Work prepared by an employee within the scope of his or her employment is generally considered "work made for hire" (that's the exact legal phrase). The employer is then considered the author of the work and the employer owns the copyright. Work created by a freelancer (work that is specifically ordered or commissioned from a non-employee) can be WFH if both parties expressly agree in a signed, written contract that the work will be considered such and that the hiree (the creator of the work) is handing over all rights to the hiring party.

Ignoring this matter can bring about hefty consequences. Consider an example in which you hire a contractor to build a video game and orally agree that you will own the copyrights. The game sells extremely well, and now the contractor claims that he alone owns copyright. Who owns the copyright? The contractor does, because there was no written WFH agreement and he created the work. Millions could be at stake. As usual, check copyright statutes or consult a professional for more information.

Independent contractors are often hired to create works to be included on Web sites; called an independent contractor agreement. Note, however, that the term *independent contractor* refers to a person's status as a non-employee and to a method of payment. It does not specify or even imply ownership by the hiree of the work. A WFH clause can be included in an independent contractor agreement to transfer ownership from the independent contractor to the hirer; as usual, consult an attorney to write up such an agreement. WFH agreements are also very commonly part of working with front-end firms, back-end developers, and other Web shops, which is a subject we cover in Chapter 10.

Trademark Tips and Tricks

A trademark is a first cousin to copyright, but there are important differences between the two. A *trademark* is a word, phrase, or symbol that identifies the source or origin of a product or a service. (A specific type of trademark is the *service mark,* which protects a word, phrase, or symbol that represents a *service,* rather than a product.) Ownership of a trademark is quite different from copyright, which is ownership of a given work. The title of a book cannot be copyrighted, but the name given to a series of books (such as *For Dummies*) can carry a trademark (and it does).

Rights to a trademark begin only when the trademark gains some relevance and commercial worth. For example, before Ronald McDonald was recognized as the mascot for the hamburger chain, he was just another clown. Now he's a trademarked clown. In fact, McDonald's claims ownership of lots of uses of the prefix *Mc,* as well as the famous golden arches. Other trademark examples include Coca-Cola's tagline *It's the real thing* and the Circle K logo used for the chain of stores that goes by that name. Of most importance to you, domain names can also be trademarked; the U.S. Patent and Trademark office attempts to treat domain names with its usual trademark standards.

The International Trademark Association (INTA), at `www.inta.org`, promotes the use of trademarks and includes convenient guides to using them correctly.

What a trademark protects

Unauthorized use of a trademark is considered a serious infringement. Keep in mind that trademark protection is available for words, names, phrases, symbols, and logos that distinguish the owner's products and services from others. A trademark that describes only a class of goods (for example, athletic shoes) as opposed to a specific product (say, GymJets) is not protectable. The statute is also clear that if a trademark (or *trade dress,* described in an upcoming section) is so similar to a trademark already in use in the United States that it might cause consumer confusion, use of the mark constitutes infringement. So while Domino Sugar and Domino's Pizza both carry trademarks, Domino's Sugar and Domino Pizza cannot.

In general, trademark laws protect your commercial identity, including goodwill, reputation, and marketing investments, by ensuring you the exclusive right to use the trademark for the goods and services you're marketing. Any person who uses a trademark in connection with goods and services in a way that's likely to cause consumer confusion can be busted as an infringer. As the trademark owner, you can sue the infringer to make him or her not only stop infringing but also pay damages.

In January 1996, the U.S. Congress passed the Federal Trademark Dilution Act to protect famous trademarks. *Dilution* is defined as the "lessening of the capacity of a famous mark to identify and distinguish goods and services. . . ." For example, you may not be able to use the trademark-carrying tag line *We Bring Good Things to Life* for your new sheep-cloning company. That line is already a trademark of General Electric. Even if your company does not compete directly with General Electric, you cannot use the tag line.

This still-new dilution statute should provide trademark holders with a more effective remedy against those who own very similar domain names. Trademark rights are usually recognized within a narrow class of goods, typically allowing companies to hold similar marks in different industries (for example, Delta Air Lines and the Delta Faucet Company).

On a related note, trademark rights are considered valuable when the trademark holds real commercial worth. This principle has set legal precedents that help protect domain names related to trademarks. For example, if a private person registers a domain name that includes a trademarked term, such as *TheUltimateDrivingMachine.com,* the original trademark owner for that phrase can usually demand and get the domain name back even if the private person registered the domain first. (Note, too, that the Anticybersquatting Consumer Protection Act makes it illegal to register, use, or traffic in a domain name that contains the trademark of another with the intention of profiting from the use. The potential liability for doing so may be as much as $100,000 per domain name.)

The Nolo.com Self-Help Law Center, at www.nolo.com, offers helpful information on patent, copyright, and trademark which includes information, forms, and other resources for understanding these topics.

The difference between ™ and ®

Did you ever wonder about the difference between the TM mark (™) and the R in a circle ®? The ® means that the trademark is registered with the U.S. Patent and Trademark Office (PTO). The ™ symbol is used when a trademark has not been registered. Registration is not required for protection, although (as in the case of copyright) it can strengthen protection considerably. (The symbol for a service mark is ℠.)

Registering a trademark

For the most effective protection you can get, file a federal trademark registration application via the Patent and Trademark Office in Washington, D.C. File your application as early as you can to gain the most protection. You can even file an application before you start using the trademark — consult a legal professional for more information on this.

Federal law protects unregistered trademarks, but protection is limited to a geographical area (the market within which the trademark is in use). If you've invested resources into making an identifier synonymous with your business, protect that investment by registering your trademark with the Patent and Trademark Office. Registration is not guaranteed; if your mark is confusingly similar to a mark already registered for similar goods or services, registration will be refused. Hire a professional to conduct a trademark search to determine whether your use may infringe on any existing marks and to determine whether your mark is actually protectable.

Trade Dress Is Look and Feel

Especially relevant to Web site pros is the idea of *trade dress,* which, as mentioned earlier in this chapter, is simply the design of a product — for example, the distinctive appearance and functionality of your Web site. According to the United States Court of Appeals for the 11th Circuit, trade dress is the "total image of a product [, which] may include features such as size shape, color or color combinations, texture, [or] graphics." Trade dress is, essentially, packaging.

The same legal standards apply here as with trademarks (see the preceding section). Courts in trade dress suits evaluate design and layout, graphics, and similar elements. It's been mentioned that the graphical user interfaces of distinctive Web pages are likely to enjoy trade dress protection.

Clip Art, Photography, Sampling, and You

Everything on the Internet is owned — if you doubt that, read all that has preceded this section of this chapter. Every scrap of art that you see is owned by someone, unless it has made its way into the public domain. Some kind souls, however, make their art available inexpensively or for the free use of others as *clip art.* Be forewarned that unless you find a statement that clip art, or any kind of premade art, is public domain, you must assume that it's copyrighted and should not be used without permission and perhaps a small payment. Of course, some clip art *is* free for you to use, and that stuff is often easy to find on any number of clip-art Web sites.

Using stock photography or graphics is also a quick and painless way to get art for your site. You can get such art through Web sites that make the images available for download, or as part of a design you commission from a design shop, or on a CD-ROM that you purchase from a software stores. Each piece of stock art carries its own licensing agreement, and you must pay attention to what you're agreeing to by buying the art. For example, it's a virtual certainty that you may not distribute the art for use by others. But it's also possible that the licensing agreement specifies use only in certain venues (print, maybe online, maybe broadcast), only for certain periods of time, or only for distribution within certain countries (which can be an issue if the license is United States only, for example, and your Web site is available to the entire world, as most Web sites are).

Another caveat: If the photos on your Web site depict a recognizable human being, famous or not, you may need to get permission to use his or her image. Celebrities profit from their images and protect them as a business asset. And all people have both the *right to privacy* and the *right to publicity,* which ensures each person control over his or her likeness, voice, biography, and overall persona. Rights of privacy and publicity are creatures of state law and the laws vary considerably. (Exceptions are made for certain uses, such as news reporting and other fair uses.)

But in general, it may be wise to get "model releases" for any photos of people you use. In fact, even if you're only posting your own family photos taken in Aruba as part of your travel-related e-commerce site, it's wise to get permission. (Aunt Minnie might not want her boss to know she was ever in Aruba.)

Today, almost anyone with a scanner or digital camera, the right software, and some talent can nab and manipulate videotapes, images, and audio. There seems to be no end to what can be created using premade images as a toolbox. The possibilities for copyright infringement are just as broad, but is there any case where altering and using the work of another is acceptable? With *very* few exceptions, the answer is no. The law seems pretty clear in this area (for once). Most instances of electronic manipulation can be litigated and can result in damages.

Of course, tampering can be done with any digital information, including audio. Digitalization, or *sampling,* is pretty common, especially in rap music that sometimes uses bits and pieces of existing works. In sampling, short fragments of composition can be easily reproduced and blended to compose new melodies or enhance them.

The main concern for the originating artist in this case is maintaining the integrity and quality of the original work. The law does not provide exact guidelines for "fair use," so you need to use your best judgment and the advice of your legal advisor to keep yourself out of hot water. The general rule: If you use another artist's work to create a new work, you may find yourself at the wrong end of a lawsuit. Our advice, as always, is to get permission to use even excerpts of another's work on your Web site.

What You Buy When You Buy Original Visual Art

There is a big difference between buying a photograph or work of art and buying a license to use the photograph or work of art on your Web site. Licensing is usually a contractual matter between you and, say, a designer or a stock photography house. (See preceding sections for more on licensing and who owns what in general.) As a single end user of stock photography, what you usually purchase is a nonexclusive, nonsublicensable license to use an image in prescribed ways. You may not sell or otherwise provide the art to anyone else, and you may not use it in any way other than that for which you've licensed it. The license agreement clearly spells this out.

A special note to Web designers: The licenses usually denote that the images you've licensed for your site cannot be detached from the page and made available for downloading or permanent storage. Also, if you license an image from a stock house, you cannot use it in the design of your trademark.

On the other hand, if you commission a photographer, graphic artist, or designer to create an original work of art, you can own the copyright provided you obtain the necessary written agreement (see the previous section on work-for-hire agreements). But there may still be copyright laws against modifying or altering the image in ways that the artist didn't intend. This applies especially in a public forum like the Web. Talk to a legal professional for more information about this complex concept.

What's in this picture?

When you purchase an original piece of art, such as a photographic portrait of your family or a sculpture from your local art gallery, you own the physical piece of art but you *do not* own the copyrights to it. All the copyrights in that piece of art (as we discuss earlier in this chapter) are retained by the artist. We know of an interesting case in which a photographer was commissioned to shoot a photo of a company's corporate headquarters for the cover of the company's annual report. The company obtained permission from the architect (yes, architecture is protected by copyright) but not from the artist who created a sculpture the company had purchased to decorate the front of the building. The inclusion of the sculpture in the photo without the sculptor's permission was found to be copyright infringement.

Linking and the Law

The Internet seems to invite unlimited public access. The very nature of the Web, in fact, is one of an interconnected network with hyperlinks that lead everywhere. In earlier stages of the Web's expansion, by putting a presence on the Web, it was often believed that you implied permission to the public to link to your page and that you, in turn, had unlimited implied permission to link to their pages.

However, it was bound to happen that some links were actually unwelcome. For example, if your Web site sells airline tickets, you may not want a consumer watchdog site monitoring air collision statistics to link to you. Or, if your site sells rich, gourmet cheesecakes, you may not want a group called the Anti-Cholesterol Coalition linking to you.

Here's another wrinkle: Some e-commerce sites encourage other sites to link to their "buy" pages (pages where you can shop around and complete purchases) because this may generate more sales. However, other sites object very strongly to "deep links" (links to pages several layers down); these sites prefer that other sites link instead to their home pages or refrain from linking to them at all. The reasons for this? The Web site may want users to view its home page and more of its top-level pages because

✔ It is earning ad revenue on those pages or wants to maximize traffic in order to attract investors

✔ It wants users to receive the overall marketing messages it delivers on those higher-level pages; deep linking disrupts this cohesive user experience

✔ It doesn't want simply to provide a service to users who "belong" to other sites; it would rather convert these users to being its own customers by showing them more of its own site

At the time of this writing, no clear legal precedents exist on the issue of deep linking. However, there have been lawsuits filed over this issue. For example, in a notable case that was finally settled out of court, Ticketmaster Online objected to Microsoft bypassing its home page and linking straight to its events and ticket information. The end result is that Microsoft no longer links to pages deep within Ticketmaster's site. But sites that want to be able to link deep cite their First Amendment right to free speech. At some point in the near future, this issue probably will be decided by the courts.

Yet another issue arises over linking liability. For example, if you're maintaining a site that you've advertised as kid safe, how deeply will you investigate the links you create to other sites? If a site you've linked to is linked to a site that's not exactly appropriate for children, are you liable? If yours is a site that calls itself kid-safe, create and post a policy for your users saying how deeply (one link deep? two?) you investigate those sites that you link to; post a disclaimer, too. Get your attorney's help with this — it's a very sensitive issue.

If you're concerned that your site is being linked to from questionable sites, monitoring is the best control. Seek out references to your page and information on incoming hits. (You can find out how to check backlinks of your site in Chapter 15.) Then send a polite e-mail to the Webmasters of those sites that you don't want linking to you, and request that the link to your site be removed. It's not a good idea to take an angry tone in this first contact; offending the other party can result in open hostilities and a derogatory link to your site, and escalating the situation into one that must be addressed in court.

What Is Your Business Liability?

If your Web site is part or all of a business, like any brick-and-mortar business, it will be liable for violations of the law or others' rights. As a business, you're accountable to customers, business partners, affiliates, the government, and the public at large. If you fail to honor any agreements, break any laws, cause damage or injury, or engage in deceitful or other unethical business practices, you may be held accountable and forced to make reparations.

It's important to note that conducting business on the Internet has presented many new twists and turns of the law, which will continue to evolve. Keeping current with the laws is your responsibility. Otherwise, you may lose customers, compromise your professional reputation, or have to pay penalties and fines. If the scenario is even worse and your liability is even greater, you could end up losing your business or being tried and jailed. For these reasons, it's critical to the success of your business to consult with an attorney at the outset and follow those laws that govern businesses. Tax law is, as of this writing, a particularly volatile e-commerce topic. We discuss taxation briefly in Chapters 5 and 14.

Freeware and shareware

Downloadable files and software are very popular online. When this stuff is literally free, it's called *freeware*. When it's distributed to others who are expected to try it and then pay a fee to its creator if they like it and want to keep it, the material is called *shareware*.

Freeware often carries with it rules for use, if not a fee. You are usually not allowed to sell, alter, or modify freeware (although there are some notable exceptions to this). Shareware carries both rules — which vary enormously — and a fee for continued use. In both cases, if you want to distribute the stuff via your site, you need to look into the rules governing the particular material that's of interest. The specific rules are usually attached to the freeware or shareware in some type of readme file.

What About Slander and Libel?

When a person says or writes a statement that *defames* (reflects negatively or falsely on) someone else, that is called *slander* or *libel,* respectively. Defamation of either sort has long been a matter of concern to journalists and others who publish information about people. The media is especially careful to verify statements before printing or broadcasting them to the world. (Defamation laws provide that the damaging or false statement must have been shared with a third party and must have caused some injury; otherwise, no resulting damages can be proven.)

As the publisher of a Web site (which you are, remember?), be equally careful to avoid defamation. In most states, if someone successfully makes a case against you, you may be forced to run a retraction and pay damages. The damages can be based on several factors, including the number of users who have seen the defamatory statement; and in an industry where we all hope for high traffic numbers, those figures can run very high indeed.

In the end, again, your best bet when it comes to the law is to be informed, make sensible judgments, and consult qualified legal professionals when in doubt.

Part II

Building: Organize, Implement, Deploy, Launch

The 5th Wave — By Rich Tennant

"THE IMAGE IS GETTING CLEARER NOW... I CAN ALMOST SEE IT... YES! THERE IT IS — THE GLITCH IS IN A FAULTY CABLE AT YOUR OFFICE IN DENVER."

In this part . . .

We wrote this part not just for the tech head, but also for Webmasters of all ilks who need a background in tech matters. It covers organizing your content and creating a framework for your Web site. Just in case you don't know HTML (or need a quick intro to XML), you can find that here. This part also gives you enough back-story to demystify servers and databases and search engines (oh my!).

This part helps newly minted tech types get their footing, but it also helps the more technically challenged to be conversant in all that tech talk you just have to engage in sometimes. Part II talks about servers (hardware and software), how server machines differ from other computers, and how firewalls work. It offers pointers for dealing with Internet service providers and hosting companies (and describes the difference between them). It also offers the skinny on database back ends, new types of databases that you may encounter, and what makes transaction systems click.

Chapter 8

Creating Your Site's Framework

· ·

· ·

The actual building of a Web site is no mysterious process. It's a step-by-step operation. First, you must come up with a basic site plan that translates the strategic decisions you've made into the basis of reality. You have to identify the different types of content and pages you'll have on your site, chart the pages and the potential links between them, sort out how navigation will work, consider whether you need a database, take into consideration how much maintenance you'll do (and how you'll do it), and then rethink your plan as you go along and all these things affect each other. Whew! This may seem like a lot of legwork up front, but trust us: Paying attention to these details now helps you create a well-organized, easy-to-use, easy-to-maintain Web site.

Getting Organized Makes Life Easier

Just as a good directory structure on your PC makes life easier, and a good file system in the office makes life more productive, a solid and understandable structure for your Web site makes site maintenance much smoother. Placing the electronic files that make up your site in a good directory structure on your server, for example, can help you identify outdated content in a moment and remove those files as soon as they're no longer needed. It also makes finding and linking to images and other items easier as you create new pages.

And a good directory structure depends on a good site map, which depends on a good overall plan for the site at hand. Note, too, that the URLs for your site, the major navigation buttons, and other important items are based on your site map. The *site map* (a chart that illustrates the site's structure) along with *storyboards* (a set of documents that detail each page and its relationship to other pages) are the beginnings of a blueprint for your site.

You can use any number of methodologies for organizing a Web site. Different Web site teams and shops have their own methods. In this chapter, we describe one way that may work for you. But don't be surprised if other people manage the process differently, and don't be surprised if you find yourself adopting some of the specific techniques we describe here but ditching or modifying others. The important thing is that you do get organized. Also, if you've contracted out site development, then those folks may come up with a way to organize your site and its files. Even so, you need to know about these topics so that you can evaluate and approve their work. Moreover, if you can go to those folks with a preliminary plan, you'll get a better Web site and may shave quite a few bucks off their fees.

Remember, even if your freelance designers and developers know more about the Web than you do, you know more about what you want the site to do today — and in the future — than they do. The structure for your site must be flexible enough to support any new content that you may want to add in the future.

Figure 8-1 shows a fairly typical process for building a Web site. (This is a detailed look at the same basic process shown in Figure 2-1.) In the earlier chapters in this book, we offered you the tools and information you need to complete the defining and strategizing stages. In this chapter, we move on to the organizing stage. Note that even when one person is responsible for the site (as opposed to the several teams shown in Figure 8-1), the basic process involves similar steps.

Figure 8-1:
Building a
Web site is
a complex
process.

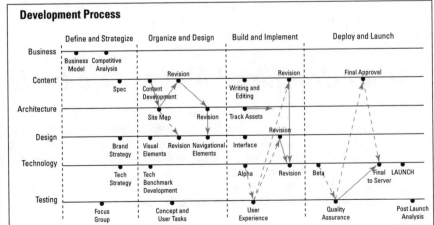

First, Pull Together Content

Where content comes from is a big question. A certain amount of what you work with will come from existing documents. For example, you can probably pull About the Company information from material created by your public relations, marketing, or human relations (HR) departments. Most companies should have scads of material describing their products or services. The customer service department probably has a list of commonly asked questions and stock answers that can easily be forged into a customer service area or FAQ (frequently asked questions) list. Look, too, for information describing the company itself, awards, key people in the company, the benefits of working for the company, and perhaps the city or community where company offices are located.

Other content will have to be created. You may have to create browsable content or interactive elements (like polls or games), and you'll almost certainly have to create the content that appears on your home page. In addition, you'll have to create content that

✔ Aids navigation and helps users find what they seek, including various index-type pages around the site as well as the search page (and the results and error pages that go with it)

✔ Helps users join in and participate in your community area

✔ Exists within your transaction system (yes, indeed, the text on the transaction pages is definitely content)

✔ Alerts users to errors that occur while they're navigating the site (error messages, in other words) and helps them use the site (the Help page)

A list of the content you have or will create is often called an *inventory of content assets*. Start the process of organizing your site by making an inventory of the content assets you have and need. Take all the papers and documents and notes that comprise your planned content and shuffle them around organizationally, considering how they are similar to each other. You can either physically shuffle actual pieces of paper or create lists of content assets. Toss out what's repetitive or unnecessary. And remember that you can always link to content instead of repeating it.

Now sketch out an initial site plan. You may want to sketch it out on a big whiteboard and just stare at it for some time, thinking things through and moving bits and pieces and even cutting and adding things as you go. Most importantly, keep your eyes squarely on the goals you've set for the site.

With your preliminary, rough ideas in hand, you're ready to structure your site. This is where the architecture begins. Up to this point, you were gathering information. But now you're headed into real-deal conceptualizing.

Group Content and Activities

The purpose of grouping content is to figure out what goes with what; that is, which pieces of content are logically related to other pieces. While grouping your content, you can also determine where you should place links, what common items can be linked to rather than repeated, and what important links should appear on your site's navigation bar. You are also taking a big step toward figuring out how to organize files on your Web server.

Identifying types of content

Look at the content. Study it like a puzzle, considering which items are logically similar to others. In doing so, consider the following options.

Grouping by subject

Perhaps the easiest and most obvious way to group the content of your site is by subject. For example, if your site is about cooking, you can group the content related to breakfast, lunch, and dinner, and then break down the dinner category into types of entrees: meat, fish, poultry, pasta, and vegetarian. You may have another category for tools (pans, knives, and so on) and yet another for seasonal menus. How you group your content by subject depends on your industry. Look to the real world for models and apply whatever logic drives your industry to the logic of your site. Figure 8-2 shows a sample list of subjects and corresponding pages for a construction company site.

```
Corporate Info
        Press Releases
        Annual Report
        Plant List
        Corporate History
        Job Openings

Construction
        Buyer's Guide
        Consulting Services
        Equipment Sales
        Hazardous Material Handling
        Demolition

Agriculture
        Farming Consulting Services
        Farm Equipment Leasing/Sales

Credit
        About Credit
        Construction Project Financing
        Agricultural Project Financing
        Equipment Leasing Options
        Credit Screen
        Account History
```

Figure 8-2:
This content
is grouped
by subject.

Try shuffling your site's content by subject, and see what you come up with. Jot down headings, and under each heading, list the bits of content you have on hand. If you find that some content doesn't fit, you may need to add a category or rethink your subject categories. If the organization is working, in the end you will have categorized all of your content. If not, don't worry — just read on.

Grouping by task

Alternatively, you may find it better to group your content based on the tasks a user may perform when coming to your site. For example, say a user hops over to your nifty software company site. The user may seek information, download the software, register it, and pay for it. He or she may also want to look into customer service, get tech support, or purchase T-shirts and accessories or books on the subject of the software. He or she may also want to download patches to the software. Hmmm — doesn't that task go in *download?* Doesn't the purchase of books go in *purchase* or *store?*

As you identify tasks that users may perform on your site, jot them down as categories. Then go through your content and consider which pieces of content relate to which tasks. Place those pieces of content under the appropriate task-oriented headings. You may find yourself adding or deleting headings as you move along. In the end, if all of your content seems to fit into this system, you're set. Figure 8-3 shows a list of pages from that construction company's Web site, grouped according to tasks. If all of your content doesn't quite fit into this sort of a system, keep reading.

Figure 8-3:
This content is grouped by the tasks users may accomplish at the site.

Managing Your Finances
    Banking
    Bill Payment
    Expense Reports
    Personal Income Tax Advisor

Managing Your Business
    Banking
    Bill Payment
    Expense Reports
    Business Tax Advisor

Investing
    Investor's Guide
    Retirement Advisor
    Mutual Fund Advisor

Mixing groupings

If you step through the group-by-subject, group-by-task exercises we describe in the preceding two sections and find that some stuff fits into one system and some into the other, you are not alone — that's often the case. You may find that the best way to go is to group some stuff by content. For example, you may group pages according to the products covered — that's subject grouping. Then you may group other pages according to the tasks that the users perform — for example, buying that product. Just find what grouping mix works for you and your industry.

Grouping by utility

Here's another grouping to consider: You may want to keep some content in one place for your convenience or your team's. For example, you may want to keep all the images in one place so they're easier to find. (Many folks call this category *images* or *artbin*. Cute, eh?) You may not have an obvious need for this sort of grouping just yet — it will probably come into play when you get to the point of arranging directory structures. Just keep it in mind for now, and if you do have some material you want to categorize separately based on how you plan use it, go ahead and plop it in that category.

Grouping by department

You may be tempted to group content based on which department of your company (say marketing or customer support) is responsible for it. Don't do this. Your site should be user-centric, not company-centric. Even if your site is about your company, don't organize your site plan around your company's organizational structure. Distinctions between departments in your company will probably make no sense at all to your site's visitors. The organization you create for your content should be geared toward the audience's experience, not toward recreating the company's structure.

Doing the grouping two-step

After identifying the different types of content, take out a fresh piece of paper and a pencil or launch your favorite word processor. With your content before you, here's how to finalize the organization of your content:

1. **Jot down the major categories under which you think you can group your content.**

   If you aren't quite sure how to arrange the content, reread the last few sections of this chapter, and think things through a bit more.

2. **Place subcategories under the major categories, if appropriate, and within the subcategories, list the content that falls into place there.**

Organizing your content is a lot easier if you consider that placing content in one category excludes it from consideration in another category. The whole point of online content is that you can link to it, so forget double placements. If you find that you've placed one document into more than one category, decide now where you think it best fits. In other words, in which *one* of those categories do you really want the document to be? (You can link to it from elsewhere.)

Establish Hierarchies Where Once There Were None

After organizing your content into conceptual groupings, it's time to turn that information into a map of the site. A *site map* describes the site abstractly. Basically, it describes (in the form of a drawing) how all the site's content and features are related to each other. A *directory structure,* on the other hand, represents how the files are actually stored on the server. A site's site map and directory structure are often drawn in similar ways, but the two items chart different information. Organizing a site map involves placing your content groupings firmly into a hierarchy.

First, consider why you need a hierarchy. When you read a book or magazine (at least in English), you read from left to right and top to bottom. It's all very linear. When you "read" a Web site, by comparison, you may jump (via links that appear mid-text), from this page to that, in an intuitive process that is anything but linear. As a Webmaster, your job is to provide the user with more intuitive paths. It's often also to lure the user down the paths your company prefers. (On a sales site, for example, all roads should lead to the products and then down a clear purchase path.) Assembling a decent site map and keeping it in order has these benefits:

- ✔ **Helps users find what they seek.** If the structure is orderly, the navigation bar will be as well. Also, users may be able to intuitively follow the URLs if they're logical and intuitive.

- ✔ **Helps you and your team maintain your site.** If you know where everything is, where to put things, and how to write a link without having to dig around too much, you'll be a lot happier.

Your goal, then, in this part of the process, is to organize your content a bit further so that it fits into a hierarchy that goes from the general to the specific, as shown in Figure 8-4.

Building the hierarchy

Note that every piece of content must go someplace in the hierarchy. If a page doesn't seem to fit anywhere, place it at the top level — just below your site's home page. Either you'll find other pages like it, or you'll find that it stands alone in some way.

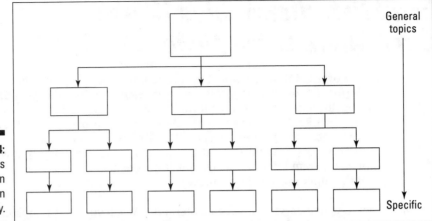

General topics

Specific

Also, as a general rule, it's best not to make your site either too wide (with many top-level categories and few subcategories) or too deep (with few top-level categories and many subcategories). If you have to go one way or the other, though, err in the direction of making your site a little deeper than wide. It's a bit easier to organize links onto a home page that way.

Remember that important items on your site should be no more than three clicks down from the home page. Remember, too, that the top-level items in your hierarchy will often correspond directly to the main buttons on your home page. The top-level items in your hierarchy, then, should be the most important categories of stuff on your site *from the user's point of view*. Having between five and seven top-level categories is generally a good guideline, though not a hard and fast rule.

If you find, as you move along, that a clear hierarchy for the material on your site is just not coming together, this may be a sign that your overall plan is weak; it's rare that a site just doesn't lend itself to some type of hierarchy. If you're having trouble, you may want to go back and review your overall plan and the groupings that you've created. Consider, too, whether the amount of content you've planned per page is appropriate.

Chapter 3 describes how to chunk pages up effectively. For the purposes of this exercise, if you're unable to group pages constructively, take a look at the content you've planned and consider whether you're including too much content on each page. If you break the pages down, perhaps they'll begin to form a more logical grouping.

Bunching pages into organized "types"

After you've sorted the general categories of content on your site by subject, task, or some other system, consider the types of pages you're going to use on your site. Some types of pages lend themselves to one or another type of content or task, whereas others offer users assistance in navigating. You'll probably find that most of the pages that make up your site fall into one of the following types.

Home page

The *home page* is the first page that a visitor sees upon entering the site — it's the site's main page, index page page, default, or "front door." The home page's purpose is to provide a quick and easily comprehensible overview of the site. It establishes the site's branding (it's recognizable identity or image) and acts as the site's table of contents. But that doesn't mean that everything on the site is linked directly from the home page. Only the most compelling or necessarily accessible items appear on the home page — these items then link to deeper areas of the site.

Some sites include subsites, or large content areas that are really robust enough to stand on their own as single sites. They, too, have "home pages." For the sake of clarity, the custom is often (but not always) to call the site's home page *the* home page and these others *index pages* — even though the filenames in both cases are often named `index.html`. (Sometimes they are called `default.htm`.) When we discuss creating the directory structure of a site later in this chapter, keep in mind that home pages generally correspond to the index file in a directory.

Navigational pages and nav bars

Navigational pages in the strictest sense are pages that help users to navigate the site. Some examples include

- ✔ A table-of-contents-style "site map" page that lists all the sections of the site (not to be confused with the site map we discuss earlier in this chapter)

- ✔ A search page that lets users dig up items of interest on the site (additional pages will be needed to display the results of the search, to offer tips on searching, and to describe to users any errors that might occur during the search)

- ✔ A portal-style page (which may look a bit like Yahoo!, for example) that acts as a directory to what's on this site or even other sites

Including *some* navigational pages can be important to your site's usability, but which of those listed you actually use depends on the style of your site. Just remember that navigational pages should not contain scads of content, because their purpose is to facilitate navigation.

Another way of handling navigation is to place links to the various areas of your site on a navigation bar (a *nav* bar) that appears on every page of the site, or at least on most pages. The nav bar can consist of graphical buttons or a set of simple text links or both.

Registration/user input page

Sometimes you want folks to register to use your site or a portion of it — for example, to get access to an area containing special content, to enter a contest, to set up an account with your online store, or as a requirement for downloading some software. Registration pages work because they're driven by a *server-side script* (a special program that runs on the Web server). To the user, the page just looks like a form.

Help pages

Help pages are designed to . . . *help*. Some sites include only a single help page, whereas others provide a whole online help area with FAQs, tips, and bells and whistles galore. Still others — the sites with complex offerings, features, or systems — need more than just a simple help page. They sometimes go so far as to use *context-sensitive* help systems, which offer tips and assistance proactively based on where the user is on the site and what the user is trying to do.

Content pages

Content pages can contain content of any type, but whatever the content is, it should be organized intelligently, and have a common look. If you produce content pages that look vastly different from each other, you may confuse the user.

The simplest way to achieve a common look is to repeat elements from page to page — some or all of the nav bar, your logo, and a color scheme you've chosen as the overall palette for your site can work. The point is that you should create a look for content pages that reinforces to users that they are on your site and haven't slipped away to someone else's.

You may want to limit the number of links going into or coming out of content pages. For some types of content, you may want to lead the user down a certain path, which is often the case in promotional sites or purchase-support sites, for example. Alternatively, you may feel that your content lends itself to more free-for-all click paths. Perhaps your content is a humor column about the Web, and the surprise of what's behind the link is the point, or maybe you're providing users with a dynamic experience within your site, and many internal links are the route you want to lay forth. In any case, you probably don't want to overwhelm or confuse the user with links, but do remember that content and links are the point of the Web.

Company pages

If yours is a company site, as many are, you need to include some About the Company information on the site. Perhaps this information is a corporate backgrounder, the company values or mission statement, press releases and a list of awards that the company has received, a list of the executive officers, and the company's location(s). In many cases, job listings and information about the company culture and the benefits of working for the company also fit in here.

Transaction pages

Transaction pages are those that are used in the process of conducting financial transactions. A financial transaction can mean purchasing a single item or a shopping cart full of items at a sales site; transferring cash from one account to another at a banking, bill paying, or stock brokerage site; making a donation at a fundraising site; or any of many other examples. We discuss transactions and what you should keep in mind in putting together transaction pages in Chapter 14.

The design of transaction pages must be clear and easy to understand, and navigation should be a breeze. As we discuss in Chapter 5, the last thing you want to do is place barriers in the way of completing a transaction. To sell, you must *remove* all the barriers. As you organize and oversee the design of transaction pages, do all that you can to make sure that users don't get confused or frustrated by your system. Include clear labels on any buttons users must click, and keep the number of pages they must traverse to complete the transaction to a minimum (six steps or less).

Results, error, and confirmation pages

When a user searches for something, he or she usually gets a result (a list of items that match the user's search criteria) and that result, you'll notice, appears on a Web page. If an error occurs, an error message has to appear, and it also often appears on a page. If and when an online sale goes through, or when a user registers or logs on successfully, a confirmation page appears. You must account for all these more functionally-oriented pages as well as the more obvious (and often more fun) types. The text on these sorts of pages is known as microcontent, by the way. Shaping microcontent effectively is discussed in Chapter 3.

Drawing the site map

REMEMBER

The site map you're about to create will provide you with a logical overview of the site, which you can use later to create storyboards and directories.

Grab a big piece of paper or launch some nice graphing software, such as Microsoft Visio. (You can even do this in Microsoft Word.) At the top center of the page, write **home page** and draw a box around that text. This box represents your site's home page.

Then, under the box representing your home page, draw a horizontal line. Next, draw additional boxes under that line — one for each of the major subject groupings you've identified as part of your content. In each of these boxes, jot down the name you used for each grouping. Figure 8-5 shows the top of a site we built — yours will look different because it will contain different types of content.

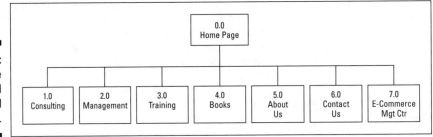

Figure 8-5:
The home page and top-level pages.

Now move through each major subject area, repeating the mapping process, going farther down level by level into your site. Where you link outside of the site, you can draw a line to an unboxed indicator. Figure 8-6 shows a more detailed map of the 4.0 Books category shown in Figure 8-5. A line leading to the word Buy indicates a link that allows users to buy books. Eventually, you have to map out every smidgen of your site, but for now, just stick to the bigger picture of which pages will go in which top-level categories.

Next, you need to number each page. For example, your home page can be 0.0, and the main pages at the second level of your plan can be 1.0, 2.0, 3.0, and so on. The pages within each of the second-level areas should have numbers that indicate their levels. For example, within 1.0, you may have 1.1, 1.2, and so on. If you go down yet another level, you can number the pages under 1.1 as 1.1.1, 1.1.2, and so on.

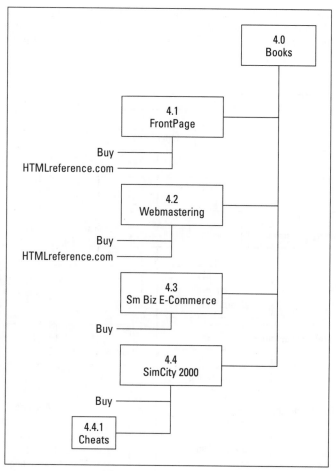

Figure 8-6:
This part of
the site
includes
several
levels of
pages as
well as
some links
leading
outside
the site.

Adding task paths

By placing all the related content on your site in the site map, you've represented ways for users to drill down to find information. However, you still have to lay out paths for users to take to follow important links or to complete given tasks on your site. How these paths go depends on the routes users should take through important content and what users will do to complete tasks when they move through certain areas of your site. For example, you'll have to plot paths through the pages for registering, downloading, or buying. This is where the task lists you made earlier in this chapter (in "Grouping by task") come in. Figure 8-7 shows some task paths drawn into the sample site map as dotted lines.

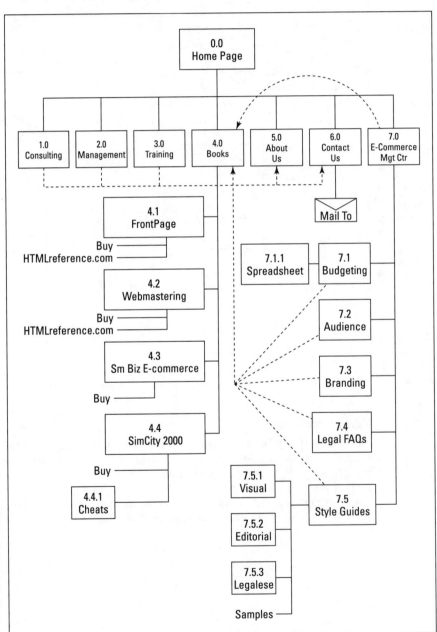

Figure 8-7:
In the completed site map, dotted lines indicate task paths.

The pros and cons of site-mapping software

You may wonder about site-mapping software and why we ask you to draw the site map yourself. Site-mapping software falls into two basic categories: tools that can read an existing site and build a map of it, and tools that allow you to create a map as you build the site. Neither type of tool helps much with planning because they both map sites after the fact. Site-mapping software can be quite useful, though, in letting you see maps of existing sites for research purposes and see a map of your site after it's at least under way. They can also be very powerful in helping you maintain your site, but they don't substitute for solid planning. Preproduction planning is the bedrock of a successful Web site.

Revising your site map

As you chart your site, you may find that the map doesn't work out quite as you imagined in one way or another. Don't worry. The purpose of mapping your site at this stage is to think things through. Once you've nailed down some specifics, the purpose of the site map will be to provide yourself, your colleagues, and any outside contractors you may take on with information about how you envision the site. For now, stay flexible — if you find you need to modify your plan, just do it. Similarly, if you find that your plan is just not working out, it's okay to scrap the site map and start the planning process over. Discovering a flaw in your logic now is much better than stumbling on that flaw later on, when you're too invested and too close to launch to turn back. Your goal at this point is still planning. It's better to plan more than less — this saves you time when you're ready to implement the site and even more time when you're maintaining it.

Create Storyboards for the Site

All kinds of people have all kinds of ways of plotting what will go on each page of their Web sites. We like to create a storyboard for each page, using a simple form that we've adapted from a model (see Figure 8-8) developed by Melissa Rach, director of content at Aveus (www.aveus.com). Again, we use Microsoft Visio for this process, although you can use Word or whatever works for you. Our form has *fields* (individual, specified areas) on it for information that shapes the page. It's not necessary now to fill in all the fields; you can do that in a moment. For now, just note that these are the fields that we use

- **Page number:** Corresponds to the number on the site map and makes it easier to track pages and their relationship to each other

- **Page name:** The working name of the page as shown on the site map

- **Filename:** Eventually, the page's actual filename goes here

- **Primary navigation:** Shows the most important links or buttons that will appear on the nav bar

- **Secondary navigation:** Links to the next level of pages down in the hierarchy (for example, in the area numbered 1.0, the pages numbered 1.1, 1.2, 1.3, and so on), and any other really crucial links that must appear (for example, the store page may require a special link to the customer service FAQ)

- **Primary content:** The content that is most important on the page — the page's reason for being

- **Secondary content:** Any piece of content that also must appear on the page; for example, a special promotion or the "cross-sell" of a product on an otherwise purely content page (See Chapter 3 for more explanation of primary, secondary, and tertiary content.)

- **Tertiary content:** Some other nugget that will appear on the page, for example, testimonials, polls or quizzes, or even some piece of art or animation

- **Footer:** The text at the bottom of every page that may include, for example, a copyright notice as well as links to the privacy policy, information about advertising, or whatever seems important enough to be on every page but not necessarily in a prominent location (Chapter 7 describes how to write a copyright notice.)

- **Maintenance:** A place to indicate whether this page is intended to be evergreen or, if not, how often it will be updated (Chapter 3 describes what makes content evergreen, and Chapter 22 discusses content maintenance.)

- **Keywords:** A few important words that must appear in the page's text and that will form the basis of the page's META tags and page title (the title that appears in the browser window to describe the page to users) (Chapter 16 discusses keywords and META tags.)

You'll want to create your own storyboard format to fit your situation. At this stage, we recommend making a storyboard for each planned page of the site. Start by making a *storyboard template* (a single storyboard that contains the information that will appear on every page in the site — the footer, for example). Copy the template again and again so you have one storyboard per page, and give each storyboard the page name and number shown on the site map.

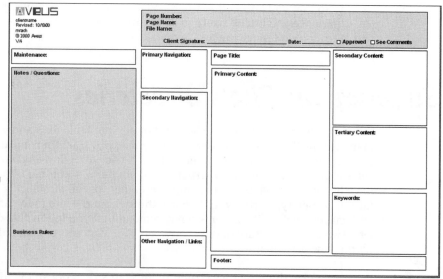

Figure 8-8:
You can use
a form to
storyboard
your pages.

Next, fill in the most obvious fields on each page. Indicate the name and number of each page, the frequency of maintenance it should get, and which three-to-five keywords best match the content on this page. (Chapters 3 and 16 describe identifying and using keywords.) Make notes about your plans for content, too. You needn't write the content — the actual writing will occur later. Right now, just indicate what the primary content should be about, what tone it should have, what important points it should make, and what goal it must fulfill. Do the same for the secondary and tertiary content. (Again, refer to Chapter 3 for a refresher on the nature of primary, secondary, and tertiary content on a page.)

Also fill in the primary and secondary navigation boxes, simply listing there the important buttons or links, based on your site map and your overall plan for navigation. This may all seem daunting, but remember that if you don't work out the details now, you'll be doing it on the fly while you build the site, and that's a whole lot tougher.

Work your way page by page through the site, filling in the storyboards. As you do, imagine yourself as the user, navigating around these pages and experiencing this site. Also consider the intended business goals for each page, and how the page will fulfill those goals. Translate your overall strategic plan into ever more detailed notes. You will uncover some places where you are compelled to make choices you didn't anticipate. That's the goal of this exercise.

Go back through the storyboards several times to refine your plan. You may also find yourself altering your site map based on what you decide in your storyboards. That's fine; again, the goal here is to create a detailed plan for the site so that you know what will be on each page and so you can plot out the experience you intend users to have throughout your site. Don't write the text yet, and don't place the art. Just make detailed notes about things.

Structure the Site's Directories

After charting your site into a clear and understandable map and working out many details through storyboards, you're ready to start thinking about how to structure the site on the server. Although you won't find any hard-and-fast rules for creating a directory structure for your site, a number of practices have become customary. For example, creating special directories to hold files of certain types that you then use throughout the site (such as scripts and images) makes life easier. We recommend that you follow this custom. Otherwise, the structure of directories on your Web server is mainly dictated by the flow of your site.

When you plan the directory structure for your site, it doesn't matter which Web server software you're using or what platform it's running on.

Some technical backstory

Before you delve into organizing files on your Web server, you should be familiar with a few technical details. These details are true regardless of which server you're using (with a couple of notable exceptions). There's nothing very heavy here — this stuff is background, but it's important background. Be sure to read this information before you move on. (For more on choosing and running a server, turn to Chapter 11.)

The directory structure on your Web server is one and the same as the directory structure that appears in the URLs that users see when visiting your site. When users access a URL either by going straight to it or by following a link, the directories and subdirectories within the file they're reaching for appear in the URL. The actual document — whether it's an HTML file, a graphic, or another item — is a file that's located on the Web server within some directory or subdirectory, similar to how a file lives in a directory (folder) or subdirectory on your hard disk.

The *root* of your Web site (the tippy top of the hierarchy of directories and subdirectories) corresponds to a directory that exists somewhere on your server. The directory is called the *document root directory.* Where that directory exists on the server depends partly on the type of server software you're using (Apache handles things differently than IIS, for example) and how the server was set up (presumably by you).

ISPs, hosting companies, and the root directory egg hunt

When you run your own server, the location of the document root directory is pretty clear — it's wherever you put it when you installed your Web server. But what if you're using an Internet service provider (ISP) or hosting company to host a virtual domain for you (see Chapter 12)? (A *virtual domain* is one that's housed on someone else's machine; often a virtual domain is on a machine that houses several virtual domains, each of which may be owned by different people or companies.)

In the case of a server housing virtual domains, the server's document root directory usually holds the service provider's Web site, not yours. The document root for your site then is usually contained within a directory called `public_html`, which is located in your home directory on the service provider's Web server. When you open your account with the ISP or hosting company, its personnel will tell you exactly where this directory is located on its server and how you can place files in it.

When a user loads a URL such as `www.acompany.com`, the *index* file or *default* file in the server's document root directory is returned. The index file is the file the server uses when no other document is specified in the URL. In reality, the Web browser just assumes that the home page's filename appears at the end of the URL. Many Web servers use the name `index.html` for the home page file; Microsoft Internet Information Server (IIS) calls the file `default.htm`.

The following example, using `index.html` as the home page file, shows the relationship between URLs and the files they access. (We don't include the document root here because the root is handled differently by different servers, remember?)

This URL . . .	*Accesses This File on the Server*
/index.html	/index.html
/projects/index.html	projects/index.html
/projects/	projects/index.html
/projects/scientist.html	projects/scientist.html

Mirroring the site's structure

The simplest way to structure files on your Web server is to mirror the hierarchy you created when you worked out your site map. To use this method, place the files that make up the topmost page of the site (the home page) into the server's document root directory. (On your site map, you can pretty much simply rename "Home Page" to be "Root Directory" and there you have it.) Then create directories under the document root directory for each section of the site, in the same hierarchical organization used on your site map. Each of the boxes you drew on your site map becomes a directory (some may have index files located in them). Consider the following special issues as you plot your directories.

Special directories for special purposes

Some files deserve their own special, separate directories. These files include resources that are commonly used throughout the site, such as images and graphic elements (the nav bar, for example), sound and video and other media files, scripts, and data files (which contain data that the scripts use when they're running). It's probably best to consider how you can best categorize these items — you don't want to toss your art and scripts in the same directory (that is, unless you only expect to ever possess one piece of art and a couple of scripts). Lots of folks call these special directories *bins*. Cute, eh? They're bins for whatever you toss into them.

Avoiding the server-side-script security pitfall

It's not strictly necessary to keep scripts in a special directory. Many servers, including Apache and IIS, recognize file extensions such as ASP and CGI, which indicate that the file is a server-side script. So technically, you can put scripts anywhere that you want.

In fact, you may prefer to store script files in the same location as the content to which they relate. For example, if you include a puzzle game on your site, that area of the site may include a page of instructions (a plain HTML file), a number of GIF images (GIF is a common file format for images on the Web) for the puzzle pieces, and the script that runs the puzzle. If you use the CGI file extension in naming those scripts, you can place the scripts in the same directory as the rest of the content for the

puzzle. That entire section of the site is then self-contained in a single directory tree. Moving that section of the site or making a backup copy is a snap.

On the other hand, using server-side scripts can open a big security hole in your site. It opens the possibility that some unscrupulous person can execute a command on your server from his Web browser. You sure wouldn't want that person executing the command `format.exe` (which would reformat your hard disk); you also wouldn't want him to retrieve password files or the log file from one of your forms. After all, would you want your competition to have access to a file containing key strategy information for your sales reps or wholesale buyers? We think not.

The CGI bin or scripts directory

CGI is used to do most of the scripting on UNIX servers. Generally, CGI scripts should go into a special CGI directory. This directory is often named *cgi-bin* and is referred to by the URL /cgi-bin. It's commonly located either in the server's document root directory or in a directory directly above the document root directory. Check your server's documentation to see where this directory should be located on your particular server.

ASP is used for most of the scripting for Windows 2000 Servers or NT Server. (Occasionally, CGI scripting is done for use with Windows 2000 Server or NT Server.) On Windows 2000 Server or NT Server machines, scripts go into a directory named *scripts* and referred to by the URL /scripts. This directory is usually located one directory above the server's document root directory. Again, check your server's documentation. (For more about servers, see Chapter 11.)

Data directories

Data directories hold data that's used in running scripts. They can hold data the script uses to generate HTML or data that's been gathered by the script. The data directory is usually called *data* and is often a subdirectory within the *cgi-bin* or *scripts* directory.

Some Webmasters like to separate the files that a script reads from the files that it writes and place them into two separate directories. Although separating the files adds some complexity to the directory planning, it also adds an extra layer of warm and fuzzy security to the Web server. The security advantage is that you can set up scripts so that they have *write* access only to the directory that holds output from the script. The script clearly doesn't need write access to the directory that holds its data. And, as a general security rule, you want to minimize the amount of access allowed, so separating files with read and write access is one handy way to limit access.

Images/media directories

Images are customarily placed in their own directory, which is often called *images* or *artbin*. And, with the explosion of other forms of media — such as video and sound — many sites have lumped images, animations, video, and audio together into a directory, calling it *media*. All the non-HTML-content files go into this directory. Alternatively, you may want to keep images in one directory and media in another — perhaps you're the sort to fold your socks and place them into neat color-coded rows when you put them in the drawer.

If you're mirroring the site's structure as you create your directory structure, each directory you create can have an *images* or *media* subdirectory within it. This directory should, in that case, hold all the media used by that section of the site.

Common resources directory

As in an office setting, it's often a good idea to place commonly used resources into a common area where everyone can get to them. Along those same lines, you may find that some files should go in a location that's convenient to every area on your site. Perhaps you want the image files that contain your corporate logo, nav bars, or identifying banners in a special directory.

Why would you want to do this? Because if that information is in an *images, art bin,* or *media* directory, every time Ursula User accesses a page that includes that stuff, she has to wait for that file to download (again). If instead you put commonly used media files into their own directory, customarily called either *common* or *resources* (at the root level of your site), you can exploit the cache that's built into many Web browsers. Users then find your site a tad faster to load. Here's why: After they've downloaded a common image for one page, it's cached in their browsers, and it pops onto the screen quickly the next time they come across a page that includes that same image.

Mapping the directories

All your organizational prep work comes to fruition when you create the directory structure that you plan to use for your site. Go ahead and sketch out your directory structure, either on paper or in your favorite word processor or drawing program. In each of the directories you've created, drop the files for that part of the site. If your site plan calls for finer groupings of files, create subdirectories as needed and repeat the process for each of these subdirectories, dropping in content and creating more subdirectories until your Web server's directory structure matches your site's structure.

You should also consider one more bit of your site structure this point. If you have a huge pile of information — maybe all the info in your product catalog or a list of resellers organized by zip code — you don't want to have to create individual HTML files for that material. In the next section, we look at databases as a solution to that issue.

Database? I Don't Need a Stinking Database — Do I?

Earlier in this chapter, we talk about how to organize and where to put *static pages* — Web pages that are created as regular HTML files. In a typical site composed of static HTML pages, the files are stored in a structure such as the directory structure we've described. However, for larger or more complex sites, the processes required for maintaining the site can become unwieldy using such a system.

Top tips for creating smashing Web pages

✔ Give your site a title that's brief, descriptive, and easy to remember. Keep the title's promise and provide any content that you say you will.

✔ Splash screens act as a barrier to entering your site. Unless your goal is to stop people at the door, don't use splash screens.

✔ When a user encounters your home page, the site's purpose and navigation should be clear. The site's identity (its branding) should also be clearly established up front and then carried forward throughout the site.

✔ Don't assume that people will scroll. Keep your content within one screen, break pages that are more than two screens long into multiple pages, or give people a very compelling reason to scroll.

✔ Keep navigational clutter to a minimum. On your home page, for example, either have between five and seven items from which to choose, or organize what you offer into between five and seven clearly defined areas.

✔ Make anything that looks like a button act like a button.

✔ Make links meaningful; avoid generic Click Here links. Instead, link on a phrase that describes what the user will get — what the payoff of clicking will be.

✔ Keep anything that's really, really important within three clicks of your home page.

✔ Keep directory names and filenames short and consistent. Use lowercase, not mixed case, directory names and filenames.

✔ Tell your users the size of any downloadable files — they need to know whether they can manage a file of this size. Also tell them the format of the files and what software they'll need, if any, to use the files.

✔ Provide an e-mail link for feedback or to a specific contact person.

✔ Test, test, test. Test concepts by showing index cards or page mockups to a focus group. Test early, alpha versions of the site before you build a beta. Test the beta before you go live. Before you announce the site, test it until you can't stand to test it another minute. Get others to test it. Find all the bugs and *squash* them. Then launch.

✔ Document, document, document. Document your plans, the decisions made as the site is built, and the specifics of how the site is created, which tools are used, and so on. See Chapter 22 for pointers on establishing good documentation and strong review and approval processes to make site maintenance easier.

Most large-scale Web sites today are built with database back ends. They often also have a directory structure such as we've described, but for the sake of efficiency, at least some of the files that make up the site are often stored in one or more databases. You may need a database under any of these circumstances:

✔ Your site includes thousands or even just hundreds of pages, and you need to update the content frequently or the content is drawn from a complex set of elements some of which change day to day.

✔ Your site includes pages that will change based on user input (maybe you have a set of pages that list something, and you want the user to be able to specify how many items are listed on a page, or maybe you are offering personalization).

✔ You plan to install a shopping-cart system that includes a catalog of products. In this instance, you need a database (or even two or three) in which to store information about the products (and the orders, customers, and payments).

When pieces of content or art are stored in a database, the HTML file can include *database calls*. These small scripts embedded in the HTML pull from the database a specified file that is then displayed on the Web page. A page that is created using content or art pulled from a database is a *dynamically generated page*. You usually need a database server as well as a Web server for these pages. You also need to create a *template* (an HTML document that defines the Web page's design and layout) into which the data can flow dynamically from the database.

Unless your site is small and your endeavor is not labor intensive, you probably need a database of some sort. Just how do you put together a database? Well, for now, look over your site plan and directory structure, and consider whether you are including a category that inclines you to need a database. If so, pencil that in on your plans, and turn to Chapter 13 to look further into the whole bag of database questions. You need to sketch out (at least preliminarily) the fields and queries you may use in your database as part of your overall site plan.

Putting Together an RFP and Specs that Work

Whether you're jobbing out the design of your site to a Web shop or just turning over pieces of the design process to members of your own staff, you must document all the planning you've done. Then you have to fork over that documentation to the people who are doing the work so they can all know and follow the plan. The documentation you create now can also form the basis of a *style guide* (a document or set of documents that sets out what conventions can and should be used on the site as it's modified and maintained; see Chapter 22).

Even if you alone are responsible for the site, you can be sure that 3, 6, or 12 months from now, you'll have only dim memories of what you decided. You need notes regarding what you decided and how you thought you could expand it to handle future developments.

Typically, when you head out to get bids for designing and building your site, you need a *request for proposal* (RFP) that outlines the project completely enough so that front-end firms, back-end firms, and any others you expect to bid on portions of the site all understand the scope of the project. Giving all the vendor candidates a good RFP will net you apples-to-apples bids from, say, all the front-end firms that are interested in working with you; that will make life a lot easier when you sit down to compare bids. An RFP generally includes

- Some information about the project's mission, it's short-term goals, and it's long-term goals (Chapters 2 through 5 talk about strategic goals.)

- A brief description of the site's intended audience and branding or personality, along with information about how the company sees the opportunity to reach the audience

- A description of the scope of the project and the deliverables. Priorities should also be described

- Any important technology requirements

- A timeline, description of the timing of various phases of the project, or at least an anticipated (and preferably realistic) launch date

- A set of questions that ask the potential vendors about their qualifications and experience as well as who'll they'll be putting on the team that works with you (Chapter 10 helps you form these questions.)

Send the RFP to perhaps five or six potential vendors. Chapter 10 discusses how to select vendors. After you choose the vendor you'll be working with (and even before that, as vendors ask and you answer questions about the project), you'll all need these documents as reference:

- **Content specs** that detail how the content should be created — for example, what types of content go here, there, and everywhere, what the point of each page should be, what keywords or key phrases must appear, what the tone of the language should be, and so on

- **Page element specs** that detail which elements will be on each page of the site — for example, a listing of all the elements your pages may include (such as titles and headings), lists (bulleted, numbered, simple, and multicolumn), text that's set off in boxes (called *sidebars*) or as special notes, any kind of special fonts that are used to indicate special text (bold, italic, or perhaps something indicating programming code on a software site), tabular information, text links, visited links, linked headlines, and so on

- **Technical specs** that detail the platform and server software you plan to use (see Chapter 11); database requirements, including the fields, queries, and reports you hope for (see Chapter 13); scripting requirements you know of at this point (discussed throughout this book); information about the transaction system you want to use, or what you want a transaction system to do for you (see Chapter 14)

We like to use storyboards (described in "Creating Storyboards for the Site" earlier in the chapter) to organize both the content specs and page element specs. Storyboarding the site also gives us a leg up on figuring out how each page will interact with others. In addition, it uncovers key issues about how users will interact with the site's search functions, databases, and other back-end systems. Tech specs are often quite detailed and lengthy, and may include charts, diagrams, and text that detail how a user's experience will be enabled by the site's technical systems.

Make sure that you share the specs with everyone who designs, implements, or posts content on the site. Sharing the specs helps the right hand know what the left hand is up to and gets everyone clear about where content should go. Doing so also lets the content people know how they should write the text on the pages that help users navigate, search, and buy, and generally makes the process of working with the whole site-creation team much smoother.

Chapter 9

HTML, Beyond HTML, and Son of HTML

*S*o you've got your site plan in hand. Now you're ready to start building. Sadly, in this short space, we can't cover *all* the nuts and bolts. But we will dash through the basics. HTML is not hard to use — it's just a bunch of code. With a few pointers and helpful hints, you can start writing HTML even if you never have before, and you can start looking at the ins and outs of what's beyond HTML.

In this chapter, we also introduce the fine control over design offered by cascading style sheets, how XML facilitates using content in a variety of media, designing for all the browsers your audience may use, and how images work on the Web. Then we zip along to the jazzier stuff: creating interactivity with Java, JavaScript, Active X, dynamic HTML, Flash, Acrobat, custom scripting, and other nifty technologies. We look at what's behind interactivity and describe what live content you can add to your already-killer Web site. (After all, if your site isn't amazing without Flash, it isn't going to be amazing *with* Flash, either.)

The Basics of HTML (Just in Case)

To be an Internet pro of any type, you need a grasp of the basics of HTML. You needn't know every obscure tag, but having a keen understanding of HTML issues can help you understand the whole business of building Web sites, from devising them to developing them. Even with all the WYSIWYG (What You See Is What You Get) HTML authoring tools on the market, most pros *hard code.* (They write code themselves, by hand.)

What's more, there is no single authoring tool that covers every detail of marking-up a Web page well. Most HTML authoring tools add odd codes of their own to the HTML they produce; and many don't handle advanced elements (like frames, style sheets, or dynamic HTML) terribly well. You simply must know HTML to understand what can and can't be done on a Web page. You'll also find it crucial to know HTML when you need to create or repurpose content for display on wireless devices, such as handheld computers, PDAs, and Internet-enabled cell phones.

You can learn HTML from CNET's Builder.com by visiting its HTML for Beginners page at `www.builder.com/Authoring/Basics/`. Once you know the ropes, use the HTML reference at `www.htmlreference.com` as your ongoing guide to HTML 4, the style sheet attributes, and the Internet Explorer and Netscape extensions.

What makes up a Web page?

A Web page is basically a text document that contains instructions for Web browsers. If you look at a Web page (in other words, an HTML document) in a regular text editor such as WordPad, you'll see a bunch of code in angle brackets and a bunch of text; that's not very exciting. When a Web browser "sees" a Web page, however, it uses these bits of code, called *tags,* to interpret how the document should look and what's to happen when certain things are clicked on.

Technically speaking, any text document that begins with `<HTML>` and ends with `</HTML>` can be read as a Web page, although other elements are essential for making a Web page that can be displayed by most browsers (see the upcoming section "Play by the rules"). A Web site is simply a collection of these text documents arranged in directories, possibly in combination with images and other media.

Whether you're a novice or a pro, you should fill your bookmark file with helpful reference sites. A few of our favorites are listed among the Webmaster's bookmarks at the very front of this book; Webmonkey (`www.webmonkey.com`), which covers everything from software to style sheets, is especially good for HTML-related information.

An HTML backgrounder

HTML is an acronym for hypertext mark-up language. The original *specifications,* or rules, for HTML were based on SGML, a language used by publishers to designate text elements such as headings, boldface and italic characters, and so on. However, as you know, HTML is good for much more than just formatting the way text looks. Hypertext is somewhat like "text plus": It includes not only text but also links to other documents and files anywhere on the Internet.

The first Web browsers enabled you to click on links to download images, sounds, video, and other multimedia objects to your hard disk. Soon after, software was designed to display *inline* images (images within Web pages), and now many other forms of media can be displayed or played directly in the browser window. Design elements such as background colors and images, tables for laying out text, and more flexibility in the look and alignment of text were added to the mix.

Now, via their Web browsers, users can experience sophisticated video, animation, and sound. Real time online collaboration and conferencing are a reality, as is access to the Internet (and online content via handheld wireless devices). HTML is still the underpinning of the World Wide Web, but to users it looks nothing like the dull gray pages of yesteryear.

Play by the rules

Every Web page has to follow a few basic rules (in terms of its HTML mark-up) to be read by most Web browsers. And Web geeks of all stripes gripe about bad, sloppy, or inconsistent code — with good reason: Bad code simply doesn't work in some Web browsers. It's also tougher to maintain a Web site that's full of messy, illegible, patched together code. We discuss how to optimize your site for various browsers later in this chapter. First, we describe some of the basic rules for writing good code.

NCSA's Beginner's Guide to HTML was one of the first of its kind (Marc Andreessen invented graphical Web browsers at NCSA), and it's still definitive. You can find the guide at `www.ncsa.uiuc.edu/General/Internet/WWW/HTMLPrimer.html`.

What's in a tag

Tags are pieces of code — text surrounded by angle brackets `<like this>` — that Web browsers read as instructions. Images, links, and formatting are all instructions that the Web browser looks for within those angle brackets. If tags are formatted properly — that is, if there's an opening and closing angle bracket — the tags themselves are not displayed as text on the Web page. If you put an incorrect or fictional tag in your code, such as `<butter>`, it also doesn't show up on the page. Web browsers that don't understand nonstandard tags simply ignore them.

What's not in a tag

Any text that is placed between `<BODY>` and `</BODY>` on a Web page (see "The essential tags," section later in this chapter), and is not included between angle brackets `<like this>`, has the potential to show up as regular text. This regular text can be modified by a variety of tags that affect how and where the text is displayed, and whether the text is a link.

An eye-opening way to learn about Web page design and HTML code-writing is to visit pages that do it utterly and completely wrong. See these sites for good examples of bad Web pages: Web Pages That Suck (`www.webpagesthatsuck.com`), and the Bad Style Page (`www.earth.com/bad-style`).

Note that in the examples we show in this book, the words within the tags are printed in all uppercase characters. Although HTML tags are not case sensitive, many HTML authors use all capital letters to make the tags stand out clearly from the rest of the document when they're editing Web pages. (XML tags, on the other hand, are case sensitive. We cover XML, which is another mark-up language, later in this chapter.)

Pairing your tags

Most tags come in pairs: an opening tag and a closing tag. The opening tag is generally a plain English word or abbreviation that describes what action the tag should take. The tag may also include additional *attributes* that describe how the tag is to act. (You can think of the main word in a tag as the verb and the other attributes as adverbs.) Closing tags include the main action of the tag, which is preceded by a forward slash (/). For example, to make the word *new* boldface, the code would look like this:

```
<B>new</B>
```

In this case, the first tag, `<B>`, indicates the start of boldface type, and the second tag, `</B>`, indicates that the Web browser should stop displaying boldface type. On the other hand, although opening tags may include other attributes, closing tags merely need to close the main instruction in the tag. For instance, to make the word *green* appear in green text, you would use the following code:

```
<FONT COLOR="#04B222">green</FONT>
```

The main instruction in this set of tags is the word `FONT`, which indicates that this tag controls how the text is to be displayed. The `COLOR="#04B222"` portion of the tag indicates what color the text should be. The closing tag, `</FONT>`, says to stop displaying the previous font instructions. (It isn't necessary to say explicitly that all the other attributes you initially indicated for the tag also have to stop now; they automatically stop when the tag is stopped.)

There are exceptions to the rule that tags must come in pairs, most notably <P> (paragraph break),
 (line break), and <IMG> (image). For the most part, however, you need to close every tag that you open for your Web page to look right.

What is the correct order of tags?

Tags should be *nested;* that is, when you open a series of tags, you must close them in reverse order. If you wanted to make a word boldface, italic, purple, and centered, and act as a link, your code may look like this:

```
<CENTER><FONT COLOR="#99038F"><I><B><A
        HREF="PURPLE.HTML">purple!</A></B></I></FONT></
        CENTER>
```

Note that the order in which you place the elements to begin with doesn't matter (although some tags should not appear embedded within certain other tags — HTMLreference.com details this). However, they should be closed in the reverse order of how they were opened. The word *purple!* in our example is properly nested.

Do you want color? Take your pick, using ColorServe Pro, at www-students. biola.edu/~brian/csapplet.html.

The essential tags

All Web pages, including yours, require a few essential tags to work consistently. When those tags are in place, you have a Web page that can be viewed with a Web browser. Many HTML authoring tools put these tags in place for you, in which case you don't need to repeat them. But when you are hard coding, you must put these tags in place. The following tags, in order, are those you need to make a basic Web page, along with a title and a line of "body" text:

```
<!DOCTYPE HTML PUBLIC "-//W3C//DTD HTML 4.0//EN">
<HTML>
<HEAD>
<TITLE>Your Title Goes Here</TITLE>
</HEAD>
<BODY>
Your content goes here.
</BODY>
</HTML>
```

The <!DOCTYPE> tag comes first and tells the Web browser which version of HTML is in play. (In our example, it's HTML 4.0.) The <HTML> tag then tells the browser that this is an HTML document. The head of the document, which precedes the body of the document, includes information that doesn't show up in the browser window, such as the title and any META tags that you may want to include. (See Chapter 16 for more on META tags and how to use them.) The title of the document, which is included within the two HEAD tags, includes the text that is to appear in the title bar of the Web browser that loads the page. The `<BODY>` and `</BODY>` tags enclose the parts of the document that the browser shows in the document-viewing window. You can include any number of other tags within the body of the document. The last tag in any document is generally the `</HTML>` tag, which indicates that the browser can stop reading the document, because it's come to an end.

Are you using HTML correctly? How can you tell? Weblint can help you identify coding problems with your pages; go to `www.weblint.com`. Web Site Garage at `websitegarage.netscape.com` will analyze your pages for coding problems and design issues.

HTML Authoring and Editing Tools

HTML authoring and editing tools give you a hand creating and modifying Web pages. Some offer WYSIWYG interfaces, some offer site management systems, some make it easy to create dynamic content. Although some have the unfortunate downside of adding odd tags and code into the HTML, others are less intrusive. Most professional Web workers prefer to hard code; that is they want the control of creating code by hand, though they often appreciate a good HTML editor or tools that help create interactivity or manage the site. As of this writing, the big players are

- ✔ **Allaire's HomeSite,** which offers raw HTML coding and WYSIWYG-style editing

- ✔ **Macromedia Dreamweaver,** which offers options for creating dynamic HTML (discussed in the section "Implementing Interactive Content" later in this chapter) and other interactivity without doing any programming

- ✔ **Microsoft InterDev,** which offers real, live developers powerful tools for programming Web applications using the same sorts of tools they'd use for other Windows software

- ✔ **Microsoft FrontPage,** which offers WYSIWYG authoring and editing and empowers people who do not know or do not want to learn HTML to make professional-looking Web pages (but is seldom used by Internet professionals)

Your many options for creating Web pages

In the process of designing and creating Web pages, lots of techniques and technologies come into play. You can certainly design and create each page individually in HTML, hand coding the pages on your site one by one. Of course, this may make your fingers hurt because it's so labor intensive. Much easier and faster ways have been invented. You can, for example use the following:

✔ Design one page as a standard template and cut and paste your content into it to create a lot of pages without having to design each one. You can also tweak your standard template as necessary to make modified versions of it and then cut and paste in content.

✔ You can use cascading style sheets (see the section "Look Stylish with Cascading Style Sheets" in this chapter) to define the look of pages. Then you can code the HTML for the pages to call on the style sheet and apply the defined look to them.

✔ You can place your content, images, and even media in a database (as described in Chapters 8 and 13). Then you can code the HTML for your pages to include a database call (a small script) that will pull out the content and images you want to appear on them. (This is known as creating pages *dynamically*, which is not to be confused with creating pages with dynamic HTML.)

You can mix and match these methods as well. For example, you can create a template that both draws on cascading style sheets to define its look and includes database calls to pull content from a database. In that case, the cascading style sheets will define the look of the page but also the look of the content on the page that came from the database.

Look Stylish with Cascading Style Sheets

The thing that drives designers crazy about HTML is the very limited control they have over the way pages finally look in a user's browser window. Designers in traditional media are accustomed to having precise control over font style, size, and placement. They call out fonts by name and specify exact sizes, like "Times 12 point." They also specify absolute positions on a page for the text and graphic elements they're laying out.

With HTML you cannot control these things. You cannot specify exact fonts — you can only list fonts you'd like the browser to use. You have no control over which font actually is used by the browser — it is a matter of what type of browser the visitor is using along with what fonts are installed on his or her computer. You also cannot specify exact font sizes like "12 point." You can only choose relative sizes that are smaller or larger than others. Finally, you have very little control over the placement of text and graphic elements on the page.

Cascading style sheets (sometimes called CSS) extend HTML to address these issues. Cascading style sheets offer Web page designers the sort of exact control over fonts and element placement that traditional designers take for granted when working with print media. With cascading style sheets, you can specify font sizes in points (instead of with HTML's relative sizing), control the absolute positioning of elements on the pages, and basically have much finer control over the final look of the pages.

In using cascading style sheets, the designer creates a design for a single "style sheet," and then all the Web pages meant to have that design are coded to call on the style sheet to define their look. Many pages can have the same design applied to them, and then when a change is necessary — say, for example, when the palette of colors is changed — the change has to be made only once on the style sheet, and it will occur on all pages with that design.

Cascading style sheets work only with Internet Explorer 3.0 or newer and Netscape Navigator 4.0 or newer. ***Beware:*** Microsoft's and Netscape's implementations of CSS are different. If you use a piece of perfectly reasonable looking CSS code on your site, test it in Internet Explorer, then look at it in Netscape Navigator, it may not look the same. This inconsistency is especially annoying because the point of style sheets is to provide easy consistency throughout the Web site. It also adds an extra level of complexity to using CSS — you have to test and tweak your pages to make them work on both of the major browsers. As cascading style sheets become more stable and both browser manufacturers move to supporting the CSS standard as published by the W3C, this issue may be resolved.

Meanwhile, all is not lost. Some companies have turned the challenge into an opportunity and marketed software that addresses making cascading style sheets that work with both browsers. Macromedia Dreamweaver is one such program.

Fast Forward to XML

HTML is, frankly, downright inflexible. It includes a certain set of tags, and you are stuck using those. You cannot add new tags. What's more, the look of each tag is already defined. For example, a long time ago someone decided that text enclosed in an <H1> tag should be big and bold. Although this was basically functional for Web sites, it left a lot to be desired.

Many organizations want to be able to publish data and content in print, online, and on CD without having to recode it and redesign it for each medium. The great value of XML is that it enables the tagging of content or data to identify it rather than to specify its look. Wouldn't it be easier if a price, for example, was coded `<price>$5.99</price>` instead of as `<B><I>$5.99</I></B>`? Then designs could be created that gave the prices one look in print, another online, and a third on CD. Additionally, the content or data could be shared, sold, or licensed to others who could apply their own look and feel to the material very easily.

XML also offers advantages in updating data or content easily and in facilitating site searches, because it's easier to find all the items tagged as a certain type than to track and find them each individually. What's more, organizations, developers, and designers can create their own custom tags, which facilitate all of their processes. Industry-wide standards are coming into view; for example, a group of medically related XML tags, e-commerce catalog tags, and others are being developed.

A brief history of XML

XML is a W3C standard language (W3C is the group that determines Web standards), just like HTML. It is basically a stripped-down, less complex version of SGML (remember that HTML is also based on SGML). SGML is so complicated that not many people were actually using it. So the creators took SGML, removed all the features they felt were not often used, and called the results XML.

In the following block of HTML code, you see how a description on a catalog page can be formatted.

```
<P><B><I>ACME Widget</I></B></P>
<P><FONT SIZE="-1"><I>$1.49</I></FONT></P>
<P><FONT SIZE="-1">This amazing widget will revolutionize the
            widget industry</FONT></P>
```

Now compare that HTML coding to how the same product description can be formatted using XML.

```
<Product>
<Name>ACME Widget</Name>
<Price>$1.49</Price>
<Description>This amazing widget will revolutionize the
            widget industry</Description>
</Product>
```

Notice in the sample XML code that no information is included about how any of the elements — name, price, or description — should actually appear on-screen. Again, with XML you can separate the presentation (or appearance) of the data from the data itself. The presentation of the data is controlled by a *style sheet,* which basically applies specified looks to different XML elements. A style sheet for the sample ACME Widget product description may call for a

Name element to appear as bold italic, a price as regular italic, and a description as a different font for a Web site. Another style sheet might call for the same elements to appear in very specific fonts, colors, and sizes (as well as in a specific place on the page) in print.

Looking Good to Everyone

So you've learned every formatting trick in every book you could get your hands on, and you've implemented all of these tricks. You've promoted your site so that it's bigger than Arnold Schwarzenegger, but you aren't getting a flood of hits — it's more like a trickle. What gives? Having a whiz-bang site that uses all the latest technology is only a halfway good idea. That's because half of the Internet population might not even be able to see your pages if you don't make some effort to cater to the many different browsers, platforms, and levels of bandwidth available to the masses you want to reach.

Who uses which Web browsers?

You're probably aware that the Web browser you use is not the only browser on the market. As of this writing, Internet Explorer and Netscape Navigator together hold *83 percent* of the market share, which is *not the same* as 100 percent. There are plenty of reasons why people use different browsers. Many schools and libraries, for example, use older computers and are forced to run older versions of Internet Explorer or Netscape Navigator. It's important to note that various browsers display Web pages quite differently. What's more, various *versions* of the same browser can display the same page differently. So ask yourself: Do you know how your pages look on the various platforms and browser versions your audience may use?

To track what's currently the hot browser on the market and who's using what, watch your own site's statistics (see Chapter 17). Also see BrowserWatch, which tracks Web software usage, at www.browserwatch.com. Get the latest, too, at CNET's Browsers Topic Center (see www.cnet.com). And before you start filling up your hard disk with new (and old) browsers to test with, look at your pages in the Backward Compatibility Viewer, which you can tweak to emulate any combination of browser features. Bookmark the site, located at www.delorie.com/web/wpbcv.html.

Making a friendly site

You must design your site to accommodate the majority of your target audience. Most will, presumably, be using the standard Web browsers. However, some may be using other browsers, PDAs, or even other devices. Such seemingly basic formats as tables, frames, background images, different font colors, and centered text, not to mention Java, JavaScript, and Flash, may not be viewable by some of your audience. Further, some folks using the standard browsers have reason to choose to disable graphics, Java, cookies, and other technologies. To create a site that's highly democratic, follow these suggestions:

- ✔ Check your site in every browser (and on every operating system) you can get your hands on.

- ✔ Offer text equivalents for every image or image map that acts as a link.

- ✔ Use descriptive ALT attributes with all of your images so people can decide whether they want them. The ALT attribute is used in many ways. It is displayed by most browsers while the image is loading, when the user's mouse moves over the image area, and in place of the image when the user has disabled image display. The ALT attribute's text also provides an alternative to images, required, for example, by special Web-to-speech browsers used by disabled people.

- ✔ If you insist on using frames, also create a nonframes version of your site, leaving all other high-tech stuff out of the nonframes version.

- ✔ Make your entire site low-end. It can still look *really* good. Many attractive sites don't have Flash or Java; they are designed to simply use HTML to its best capabilities.

Designing for wireless

Building pages for wireless (handheld computers, PDAs, and Internet-enabled cell phones) requires special attention because each device has its own quirks. One challenge is the teensy little screen size. Any content that's delivered to most wireless devices has to appear in a small LCD display — that's not much real estate. Displays that are limited to gray scale and don't allow for much in the way of graphics lead to more challenges. What's more, the itsy-bitsy keypads limit the ability of users to navigate or enter data. You have to design navigation of the content so that someone with a phone keypad can easily move from page to page, keep the choices presented on each page simple, and pretty much forget about forms, graphics, and so on. PDAs are like the earliest of Web browsers, but shrunk down to handheld size.

Converting your Web site to display it on a PDA is easier than getting it down to cell phone size. Note that as of this writing most PDAs use HTML 3.2, while most Web browsers on desktop computers recognize HTML 4. Of course, HTML 3.2 is a subset of HTML 4.0. If your Web site is created with HTML 4 and viewed using a Web browser or PDA that recognizes only 3.2, the pages lose some formatting, but they are at least visible. (Whether what's on the pages is large enough to be seen is another matter.)

Other design and layout features also may be lost in the shuffle to PDA. For example, some PDAs don't display tables, have only gray scale, and have limited graphics. As things go forward, this is all bound to change. However, desktop computers will always have larger screens and more power. Fortunately, the bottom line is that if you write good HTML code, it will display on a PDA, but as things shake out in the wireless market, techniques will be devised for making design more functional for PDAs. It's a virtual certainty that you'll have to monitor what wireless capabilities your audience has and tailor your offerings just as you do for Web browsers on desktop machines. You may also have to create a traditional Web version of your site, a somewhat stripped down PDA version, and a very simple, very small-screen cell phone version.

What's up with broadband?

Ironically, as some screens are growing smaller, the advent of broadband (very fast) access allows for more sophisticated content delivered via the Web. More and more users already have their Internet access via DSL and cable modems rather than slower modems. The pipelines that deliver Internet content are only getting bigger, and as they do, bigger files (such as those necessary for fancier graphics, video, audio, and slick animations on your Web pages) become less burdensome. Furthermore, the boundary between Web pages and desktop software is blurring.

Many gyms already have exercise bikes that include screens with Web browsers. Cars and refrigerators may be next. Soon, people will be looking at things you've built for the Web today using browsers and platforms that have yet to be imagined. Of course, we'll all cross that bridge when we must. In the meantime . . .

Graphics, Images, and Art

Images are commonly used on Web pages to create navigational elements that are easily identified (buttons, in other words), highlight certain areas of a page, or to add visual material that helps support the content of the page. You might want to add a background image to your page, use very stylized text as buttons or headings, or toss in a clever but simple animation. All of this can be accomplished using images.

Avoid using images where they are not really needed — don't place an image on a page simply to include an image. Always remember that the point of including images is to help communicate the ideas on your page to your visitor. Many Webmasters overestimate how much bandwidth is available to their sites' users. Ma and Pa McGillicuddy in Mt. Aukum may look at your site using a funky modem and an old machine. They are not going to want to wait half an hour for your pages to load. And if you go wild with images, the viewers may end up having to turn off automatic image loading or use a text-only browser. (In the E-Commerce Management Center at www.tauberkienan. com, you'll find a chart that shows relative download times for various types of connections.) Keep in mind, too, that the World Wide Web is, after all, worldwide. If you want folks in Europe, Asia, and the rest of the planet to see your site (as well as the McGillicuddys), follow these guidelines:

✔ Make sure your site doesn't depend entirely on images to be useful.

✔ Make your image sizes small enough to load quickly. (10K or less is the norm for a banner ad; photos can easily exceed 12K.)

✔ Keep total page size (that is the sum of the size of the HTML file along with any graphics) below 50K. (Okay, you can go up to 70K if you really think it's worth it.)

✔ Always include a description of the image in the ALT attribute's text.

✔ Remember that auto-translators (which convert Web pages from one language to another) can interpret only text, not images.

We're not saying, however, that art isn't a good thing. It's a very good thing. It can help dress up a Web page, make it easier to see what's what, and, well, step in here and there for a thousand words (as the saying goes).

Image types you will encounter

Web site art is digitized art; and to be digitized, an image has to be converted into a lot of tiny little dots of color. (Even black and white images have color; the colors are *black,* and *white.*) When there are more colors, more complex colors, or more subtle gradations within a piece of digitized art, more digital work must be done (by the computers involved) to make the dots and the visual effect look right. The more dots there are (or the more colors are involved), then, the bigger the file is. The bigger the file, the slower the download. And your goal is faster download, so you want as few dots as possible without sacrificing the visual effect you need.

Digitized art can be stored in a variety of file formats. You have to decide which format to use under what site design circumstances, how you are going to achieve optimal effects with images (there are lost of tricks for doing nifty things with graphics files), and finally what software to use.

The standard file formats for art used on Web sites are GIF (which has the file extension GIF) and JPEG (which has the file extension JPG). Each format actually translates images into electronic files by compressing the image. GIF files are good for storing graphics that include solid blocks of color rather than subtle gradations. JPEGs are better for photographs, which generally have subtle gradations, even if they are black and white photos.

The bottom line is that a photographic image stored as a JPEG results in a much smaller file than the same image stored in a GIF file. This means you get a higher quality image with a smaller file size (which translates into a faster download).

In addition to the ordinary GIFs used for static, graphical images, some variations exist:

- **Transparent GIFs** are those that have a "clear" background that enables some other image or a background color shine through. For example, a GIF file with a logo in it might have a square, clear background surrounding the actual logo image. When that square image is placed on a page with a blue background, the blue shines through and appears to completely surround the logo. When you save a file as a GIF, you can opt to make it transparent.

- **Interlaced GIFs** load in several subsequent passes; each pass clarifies the image. Again, when you save a file as a GIF, making it interlaced will be among your choices.

- **Animated GIFs (also known as GIF 89A),** consist of a series of images that are displayed one after another to create a simple flip-book style of animation. Many drawing programs offer the option to make animated GIFs.

GIFWizard is simple tool that can help you reduce the file sizes of your GIF images. Check it out at www.gifwizard.com. For information about making your Web pages accessible to those with disabilities, see the WC3's Web Accessibility Initiate at www.w3.org/WAI.

Two other types of images commonly appear on Web sites (these are not file formats; just types of images):

- **Thumbnails** are postage-stamp-sized images; they're usually linked to bigger versions of the same image (on a separate page). You generally have the option to make art a thumbnail (usually it will be a GIF for a Web site) when you create the art with a drawing program.

- **Image maps** are large images with clickable sections usually linking to related information on other Web pages. (The first image maps were actually geographic maps.) You can use HTML authoring software or any of several utility programs to create image maps.

Preparing images for the Web

If you create art using drawing software (such as Adobe Photoshop or JASC Paint Shop Pro), you can easily save it as a GIF or JPEG. Similarly, if you scan hard copy of art, you can easily save it to the right format. You must avoid *dithering* (the effect of two dots of color appearing near each other to approximate a third color) when you save art as a GIF; dithering bloats files and ultimately looks lousy. It isn't an issue for JPEGs, which don't actually use dithering to achieve their effects.

Photoshop and Paint Shop Pro not only enable you to create images, they also let you tweak art for use on Web sites. You can use them to scan images, modify existing scans, and manipulate images with effects such as blurs, borders, cropping. You can learn about Paint Shop Pro and even download an evaluation copy from JASC's Web site at www.jasc.com. The Adobe site (at www.adobe.com) includes Photoshop tutorials, user forums, sample images, and technical support areas.

Why Even Include Interactive Content?

Some people worry that the Web increasingly resembles television. The problem with TV is that all you do is sit and watch it. Television isn't interactive, and the concern is that Web sites ought to make more of an effort to engage their readers than an episode of *Cops.* The more a visitor is engaged, the more he or she sticks around (or comes back). They are *using the Internet* instead of just being online.

Interactive content doesn't just mean Flash, Java, or chat. Although it can and does generally mean that you've added something more than just the hypertext and images that you see on virtually every Web site, it's also important to remember what the two keywords *interactive* and *content* mean. *Interactive* doesn't necessarily mean high-tech. It means that your visitors are able to interact with what's on your site. *Content,* our second keyword, should be self-explanatory, but people often confuse *any text* with *content.* Don't throw just anything up on your site; pay attention to the quality of your content. You have to start with good cucumbers to make pickles that people want to eat, and you have to start with interesting ideas — ideas that are based on your site's goals and mission — to make good content. See Chapter 3 for more on the nature of good content; in the sections that follow we discuss making interactive content happen.

Implementing Interactive Content

Most, if not all, really interesting live content involves some heavy-duty multimedia editing and possibly top notch programming. Having a good Web designer in-house, along with a programmer, may be advantageous if you're undertaking a huge project that needs constant maintenance. But in most cases, you can outsource much of the design and programming to independent contractors or consulting firms. (See Chapter 10.)

Whoever is in charge of implementing your site's hardware should be intimately familiar with your plans to extend the site. You may need to consider security issues for media like RealVideo and Java, and there are disk space and bandwidth issues involved in broadcasting things other than text.

Make sure, when you undertake to make a large part of your site dependent on any sort of non-HTML programming, that you have the staff or the contractors to maintain the site after it's launched. Things break, new quirks arise, and the Flash animations and script that work fine today may not be able to meet your demands six months from now. Some of the most popular options for livening up your site are described in the sections that follow.

Java

Java isn't a hit-getter or even an attention-grabber unless it's used wisely. Java is just a programming language, albeit a platform-independent, incredibly flexible one. Java has two main applications on the Web. First, on the client side, Java is used to create applets that can be added to a Web page to embed interactive content on a page. Second, on the server side, Java is used to write scripts that run on the Web server and generate content that is sent out to a Web browser.

Client-side Java isn't limited to animated dancing bears and lit-up tables of contents, though those are certainly popular gimmicks. Java is also an incredibly efficient method of interface design, especially where databases and the Web intersect. You can create entire freestanding applications, make your advertisements automated, or simply spark up your pages using Java. But doing so generally requires a knowledgeable programmer to create something really remarkable or complex. Server-side Java is often used to create customized portals and applications such as e-mail sites (sites where you can read and create e-mail).

Johns Hopkins University's Java Programming Resources collection (www.apl.jhu.edu/~hall/java) is a great place to start learning about Java programming. If you would rather look at some of the best applets, try Jars.com at www.jars.com.

JavaScript

JavaScript, although not as robust a language as Java, has several advantages, primarily that it's not as difficult for nonprogrammers to learn. JavaScripts are generally placed within the HTML document for the Web page itself so that after the page is loaded, the JavaScript is enabled. Java applets, on the other hand, can take several minutes to load. JavaScript can be used for mini-applets, animations, navigation and interface tools, and all kinds of other functions, including error checking.

The Netscape guide to JavaScript can be found at `developer.netscape.com/docs/manuals/javascript.html`. The JavaScript Tip of the Week site (`webreference.com/javascript`) has a nice repository of useful and fun things you can accomplish with JavaScript.

Dynamic HTML

Dynamic HTML (DHTML) enables you to make elements on the page respond to your visitor's actions. Menus can pop down when the visitor rolls the mouse over them, text can change color when the visitor points at it, boxes full of text or images can appear and disappear. DHTML uses JavaScript to control cascading style sheets (CSS, covered previously in this chapter). Internet Explorer and Netscape Navigator implement DHTML in differing ways, which makes creating DHTML code that works on both platforms (as usual) more challenging. Some authoring tools, such as Macromedia Dreamweaver, provide easy WYSIWYG editing of DHTML pages and can create pages that work in both browsers.

ActiveX

Microsoft's ActiveX uses Microsoft programming tools already familiar to many programmers, such as Visual Basic (for software authoring) and OLE (for interapplication compatibility), to build doodads that then can appear in Web browser windows (specifically, in Internet Explorer windows). ActiveX is used to create many fine games and fancy animation effects, and it's also a gateway into real online collaboration. Using ActiveX, you can make Microsoft Word and Excel documents accessible to an Internet or intranet community so that people can change the content of an online document in real time. A lot of what can be done in Shockwave can also be done in ActiveX: multimedia presentations, Web site navigation, interfacing a database, and so on.

Flash, Shockwave, Acrobat, and RealPlayer

Flash, Shockwave, Acrobat, and RealPlayer all require users to have plug-ins to experience them. Plug-ins are programs that, rather than launching as separate software from the browser, display (or play) non-HTML media (for example sound, video, or animation) within the browser window. No fuss, no muss — browsers simply display a dialog box saying that a plug-in is needed and offer the user the option to get it. If the user elects to get the plug-in, it's downloaded and installed automatically. The user is often unaware that another program has launched. He or she simply sees the video, hears the music, or whatever.

Through the implementation of plug-ins, developers can extend the usual capabilities of Web browsers. Macromedia and other companies have created plug-in software that makes high-quality multimedia movies and games accessible on the Web. With the help of such software, Web site designers have flexibility with the content they put online. Some examples are

✔ **Macromedia's Flash** enables Web designers to create flashy (excuse the pun) animations that can respond to a user's actions. A simple line-drawing animation might, for example, follow the user's mouse around the screen. Flash is also often used for animated "splash screens" that appear when a user enters a site as well as to create cute games and effective online product demonstrations. Flash files are small, so you can do a lot with Flash without slowing down access to your site. The software for playing Flash animations is free and comes with many computers. To create the animations, you'll need Macromedia Flash.

✔ **Shockwave,** like Flash, was designed to display multimedia. Before Flash, it was the hot game in town, and lots of designers whipped up Shockwave content. Shockwave packs more power than Flash — it can be used to create stunning multimedia presentations. Product demos created in Shockwave are especially slick. However, all that visual sophistication comes at a price. Shockwave files are hefty, and best delivered on CD-ROM or DVD-ROM rather than via the Web. Shockwave movies can be viewed using a plug-in and are created using Macromedia Director.

✔ **Adobe Acrobat** was designed to convert print document pages to a digital form that can be displayed online. The online versions look pretty much just like the print ones. The fonts, layout, alignments, page breaks, and other elements on the pages remain exactly as they were on the original. This has the advantage of retaining design exactly. Many companies use Acrobat to store documents that need a greater level of formatting than can be achieved with HTML, for example, corporate reports, product specifications, and marketing materials. Acrobat files have to be downloaded from Web sites (as PDF files). They can then be viewed (within a browser window via a plug-in) or printed. Forms such as IRS tax forms are very handy to get as Acrobat downloads. Material that is meant to be read online, though, is usually better displayed as a Web page. Adobe offers several programs that turn Windows or Macintosh documents into Acrobat files.

✔ **RealNetworks' RealPlayer** enables you to incorporate audio and video into your Web pages. A technology called *streaming* media enables video and sound to play on a user's computer before the video or sound has completely downloaded. Long video or audio segments become a possibility, unlike the days of yore, when the whole file had to be downloaded first and then played. RealNetworks makes available RealServer — the server software required to serve the content — as well as authoring and converting tools that let you get audio or video into the Real format.

Custom scripting

If you have access to a wily programmer (or several of them), you can get just about anything done. Smart folks online have written their own Web software that works within the HTML environment to accomplish many things. Here are some ideas you may have already considered

✔ A logon system that offers perks or customized content to registered users

✔ Browser cookies (explained in Chapter 17) that track visitors and remember who they are and what they did the last time they visited

✔ Shopping-cart systems (explained in Chapter 14) that keep a log of what people bought — and what they considered buying

✔ So-called intelligent agents, which compile sets of preferences and retrieve information based on customer preferences and profiles

✔ Randomization scripts that change the look of the site with every visit

✔ Message boards or chat areas that offer your users the chance to communicate with fellow users

✔ Fun gadgets such as games or calculators

All of these features and options (and more) can be created through the use of scripts, specifically server-side scripts (those that run on the server rather than at the client end — the Web browser end). The popular platforms for writing server-side scripts associated with these features are Active Server Pages, Java Server Pages, and PERL. Here's the differences among them:

✔ **Active Server Pages (ASP)** is Microsoft's technology that lets programmers embed VBScript code (similar to Visual Basic) inside HTML documents. ASP can be used only with Microsoft servers.

✔ **Java Server Pages (JSP)** technology is similar to ASP, except that it uses Java as the programming language instead of VBScript. JSP can be used with a wide range of Web servers and platforms. It's also more scalable than ASP.

✔ **CGI** is the longest standing programming technology used on the Web. CGI is usually used along with the PERL language to write custom programs that generate HTML that is then displayed by the Web browsers. For example, when a user clicks a Search button, and a list of results appear, CGI and a PERL script are at work.

All three of these technologies are frequently used to create dynamic content, pulling information out of a database (usually based on user selections) and displaying it in a Web browser. They can also be used to collect information from users and log that information back into a database for future analysis as well as to convert XML documents into HTML format for display in a Web browser.

Chapter 10

Jobbing Out to a Web Shop or Developer

Maybe you have a staff, and maybe you don't. Maybe yours is a virtual organization that pulls together skilled people from various venues depending on what type of projects you have going. Whether it's for a short-term project or with a long-term understanding, and whether a whole site is under construction or just a bit of programming needs to be done, plenty of Internet pros work with lots of outside vendors. Knowing how to choose the right companies or individuals and knowing how to handle those oh-so-important contracts and relationships can be a big part of Webmastering.

The Pluses and Minuses of Outsourcing

Whether to *outsource* (job work out to a vendor or an individual) is a question that often comes up. Outsourcing is an obvious option when you have more money than time, but it's also effective in netting expertise. Hiring people who know the ins and outs of building transaction systems or advertising online may save you the effort of climbing a steep learning curve yourself.

Further, outsourcing is sometimes actually cost effective. For example, if you aren't prepared to commit to the expense of computers, office space, and so on (the infrastructure needs of a staff), you may find it more expedient and cheaper to outsource to some existing company or to build a short-term virtual staff of freelancers who work strictly on one project to completion. (If you choose that last option, though, make sure you're complying with government regulations. In the United States, the IRS has "twenty rules" that define independent contractors; know them before you step in hot water.)

Some folks think that outsourcing has various disadvantages. Arguments go that you may lose control of the project if you outsource, that you may lose the learning opportunity inherent in ascending that learning curve, and that management overhead can increase when an outsourced vendor or team is engaged (because those folks have to learn to navigate your company and communicate with it). Of course you must assess the risk for your situation. However, keep in mind that if you keep good, overarching management of the outsourced venture in-house, you should be able to monitor the project (and not lose control); you may well learn a lot from the expertise you're paying the outside people for; and the management overhead of hiring, training, and getting an in-house team up to speed is no small matter, either.

Types of Shops You May Encounter

No two Web shops are alike in every aspect. Even two shops that seem on the surface to offer identical services have different slants on things — this is true in every field, right? Yet Web shops do fall into some general categories, and understanding what these are can be your first step in choosing among them.

A Web-shop success story

Web site coordinator Marcy Lyon says, "We contracted out for the development of our entire site, from HTML to graphics to database programming. The main advantage was that we got ten professionals in different areas working on our Web site: a database programmer, two types of designers, an HTML person, a technical writer, someone who specialized in Web site navigation, and a slew of others whose roles I don't even know. They did a fantastic job, and the company provided all the paperwork and managed another firm that provides quotes for our Web site. They had clearly defined goals and milestones and more documentation than most people would think you would need, although it's really paid off in the final analysis."

Front-end shops and back-end shops

Once upon a time, building your big-time Web site involved calling up one of the dozen or so known design firms, getting a quote, and getting rolling. The design firm did everything, soup-to-nuts, including identity, design, coding, developing any necessary back-end systems, and sometimes even announcing and promoting the site. Not so any more. These days, the whole Internet industry is segmenting, and it's far more typical to hire separate, specialized front-end and back-end firms to work together on your Web site. Remembering that *front end* is like "front stage" in the theatre (it's what the audience sees) and *back end* is like "back stage" (it's what's going on behind the curtain to enable what the audience sees), you can easily imagine that the front-end firm does the look, and the back-end firm does the database, transaction system, content management system, and so on.

Note the omission of coding. We have actually seen a situation where a company neglected to realize that neither its front-end firm nor its back-end firm had included the HTML coding in their bids. The client company had started the project believing the front-end firm was going to do it and had accepted its bid (which was $100,000 less than its competitors') on that basis. Six weeks before launch, at a roundtable meeting of all parties, the front-end firm said to the back-end firm, "When you start the coding . . ." and several mouths fell open. We hope you avoid this situation, among others, after reading this chapter.

Some specialists are very special

As time marches on and the Internet professions segment themselves into an increasing array of specialties, some companies are focusing on providing a deep level of expertise rather than a broad range of services to their clients. In addition to front-end firms and back-end firms, you find firms (and consultants) that specialize in *branding* (creating a recognizable identity for the site or its offerings), *usability* (making sure the site works smoothly in the experience of the users), *testing* (conducting quality-assurance and focus-group testing before, during, and after the site is built), *traffic analysis* (finding out who uses your site, when, and how), and so on.

Integrators (companies that create the back end of a site by integrating or combining software and other technology developed by other companies) are commonly used these days. They sometimes write original software (primarily to glue together the products of other companies), but in general, their task is to write a minimal amount of original code. Integration has become increasingly important; even technology companies that don't call themselves integrators do integration as part of creating a Web site's back end. When you're hiring an integrator, make sure (as you would with any back-end firm) that it has experience with the mix of technologies and products that fit into your plans.

Big-time consulting companies like Arthur Andersen (www.arthurandersen.com) and PricewaterhouseCoopers (www.pwcglobal.com) offer a very broad range of consulting services segmented into groups. If you were a telephone company, you'd work with the telecomm group; if you were a manufacturer, you'd work with the manufacturing group; and so on. The services offered are broad, ranging from ongoing management consulting to actually supporting your business or online activities, to building systems (sometimes including Web sites) or reengineering the whole company. Most of the clients of big-time consulting companies are on the Fortune 500 list. Working with these consulting companies may gain you access to a wide range of skilled professionals with lots of real-world experience in their particular segments.

You can also contract out such services as media buying, human resources, administrative services, customer service, specific tasks such as freelance editing or writing, and even the procurement of office furniture and cubicles. In this chapter, we focus on hiring a generic, do-it-all design firm because that allows us to describe the many issues relevant to building a site. Whatever the task you're jobbing out (or its scope), this chapter should help. We give a particular nod to specialists here and there, however. And we devote an entire chapter of this book (Chapter 12) to dealing with ISPs and others (Chapters 13 and 14) to dealing with databases and transaction systems.

About ISPs and Internet presence providers

IPPs (Internet presence providers) offer their clients design and implementation as well as Web site hosting. Some even do consulting in specialized areas. ISPs, by contrast, sometimes offer Internet presence services but generally focus closely on offering connections rather than design or other services. (See Chapter 12 for more on ISPs and hosting.) An IPP's computers are usually connected directly to the Internet, and many businesses find that storing (or *hosting*) their sites at an IPP is an economical or business-savvy alternative to purchasing and maintaining their own Web servers or storing their sites at a hosting service.

In cases where the IPP says it provides a range of services that includes content development, design, implementation, and so on, ask the IPP personnel (and yourself) whether the IPP has a fully staffed design and development team that works independently of the site hosting team. Or (shudder), is the IPP's "design" staff just Tom in tech support who is going to be working on your site between calls?

Be sure to interview a potential IPP (or any other Web shop) carefully. Answers to these key questions may foreshadow your experience in working with a given IPP:

- ✔ How large is the IPP's design and development staff? Who's on staff, what do they do, and what sort of relevant background do they bring to the project?

- ✔ Are Web site design and development the IPP's only function? If not, what else does it do? What percentage of its time is devoted to which functions?

- ✔ To have access to the design and development staff, do you have to purchase site hosting services at the IPP? What sort of packages or short- or long-term deals are available for each?

- ✔ What level of service is provided for in the hosting agreement? (See Chapter 12 for the skinny on this.)

Working with an IPP for both your hosting and your site design and development needs can seem an ideal solution for those who can't take on the responsibility of having a staff (equipment, hiring and training, benefits, insurance, and so on). No one knows the ins and outs of a specific Web server better than the people who own and run it, and if the IPP is a reputable one, it is presumably up on the latest technologies and techniques. The downside, however, may come if the IPP's design and development group is poorly staffed or underdeveloped, or if site production takes a back seat to urgent matters on the hosting side. Often an IPP is covering so many bases for so many sites it's just plain spread too thin.

It's crucial that someone on your staff be savvy enough to manage the IPP. That person can be an in-house site manager or producer or Webmaster; he or she must be trained in enough technology to make shrewd decisions (rather than leaving everything up to the IPP). The in-house site manager must also be skilled enough in project management to monitor your budget, timelines, contracts, and the fulfillment of your expectations.

We have heard of one case where a company handed over increasing levels of responsibility for its site to an IPP. The in-house site manager was a marketeer with no tech knowledge; he was a smart fellow but not deeply Web-savvy. As the IPP made changes to the site and its back-end systems, no one was requiring or writing documentation. Further (and unbeknown to the site manager), the IPP began using proprietary tools and coding on the site. Eventually, the client company began to worry that the IPP was not keeping up with changes (it now had a lot of clients) and was not maintaining the site properly (it kept crashing). The relationship soured, but the IPP had the Web site, as well as owned the proprietary tools and code. The client company eventually hired an expensive technical consultant to watchdog the IPP. First on that consultant's To Do list was firing the IPP, but to do that and avoid alienating the soon-to-be-history IPP, she had to rebuild and relaunch the site. This undertaking was very expensive to say the least.

Again, the goal of this chapter is to help you avoid such scenarios. The keys to having a good relationship with an IPP (or any other vendor) are a solid understanding of the scope of the project, a well-constructed contract, and sharp management of the vendor by your in-house staff.

Ad agencies as front-end firms

If your company retains an ad agency, having that agency create or oversee the creation of your site may not be a bad idea. The agency presumably knows the media message and style you feel are appropriate for your company's marketing mission, and it probably employs many creative and talented people. As time goes on, more and more ad agencies have hired capable staff with the right experience and training to plan and design Web sites.

However, working on Web stuff is often a sideline for ad agencies. Sometimes they see the Web site *only* in the context of their commitment to branding and advertising. And in a worst-case scenario, they may not understand the difference between creating ads or brochures and producing compelling content that brings in traffic.

Before you turn over responsibility for designing and building your site to an ad agency — even a reputable, familiar one — make sure that it has people on staff with real online experience. If the agency you have on retainer or often work with doesn't have good, previous Web experience, but you want to keep the agency in the loop for the sake of continuity in your overall media presence, we recommend that you have the agency work on the look or concept for the site (you can often retain the agency as just a branding consultant for the project) and then turn over the actual site design and implementation to another, more Web-savvy company.

Either the ad agency or you can hire the Web shop. However, if the ad agency does the hiring, it will most likely feel it should control the Web shop. Perhaps a better strategy is to manage the project yourself, with the ad agency providing input and the Web shop also providing input into what can work (at least technically) on the Web site.

If the ad agency you work with is genuinely Web-savvy, you're set. You may find that having the agency do your site is the route to an overall media presence that sends just the right message to all fronts.

Design firms large and small

Web site design firms come in different sizes and configurations, from the big, famous types that charge high fees and accept only those clients they see as cool or furthering their portfolio, to the small, independent operators (and even virtual organizations) that pull together talent from a pool of freelancers, to individual freelancers themselves. Which type works for you (if any) is a big question that brings into play your budget, how much outsourcing you really want to do, and your site's overall goals.

Big, exclusive design firms

Big-name design firms (like Organic Online, Razorfish, and a host of others) almost always have many people on staff who are skilled in all the hip and happening digital design techniques. You can expect their staffs to include marketing moguls; programmers and database developers; video and sound producers; public relations pros; usability experts; information architects; dozens of artists, typographers, and multimedia whizzes; and the usual crew of assorted production folks. Often, these firms have their own style. That's not a bad thing — like some big ad agencies, these top-shelf firms frequently establish a certain style that they market to their clients.

If reaching your audience demands working with the highest echelon of front-end firms, this may be the path to success. Your site will probably be stunning and very navigable, with strong technical underpinnings, but plan to pay a hefty price for this service. These firms are able to screen their clients and accept only a chosen few — their services often can be had for no less than a $200,000 commitment and then only if you, the client, seem as prestigious to them as they seem to others.

Boutique shops

A *boutique shop* — one that has, say, 10 or 20 employees on staff — also often specializes in a specific design style or type of client. Here, again, you generally find in-house design and implementation staff, including those performing specific jobs such as converting video and sound files to the appropriate Web site formats and implementing cutting-edge programming and database techniques. When you sign up with a shop like this, a handful of people may be deployed as a team for producing your site. These folks may or may not actually be on staff; they may be pulled from a pool of freelancers. The team may include some or all of the following:

- ✔ **A producer,** or project manager, who manages the design and production process
- ✔ **A designer**, who creates the site's look and feel, including the theme, metaphors, palette, typography, and special element placement (sometimes a creative director or senior designer oversees this process)
- ✔ **Artist(s),** who create and/or edit graphics to be included in the site (often with direction from the designer)
- ✔ **Programmer(s),** who implement the programming and scripts needed to make forms, Java applets, message boards, chat areas, or other specialized applications that run on the site (sometimes this is all done by another vendor working in tandem with the front-end shop)
- ✔ **Production staff,** or coder(s), who translate the output of the designer and artists into HTML (again, this task may be assigned instead to the back-end firm)

The titles of Web site design and development staff vary among companies. You may be assigned any configuration of folks who have an array of titles. At a minimum, you should be assigned a producer or project manager who then acts as your primary contact throughout either the project or your entire relationship with this firm.

Boutique shops can be a good choice when you don't want to pay the big bucks to a big-name design firm but want and need the security of working with a proven team that can function like a well-oiled machine. Prices vary widely for these firms; our advice is to read through this chapter to get insight into the jobbing-out process and then get a few bids before you settle on finalists.

Small, independent operators

In the late 1990s, small, independent operators in the Web site design business popped up like video-rental stores did in the early 1980s. Many have been folded into larger firms, but many more have since hung out their shingles.

Often, these outfits consist of an owner, and . . . well, that may be it. Or a pool of freelancers may be backing that person up. If the owner of a small shop has a pool of freelancers he or she works with regularly, that again offers the advantage of working with a proven team. Keep in mind when you work with a small shop that the owner's skills often define the primary skills of the shop. If you want Flash and dazzle in a particular project, you want to find someone with a dazzling portfolio of Flash on her client sites. If you're going to have a big database component, someone who work well with an experienced developer of robust databases is important. If you need more help with content, a designer who has access to a clever content developer may be the hot ticket. In any case, when you investigate small shops, look into how relationships between the primary shop owner and any freelancers are defined, and whether the principals understand the processes they're subcontracting out.

Small shops may take on only one large project at a time. If so and if your site is that project, you have the shop's full attention from beginning to end. On the downside, if a small shop is mid-project when you approach it, the shop may be unable to get started right away. In some cases, small shops can be a very economical alternative. They can also offer more personal service, and for small-to-midsize projects, they may be a good choice, especially if you find one with which you can maintain an ongoing and successful relationship.

Finding Qualified Web Shops

As is true in many other areas of life, word-of-mouth referrals are often the best source of information about Web shops. Contact sites you admire and ask their managers, producers, or Webmasters who designed the sites and how to contact those firms. (Of course, you may run into some sites that do all of their development work in-house!) You can also get referrals through inquiries to discussion groups populated by Internet professionals; such groups are described at the end of Chapter 18.

Yahoo! (www.yahoo.com) lists Web shops, including designers and others. The Firm List (www.firmlist.com) and DesignShops.com (www.designshops.com) also list designers.

If a design firm you like doesn't have room in its busy schedule for your project, it may refer you to others who might. Through referrals from designers, you can also usually find back-end firms and other specialists.

As you seek a design or development outfit, refer again to your mission statement (Chapter 2) and your specs for the project (Chapter 8). Keep your business, content, and usability goals in mind as you review each shop's style, experience, skills, and references. If your primary mission is to provide technical support for your products, a shop that specializes in slick, mood-driven design and postmodern copy may not be the one for you.

How do you figure out who is worth working with when you have a few candidates in mind? Send out the same RFP (request for proposal; see Chapter 8) to all the candidates so they will all be bidding on the same clearly defined project. Send your RFP to perhaps five or six candidates (a few may respond to say they can't meet your schedule or some such; you want to wind up with at least three good candidates).

In your review of their proposals, don't just automatically take the one with the lowest price. You must judge how the services they offer compare to those of other firms, as well as their individual experience and style, and the depth of their abilities. We cover those topics next.

Judging experience

As with hiring an employee or contracting with another vendor, you have to evaluate the experience of potential Web shops before you hire one. Any shop with even basic public relations and marketing skills is more than happy to tell you what it does best. You'll want to know answers to these questions:

- ✔ **Where did these folks come from?** With e-commerce and the Internet services industry still in their youth, most people who are employed in these fields bring with them some background from another field. (We cover this in Chapters 1 and 18.) Some people have rich experience gleaned in related fields such as publishing, print design, marketing, and traditional programming; others were plumbers. We're great believers in the transferability of skills, and as we point out in Chapter 18, there aren't yet lots of standardized degree programs available in any aspect of site creation or management. But you must make sure that the staff at your prospective Web shop actually has transferable skills or that those people have taken the appropriate training and combined it with the correct level of experience. You may want to review Chapters 1 and 18 to get the lowdown on the skills that various Internet pros must have and what fields these folks may come from.

✔ **Does their background translate to ability?** Many skill sets lend themselves to creating and managing Web sites. (Again, see Chapters 1 and 18.) The catch here is to know how well those skills have been adapted to the unique requirements of the online world. Artists in the online world have to be concerned with the limitations of color depth and density that arise in Web site design. Print publishers simply must relax the layout control they're used to having and come to grips with the inflexible nature of HTML layout. They also have to learn to write for scannability and ease of navigation rather than flowing narrative. Advertising and marketing pros are faced with a medium that combines some of the best — and the worst — of all the media they've previously worked with. Techies have to become more conversant in visual design issues than is generally needed in traditional programming and MIS fields.

✔ **Does their background and focus fit your goals?** Remember that mission statement that you drew up in Chapter 2? Pull it out again, and shape it, along with what you determined about the site as you planned it and organized it, into an RFP. Review your RFP side by side with each prospective shop's offerings. A shop with a solid background in advertising or marketing may be a good match for a site whose purpose is to inform and excite. A technical shop should do well with a site that's geared toward user support for your new widget product line. Make sure that their focus is compatible with yours, and that their bid covers all the bases and issues you described.

Obviously, artistic talent is necessary in producing a site whose goals make a designerly look a requirement. If that talent isn't present in the prospective Web shop's principals, design can be subcontracted without a problem. But should the subcontracted artist be required to have extended years of experience in *computer-created* graphics? Designers and artists in the print and advertising worlds have skills required of all artists: an eye for color, a sense of placement, and knowledge of visual balance. To do Web site graphics, these people must also understand the Web-safe palette and other unique issues of preparing digital art for Web sites. Adaptability to the constraints of creating Web sites is key. Knowing how to convert graphics that are deeply saturated with color into files small enough that they don't choke a user's modem separates the standard artist from the Web site artist.

On the technical side, one may think any programming experience is acceptable, but again, programming for Web sites takes many forms. Someone with experience developing spreadsheet applications or video games may not have the programming skills and experience mix necessary for Web site programming. New languages (Java, JavaScript, and VBScript) and technologies (Flash, ActiveX, cascading style sheets, and more) have been introduced to Web developers at breakneck speed. It takes a talented and impassioned technical staff to keep up the pace and to separate hype from real utility so they can focus on what's important.

Time and the Web

The Web has only been around for a short time. Almost no one got into the industry right away, and anyone who tells you that he or she has ten or twelve years of Web site experience is probably full of hogwash. If some shop claims experience that took place before the mid-1990s, ask people there to define that experience. Do they simply mean that they had an e-mail connection for many years? (That's not very impressive.) Were they actively publishing content on *gopher servers,* a forerunner of Web sites, for the first six years of the shop's ten-year history? Have they been on the graphics side of computer game development for four years before migrating to full-fledged multimedia CD-ROM production and finally to Web site development? (Games and multimedia are not the same as Web sites.) "Years of experience" can mean many things, but experience on Web sites that occurred before 1995 is well nigh impossible, and it's the rare bird who's actually been around since day one.

Quantifying experience and success

How many accounts a shop has handled doesn't necessarily indicate the quality of that shop's experience, but knowing this information can help you define the breadth of its experience — especially if the accounts have been for a widely diverse or an intensely focused client base.

In Chapter 2, you considered briefly what would qualify your site as a success; you can get more information about that in Chapter 17. Get a clear picture of what will qualify as success for your site. Then ask the prospective shop to tell you how success was defined in each of the sites it feels most proud of, whether those success benchmarks were reached, and how long that took. If you're planning a site that will include online sales, ask the prospective Web-shop folks what sites they have done for online merchants and what impact their input had on that aspect of the project. Did sales increase as much as or more than predicted? Did the customer base grow into previously untapped markets? Has the client been satisfied with the process of delivering and handling those sales? Did the shop even follow up or find out about success?

References are paramount

Prospective shops should be able and willing to provide you with at least three references from current or recent clients. Get the name of the decision-making contact, an address and phone number, and a URL for the Web site the shop created for that client. First, investigate the site that was created (more on this in the next section). Then when you contact the reference, interview your contact with these questions in mind:

- ✔ Who was your primary contact at the Web shop? Was this person professional, and how did he or she handle any problems that arose? Did you deal with anyone else, and if so, what was that person like?

- ✔ Was the site delivered on schedule? How was the schedule organized? Were alpha and beta versions of the site delivered as expected?

- ✔ Was the site delivered within the allotted budget? What glitches or surprises occurred? They always do — the real question is how did the shop handle them?

- ✔ Did the shop perform as expected? Did the quality of what it produced match its promised expertise?

- ✔ Would you do business with this shop again? If not, why? If so, what would you like to have done differently the next time?

Because vendor references aren't as legally sensitive as employee references have become, you should get good information from contacting a prospective shop's references. Ask specific questions and make sure you take notes.

Judging style and substance

So you have those handy references in your mitts, now what do you do with the URLs? Fire up your browser and go forth to look them over, that's what. Study them in detail but don't stop there. Most Web shops maintain their own Web sites. Forget looking at the site itself — look at the clients' sites. Not just the screenshots of the clients' sites that appear on the shop's site, but *the actual clients' sites*. Review these sites as well as those of the companies you were given as references, remembering that these are the projects the shop is most proud of.

Can you clearly see what the mission or purpose of one site or another may be? What did the shop do (or not do) in designing and implementing the site to further that mission? On reviewing the site, have you learned something about the company that owns the site? Does its products or services or content interest you? Have you been persuaded to make a purchase or request more information or do whatever the site seems to be geared toward you wanting to do? Your own responses to other sites can be a valuable indicator of the response that others may have to this shop's work.

Plays well with others

How vendors — including your potential Web shop — interact with in-house staff and even other vendors has a big effect on the success of your endeavors. Points to ponder as you think this over include not just how often but *how* (in what style) they communicate, how willing they are to maintain communications with others, what office hours they keep, and what client-to-producer ratio they maintain. (Will your Web endeavor be put on hold for another deadline?) Avoid the arrogant, crabby, or blaming Web shop in favor of one that is respectful, communicative, and responsible.

Ask specific questions, including (as applicable) whether the shop will work directly with your ISP, hosting service, or in-house IS group to coordinate installation and future updates. Does the shop expect you to handle all of those communications? It's okay if you're going to handle these tasks as long as you know this up front and the shop provides you with all the information you need. This is something you can explore during an early interview with a shop; pay attention to whether its personnel respond completely or offer only half-baked comments.

We saw a case where shop A was hired to revamp an existing site, and well before the contracts were signed, it became clear the shop was going to have to work with shop B to coordinate the sharing of a big database with a sister site. Shop A visibly balked when this was mentioned, while shop B responded cooperatively. Shop A was hired and did the site's front-end revamping, while shop B worked on the database. Throughout the whole project, shop A balked and complained about many matters large and small, while shop B kept a very calm and cooperative attitude. The project was finished, and one vendor was retained to maintain both sites. Guess which one.

Here are some more questions to keep in mind:

- ✔ How proactive are the shop's people in coordinating with your marketing, public relations, and other staff?

- ✔ Do the personnel expect perfectly complete and final copy to be delivered to them, or can they reach out and ask questions and accept a few last-minute alterations?

- ✔ How will the people deliver the site and get your final approval?

- ✔ How will the site actually get onto your server? Will they upload it or will you?

View awards with caution

Awards can indicate experience and quality, but only if the awards are recognized and respected and if they are based on clearly defined criteria. See Chapter 17, where we talk about measures of Web site success in general. When you're judging Web shops, consider with caution any awards they've received. You may want to review the awarding organization's methods for selection and judging, as well as its credibility, before you decide that an award validates the shop's capabilities.

They listen, but do they hear?

During your conversations with Web shop candidates, beware of these red flags that should inspire you to consider another choice:

- Are you presented only with predefined templates to choose from rather than having a considered and carefully constructed plan for your site based on information you gave these folks? (Chapter 8 describes how to make a site plan and write an RFP.)

- Do the shop personnel try to shoehorn your site into addressing just one goal — even if your mission statement covers several? (Chapter 2 covers setting goals for your site.)

- Do the personnel try to copy a competitor's site with the intent of mimicking that success rather than taking an original approach?

- Do the people quote prices or present a proposal without first discussing your site with you in detail?

If any of these flags pop up during conversations with a prospective Web shop, don't immediately exclude that firm from consideration, but investigate the area that gives you pause in much more detail by asking more questions and by making clear the intentions for your site. Do your best to get your answers in writing.

The day after: Now what?

It's easy to focus your attention on launching the site while forgetting what's going to happen the next day and thereafter. This is a pitfall both for the in-house site manager, producer or Webmaster, and for many Web shops. You may actually have a sterling plan for site maintenance and need no help with it, or you may be planning to job some or all of that task out to the shop that's building the site. What, in that case, happens after launch?

In a "cash-and-carry" situation, the Web shop may be interested only in producing the site, and it may plan to hand all other concerns thereafter back over to you. If you and your staff have the skills for dealing with this setup, that's fine. Just be sure you write into your contract the criteria for acceptance and approval. Make it clear, too, that you require time period during which the shop is required to fix any problems that crop up.

Some shops offer basic training to your staff, agreeing to deliver the site and then spend time training you or your team in making minor changes and handling small maintenance tasks on your own. The shop may provide templates, written instructions, or even on-site, hands-on training. Insist on receiving thorough instructions before this objective is considered complete. Also, be sure to define how requests for assistance will be handled after basic training.

In a full-service setting, the Web shop delivers the site and remains involved in the day-to-day maintenance of the site. The shop may provide daily updates if the site calls for it, perform scheduled maintenance, provide detailed analysis of the site's performance, and more. This type of ongoing relationship requires that a clear maintenance contract or retainer agreement be put in place in addition to or as part of the contract for creating the site. We discuss more on this topic in an upcoming section on contracts.

Defining the Project

As you go about selecting the shop you plan to work with, you must have a clear picture of what various shops do and don't do as a matter of course. (Even what various design shops do varies; know what your candidates see as the scope of their jobs.) To make sure what they do matches what you want, you must be able to tell them clearly what your project is and what you expect of them. Poorly defined or undefined expectations can easily lead to disappointment in the final product (your Web site).

So, how can the intrepid Internet professional make sure that what's expected by both sides is clearly defined? *Put it in writing!* This sounds simple, but it's amazing how much people assume and how much folks don't seem to know about what needs to be put in writing. In your conversations (and written communications) with the shop of choice, make sure you cover these points:

> ✔ **Clearly define the deliverable product.** Be as descriptive as possible. Instead of writing a basic work order, express how you expect the site to look and perform. Be very specific about your needs, referring to the planning you did based on earlier chapters. In fact, you did that planning partly so you could communicate to whomever was going to work on the site what the site was supposed to be and what it should accomplish; attach that document to a brief summary and fork 'em over.

✔ **Lay out each step in the production process.** Each shop is likely to have its own version of the production process; get this information from the shop. Review the process with the shop's personnel, inserting any additional approval points or benchmarks that may be required on your end — for example, sign-offs from executives, your marketing department, the sales or human resources folks, and so on. (Don't forget legal reviews.) In Chapter 22, we talk about the review process. Make sure you understand how this particular shop defines various stages (alpha, beta, and final) in the site-building process (see Chapters 3 and 8 for more on that).

✔ **Agree on timelines.** With your outline of the production process in hand, set a timeline that marks when each step must occur. Make sure both sides understand whether the timeline represents goals or true deadlines. Establish what the consequences of missed deadlines are for either side. (We prefer the more positive message that offering bonuses for achievement sends rather than the punishing notion of docking payment for any missed deadlines.)

✔ **Consider potential "gotchas."** Don't forget to assign responsibility for the incidentals that come with launching a new Web site. What happens if something goes wrong somewhere along the way? Figure out just who must do what. You may not want to think of the worst, but as site manager, producer, or Webmaster, you have to.

✔ **Understand when and how payment is expected.** Payment to the Web shop is often tied closely to the timeline. You must agree on whether payment is due upon delivery of a given step or upon *approval* of the component delivered in that step. (*Hint:* It's more to your advantage to pay on approval.) Whose approval is needed? How will it be indicated? When payment time rolls around, remember that 30 days means 30 days. If your company cuts checks just once a month, let the Web shop know that up front, before the project starts. This may be an issue if you're dealing with an independent operator, whose cash flow perhaps isn't what a big outfit's might be.

✔ **Come to terms with what may happen after launch.** How is the end of your relationship defined — or is it defined? Many contracts neglect provisions for maintenance, updates, or a certification of services and functionality. Don't get yourself stuck in an open-ended, ill-defined relationship — make sure you put these matters in writing.

What You Are Going to Pay

Pricing within the Web site design and development industry can be very fickle. As of this writing, standards aren't firm, and the pricing models of various shops differ, even in the same categories or skill sets. Overall, assigning value to the production of a Web site can be a tricky and sometimes arbitrary business. Defining the project and getting apples-to-apples bids will help you, but you also should know what generally drives rates.

Some front-end firms and individual designers base their pricing on a per page model (charging you, say, $100 or $125 per page). But that model doesn't allow for the differences among pages that require lots of design but have no text, those that require little design and have little text, and those that have complex design, loads of text, *and* a few zippy elements that require programming.

For your Web site, it's better to get a bid than an estimate. A *bid* proposes a certain scope for the defined project and provides a cost beyond which the project will go only in certain circumstances that are generally spelled out. An *estimate* says, "we think it's going to cost this much" but generally offers no guaranteed cap. Again, getting a bid offers you a better sense of what you'll pay, but in order to compare one bid to another, you need to be savvy about what may make one bid for building your site come in at, say, $125,000 and another come in at $200,000.

What drives rates

Other than the scope of a project, how many people hours it may take, and what the real costs are, five major factors drive a shop's prices:

- ✔ **Experience and accomplishment.** Your review of the shop's skills and the breadth of its accomplishments can help you evaluate its fees. Has it had clients in your specific industry? In related industries? Has it been able to produce successful sites for businesses the size of yours? Has it captured the essence of each company within that company's site? High marks in these areas allow a shop to command higher fees than its less-accomplished peers. However, an impressive portfolio doesn't necessarily translate into high fees. Make sure the quality of the work justifies the quantity of the bill, and get the best you can for your budgeted dollars.

- ✔ **Level of service.** Review the information you gathered earlier in this chapter regarding what a shop can and cannot provide for you. Does it produce only templates from which your team will build, or does it produce the entire, original site (coding and back-end integration included)? Will it be training any of your staff? Will it be an ongoing partner in the development and success of your site? Shops providing more services for longer stretches of time merit higher fees.

- ✔ **Geographic location.** In any industry, the country, state, city, or neighborhood that a business is in can inspire higher or lower fees. You pay more to go to the theater in New York than in Seattle, and you pay less for tomatoes in January in Texas than in New Jersey. In the Web site design and development industry, the costs of doing business (commercial rentals, state and local taxes, availability of enterprise zones, the cost of utilities, and the overall cost of living) contribute to setting base fees. Web shops located within high-tech centers, such as California's

Silicon Valley, San Francisco's SoMa district, and New York City's Silicon Alley, may also charge a premium simply for being where the action is. Because they are where the action is, they may indeed be the savviest of them all, but many talented, smart, hip and happening Web workers reside in Minneapolis, too.

✔ **Status, fame, and positioning.** Has the firm positioned itself as one of the online elite, or is it marketing itself as an affordable alternative? If it's the former, is the shop worthy of being included, and do you want that status for the associated abilities enough to pay more? To find out if a prospective shop is truly high-profile, ask other Internet professionals who they would include on a short list of premier Web shops. Does your candidate show up on those lists? If the shop you're considering promotes the value of its services rather than its status or fame, do you agree after your evaluations that it offers a great value?

If you find that a shop's prices are either higher or lower than those of its local competitors and peers, consider that to be a red flag. A high price may indicate that the shop holds an inflated opinion of its worth. A low price may indicate inexperience or naiveté, or that the shop is in financial trouble. Look for a shop whose fees are in your acceptable range, and consider that your best bet.

Negotiating fees

While the Internet professional world is no flea market, pretty much everything you contract out is flexibly priced — at least at first. There's often a bit of room in an estimate to get a justified discount. At the very least, you can request that the project be priced in pieces (x dollars for this portion and y dollars for that) so that you can scale back your plans, if necessary, to stay within your budget. We've had our best successes, though, in staying within budget by fully specifying projects and providing adequate information to the vendor. Making the vendor's job easier avoids increased billable hours.

Use a one-stop shop or specific vendors?

In general, using multiple vendors often means that management overhead increases exponentially on all sides, sometimes driving your costs (and maybe your blood pressure) through the roof. Hiring a front-end firm and a back-end firm is fine, but hiring three or more companies and asking them to work together can get very tricky.

Get the executives of the various vendors on board, make sure they understand the scope of the project(s), and make sure the people you will work with most closely at each firm are the type of people who work well with others.

You or someone on your team may have to coordinate the efforts of the various vendors. You may also have to establish, at least implicitly, who among the vendors is top dog. It generally makes sense to assign this spot to the vendor with the largest or most important role in the project.

"Feature creep" can really cost you

So you make up your mind that you're going to buy a new car and head to the dealer that offers a great price on a cute little sedan. When you get there, you find that the sedan has no stereo. You decide you really want one, and then the pal who's with you suggests a moonroof. The sales rep walks by, and you ask about performance. You learn that the car has a four-cylinder engine, while you were hoping for more power on hills. A moment later, you find yourself looking instead at the red convertible with the leather interior and V-6 engine. That's called *feature creep*.

Feature creep drives up costs. That cute little sedan is a lot cheaper than the red convertible, and that's no accident. As you add bells and whistles to your site, costs go up, and it's a rare Web shop that halts its work to give you a new estimate based on all the stuff you or your higher-ups have started thinking would really make the site special since the contract was signed.

Don't be pressured by your shop to include features that aren't in the best interests of the site. Don't let your higher-ups think that they can add personalization or convert the content to wireless without consequences, either. Get estimates for any additional features, and consider those estimates in the context of whether that stuff is going to contribute to the success of your site. Find out what alternatives exist for accomplishing the same goal without the added cost. The price your shop quoted at the outset of your project was based on the specifications you provided and on the shop's understanding of the scope of things. Although most shops budget for the minor changes and corrections that almost always occur in the approval phase, major changes or feature enhancements increase costs. It's your job to keep them in line.

If you receive an estimate that's seriously beyond your budget but you really want to work with that vendor, you may want to review the production to see which (if any) preproduction or approval steps can be reduced or eliminated. You may be able, for example, to scan your own art or rely on a simpler two-step approval process instead of endless rounds of review by a variety of players. Using your in-house staff to do testing may also be an option.

Although we don't recommend low-balling a prospective vendor, you can and should ask if the price quoted is its best price. Offer what you consider to be a reasonable alternative amount in response. Feel free to negotiate, but don't get silly about it. A counteroffer of perhaps 20 or maybe 30 percent less than the shop's bid is reasonable. The shop will obviously come back to you with its own counteroffer, and off you go, negotiating 'til you reach an agreement.

Deciphering Contracts and NDAs

The fact that you need a signed contract in hand before the project begins is probably clear by this point. The contract must outline what you expect from the vendor and what the vendor expects from you. It must also establish what occurs if those expectations aren't met. At the time the contract is signed, no important questions should remain unanswered.

It's always prudent to have your company's legal staff or corporate counsel review contracts prior to signing. They see things you don't — ambiguities and opportunities for misunderstanding — and they can clarify the language.

Nothing is carved in stone (until it is)

A contract is a document of mutual understanding and agreement. Up to the point when it's signed, much of what's in the contract may be negotiable, but contract negotiations can slow down progress in any project. At the outset, define which terms are non-negotiable to you and have these deal-breakers in mind when you're wheeling and dealing. Remember that the prospective Web shop will also have deal-breakers on its side.

You can start the contract process by putting forth your standard contract or by letting the shop put forth its contract. Yours is probably written to your benefit, but the shop's contract may provide you with clues to its business practices. Most shops have a standard contract from which they operate. Have your legal counsel review this contract at the outset for any clauses contrary to your company's standard policies. Find out what points you can and cannot, in your company's view, negotiate on, and whether you use the vendor's contract as a starting point or use yours.

Intellectual property and copyrights

Just who owns the final product? If you aren't experienced at hiring someone to create intellectual value for your company, this may sound like a preposterous question. However, it is one that lands many Web shops and their clients in plenty of boiling oil. It's common practice for back-end firms to retain ownership of code and tools and simply license their use to clients. Front-end firms may offer only narrow rights or broader rights. Review Chapter 7 to find out more about these important matters.

Nondisclosure agreements

A *nondisclosure agreement* (NDA) is meant to protect confidentiality. NDAs are a standard feature of many modern contracts, even employment agreements. They can also appear as stand-alone documents to be signed before a particularly confidential project is described. When a vendor signs an NDA, he or she is agreeing not to disclose whatever is labeled through the NDA to be confidential. Especially if your site will feature an as-yet-unannounced product or service, keeping that information under wraps may be a priority, and you must be sure NDAs are signed and filed. Web shops are often also interested in keeping their design and bidding processes confidential. You may actually be asked to sign an NDA before the bidding or contract negotiation phase begins. As with the overall contract, the NDA is an explicit statement of expectations. Decide what can be disclosed to whom and at what time or under which circumstances, and that shapes your NDA.

Maintaining Vendor Relationships

Finishing a project and ending the contract on a positive note is great for both parties. When it's all over, you may well have established a business relationship that continues, and the Web shop can add you to its roster of happy clients who can tell others of their good experience.

Working with a shop you know — one that has done good work for you and now knows your site inside and out — can be a huge time and energy saver. The shop that knows you can immediately pick up a follow-up project with little prep time, and you know what to expect in working with its people again.

This type of good relationship is definitely a two-way street. It's up to the shop to deliver as promised, but it's up to you to make the scope of the project clear in advance, to manage expectations and keep the budget in line as the project goes on, and to resolve any misunderstandings or glitches as quickly and professionally as possible. It's also a good idea to pay promptly (30 days means just that), assume good intentions first (rather than assuming the people in the shop are mean, stupid, or crazy), learn the lingo of the industry, make no assumptions, and always communicate clearly.

Do these things, and you are at least in the right. You may also (if the Web shop keeps its end of the deal) end up with a valued partner.

Chapter 11

Under the Hoods of a Few Good Servers

*Y*our server serves your Web site to the world. That alone should be a persuasive argument that you ought to understand your server. Which server hardware and software you select has profound impact on what you can offer (in terms of content, technologies, and features). It also has impact on how much traffic you can withstand and how robust and reliable your site will be. Whether you plan to run your own server or have a hosting company host your site (*hosting* is simply housing the server; see Chapter 12), you need to know a bit about Web-server software — the actual software that turns your server machine into a Web server.

A number of Web servers are now commonly used, and each offers its own set of strengths and weaknesses. In this chapter, we walk you through what makes some popular server options good, as well as discuss their relative weaknesses. Then we look at what's involved in running your own server, why you may want to do that, and what it's all about.

Servers and Platforms and Software — Oh My!

Your "server" actually consists of hardware, an operating system, and software. The hardware can be a machine as simple as a desktop PC or as complex as a big, expensive, multi-processor server such as a Sun Enterprise server. The *operating system* (also referred to as the "platform" on which the server software runs) is the software that controls the basic functioning of the hardware. Linux, UNIX, Windows 2000 Server, and Windows NT Server are all commonly used platforms for Web sites. Finally, the server software itself is the software that performs the specific, fundamental tasks necessary for serving Web pages, running a database, or a variety of other functions.

Note that you can run several types of servers on a single machine — perhaps a Web server, an FTP server, a database server, and an e-mail server. Each of those servers would have its own server software running on the machine, although they would all be running on the same platform.

You can also spread one Web site across multiple server machines (see Figure 11-1). In this case, the Web server, database server, and e-mail server may all be on separate machines, two of them may be on one machine while the third is on another, one may be on two machines with the other two also on one of those machines. In fact, some altogether different combo may be going.

In this chapter, we concern ourselves mostly with Web servers and a few other closely related types. For information about database servers, turn to Chapter 13. For information about other servers, turn to bigger books on the topic — there are plenty of good books about server software. Our goal here is to help you through the maze of information about Web servers and discuss how to choose one.

The purpose of a Web server is to respond to requests from Web browsers. This usually means locating a file on the server based on the URL that the browser provides and then returning the contents of that page to the browser. It can also mean executing programs that run on the server. These programs, in turn, may direct queries to the database server and execute database queries. Basically, a server serves what the client software (the Web browser) requests.

Most commercial sites "split the load" (spread the burden of serving the site) among a bunch of Web servers. In this case, requests that come into the site via its main URL are automatically redirected to one of the many servers. This scheme allows a big site to handle much more traffic than a site with a single Web server. It also allows the site to continue to function even if one of the Web servers crashes.

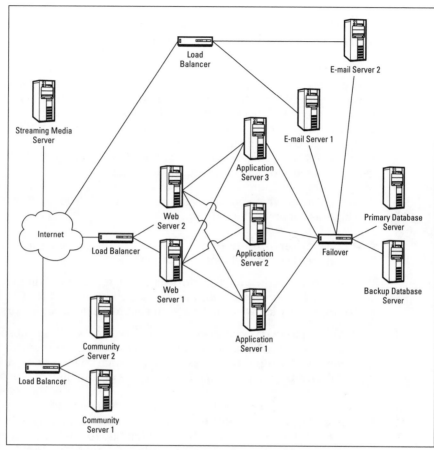

Figure 11-1:
A Web site can consist of many types of servers on several server machines.

To some degree, whether you first select the server software or the platform is a chicken-or-the-egg question. You can choose the server software and let that dictate your platform, or you can select a platform and let that limit your server options. If you or your team have experience with a certain server or platform, you're likely to go that route. If your chosen hosting company (see Chapter 12) works only with a certain platform or certain servers, that may have an effect on your choice. If all of your options are open, however, you can make choices based on other factors in your situation. In any case, understanding server options is key to making wise decisions.

Selecting a Server Platform

People get religious when it comes to operating systems. We don't want to step on anyone's intensely held beliefs, and anyway, we believe that Windows 2000 Server, NT Server, UNIX, and Linux are all great choices for

Web server operating systems. Each has solid strengths as well as weak-nesses. We aren't going to recommend one over the others here. Instead, we'll tell you what's what so you can choose.

Note first that Windows 2000 Server is similar to NT Server in that both are high-end Microsoft products that offer an easy graphical interface and work well with other Microsoft products. Windows 2000 Server is, in fact, simply a newer version of NT Server. UNIX and Linux are similar to each other in that both are non-proprietary products (no one company owns UNIX or Linux, although various companies own or distribute various forms of UNIX and Linux). UNIX and Linux both have text-based interfaces and are tougher to get acquainted with but offer value and flexibility.

As you consider which operating system you should run on your Web server machine, ask yourself the following questions:

- ✔ Does the server software you want to use run under a specific operating system? If so, your choice may be clear.

- ✔ Are your system administrators already familiar with Windows 2000 Server, NT Server, or UNIX/Linux? If so, you may want to stick with what they already know. (Of course, you should weigh other factors.)

- ✔ Will you have physical access to the server, or will it be housed in an off-site location? UNIX and Linux are easier to administer remotely than Windows 2000 Server or NT Server, although one does have to know UNIX/Linux pretty well to take advantage of administering remotely.

Desktop operating systems, like Windows Me, Windows 98, and the Macintosh OS, are unsuitable for running your Web server. These operating systems, for all their other capabilities, aren't up to the job of staying up and running 24 hours a day and 7 days a week (often referred to as *24/7*). In the sections that follow, we look at the pluses and minuses of Windows 2000 Server or NT Server versus UNIX/Linux.

Windows 2000 Server or NT Server

Microsoft Windows 2000 comes in several flavors: Professional, Server, and Advanced Server. The Professional version is for use as a desktop operating system, so we don't cover it here. Windows 2000 Server is most commonly used as a Web site platform, while Advanced Server offers high-end features (which are omitted from the Server version) that make it appropriate to the most powerful server hardware and for the most complex, large-scale sites. Because Windows 2000 Server is most commonly used for Web sites, in this book we focus on it to the exclusion of Windows 2000 Professional. Windows 2000 Server is actually a more recent version of NT Server, although NT Server 4 is (as of this writing) also still popular.

Both Windows 2000 Server and NT Server are robust and reliable operating systems that are often used to run handy servers such as database, file, and Web servers. Microsoft bundles Microsoft Internet Information Server (IIS), and Microsoft's Web-server software, with both Windows 2000 Server and NT Server.

Both Windows 2000 Server and NT Server come with the now ubiquitous Windows interface, which means that most people can sit down in front of a machine running Windows 2000 Server or NT Server and know at least how to do the most basic functions. For simple activities like saving files and other familiar tasks, using Windows 2000 Server or NT Server is a lot like using Windows Me or Windows 98. Windows 2000 Sever and NT Server are popular operating systems for the local area networks (LANs) that many companies use in their offices. If your company uses Windows 2000 Server or NT Server for its LAN, you probably have access to a lot of internal expertise (yours or your colleagues') that can be leveraged in the course of running your Web servers. Additionally, Microsoft provides a lot of support and training for its products, which, in combination with the easy interface and easy integration with other Microsoft products, makes it a snap to get set up with Windows 2000 Server or NT Server (at least compared to UNIX or Linux).

The two biggest drawbacks in using Windows 2000 Server or NT Server are that their hardware requirements are kind of hefty and their remote administration capabilities are limited. Running a Web server using Windows 2000 Server or NT Server, you need more robust hardware than you would to handle the same traffic load running a Web server using the various versions of UNIX or Linux for PCs. The bigger machine will cost you more moolah, too.

Remote administration (which, you'll recall, is not the strong suit of the Microsoft server products) can be very handy — if you can change directory names from your desktop without having to run down to where the server is physically located, you may be a happier camper. In the area of remote administration, Microsoft has made improvements in Windows 2000 Server over its predecessor, NT Server. But on the whole, you still have to be sitting in front of the server machine to do plenty of the tasks you could handle remotely if you were using UNIX on your server machine instead. Remote administration may sound like a luxury at first, but it can become a headache if you are responsible for maintenance and you have to do it when no one is accessing your site — maybe at 4 a.m.? — you'll end up driving to where the machine is instead of sitting at home in your jammies sipping cocoa and taking care of business remotely. That said, the convenience of setting up an NT machine as a server may make the choice plenty attractive.

UNIX and Linux

UNIX has always been a popular operating system for running server and other mission-critical software such as Web servers — in fact, the Web was originally built on UNIX machines. Until a few years ago, running a Web server basically meant having to have a server machine running UNIX. Many Webmasters still think that UNIX is the one and only operating system to use for Web servers, although more recently, Linux (a younger cousin of UNIX) has also become popular. UNIX is a commercially developed and distributed operating system, while Linux (at least in its purest form) is a freely available operating system that was developed on the *open source* model. The open source model allows anyone to take, use, and change software within certain restrictions set forth by the software's creators. Variations of Linux are sold or distributed commercially; from a functionality viewpoint, UNIX and Linux are almost indistinguishable.

Among the advantages of using UNIX or Linux (hereafter known as UNIX/Linux) is that UNIX/Linux has been around a while. It's more stable, more robust, and better developed than Windows 2000 Server or NT Server. Quite commonly, a machine running UNIX/Linux can run for months nonstop with minimal maintenance; this is way more than can be said of just about any version of Windows, although Windows 2000 Server is no slouch.

A vast collection of freely available software exists for use with UNIX/Linux. This software ranges from tools you can use to develop your Web site to actual Web server software, such as the highly popular Apache.

Remotely administering UNIX/Linux machines is a breeze (if you know UNIX/Linux). Sitting in Santa Monica or Altoona, you can install software and make changes to a machine in Oswego, Bala Cynwyd, or Spokane without trouble. This makes installing software on your machine at a hosting facility simple. It also makes maintaining your Web server easy, even at midnight hours when the machine is not being heavily trafficked and you just can't bear to pop on your parka and brave the storm outside.

Should you choose to use UNIX/Linux as your OS, you have to learn the ways of UNIX/Linux, a text-based OS with its own ins and outs. You also have to do some work to configure your machine. However, you get a robust and reliable operating system. Like most things in life, it's a mixed bag.

The Many Types of Servers

Most of today's commercial Web sites rely on many servers to create what people experience as a single Web site. Each of these specific servers performs a different function. Depending on the Web site's features, you may need some or all of these types of servers:

✔ **Web servers:** Every Web site must exist on at least one Web server, which functions to serve (surprisingly enough) Web pages. A basic Web server receives a request for a Web page, retrieves that page from its file system, and sends the page over the Internet to the user's Web browser for display. Web servers also run server-side scripts and interact with application servers (in that they determine when a request from a user should be passed along to the application server for processing).

✔ **Database servers:** Database servers provide access to large amounts of data, which is stored in a database on the database server. The data can be product information, Web site content, information collected about site visitors, or any of a lot of other stuff. Usually, data in a database is accessed via special software running on an application server. You can read more about database servers and databases in Chapter 13.

✔ **Application servers:** Application servers are designed to allow for the running of specialized, complex Web-based programs such as e-commerce transaction systems, auctions, and community-technology systems (such as chat). Since the early days of the Web, programmers have been writing programs that run on Web servers to accomplish certain tasks — to access data in a database, provide calculators, or capture information that visitors enter into forms. Until recently, these programs were written using technologies such as CGI. Although these technologies were great for developing simple programs, they fell down on the more complicated jobs that are becoming commonplace online. Usually application servers function behind a Web server. That is, when users comes to the Web site, the server they first encounter (behind the site's interface) is a Web server. The Web server then passes requests to and starts processes on application servers as needed. The result is that the Web server and any application servers work together to provide what looks to the user like a single interaction with the Web site.

✔ **Mail servers:** Mail servers serve e-mail. Many Web sites incorporate e-mail into their functionality — by sending outbound e-mail (newsletters, order confirmation notices, and so on) to users or by accepting incoming e-mail from users (often via forms). Mail servers, none too oddly, come in two types — one that sends out e-mail and one that receives e-mail. Many sites incorporate one or both of these types of servers into their systems. Truth be told, e-mail often becomes such a vital force on a large Web site that several machines are dedicated just to running the software to support e-mail.

Other specialty servers exist to handle streaming media (audio or video), community technologies (discussion groups, message boards, and chat), personalization, and various other features of Web sites.

A Thing or Three About Application Servers

Application servers don't emerge from the box all divvied up as transaction system servers, auction servers, and whatever else. Some developer has to take in hand some fairly all-purpose application server software and develop it into a server for a specific application. Step one is choosing the right application server. You can and should consider the usual server issues (cost, stability, platform, and so on). Beyond that, noodle on whether the Microsoft solution or the Sun solution will be best for you.

What Microsoft and Sun offer

The Microsoft solution is based on Microsoft technologies and is sold as Site Server and Site Server Commerce Edition. The usual advantages of Microsoft solutions apply — the interface is easier, the tools are familiar, and Microsoft technologies all work together nicely.

The Sun solution bases application servers on Java. (Sun invented Java.) Sun doesn't actually sell the applications servers; other companies (BEA, IBM, iPlanet, and others) do. The main advantage here is that Java is cross-platform and anything created with or for Java runs under Windows 2000 Server, NT Server, UNIX, or Linux. Because of this, it's possible to migrate from one operating system to another should you decide later to do so. Developing applications for the Sun-type application servers is familiar to Java programmers.

Other, more accessible options

Both the Microsoft solution and the Sun solution require skilled programmers to develop applications and integrate them into the Web site. They're both geared toward big, busy sites with complex applications. However, some less challenging solutions exist for sites that have respectable traffic and less complex systems. Many such sites are built using Allaire Cold Fusion, which offers the advantage that everyday people sans programming degrees can easily develop the skills needed to write programs with it. Cold Fusion is cross-platform and is much less expensive to implement and use than either the Microsoft solution or the Sun solution.

Zope is an open-source Web application server that has particular strengths in storing content in a database and turning the stuff in the database into Web pages when needed. Many developers like working with Zope because it is open source, which means that you can access the actual programming code that makes up the system (something you can't do with most other application servers). This allows you to modify and extend Zope to meet new challenges. Technical support comes in the form of a large and enthusiastic online community of open-source software devotees and free advisors.

All the Best Web-Server Software

Plenty of server software exists to turn a computer into a Web server, but they aren't all gem-like wonders. Here we concentrate on the more popular and robust packages. You will most likely use one of these to run your Web server.

You can find out all about recent versions of popular Web servers, along with information about other add-ins and tools you can use to maintain your site, from Server Watch at www.serverwatch.com. A feature-by-feature comparison of Web-server software is available at webcompare.iworld.com. Through Netcraft (www.netcraft.com/), you can find out what server software any site on the Internet is running as well as which server is most popular at the moment.

Microsoft's Web-server software

Microsoft is, naturally enough, in the server software game. Its entry is Microsoft Internet Information Server (IIS for short). IIS is included with (and only available with) Windows 2000 Server or NT Server. You cannot run IIS under any flavor of UNIX or Linux.

Because IIS runs under Windows 2000 Server or NT Server, when you use it, you get all the usual Microsoft advantages (interface, easy integration with other Microsoft products, you know the drill). On the downside, IIS can be a royal pain to administer remotely. You say you need to reboot your NT machine so those changes that you made to the server can take effect? Great. Hike over to where the machine is located and do it. You say it's 1 a.m., and the company hosting the machine is closed for the night? Tough luck, compadre.

IIS integrates nicely with other Microsoft products, including BackOffice, for example. (BackOffice is a whole suite of server products.) It can use the same security features that are found in Windows to secure transactions on the Web, so you're set there. In addition, you can easily create Web applications that use BackOffice servers such as the highly popular SQL Server, Microsoft's database server, along with IIS.

Apache Web-server software

According to Netcraft's Web-server survey, Apache is the most widely used Web server in the commercial world. More dot-com Web sites use Apache than any other server. Apache has gained this status despite — or maybe because of — its freely available and unmarketed nature. Like Linux, Apache was developed by a large group of volunteers who were mainly interested in making it good.

Apache is primarily a UNIX-based server. (Although it's also available in Windows 2000 Server, NT Server, and even OS2 versions, the vast majority of sites that run Apache run UNIX/Linux as their operating systems.) You can find downloadable versions of Apache as well as extensive documentation at www.apache.org.

Unlike Microsoft's server, Apache does not include any graphical utilities to help you set it up. You have to edit the Apache configuration files with a text editor, and you need to be a UNIX/Linux head to get this done. One more yummy aspect of Apache is that you can use all that good UNIX/Linux stuff with Apache. Much of that stuff is free, but again, if you aren't UNIX/Linux-adept, it may be challenging.

iPlanet's Web-server software

iPlanet is a joint venture between two of the biggest names in Web software — Sun (the folks who invented Java) and Netscape. iPlanet offers two Web server products: You can find out about iPlanet's servers and other developer products at the iPlanet Developer site (developer.iplanet.com).

- ✔ **FastTrack Edition** is iPlanet's entry-level Web-server software. It includes all the necessary features for a basic Web site. It can serve up HTML pages and execute server-side scripts just fine, thank you. With FastTrack, you can administer the entire server right from a Web browser. iPlanet offers versions of FastTrack server for Windows 2000 Server, NT Server, and many versions of UNIX/Linux. All of these versions of FastTrack have the same features, behave similarly, and look practically identical.

- ✔ **Enterprise Edition** offers all the features of FastTrack, with many added features in the areas of increased reliability, scalability, and security. Enterprise can also integrate with iPlanet's application server for serving more complex Web-based applications. Enterprise is one of the most often used servers for high-profile, big traffic Web sites. If you plan to support many millions of page views, offer secure transactions, or serve complicated Web-based applications on your site, consider Enterprise server. Many folks have experience administering it, and it's very robust.

Running Your Server Yourself

Now that you know about your options in choosing a server, you ought to think about who is going to run the thing and where it will be located. The answers are not automatically you and in your own cramped cubicle. Basically, the server can be housed at your location — that is, attached to your corporate network, which is in turn attached to the Internet — or it can be located at an ISP or hosting company.

 If your server is located at an ISP or hosting company, your site may be housed on one of that facility's servers — in which case yours may be one of hundreds hosted on that same machine. (This is known as a *shared server* scenario.) Or your site can be on your machine (or a leased one) at a hosting company's locale. (Depending on the level of service you have, this scenario may be called *co-location* — colo for short — or managed services.) Chapter 12 talks about the ins and outs of having an ISP or hosting company house your site. As in most matters, there are pros and cons — enough so that we gave it its own chapter. Here we talk more about the ins and outs of hosting your site yourself. If you do plan to go the hosting facility route, read on in this chapter anyway to get a small mountain of information that can help you in talking to your vendor about your server.

To some people, the very nature of being a Webmaster is one and the same as running a Web server. Some folks think that a Webmaster is primarily a server administrator. (We don't think that way, but if you do, turn to Chapter 1 for more on all that a Webmaster is and does.) Running your own server does, however, offer some distinct advantages over entrusting it to the care and handling of a hosting company. On the other hand, it can be a bit of a pain. We'll start with the upside.

Why bother?

The first question to ask yourself in assessing whether to run your own server is *why bother?* With so many companies now offering hosting services, the need to run your own server may seem less compelling now than in years gone by, when you basically had to maintain your own Web server to have a site at all.

Your own server = total control

Running your own server in-house gives you total control over the machine. You, the Webmaster, can decide what software is used, when the machine needs to be upgraded, and when a second server is required. (Okay, so you may still experience budgetary constraints, but that's life.) Some hosting companies allow you to run only server-side scripts that they have approved, whereas others don't let you run any server-side scripts at all (for fear of security holes and a drag on server performance). When you own the machine, you don't have to worry about these restrictions.

Running your own Web server also means that you can install additional servers as you need them. Many of the more technologically compelling forms of content — streaming media, real-time chats, and so on — require special server software. If you're using a hosting company to house your site, you may have to persuade or even bug the provider to install the additional servers you need. It's hard to find a hosting company that offers such a broad and inclusive mix of servers that everyone who wants something special is pleased. When you're running your site from your own server, you can install additional, specialized servers as you need them.

Your own server = responsibility

But (and this is a big but) having full control of the machine also makes you fully responsible for it. You, not the hosting company, have to keep the machine and the Internet connection running all the time — 24 hours a day, 7 days a week — come fire, flood, or pestilence. You are the one who has to get up at 3 a.m. when the boss (who is in London, where it's a decent hour) notices that the site has gone down and calls, and you must figure out what to do about the problem. (Turn to the section "Keeping Your Server Running 24/7," later in this chapter, for clues.)

The hardware you need

You can run a Web server on any of several hardware choices. We have seen Web servers running on computers ranging from Pentium-based PCs that cost about $1,000 to Sun Enterprise servers that cost upwards of $1 million. Of course, the $1,000 PC can handle only miniscule traffic compared to the $1 million server, yet nearly everyone would rather use the $1,000 PC if it could do the job. So on what basis can you decide where you fall in the continuum? The big determining factors are

 ✔ **The type of content that comprises your site.** If your site is almost exclusively comprised of static HTML files, you can get away with a less powerful machine. If you'll be running lots of server-side scripts that take up processing time on the Web server, however, you need more juice. Connecting databases and fulfillment systems, or running cool stuff like streaming media, ups the ante even more.

 ✔ **Whether you plan to run additional servers — say a database server or a media server.** You can run a Web server and a database server on the same machine if it has a powerful processor or more than one processor. The machine needs plenty of memory for multiple servers, too. You may even need multiple machines for this scheme — and the more traffic you anticipate, the more machines you need.

✔ **The amount of traffic you expect.** The more people you expect to visit your site, the more pages you'll need to serve and, in turn, the more powerful machine you'll need. Every simultaneous user takes up memory on the machine. A simple PC can handle a few visitors at a time, but for a commercial site that may have even just hundreds of users simultaneously, you need more memory, and for thousands, you need multiple machines.

✔ **To what extent you can live with your site being down.** A cheap desktop machine doesn't have much in the way of *redundancy* (intentional repetition of systems so they can act as insurance against each other's failures). If something breaks the machine stops working. More expensive servers include redundant systems so they can continue running like nothing has happened even when a hard disk or power supply fails.

Bear in mind that you get more bang for the buck (or for the CPU) using computers running UNIX/Linux than computers running Windows 2000 Server or NT Server. In other words, the same server machine running UNIX/Linux can handle more hits than it could if it were running under Windows 2000 Server or NT Server.

Also, don't skimp on hard disk requirements. Two types of hard disks are commonly used today: IDE and SCSI. IDE is cheaper, and SCSI is more robust. Most desktop machines come with IDE drives. IDE drives are fine for desktop PCs, but they slow to a crawl under the burden of a server's load. Get a SCSI drive, even if you use the stodgy $1,000 PC option. The extra cost of the SCSI drive is well worth it in increased speed and reliability.

Finally, the same software-is-a-memory-hog rule applies here as well as on your desktop PC. Get memory — lots of it. No matter what hardware you choose, load your machine with all the memory it can handle. More traffic is a heavier load, and more scripts represent a heavier load. Heavy loads are a burden that slows delivery of Web pages. You don't want your pages to appear when they get around to it — you lose traffic that way.

All about administration

Running a Web server is not a matter of setting up the machine and heading for Hawaii while the thing hums nicely along. Keeping a Web server up and running all the time takes a unique set of system administration and networking skills. To keep your server running, you must have someone on board who can keep the Internet connection going all the time — someone who knows about TCP/IP networking and more specifically about the type of leased line you have connecting to the Internet. (TCP/IP, by the way, is the networking scheme that holds the Internet together.)

This person can monitor your connection to the Internet and can get on your ISP or hosting company's case if and when the connection goes down. (You need an ISP or hosting company even if you run your own server — right?) This person may also have to coordinate visits from the phone company to maintain the leased line. The administrator can also review the system's log files (see Chapter 17), looking for anything out of the norm and keeping an eye on disk usage and security.

These matters need vigilant attention — don't relegate them to an over-worked techie whose first priority is fixing the CEO's computer. (Most system administrators opt for the CEO's computer if forced by time constraints to choose.) To keep your server in top, reliable condition, you need to attend to its maintenance as if it were a fine car. Get a knowledgeable, diligent administrator with both system and network administration skills.

Connecting to the Internet

Running a Web server is not like hooking up your desktop PC to the Internet. When you run a Web server, many people (you hope) will be accessing the machine at once. You need a *permanent* (that means a 24-hour-a-day, 7-day-a-week) connection to the Internet that can handle some traffic. And even if you run your own server in-house, you need some kind of ISP account, so you need a good ISP and a good relationship with that provider. *Connectivity* (how you're connected) is crucial to your Web site operation.

Your ISP can help you determine the best option for connecting your corporate LAN to the Internet. Whatever technology you wind up using, it's important that your ISP is already familiar with that option. You don't want to be its first customer using a new technology that your ISP is just getting the hang of. Tackling the question of what type of connection you need means considering bandwidth and speed and how to cope with your firewall, if you have one.

Bandwidth and more bandwidth

Different types of connections afford you more or less bandwidth. You want as much bandwidth as you can afford. (This is kind of like memory in that way.) *Bandwidth* is a measure of the amount of data that can travel over your connection to the Internet. Bandwidth is usually measured in *kilobits* (1,024 bits) per second or *megabits* (1,024 kilobits, or 1,048,576 bits) per second. The abbreviation for these measurements are *Kbps* (kilobits per second) and *Mbps* (megabits per second).

Bandwidth usage usually comes in bursts — it isn't spread out neatly around the clock. It's common knowledge that most folks use the Net during lunchtime, so there's a big surge in bandwidth at that time, for example, and the surge travels westward just as time zones do.

All about bits and kilobits

It may surprise you that 2 Kbps is not 2,000 bps. That's because 1K (one kilo) is actually 1,024 bps — 2K then, is 2048 bps. Likewise, 1M (mega) equals 1,024K, and 1G (giga) equals 1,024M.

Going backward, 1G = 1,024M = 1,024 x 1,024K = 1,024 x 1,024 x 1,024, which equals 1,073,741,824. In other words, 1,024 Kbps equals 1,048,576 bits. (Did you really want to know all that?)

Most options for getting bandwidth are based on using telephone technology, with the notable exception of cable modems. Check with local ISPs and cable companies to see what's available in your area.

Yes, you really need a T1 line (or better)

The first question you may have is: What is a T1? A *T1* (also called a DS1) is just a big phone line (big in the sense of having large capacity). If your company has a PBX and multiple phone lines, it probably already leases one or more T1s from the local phone company simply to handle telephone calls. This same phone line technology (that is, a T1 line) is used to make a dedicated connection between your corporate LAN and the Internet, although you don't want to use the same T1 your company's phone system is using for your Internet connection. You need a dedicated line.

Other connections that are slower or faster are available. For more bandwidth and faster serving of your site to its users, get the fastest connections and consider getting more than one dedicated line, too. Table 11-1 shows various types of connections that are available and the amount of bandwidth each of them offers. Note the following points as well.

What do you connect to?

If you keep your server in-house, you need a dedicated Internet connection. So what exactly does your dedicated Internet connection connect to? Well, it usually connects you to your ISP's network. Your ISP's network, in turn, uses dedicated lines to connect to one or more of the Internet's backbones.

In interviewing potential ISPs (see Chapter 12), check what type of bandwidth they have and how many other customers are using that bandwidth. The ISP should have more bandwidth than

it's using. In a perfect world, there would be more bandwidth between the ISP and the Internet than there is between all the ISP's customers and the ISP. (If you find an ISP like this, please . . . let us know. They're rarer than honest politicians.) You can use the ratio of the ISP's bandwidth to all the ISP's customers' bandwidths to compare one ISP to another. Choose the one with the lowest ratio. Chapter 12 offers insight into dealing with ISPs as well as hosting companies.

Table 11-1	Connection Types	
These Connections	*Offer This Much Bandwidth*	*Suitable for Hosting a Site?*
Frame relay	56 Kbps–1.5 Mbps	Yes, but only at higher speeds
ISDN	56 Kbps–128 Kbps	Yes, if traffic is low
DSL	328 Kbps–1.5 Mbps	Maybe, depending on how ISP configures the connection
T1 (a.k.a. DS1)	1.54 Mbps	Yes
T3 (a.k.a. DS3)	45 Mbps	Yes
Cable modem	10 Mbps	No, because Internet protocol for cable is not tweaked for publishing information

✔ **Frame relay** was a commonly used technology some years ago but is fading rapidly. It's slow and expensive, yet some companies have it in place and have not yet given it up.

✔ **ISDN** is really only an option for running your own server if you expect very low traffic, say in the dozens of users. It's often not economically feasible to keep an ISDN line running 24/7. This is because usage on an ISDN line is metered. (You pay for what you use, and you'll probably use a lot.) For a company Web site, ISDN is really not practical.

✔ **DSL** is also usually not a good option for running a Web server because most DSL connections are *asymmetrical*. This means the speed that data goes from your ISP to your computer is much faster than the speed that data goes from your computer back to your ISP. This setup is great for how most people use the Internet — they browse the Web. But, it's not great for serving Web sites. When you serve a Web site, you're sending a lot of data back to your ISP — which is the slow direction with DSL.

✔ **T1** is the most commonly used dedicated connection. Although the T1 is leased from a phone company, your ISP can often handle the details of ordering it and scheduling its installation. When the T1 is installed, it is routed directly to your ISP instead of through the phone company's central office. The entire capacity of the T1 is used to handle Internet data. You ought to have at least a T1 (or some faster connection) if you're going to host your own Web server.

✔ **T3** (also known as a DS3) is a bunch of T1s bundled together. A T3 can be used for telephone traffic or for connecting your corporate LAN to the Internet. A T3 gets you gobs more bandwidth than a T1 — perhaps 40 times as much. Some big sites use multiple T1s when they need more capacity than a single T1 but less capacity than a T3 provides. Use of T3s is actually pretty rare; usually only the biggest Internet software companies and huge ISPs or hosting companies use T3s. In some cases, you can lease part of a T3.

✔ **Cable modem** connections aren't appropriate for hosting your Web site. Although a cable modem connection can be as fast as a T1, the bandwidth it offers is not divided evenly between data going into your computer and that going out of it. Basically, a cable modem gets you lots of bandwidth to browse and only a little bandwidth to publish.

Getting around the firewall

A *firewall*, generally speaking, a combination of hardware and software that's designed to isolate your corporate network from the Internet. If you're setting up your Web server on a network that exists behind a firewall (and if your corporate network is connected to the Internet, it *should* have a firewall), you have to do some special configuring to make everything work. The basic challenge is deciding where to locate the Web server — inside or outside the firewall.

Many companies have security committees. These good people are responsible for network security. If your company has such a group, you may have to get the group's approval for the way that your Web site is set up. This is especially true if your site will interface your existing in-house corporate systems or if your server must house confidential information. Remember that it's this august group's job to keep the company's data and resources safe. It is not the group's job to keep your Web site jumping with cutting-edge technologies. They are likely to be conservative in their judgments, and rightfully so, given their mission.

Looking into firewalls

The point of a firewall is to allow people on the corporate network to access the Internet (perhaps with restrictions as to who can do so or what they can access) but, at the same time, not allow people on the public Internet to access resources on your corporate LAN. Basically, a firewall acts as a gateway through which all your Internet traffic must flow. The firewall's job is to allow and disallow traffic on a case-by-case basis, obeying rules that are set up by the network administrator.

Firewalls work well in limiting access from the Internet to your corporate LAN. They do not always work well when you want to run a Web server, want everyone in the world to be able to access the server, and want people on your corporate LAN to access the Web server, too. If, on top of all that, you also want your Web server to be able to execute queries against databases that are behind the firewall, things get very interesting. And given that those are all perfectly standard things to want if you're running a Web site, the firewall is likely to be the subject of much of your attention.

A firewall can exist at some point or another in the configuration of your network. Everything on your network that's directly connected to the Internet is said to be outside of the firewall, even if it's in the building, whereas everything that has to go through the firewall to get to the Net is considered to be inside the firewall. A firewall treats any computer outside of it as an unknown (and therefore suspect) machine. Figure 11-2 shows a typical firewall setup.

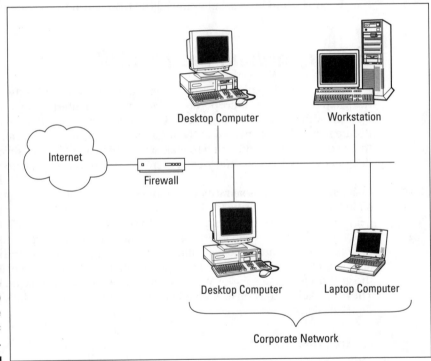

Figure 11-2:
The firewall marks the line between the corporate LAN (inside the firewall) and the public Internet.

Where you place your Web server is among the bigger choices you must make (unless your network administrator or security administrator makes the choice for you). Technically, you can place your Web server inside or outside the firewall. Each choice has its pros and cons, as with most things in life.

The work of configuring the firewall usually falls to the network administrator. We hope to give you enough information here so that you can talk to that person about your options and work together to place your Web server in the best location for your particular network and Web site requirements.

Placing the Web server outside the firewall

Putting the Web server outside the firewall is at first blush the easiest and most secure way to go. This option makes it easy for folks outside the firewall to access your site, but it's harder for those within the firewall to gain access. To get around this, the network administrator must set up the firewall to allow people within it to access the Web server. Be forewarned, though, that doing this can introduce a problem if people on the local network are not usually allowed to access material on the public Internet. Likewise, if your Web server needs to access resources inside the firewall — say a database server, for example — the firewall must be configured to allow this access. You may have to negotiate with your network administrator to get the access you need.

Outside the firewall, you can place not only the Web server but also any other servers your site may require — say, a database server. You can even replicate data between a database server inside the firewall and one outside the firewall. These options introduce many security concerns, however, which your network administrator has to address.

Placing the Web server inside the firewall

If you place the Web server inside the firewall, your network administrator must configure the firewall to allow people on the Internet to access the machine; otherwise, you'll have a Web server that only people on your corporate network can access. (Hmmm, isn't that an *intranet?*) Most network administrators frown upon putting the Web server inside the firewall, because this means that they have to open a hole in the firewall to allow outsiders to access the Web server. The more holes that you put in your firewall, the more it resembles the Jarlsberg cheese of security.

Placing the Web server in the DMZ

You can have it both ways — maybe not always, but about this topic. Figure 11-3 shows a setup consisting of two firewalls, which create an area know as a DMZ. The advantage of this configuration is that users on both the corporate LAN and the public Internet can access the Web server. The network administrator does not have to compromise the security of the firewall, either by letting people on the public Internet access the corporate network or by letting people on the corporate network access the public Internet. This configuration keeps the security committee happier and more cooperative, too. It also makes it possible to give the Web server extra access to the corporate network while still preventing this access from the Internet itself. This type of configuration is very common on corporate networks.

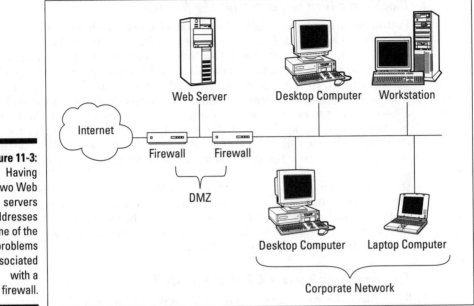

Figure 11-3:
Having
two Web
servers
addresses
some of the
problems
associated
with a
firewall.

Keeping Your Server Running 24/7

Running your own server means keeping it running 24 hours a day and 7 days a week. Someone must be available at all hours to fix the server if something goes wrong. Weekends, holidays, you name it — someone has to be responsible. Servers don't take vacations. However, this is not as daunting as it seems. Paying attention to the server during your working hours goes a long way toward your confidence that the server can run smoothly after hours.

Backup hardware also helps. Have a second machine ready to take over the duties of your Web server at a moment's notice, and you can quickly get your site back up when a hard disk crashes or another major hardware problem occurs. Just remember that your backup machine must have on it the same, current files (content, scripts, and so on) as the original machine. Ideally, the two machines will have identical systems and content on them. This means posting the same files to both machines, which is labor intensive and opens the door to human error unless you use software to sync things up.

Computers — like children and puppies — don't consider your schedule or convenience when they act up, and you need someone on call to reboot and fix things 24/7. But that person needn't sit by the machine around the clock — the server may never crash.

We once ran a Web server that hummed along 24/7 for nine months with no crashes. Routine maintenance for this machine consisted of about 15 minutes every weekday reviewing log files, and then random remote checking of the machine on occasional nights and weekends. When the server finally went down, it was because of a countywide power failure. (The server, by the way, was running on Linux.)

Even a power failure can be sidestepped with adequate investment of resources. Quite commonly, ISPs hosting companies use a UPS (uninterruptible power supply) to fend off the effects of a power failure. Some also often have diesel generators on hand. And direct multiple connections to various Internet backbones are de rigueur. All this is meant to ensure that the Web sites and servers hosted by the ISPs and hosting companies continue to run uninterrupted even in the event of a long-term power failure.

A good compromise measure that can get you both the benefits of running your own server and some nice 24/7 support is to co-locate your server at a hosting company. In this scheme, you usually lease or buy a server machine and place it at your hosting company's facility. It plugs into the hosting company's network and backbones — giving it full access to all the hosting company's bandwidth. Then, because the hosting company usually has a system administrator on site 24/7 to do emergency maintenance, you're covered. Chapter 12 (that's the next one) covers dealing with hosting companies.

Chapter 12

Dealing with ISPs and Hosting Companies

Choosing the company that serves your data to the world is a crucial decision. You want users to be able to access your site on the first try — if this doesn't happen, they may never try again. You also want to relax, right? You don't want to worry. You want your site humming happily along 24/7 and 365 days a year. The level of connectivity and service you get from your ISP or hosting company will have a deep impact on whether or not you get your wish. *Hosting* is, quite simply, providing some combination of the hardware, server software, connection, and services necessary to serve your site to the public. Your Web server is likely to be hosted at an ISP or hosting company; if you have other servers (see Chapter 11), they may be as well.

You're probably familiar with ISPs (Internet service providers). An ISP focuses on providing people and companies with access to the Internet. Web site hosting is one service ISPs offer; e-mail may be another. Some specialized hosting companies, on the other hand, offer much higher levels of support and security to their clients. These higher-end hosting companies are often geared only toward hosting large-scale sites. They seldom or never offer e-mail services, for example. Either an ISP or a specialized, high-end hosting company can be referred to generally as a hosting company.

The hosting company you select should be flexible, competent, and trustworthy. *Comparison shopping is essential* when choosing a hosting company. This chapter focuses on how to choose the right company to host your site. (For information on types of Internet connections and how you can run your own in-house server, turn to Chapter 11.)

The Typical Services Offered

Although the services offered by hosting companies vary as much as the companies themselves, most offer a range of basic features and services. Each has a data center (or multiple data centers) which is a facility for housing servers. The data center may be as tightly secure as a fortress, or more lax. The best data centers are those with the closest connections to the Internet's backbones. The very best have multiple connections. A good hosting company's data center also offers

- ✔ Leasing of a server or server space along with other hardware required to get your site up and running

- ✔ Reliable electricity for the server, including diesel generators to keep things going if and when the lights go out

- ✔ Physical security (sometimes even armed guards!) to keep your competitors from poking around on your server

- ✔ Automatic monitoring of both the hosting company's network and your servers to ensure that they are available 24/7

- ✔ Network and server monitoring 24/7 via a Network Operations Center (NOC) that can handle telephone calls from you

Some hosting companies also offer consulting services. Of course it's always handy to have professional advisors to help you get your server optimally configured.

Note that the ISP through whom your company has its general Internet access is not always the same company as your hosting company. The criteria used for selecting a general purpose ISP differ from those used for selecting a hosting company. The major difference is that when you select an all-purpose ISP, you look primarily at how top-notch the connections to the Internet are; when you select a hosting company, you also look at the data center and security levels. And, you look for much higher levels of support.

Your Level-of-Service Options

As we mentioned, hosting companies come in a variety of shapes and forms. Hosting options, however, basically boil down to these classes or levels of service:

- ✔ **Shared server:** Leasing space on a server that also acts as the server for sites operated by other people or companies. Generally, the hosting company handles server administration, but only based on the necessity of simply keeping the server going for the dozens or perhaps hundreds of clients sharing the server. They don't do custom work on the server for individual clients. They may limit server-side scripts running on your site, they won't install special software (such as a streaming media server) for you, and they don't offer a lot of round-the clock technical support. Shared server scenarios do have the advantages of being inexpensive and quick to set up. However, shared server situations are not the best option for bigger commercial Web sites.

✔ **Server co-location:** Leasing space in a data center and storing your server there. Your server in this case may be owned or leased, but it is not shared with others. Usually, the hosting company does not manage or administer the server itself. That's up to you. The hosting company does maintain the connectivity to the Internet. Generally, this connectivity will be faster and more reliable than shared server connectivity. It also runs a secure data center, with trained personnel to monitor service day and night as well as backup generators to provide electricity in a power failure, for example.

✔ **Managed services:** Leasing both a server and the space in a data center to store it from the hosting company; in this case, the hosting company also manages and administers the server, and provides pretty much a full-service package of connectivity, hardware, software, and service. In addition to the level of services offered by a server co-location outfit, the managed services company usually offers a guarantee that your site will be up and running all the time no matter what (except for specified maintenance periods). Managed service companies also often provide dedicated security teams who protect clients' servers from both known and potential threats of breaches, holes, or break-ins.

It's also quite possible to maintain your own server in-house with a direct connection; this nets you both full control of the server and full responsibility for it. We talk about issues related to do-it-yourself hosting in Chapter 11. The following sections discuss these four options in greater detail.

Introducing application service providers

Application service providers (ASPs) are specialty companies that provide particular services for Web sites. For example, some ASPs concentrate on providing transaction systems, some offer Web-based e-mail, or calendaring, or those nifty little electronic postcards people e-mail around to each other. Just about any *application* (software or system that solves a specific problem or does a specific task) can be offered by one ASP or another. As part of their services, these companies provide the application; they also host the application server and they help you integrate the application into your Web site systems.

Questions to Ask an ISP or Hosting Company

Consider what you want from a hosting company, and then choose a hosting company that offers those features. Choosing a hosting company based on price alone is not your best bet, because many hosting companies offer radically different services and features. What's more, changing hosting companies later is a hassle that you want to avoid. What to look for? Well, you need to find a company that responds to questions quickly, that's easy to work with, that can help you make decisions confidently, and that offers specifically what you need. Ask for customer testimonials (and corresponding e-mail and Web addresses). Ask your friends or business contacts in the trade who they recommend and (perhaps more importantly) who to steer clear of.

The following list contains questions you ought to ask of any potential hosting company. Use the answers to these questions to compare hosting company candidates. Note that your priorities and your budget will affect the weight of each question when you're making your decision. Start by asking how much bandwidth you'll get at what price, and then consider these additional points:

✔ **How reliable is the service?** You want your site up and running, so you want your hosting company up and running. How much downtime per week (in hours) does it suffer, and how will that affect your business? How will they notify you of downtime? Does the hosting company provide server backup of systems and files and, if so, how often? Does the company have back-up generators so it can keep operating during power outages, floods, fires, famines, riots, and pestilence? Does it have strong customer service? Does it return phone calls and e-mail quickly (say, within 30 minutes) and follow up on the tough questions? And finally, is the company willing to sign a service level agreement (SLA) that outlines its obligations in all these areas?

✔ **If you're using a shared server, how much disk space on the server do you get for the site?** The amount of disk space your site needs depends on the kind of site you're running. If you plan to include large files, such as movies or downloadable software products, you need a lot more space. And if you have plans for expansion (who doesn't?) you need to know what it will cost in the future to get more space. Don't forget, too, that the space needed for databases and large e-mail archives may fluctuate as the databases or archives grow. Payment for that space is often figured differently from that for HTML documents; discuss these issues with the hosting company before you sign on.

✔ **What type of access do you need for maintenance?** Some Webmasters need a lot of access to a machine to maintain a site, whereas others can manage their sites just fine using routine FTP operations. You need to be sure that your hosting company provides the type of access to the machine that you require.

✔ **Do you need a Windows 2000 Server, NT Server, or UNIX-based system?** You may have a site that requires some technology that is available only under one of these operating systems. Be sure that your hosting company supports the operating system you require.

✔ **Do you need the capability to install and execute server-side scripts?** Server-side scripts can enable a lot of interactivity, randomization, redirection of traffic from page to page, and other nifty site features. If you think you'll need to run server-side scripts, make sure that you choose a company that offers you this option. You should also be sure that the company supports the particular technology you intend to use for your scripts.

✔ **Do you want prepackaged Web site service?** Some hosting companies offer their customers preprogrammed Web site functions such as forms processing, site-specific search engines, chat capability, and transaction systems. Some companies go as far as to offer templates that you can use to design extremely simple Web pages. Make sure that these tools (or toys) are up to snuff. And find out how customizable they are before you get too excited about them.

✔ **Does the company provide a 24/7 Network Operations Center (NOC)?** Your hosting company should have a Network Operations Center (NOC) that is staffed 24/7. It is from the NOC that hosting companies monitor their network and ensure that your site is always accessible to your visitors. Hosting companies should also provide you with a way to contact the NOC at any time to report trouble with your site or to get updates on problems.

✔ **Do you plan to run a high-traffic Web site?** Although everyone wants his site to be popular, you must acknowledge the minimum and maximum goals for the size of your audience when you're considering a hosting service. Running a site that has mass appeal for a specific niche of people (like gardeners or ex-Marines) is quite different than creating the next Yahoo! competitor. Talk to your hosting company about how many clients it has and how much Web traffic it handles each month. Also, many hosting companies charge partly on the amount of traffic to your site. Find out how your cost increases as your site gets more popular.

✔ **Are you using the site to sell a product? Do you need to provide secure transactions?** If you're relying on your hosting company to provide a transaction system, you should be sure it takes the security of your data seriously. Protecting things such as customer records and credit card numbers can make or break your company if you sell online. (See Chapter 14 for more on security and selling online.)

✔ **Are you going to have a database or any special applications as part of your site?** Can the hosting company support the specific database you need? Is the company's staff already familiar with working with it? (You don't want to pay for the learning curve.)

✔ **Do you need multiple domain names?** Registering a domain name should be relatively painless. But having your hosting company set things up to handle multiple domain names may be tricky. Some hosting companies require you to open separate accounts for each domain name you want to host and may not be able to redirect one domain name to another (for example, redirecting `www.mycomapnyinc.com` to `www.mycompany.com`).

✔ **Are you counting on using your hosting company for consulting as well as hosting?** Some hosting companies offer routing consulting on networking, administration, server-side programming, HTML, and other aspects of a site. Others simply do not, and they ignore all requests to that end. Make sure that you establish your hosting company's position at the beginning of your relationship to avoid any misunderstandings. Often if the hosting company doesn't do consulting work itself, it can recommend one of its own clients who does.

✔ **Do you have any use for additional offerings?** These bonus features or extra packages can include things such as Web page design, Internet marketing support, business-partner connections, custom advertising servers, catalog servers, or database packages. Look at the descriptions of what the hosting company offers, and decide if anything looks essential.

In general, it's best to choose a hosting company with a solid background and reputation. Occasionally, investing in the new kid on the block can be a great move and the best inroad to innovation, but unless your gut says otherwise in a resounding voice, go with a more established or a widely recommended provider.

The Webmaster's role in setting up a network

Although setting up an entire office network system is not usually within the scope of a Webmaster's duties, you need to make sure that you're in on the decision-making process about the company's network works in conjunction with the Web site's servers. If you are not the company's network systems administrator *(sysadmin),* make sure that you befriend this person and agree to keep each other informed on decisions involving the Web site's connection to the world.

Decisions such as where the servers will be located (on-site or at the hosting company), how much server space and bandwidth will be reserved for the Web site, and who has password access to the servers can certainly affect the Webmaster's daily routine. Be sure to use the checklist in "Questions to Ask an ISP or Hosting Company" section in this chapter when discussing server and network options with your sysadmin or with a network consultant.

Internet bandwidth: The condensed version

You've probably heard the much-told fable of how the Department of Defense first set up the Internet 30-odd years ago as a communications platform able to survive a nuclear attack. Today's Internet isn't a military project (nor is it a centralized, government-run network), but the principle is the same now as it was then: Each piece of data that's sent over the Net must be able to get from point A, the origin, to point Z, the destination, without relying on another network station in between. Each piece of data, divided into packets, finds the most expedient way to reach its terminal. If a few packets get into a traffic jam outside of Chicago and the rest of the packets divert themselves south to Chapel Hill, they all get reassembled and delivered as a whole, wherever they're supposed to wind up.

To make the best use of the existing Internet, the fewest possible number of "hops" should occur along the way. Each time data is routed through a computer, that's a hop. It's kind of like riding the bus: The more transfers you make from bus to bus, the longer it takes you to get there. Additionally, you get across the country faster in a 747 than in an old Escort, so the quality of the machinery involved, both computers and cables, contributes to the speed of the transfer.

The original Internet had a single *backbone,* but now there are many backbones — thick pipes of telephone cable bundled together — that all other networks on the Net are connected to. The original groundwork laid out 30 years ago is still there, although other backbones have been built since then by telecommunications companies and high-end Internet service companies. The closer an ISP or hosting company is to a major backbone, the faster its transfer rate is. Additionally, a good ISP or hosting company is connected to more than one backbone and is connected to backbones operated by different carriers, so if, for example, AT&T's service fritzes out at a central location, MCI WorldCom's lines can pick up the slack.

Ask your prospective hosting company which carriers it uses, how close it is to major backbones (also called *pipelines*), and what its contingency plan is in case of connectivity outages from the major carrier. Ideally, you want to choose a hosting company that has multiple T1 or T3 lines that are linked to different major carriers.

 You can find out a lot about thousands of hosting companies by searching The List of Internet Service Providers, also known as The List at thelist.iworld. com. You can also check Yahoo! (www.yahoo.com), and CNET has a section about Web hosting (webisplist.internetlist.com/html/aisles/Web_Hosting. asp) that offers information about hosting options and services.

How Hosting Service Costs Compare

Prices for hosting are as varied as the companies that offer them. You may get access to a shared server for a small, simple site as part of your $20-per-month Internet dial-up account, or you can pay thousands of dollars per month to host your large commercial site at a managed services company.

The contingency plan

Storms, earthquakes, fires, a guy tripping over the power cord, telecommunications outages, tornadoes, rains of frogs, and other emergencies are hard to prevent. When they do happen, what's Plan B? The more prepared a hosting company is to cover your Web site in such an emergency, the more that service may cost. At the very least, your hosting company should back up all data at least once a day. (Find out what backup files they'll actually restore. Will they restore a specific file at your request or will they only restore all of the files after a problem has occurred?) Backup generators, multiple backbone access through different carriers, and multiple site storage for backup servers can help transcend physical breakdowns of electrical and telecommunication equipment, and those features become more important to you as your site grows. Some companies go beyond that, providing multiple backup generators and storage facilities that are nuke-proof. However, you pay a pretty penny for goods like these, so make sure a little downtime really is going to be a crisis before you shell out huge sums of money.

Long-distance hosting

You needn't limit your search for a hosting company to your particular locale — your site is just as available if it is served out of California, Illinois, or New York. If you don't need physical access to your server (which you would need in a co-location scenario) and you can conduct remote administration (in other words, if you're using server software that allows remote access), you can maintain your site remotely wherever it is. You can then consider companies in other cities when you compare pricing. The one caveat to selecting non-local servers is the international question. If you are targeting a specific country, place your servers at a hosting company in that country. If you are targeting multiple countries, then (because most countries have good connectivity to the United States) a U.S.-based hosting company is your best bet.

Leasing a server

When you create a site that offers enough data and experiences enough traffic to warrant living on its own server, you may want to lease that server instead of buying one. Leasing has the financial advantage of spreading costs over time rather than requiring a lump outlay up front. Also, because hardware becomes obsolete all too quickly, leasing allows you to pay for the hardware only while you're using it; you can then fit your hardware budget into a planned upgrade cycle. Sometimes you can lease a server through a hosting company that you're co-locating with or through a managed services company; otherwise, you may be able to lease a server through a reseller or computer rental company. Server leasing may be a big part of your hosting bill — often accounting for over half of all charges.

Getting quotes and haggling

Depending on the hosting company's level of service and the complexity of your hosting requirements, you may or may not find specific pricing information posted on the Web sites of the hosting companies you're considering. Contact hosting company candidates directly to get a price quote. Generally, any prices quoted immediately are for the most popular packages the company offers. You may have specific needs that differ from those packages. That's fine, just spec out what you need, tell the hosting company's rep, and get a quote.

Be ready for a period of give-and-take as your potential hosting company starts to understand what you're trying to do and what you want. During this process, brace yourself for haggling. You can negotiate no matter what your needs are, but if you are going to be a higher-end client with more complex needs and a bigger monthly bill, you may be able to wheedle some extras out of the hosting company. The more money you're spending with a hosting company, the more benefit you may get from persuading, bargaining, and badgering. Don't hesitate under any circumstances to mention what various competitors are offering. Hosting companies are like car dealers in that they post a "sticker" price and then actually have a minimum price they will bicker down to if you know you can do that.

Painful Pitfalls and How to Avoid Them

When choosing a hosting company to host your Web site, consider your decision to be a long-term one. Changing providers midstream is a huge hassle. Such a move could involve not only relocating the contents of the Web site but also reassigning domain names, redirecting users to a new site address, changing e-mail addresses, and possibly losing visitors at every step in the whole annoying process.

When you select a hosting company, think not only of the site's immediate needs but of any future needs that may come about because of the growth of your site. If you cut a few corners now, you may regret it six months down the road. In short, make sure the hosting company you choose now will still be the hosting company you would choose a year or more from now. Think of the choice as a marriage — divorcing from a hosting company is messy, expensive, frustrating, and no fun for any of the parties involved. The sections that follow help you look at several problems that could crop up.

The bandwidth follies

You want your site to grow. Ideally, you want your site to be terrifically popular. Even if you aren't reaching for worldwide notoriety and a cadre of devoted daily visitors, you surely want as much traffic as you can get. What happens if you achieve Net fame and your hosting company isn't prepared to handle the traffic? Repeated Internet "busy signals" and snail's-pace download times drive visitors away from your site in droves.

If your hosting company has fast, dedicated connections to the Internet — say multiple T1s, T3s, or preferably even faster lines — that's a good sign that the hosting company can handle a lot of traffic. Impressive connections to backbones are important. Ask prospective hosting companies about their proximity to major Internet backbones and (just as importantly) whether they're connected through multiple routes so that if one segment of the network crashes, they can keep your site up and running.

Similarly, ask prospective hosting companies about their plans for growth — in terms of bandwidth, equipment, and staff. The physical servers and routers must have excellent response time, even during peak hours like lunchtime and happy hour, to guarantee that traffic flows smoothly. You're in good hands with a hosting company that is already stable and efficient and has a strong commitment to growing and helping you grow with it.

Counting the clock ticks

Your hosting company is composed of both people and machines. The people are an important element in that they plug things in, fix problems, input data, register domain names, set up your account, and bill you. They're both the man behind the curtain in the *Wizard of Oz* and the folks who handle every question you ask them, from account setup to questions about adding or improving services. Some hosting companies go the distance, setting up mailing lists and newsgroups that their staffs monitor for questions and concerns. Make sure your hosting company has a good reputation for timely customer service at every level, from billing to tech support. You don't want to be sitting in your office biting your nails, wondering when that domain name registration is going to go through. You want to be confident that the folks at your hosting company are on top of things and that they care and take action when glitches occur.

Doing the hosting company shuffle

We've cautioned you that changing hosting companies after your site is up and running can be a big headache that you're better off without. Occasionally, however, what once seemed like a good company is unable to fulfill its promises for some reason. Sometimes, too, hosting companies, like other new businesses, can't meet the financial strain, and they fold or get sold. Sometimes the one employee who really held things together with organizational or technical expertise leaves the company, and the hosting company is never the same. And sometimes new companies just take on more than they can handle, lose sight of their goals, or simply burn out.

You can't really predict these kinds of human weaknesses — they happen to the best of us occasionally. And, of course, some hosting companies don't go downhill but rather present themselves to be much more competent or responsive than they really are. If your hosting company goes belly up or falls asleep on the job, or if you get overly frustrated with your hosting company's level of technical support or customer service, you may have no choice but to change hosting companies and hope that your new choice outdoes your first. What is involved in changing hosting companies and how to make the move as painless as possible are the subjects of the next sections.

Physically moving (the server machine)

After you've found a new hosting company that has at least the same level of bandwidth as your initial provider and that meets your criteria for service quality and options, you need to move both your data and any equipment the hosting company currently holds to the new hosting company. If you own or lease a server, the process may be as simple as picking up a box (the computer) and driving it across town. There is a possible trap here, however: Just because you own the machine, for example, don't assume that you own all the software that's on it. What you do or don't own and what you are or are not leasing varies depending on what level of service you have (shared, co-location, or managed services, as discussed earlier in this chapter). It also varies depending on your specific contract.

Make sure you know who owns the Web server software as well as any essential extras such as database packages and servers, multimedia transmission software, server-side scripts, and security software *before* you tell the hosting company that it's over and you're leaving. Determining ownership may be more complicated if you're leasing your hardware from your hosting company as opposed to leasing it from a third party. In this case, you probably won't be able to relocate the actual hardware to your new hosting company — you'll need to deploy new hardware with the new vendor.

Whenever you move your server, don't forget to back up your data beforehand! In fact, make backups often anyway — most likely you'll need to restore from a backup one of these days for some reason or another.

Take your time: A moving story

Wendy Van Wazer was involved in two hosting company moves while working as system administrator at a big publishing company. Her advice? "Don't rush into it. Take the time to ask all the right questions. If you find at the beginning that the hosting company does not return phone calls regularly, that indicates what it may be like to work with later on." One hosting company was being bought out at the time of the move, so it couldn't help much, and Wendy's horror story even includes transporting a server in her car and having the brakes fail!

Another pitfall that Wendy ran into at the time of the move was finding out that her company didn't own either the Web server software or the database package that they had been relying on. "The ISP stopped responding to our tech requests, it stopped returning our calls, and it had been the one doing the administration. The

system software hadn't been updated, and we discovered that we didn't own any of the database software. We had to update the system and redo the entire database." You can avoid these problems by talking to the ISP about these issues from the beginning. "Communicate with the ISP about who owns the hardware, who owns the software, and what software it is using for its servers," Wendy advises.

She also recommends owning your own hardware and having a hand in keeping the DNS records, as well as maintaining at least one DNS server at all times to aid in reseeding the Internet with the new IP address associated with your domain name. "The old ISP needs to guarantee the rerouting of your domain name," says Wendy, "but you must be explicit about what recaching information is included in your DNS records."

Virtually moving (only software and files)

Moving a physical server machine can be easy compared to transferring all the data that's involved in a Web site. It's like packing up your entire household and cramming its contents into your car. The task is difficult, and you're sure to forget something. What's more, you may not know what it is you forgot until you're finished unpacking. Make an agreement with the old hosting company not to completely erase your data until an agreed-on period of time after the move — try for 90 days. Here are some other things to deal with during the move:

- ✔ Files containing information about your domain name and its administration

- ✔ Password files and username records; e-mail archives for both users and mailing lists; and configuration files for chat, message board, and discussion group software

- ✔ Any server-side scripts, executables, or other programs

> ✔ Software and licenses that you own, along with any electronic keys needed for them
>
> ✔ All the HTML files, the images, the sounds, and the multimedia files that make up your site, as well as anything that's archived on the FTP site
>
> ✔ A copy of all the log files you have stored on the server

Don't take no for an answer. Unless you signed a particularly poor contract with the hosting company, you own your data.

Expanding your universe

Someday, you may decide to jazz up your site. You may want to add online transactions or streaming video. Can your hosting company keep up?

Suppose you want to start selling ad space. Or you think it would be really cool if a user could register his or her interests with your site. Wanda Webuser can register, and the next time she visits, she'll see her areas of interest in bigger letters, the ads on the page will reflect her tastes in music (or books or cars), she'll have the opportunity to hear a streaming audio interview with her favorite hockey player — and then she can even purchase a copy of a Great Moments in Hockey video using an order form.

This type of setup, depending on how you execute it, may require a custom database. It may demand several sophisticated server-side scripts, a streaming media server, and enhanced site security for online ordering. It may also capitalize on an automated mailing program and a site-wide search engine, and it certainly requires a lot of storage space on the Web server.

So you call your hosting company. The news isn't good: No server-side scripts are allowed, no streaming media server is available, and no secure transactions are accepted. You cajole and you threaten, but it's no go. Then you simmer down and consider whether it's worth the effort to drop the hosting company like a handful of boiling beans.

Head this type of thing off at the pass. In the end, you'll do far better in selecting and working with a hosting company if you know as much as you can about its services and connection options up front. Get the most robust hosting you can. Read Chapter 10 for tips on dealing with any vendor. Look at Chapter 11 to familiarize yourself with server and connection basics. Hosting-company folks, just like car mechanics, take you more seriously and listen more if you can speak their language.

Chapter 13

Databases for the Masses

. . . .

In This Chapter

▶ Defining databases and their components

▶ Looking behind the Web site database scene

▶ Comparing flat-file, relational, and object databases

▶ Distinguishing among database products

▶ Selecting database servers

▶ Talking to database designers

▶ Maintaining your database

. . . .

*U*nderneath the glitz and hype, the Web is all about information, interactivity, convenience, and functionality. It's about organized, accessible content, and lots of it. As you add content to your site and it grows and grows, keeping things current and helping users find what they seek becomes an increasing challenge. What's a Webmaster to do? Behind many Web sites big and small — whether their goals are sales, information delivery, product distribution, purchase support, or whatever — lies a solid solution: a *database*. Databases enable not only content storage and management, but also interactive tools and toys, personalization, and the online-catalog-shopping convenience users have grown to trust and love. Behind the scenes, databases drive an awful lot of Web site functionality.

What Exactly Is a Database?

It's really pretty simple. You could keep your clothes in a heap in the corner and sort through the whole pile every time you wanted to find a pair of blue socks, or you could buy a dresser, make one drawer the sock drawer, and look there when you want your blue socks. Knowing that this was the *sock* drawer, you'd just search for the color *blue*.

A *database* is a system that lets you organize and store pieces of information in a file so they're easier to find and use. It's more complicated to arrange than your dresser, but it operates on fundamental principles that are as simple as organizing drawers.

The difference between data and information

There's a big difference between data and information. Basically, *information* is useful and meaningful, whereas *data* is broken down information — just pieces of stuff that can be manipulated and that, when compiled in some organized way, become information. For example, a list of first names (not the first names of actual people, just *first names*) is data. When the first names are combined with last names so they describe actual people (or when you can imagine faces that go with the first names), those two pieces of data — the first name and the last name become *information.*

Consider another example: Joe keeps the names and phone numbers of his friends and associates on scraps of paper in his wallet. One scrap to a person, each has a name, a phone number, and maybe an address on it.

Each of these scraps is what's called (in database lingo) a *record. Data* is what is scribbled on the scraps. If Joe organized all that data in alphabetical order into an address book with a-b-c tabs along the side, he'd have a *database.* (But not an electronic one.) A database is just a bunch of information broken down into discrete pieces and organized in a way that's easy to use. An encyclopedia is a database. So are recipes on index cards in a box. A magazine is *not* a database, because, although it is full of information, the material is not broken down and organized around a reference point (it's not arranged alphabetically, or by number, or by any other system that makes it easy to look things up).

Joe, with his wallet full of loose "records," can write down information on the papers in his wallet in any order; it doesn't matter. When he wants to call up Lana Cartwheel, he looks at every scrap of paper to find the one with Lana's number on it.

If Joe used an address book, he could instead turn to *C* for Cartwheel, and there he'd find some boxes on the page, including one where he'd written Lana's name on one line, her address on another, and her phone number on a third. In database lingo, each of these lines of data is called a *field.* Every record in a database includes the same set of fields. When Joe gets a new address book, all the boxes, which are *records* on the page, have identical fields — and that, along with the alphabetical tabs on the edge, makes it easy for Joe to look up his friends' addresses and phone numbers. Asking a question of a database is a *query.*

A *table* is just a collection of records with the same structure: All the records in the table contain the same kind of information. A database can consist of one table or of many tables. Here are the three basic types of database systems:

✔ A *flat-file* database allows you only a single table in which you store all your information.

✔ A *relational* database allows you to create multiple tables that can then be linked via shared fields, making it possible to create complex relationships among data in the tables.

✔ An *object* database allows you to specify relationships among kinds of data. Unlike a relational database, the data in an object database is not stored in a table with related tables and unlike a flat-file database, the data is not stored in a list. It is simply stored as an "object." (An *object* is a combination of data and procedures for using the data, all stored together as one item.) The development process includes both defining the objects and determining how they'll be related to each other in the database.

As of this writing, relational databases are predominantly used for Web sites, so in this chapter we focus primarily on that type. We do, however, touch occasionally on flat-file and object databases.

Regardless of which type of database system you use to store your data, to make your database system work, you need ways to work with and manipulate the data, including ways to

✔ Add an entry (say, for example, a record for a new customer)

✔ Delete an entry (if, for example, you lose a customer)

✔ Update the data in an entry (if the customer moves or changes phone numbers, for example)

✔ Find, sort, and display the data

All the database products that we describe in this chapter are programmable and customizable. A big part of actually deploying them involves creating special programs or *scripts* that pull data out of the database, slap some HTML around it, and display it as a Web page or form that appears on the user's Web browser screen. The user does not see the database, but only the Web pages generated using the data in it.

A database, then, typically includes a *back end* (the database itself and any other pieces of it that live behind the scenes) and a front end (the interface to the database). (As you know, a Web site also has a back end and a front end.) Often a database has more than one interface — for example, those who enter data into the database use one interface (usually quite utilitarian looking) and who *use* the database see another interface (with nice graphics and an attractive on-screen layout). In a Web site setting, the front end that the public sees appears in the form of Web pages.

A Good Database May Be the Backbone of Your Site

A good, sturdy database can easily become a Webmaster's best friend (next to a humming, never-fails Web server). Whether your role is content, production, tech, or exec, you're likely to find that a database eases your load and makes maintaining content as well as the whole site a far simpler matter. If your content consists of a lot of related information — as is so often the case — organizing the data that makes up that information in a handy database is probably the way to go.

What your Web site database contains can vary widely. In the case of a big search site (AltaVista, Google, and the rest), the database contains data about other sites on the Web. In the case of a site like Amazon.com, the data in the database is all about the products that are available for sale.

On a content-driven site like CNN.com, the database holds the articles, interviews, images, and other media that make up the content of the site. Within the HTML code that makes up each page, one or more *database calls* (scripts, really) pull from the database various pieces of content. That stuff is then assembled (again by a script) into a Web page. The page (which is known as a *dynamically-generated page*) looks to the user like any ol' page generated in regular HTML. Any given piece of content (or any image) stored in the database can appear in many places on the site looking different each time. When, for example, those Webworkers maintaining the site need to make a change in the content, they can do it once and the change will appear everywhere the content appears. This is obviously a big timesaver. (Chapter 8 discusses the advantages of placing content, images, and media into a database and generating pages dynamically.)

Big content-driven sites often use special content management systems to track content assets and workflow. Content management software often works in tandem with a database to do its job. Chapter 22 goes into more detail about content management systems.

Personalization (the ability of a user to set up and view his or her own customized version of a specific Web page) requires that a database be in place. The bits and pieces of content among which a user chooses in the process of personalizing his or her page are pulled from a database via scripts the user never sees.

Take a quick look at these examples of successfully implemented Web site databases:

- ✔ Travelocity (www.travelocity.com) places tremendous information at users' fingertips, including worldwide availability of air flights and more. Travelocity uses a quick, robust database to bring up flight information and track the folks who register and use the service.

- ✔ Ticketmaster Online (www.ticketmaster.com) also has an impressive online system, built around a huge entertainment database.

- ✔ On a smaller scale, Foothill College, a community college in the heart of Silicon Valley, posts its course schedule at wwwfh.fhda.edu/FMDB/ FHSummer.html. Of course, Foothill College could have simply created one or several static HTML pages listing each course's name, number, description, and meeting times, but offering a searchable database and a nifty fill-out form makes things a *lot* easier for users . . . er, students.

WebMonkey offers an entire area dedicated to describing how to get a database up and running on your site. Go to hotwired.lycos.com/webmonkey/ backend/databases.

Understanding Types of Databases

The term *database,* then, can refer to a single, stand-alone table of data; to a group or system of many related tables; or to a group or system of objects containing data along with instructions for how computers will use that data. Databases can be simple or extremely complex; which is appropriate when it depends on what the data is and what sort of information it's meant to convey. Of the many database products available, some are relatively simple and inexpensive, whereas others are more sophisticated and (of course) more expensive.

About flat-file databases

The table that actually comprises a flat-file database is very commonly stored in a plain text file (although this is not a strict requirement). If you were to open up a customer information file using a word processor, you may see something like this:

```
Lori Grant 456 Elm St. Clanton OH 55556 #3378887
Jessica Buehrle 285 Oak St. Bayshore FL 09876 #7787447
Kevin Cunningham, Jr. 83 First St.Palo Alto CA 98474 #8976235
```

As you can see, the table is a collection of records, one record per line. Each record contains several fields, or items of data, and in the example shown, each record is simply a collection of data about one person. The records shown aren't even organized alphabetically, but rather in the order they were entered into the database.

Basically, if you have a very simple list of data to work with, a flat-file database will probably work for you and may keep things quite simple. For quick and simple jobs, a flat-file database has some advantages:

- ✔ **Development is easy.** Anyone who's familiar with a programming language like Perl or Visual Basic can probably build a flat-file database in just a few days.

- ✔ **Access time is quick.** If your flat-file database is small, you can generally add, alter, and retrieve data very quickly. (If it's big, you've got a problem.)

If you have no existing database from which to start, getting a database up and running using a flat-file system is a quick and dirty option. Remember, however, that these advantages are true only if you have a single table of data to manage. Here are some disadvantages of going the flat-file route:

- ✔ **A flat-file database is rigid in its structure.** A list is a list, and a flat-file database, once implemented, is very rigid. It's just not able to expand its capabilities to handle future requirements as they arise. Even the simple process of adding a new field to the database can involve excessive programming and testing time. It may also involve converting the existing data to a whole new flat-file database that includes the new field.

- ✔ **The database can quite easily grow bloated.** A flat-file database is okay for lists, but in plenty of cases, keeping a simple list is not a good idea. For example, look at a simple sales system. If a single customer places two or more orders, the same data — the customer's name, address, and other identifying info — has to be repeated in each order. Each individual record has to be larger (to include all that customer info), so excessive data is being stored. What's more, each record has to be entered separately, so there's plenty of room for mistakes (for example, the spelling of a customer's name may not be repeated consistently).

- ✔ **As your database grows, it will slow down.** Over time, your database may grow to be pretty big. And, the more it grows, the more slowly it performs. In a typical flat-file database, a search must look through every line of every record — that's just the nature of the thing. If, for example, you conduct a search of a customer database looking for everyone with the last name of *Smith,* the search has to sift through every line of data in every record to find all the Smiths. Searching through 100 lines of data is clearly a lot faster than searching through 10,000 lines; a bloated flat-file database is going to be very, very slow.

If you have complex needs in using a database — for example, for a product catalog or sales system — the relational database solution quickly gains appeal.

About relational databases

A relational database, as described in earlier sections, allows you to set up tables of data and *link* them to other tables of data. Think of tables as the building blocks of your relational database.

It's like this: Priscilla maintains a database for her small business (in the real world, not online). In her database, she has one table that functions as her *customer address* book. It's pretty basic, a lot like Joe's address book, which we described earlier in this chapter. Then she has another table that functions as her *invoice* book, in which each record contains the particulars of an order. The Customers table in her database, which tells her *who* placed the order, is linked to the Invoice table, which tells her *what* was ordered. (In Priscilla's order-entry system, every invoice is linked to a customer, but not every customer is linked to an invoice.)

Remember that all the records in a table contain the same fields. (In other words, each record in the Invoice database contains lines for Date of Order, Product Ordered, Quantity Ordered, Price, and so on.) Figure 13-1 shows a set of related tables that are linked to form one big relational database.

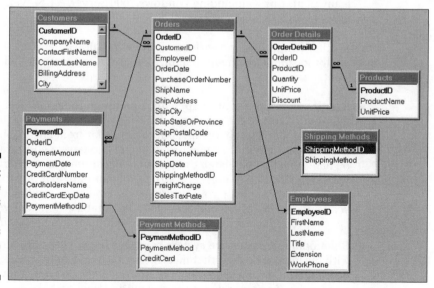

Figure 13-1: Each table in this relational database is linked to other tables.

In a relational database, the data in several tables is linked through one or more fields that they have in common. For example, the names, addresses, and phone numbers in Priscilla's client list are the same as those that appear in her invoice list. When Priscilla writes invoices with her Invoice table, the database automatically pulls the customer's name and address from her Customers table. It's probably easy to see that Priscilla's relational database system could translate into a Web site operation, and that if she went that way, using her relational database system would be a big advantage over using a flat-file system.

Relational databases are very powerful tools — they are robust and expandable, and there are many to choose from. Here are some of the advantages they offer:

✔ **If you can dish it out, a relational database can take it.** Relational databases are expandable; you can add as many tables of related data as you need, ad infinitum (well, almost).

✔ **A relational database can be customized to do all sorts of tricks.** Because relational databases have their own standard programming language — Structured Query Language, or SQL — they can be programmed to manipulate data and display it in all sorts of nifty ways. The more powerful, expensive packages (see later sections in this chapter) can really do some cool things.

✔ **Just about everybody offers a relational database product.** From Microsoft Access running on a desktop computer to the big guns like Oracle and PostgreSOL, relational database products are available for many platforms — including Windows 2000 Server, NT Server, UNIX, and Linux — and for many prices.

On the other hand, those powerful and robust relational databases are not usually so simple or cheap to implement. Here are some of their disadvantages:

✔ **Relational databases are expensive and tough to install/design/ maintain.** A few of the relational database products available today won't cost you a small fortune, but most are far from cheap, and some are *very* expensive. Plus, you probably need to have a consultant or two on hand to help you install the system, to customize it to interface with your Web site, and to correctly structure your data in a way that makes sense for today and for your future needs. Finally, depending on the scope of your database and the relational database software you choose, you may need a DBA (database administrator) on staff.

✔ **Relational databases are system resource hogs.** These are big programs with big jobs to do, and that means they take up a hefty chunk of hard disk space and they need plenty of RAM to chew on while they work. If you expect big-time traffic, consider putting the database server on a separate machine.

About object databases

Objects (brace yourself, to most people, this is very abstract) are self-contained items that include both data and procedures describing how a computer should use or otherwise deal with that data. Object databases (also sometimes called object stores or hierarchical databases) are the new kid on the database block. They are conceptually similar to object-oriented programming and languages (such as Java) in the sense that the technology involved allows database developers to create objects and store them in the database. As is the case with object-oriented programming, each object in an object database can contain whatever data makes sense for the object. For example, if you create an object for a cat, you may include information about the cat's name, age, and breed as well as an "eat procedure" that describes how the cat eats.

When an object is stored in an object database, it is not stored in a table with related tables (like in a relational database) or in a list (like in a flat-file database). It is simply stored as an object. When a developer creates the database, he or she determines how objects of what sort are related to each other and how. The relationships can be quite simple — as simple as a list. Or they can be as complex as parent-child-siblings relationships in a hierarchical chart.

On a Web site, an object database may be used to store large quantities of complex content. The content can then be manipulated, used, and displayed based on the procedures that are embedded in the objects.

Light-Duty Databases and Their Uses

The databases described in the following two sections work really well for many lighter duty Web sites. They generally cost a lot less — both in terms of up-front licensing cost and in terms on ongoing support and hardware — than their bigger brothers that are discussed later. They are also both SQL databases, so you can start using one of these and upgrade to a bigger database when needed without rewriting all your database code.

mSQL

Mini SQL, more commonly known as simply mSQL, is a light-duty relational database for UNIX/Linux that is available for download from www.hughes. com.au. mSQL ships with a database-to-Web module called w3-msql, as well as a simple-to-use interface programming language called Lite. Using w3-msql and Lite, you can link mSQL to your current Web server. (This is particularly easy if you happen to be running the Apache Web server, which is described in Chapter 11.)

mSQL is great for small databases because it's simple to set up and use. It does, however, have the drawbacks that it cannot cope with large fields. And although mSQL uses standard SQL query commands (SQL is a standard language for manipulating relational databases), it does not support the full set of SQL specifications. mSQL is a fine choice for database dabblers and novices, or companies that really need a relational database but just can't afford one of the bigger relational database servers.

Microsoft Access

Most people know Microsoft Access as a friendly relational database program that they can run on their desktop computers. But, Access is also a real database server (albeit one that can handle a lot less data and transactions than its bigger cousins). Access is a terrific option for a very lightly-trafficked database that needs to include only a few thousand records. You can't use Access running on your desktop computer as a Web site database. It has to be on a server machine. But it can be on the same server machine as your Web server software. Upgrading from Access to the big bruisers we describe in the next section is quite possible and sometimes even smooth. That's because Access is a SQL database server, and the powerhouses among relational databases are also SQL databases.

The Big Bruisers and What They're Good For

If you need a little more bang than a database like mSQL or Access can offer, investigate the next big step up — larger, more functional relational databases. In the sections that follow, we give you a quick rundown of the heavyweight champs of the relational database world. All the products we describe can be used for Web site back ends as well as other database applications; which one is right for you is a pretty big question that we hope you'll be better prepared to address after reading this material.

As you consider these products, keep in mind that your organization may already have one or more databases in place. Check which products those databases run on; using them in your Web endeavor will afford benefits including that a skilled in-house staff person is probably in place, and perhaps even the data you need to get started is there and in the correct format.

Also bear in mind that to implement any of these products, you need a professional database developer (unless you are a professional database developer). Don't imagine you can skimp on this; if your database is important enough to your Web endeavor to consider these impressive options, get a pro to put your database together.

For online answers to questions about SQL and relational databases, ask the SQL Pro (www.inquiry.com/techtips/thesqlpro).

Oracle

When it comes to heavyweight champion databases, none is heftier than Oracle (www.oracle.com). In the real world, every time you use a credit card or an ATM machine, odds are that you're interacting with an Oracle database in some way (without even knowing it). Oracle produces high-performance databases that can handle hundreds of thousands of transactions per second. Oracle ships with Oracle's database-enabled Web server, aptly named . . . WebServer. WebServer is fully functional, is available for UNIX/Linux and Windows 2000 Server or NT Server, and supports both static Web pages and dynamic Web pages (which combine the usual static text and graphics with information that's queried from an Oracle database). In addition to working with Oracle's WebServer, Oracle will work as a database back end for almost any of the third-party tools we discuss in the "Middleware: The Glue That Binds" section, later in this chapter.

Oracle itself is very expensive, and you'll need someone with Oracle experience to help you install and build your database. For normal, day-to-day operations (such as adding new records, retrieving data, updating data), you don't need a DBA, but it is a good idea to have one on call just in case. When you want to add new kinds of information — the kinds that would require you to add another table — you do need to call on a DBA or database developer.

Microsoft SQL Server

Microsoft SQL Server is a relational database designed specifically for Windows 2000 Server or NT Server. SQL Server comes with easy-to-use Windows-based tools for maintaining and monitoring your SQL Server database. Like all Microsoft products, it works well with other Microsoft products, such as IIS (Internet Information Server).

Hiring a database developer

Cordell Sloan, a systems architect, advises, "In database development, bet on experience. Getting the job done quickly and correctly requires that. It may cost you more per hour to hire a pro, but it will cost a lot more in the long run if you don't. You want someone who will hit the target in one shot; you don't want to pay for someone else's learning curve."

One copy of a database is enough; two is too many

We once found ourselves managing a situation in which a company that had two Web sites wanted its online catalog database to appear on both sites. This may sound like a piece of cake, but a strange hardware setup (one site ran on a UNIX machine, the other on a Windows NT machine) combined with custom database configuration on one made it difficult for both sites to physically access the data. As a result, the company decided to keep one copy of the database on the UNIX server and make a second copy on the Windows NT server. This was a recipe for disaster!

The data in one database was always a day behind the data in the other, and the company always had to worry that customers at one site were getting less (or incorrect) data if they were coming in from the "secondhand" site. Luckily, this company was actually updating only one database and then making a copy. Had the company also decided to allow its staff to make changes in both databases, the data would have been out of sync then and forever. What a mess!

We strongly advise you that a basic principle in database design is that you must never, ever imagine that you can keep up two copies of a single database. Both human errors and machine glitches will creep into both systems, and they will never be right. Trust us, and don't try it.

SQL Server is fairly simple for a developer to install and provides a powerful relational database application for Web sites. It's pricing structure is Byzantine, but SQL Server is a lot less expensive than Oracle. Of course, to actually implement a SQL Server solution you must have pros to get the thing set up. SQL Server, like Oracle, can work as a database back end for almost any of the third-party tools we discuss in the "Middleware: The Glue That Binds" section, later in this chapter.

All in all, consider choosing SQL Server as your database back end if you already use or plan to use predominantly Microsoft technology for your Web site. The folks at Microsoft have worked to integrate SQL Server with other Microsoft Internet technologies including Active Server Pages, Microsoft Transaction Server, Visual InterDev, FrontPage, Office, and BackOffice.

PostgreSQL

A very popular open-source database, PostgreSQL, is a fully functional SQL-based database that runs under most versions of UNIX/Linux and Windows 2000 Server and NT Server. Because PostgreSQL (unlike the rest of the databases discussed in this chapter) is open-source, when you get PostgreSQL, the full source code comes with it. This allows any programmer (if he or she is so inclined) to modify PostgreSQL itself. PostgreSQL is, like most open-source software, *free*! Oracle is a more reliable option for large sites with heavy traffic and complex content. PostgreSQL compares quite favorably with SQL Server, although it doesn't integrate as smoothly with other Microsoft products.

The PostgreSQL Web site (`www.psotgresql.org`) offers information about PostgreSQL's continued development and ways you can help with that. It also offers documentation, links to companies that provide commercial support for PostgreSQL, developer discussions, and (of course) the software itself for download.

Middleware: The Glue That Binds

Your database, your Web server, and the user's Web browser don't automatically and seamlessly work together — they need introductions, they need lines of communication, they need *middleware*. Middleware is software that allows Web pages to be created from the data in a database. These pages can be created dynamically on the fly or based on user input. (For example, when a user visits a site, he or she can fill out a form, and that information is used to query the database. The user then sees the result in the form of a Web page.) In any case, middleware does the work.

In general, middleware falls into two categories:

✔ **Drivers that allow server-side scripts to access the database.** The addition of the proper middleware driver for a specific database allows a programmer to write scripts that query and store information in the database. Drivers exist for most databases that work with C, C++, Java, or Perl. Most databases also come with ODBC drivers, which allow you to access the database with any programming tools or software that supports ODBC.

✔ **Special HTML authoring tools that allow you to integrate data from the database into the pages you create.** Generally, you don't have to be a programmer to use these tools.

Some database products come with middleware. This is perfectly good stuff and can be used to publish many types of information and content on the Web. But using what a database product comes with isn't your only option. You can also get and use third-party tools as discussed in Chapter 9. Fusion from NetObjects (`www.netobjects.com`), for example, is a full-scale WYSIWYG (What You See Is What You Get) HTML editing system that also includes the ability to publish the contents of a database as part of your Web site. Fusion is not simply middleware, but it can be used as middleware with many popular database products.

ODBC: Microsoft's database access standard

Different database programs do things differently — they're just all wired up differently. Data could not be shared among database systems (or between databases and Web servers) if not for ODBC (Open Database Connectivity), a Microsoft standard that inserts a middle layer between a database and any ODBC-compliant program. Database developers and administrators work with ODBC to connect Web servers to database servers. ODBC is also the technology that enables scripts to access database servers — at least in a Windows 2000 Server or NT Server setting.

Middleware is somewhat like an authoring tool, except that it allows you to create templates for dynamic Web pages — pages that combine static text and graphics with data pulled from the database. It allows you to create one "page" that becomes thousands of pages based on various combinations of data from the database.

Requirements for Database Server Machines

Many of the databases discussed in this chapter require a dedicated computer acting as a database server. That computer has to be up to the job. Even with technologies such as ODBC, which make it a little easier to move data from one database to another without rewriting a lot of code, changing databases or database servers is a pain. And selecting a database server is quickly followed by investments of time and money in licensing the software, developing the system, and training people to use it. If and when you change database servers, all that investment will have to occur again. Go into the database selection and development process with a clear picture of your projections for future traffic and content.

The details vary depending on which database software is going to run on the computer, but in general a database server must be:

✔ **Reliable:** Downtime is bad — users don't stick around and often don't come back to a site that goes down. On a server, physical systems tend to wear out after time. A server's disk drive, power supply, or network connections can fail, causing the server to crash. As insurance against this, redundancy (having multiple physical components) is good. If something (such as the disk drive) fails, the machine switches to the auxiliary drive and keeps going. (Having multiple servers is a great idea for the same reason — if one server goes down, another can take over without interruption.)

✔ **Fast:** The speed at which a site's database server can serve data directly impacts how fast the Web site seems to users. More memory, faster disk drives, and a faster processor make a server fast; get as much memory and speed as possible. Also note that a desktop computer has only one processor, but a server can have many. Processors are expensive, so you'll have to balance your needs against your budget, but get at least two processors.

✔ **Expandable:** As your site and its traffic grow, your database server may have to work harder and harder to keep up processors, you can bolster your server's performance. Get a machine that has room to install more processors later. It should have twice as many slots for processors as you initially need.

A robust (reliable, fast, and expandable) database server makes all the difference in the world. A robust database serves more data or content faster. Don't skimp on your servers. Scaling down your database server's capabilities may seem like a simple method for saving costs now but it will only wind up shortchanging your ability to serve your site effectively in the future.

Talking to Database Developers

Databases offer a powerful way to organize data and maintain the information offered on a Web site. Database design is a specialized skill that is different from programming or any other form of Webmastering. The job of a database designer or developer is to create and implement an orderly definition of the data you'll be incorporating into your Web site. (An *integrator*, by the way, is a person who works with database developers and fulfills the special function of integrating database systems with the other systems that make up your Web site, for example transaction systems.)

To be successful, the database developer has to understand your site's objectives, know which database product or solution to use given your purpose and time or budget constraints, know how to translate your needs into a database design, and know how the database needs to evolve in the future. To enable the database developer to do his or her job well, you need to provide this person with a clear picture of your content and resources.

Give your database developer a copy of the site specs you created in Chapter 8; highlight those portions of the specs that particularly concern the database issues, and provide a special summary as a cover sheet. Prepare the answers to these questions, which you are sure to be asked:

✔ What platform does your server run on? Windows 2000 Server, NT Server, UNIX, or Linux?

✔ What kind of Web server software are you using or planning to use?

✔ Where is the data right now? Is it already stored in a company-run data-base? If so, what kind of database? (Provide as many details as possible.)

✔ How do you plan to allow users access the data? Do you want users to register or otherwise fill out forms in the course of accessing the data? Do you want text links to the database data?

✔ How do you expect users to query the database? What kinds of data or information do you want them to be able to get? Which fields do you want them to be able to search? Are there any fields they should not see?

✔ Will users be entering data into contest or site registration forms?

✔ Will this database be used in conjunction with any others? With an online transaction system? (Again, provide all the details.)

✔ How do you expect your database needs to change in the next six months? In the next year? In the next two years?

Finally, you should know and be able to describe or even sketch out what kind of data your database will hold. Put together a chart that lists the specific fields that will make up a record, as well as how you imagine tables will work together. Doing so will help you (and your database developer) to see things more clearly.

When you sketch out the records, estimate how many characters or words you expect each field to contain, describe what sort of data (text, numeric, other?) will be in each field, and note any peculiarities that may help the database developer anticipate problems. Here's an example:

Field	Size	Type	Notes
Last name	20 characters	Text	
First name	20 characters	Text	
E-mail address	25 characters	Text	
Phone number	10 characters	Text	Place hyphens after area code and prefix; use text because this won't be a number on which math will be performed.
Amount of most recent purchase	Varies	Numeric	Math may be performed on this number, so it should be numeric.
Opinion of electronic commerce	40 words/ about 200 characters	Text	Some people may write more; should we cut them off at 40 words, or allow for the potential of more data than we expect?

What's it going to cost?

A database solution may well represent a major piece of your site budget. In planning for the costs associated with creating and especially maintaining your database, you need to remember to factor in these costs:

✔ The estimated cost of day-to-day maintenance, including not just the big-ticket maintenance but simple data entry and the deletion of dead records.

✔ The cost of bringing in a DBA or developer to accomplish the improvements you've planned.

✔ The cost of occasionally bringing in a DBA or developer to troubleshoot. (Don't imagine you'll never need a DBA; plan at least a few visits per year.)

✔ The cost of upgrading software and hardware.

✔ The cost of creating backups and (preferably) storing them off-site.

Remember that last one especially — don't let the cost stop you from protecting your valuable data by making and storing backups off-site.

Keep in mind as you talk to database developers that although they know databases, they don't know your business or your needs. You must communicate this information to them and iron out any wrinkles that appear along the way. Offering the database developers clear information up front is the best way to avoid confusion later.

A Few Words on Database Maintenance

You needn't be a database developer or DBA to do most database maintenance. In fact, in the course of setting up your database, systems and processes should be put into place such that you or someone on your Web team (even someone who isn't necessarily a database whiz kid) can take care of these operations:

✔ **Adding new records.** You should be able to add new records and the data they contain to your database whenever necessary.

✔ **Editing records.** You must be able to make corrections in existing records at will.

✔ **Deleting records.** You should be able to delete records at will. Furthermore, if you expect records to expire on a regular basis, you should have a feature in place that automatically removes expired records for you.

✔ **Making regular backups.** Backups are *very* important. Depending on which type of database you implement, your data may be backed up automatically when your Web site is backed up, or it may require a separate backup procedure. Arrange a backup plan with your Web site administrator and/or database developer at the outset of your database project.

✔ **Keeping an eye on performance.** Make a point of using your new database application regularly, and when you first launch it, pound on the thing mercilessly. This is the best way to detect and correct problems with the database itself. It's also a good way for you to determine if your database is getting so much use that it's slowing down the machine it lives on.

From time to time, you'll also probably want to make minor or major improvements to your database. Unlike routine maintenance issues, which you can usually handle yourself, you're likely to need to bring in a DBA or consultant to help you implement improvements. Improvements you may want to make include:

✔ **Creating new kinds of queries.** As you and your site's visitors use your database back end, you may discover ways that you or they want to access the data that you didn't anticipate at the beginning of the project.

✔ **Adding new types of data.** Say, for example, you've launched an online catalog of your company's T-shirts in the form of a database. Six months later, the hard-copy catalog starts printing both U.S. prices and Canadian prices. Now you need to add the Canadian prices to the online version of the catalog.

✔ **Upgrading the software.** Software developers love to release new and improved versions of their products, usually about once a year or so. At some point in your database's lifetime, you'll probably want to upgrade to a newer version of database software — there's bound to be a new feature you'll decide you need. Sometimes upgrading is a snap; sometimes it isn't.

✔ **Upgrading your hardware.** With luck, your Web site will become so successful that the hardware you've set it up on will become bogged down. At that point (or whenever you get the opportunity), you may want to upgrade to a more powerful server.

All these tasks signal the time to call in a DBA or developer. Make sure when you do that you both have a current backup of your data socked away and that you call someone who has professional experience with the specific database product you use.

Chapter 14

Transaction Systems Made Easy

• •

In This Chapter

▶ Understanding how online shopping works

▶ Understanding security and commerce

▶ Establishing business rules

▶ Tackling secure servers and transaction systems

▶ Mastering the challenge of fulfillment

• •

Selling on the Web can be dicey business. In this chapter, we discuss the special issues that surround selling online. We start by looking at security and how security impacts e-commerce. Then, we go into how you can get set up to sell online by building, buying, or renting the right system for you. Finally, we discuss *fulfillment* — getting your product to your customers in a timely, reliable way.

How Online Shopping Works

Picture yourself as Wanda Webuser. Seeking out widgets, you go straight to Acme Wonderwidget, the industry leader. One by one, you view Acme's fine widgets, and when one strikes your fancy, you click on a Buy button to plop it into your virtual shopping cart. After a while, you think, "I wonder how many Wonderwidgets I have in my cart?" You click on the handy What's in My Cart? button, and change your mind about one or two items. Then, with the click of another button, you head for the checkout page, where you provide some simple information via a brief set of order forms, pony up your credit card number, and *click* — you're done. In most cases, Acme sends you an e-mail confirmation of your order, and the order itself arrives within a specified time, via a real-world shipper.

Shopping-cart systems like these consist of a front end that's composed of a series of Web page forms, a bunch of server side scripts that enable the user to add and remove items from the cart (as well as just peek into it), and usually a database of products. All of those components enable a Web site to offer online sales. Again, when an online sale occurs, a transaction takes place, meaning that an order is taken, payment from the buyer to the seller occurs, the item is shipped, and the item is received.

But another aspect of that transaction is the process of the seller accepting a credit card from the buyer. To users, the complexity of the process this event triggers is not apparent. To sellers, their banks, and the buyers' banks (the banks that issued to the buyers the credit cards they use in the transaction), the process of getting payment is crucial. Figure 14-1 illustrates the transaction process from the viewpoint of sellers and banks.

When you set up your transaction system, you'll have to set up a merchant account with your bank. Tell them that the account is meant to handle online transactions. Set up this account before you start to build your transaction system. You'll need to have account and bank routing numbers on hand as you build the system. You'll also need to know that the way your bank processes credit cards is compatible with the way your transaction system does. Your business relationship with your bank is a cornerstone of your business relationships, so start with the choice of bank and go from there.

As you make decisions about your transaction system, you'll need to understand security. Security in e-commerce transactions has been bandied about a lot, and sometimes it's been sensationalized. Usually, the discussion has centered around the security of user information, including users' credit card data. As you can probably guess from perusing Figure 14-1, security is an issue throughout the process of selling and collecting payment. When credit card billing occurs between the merchant, the merchant's bank, and the bank that issued the credit to the customer, electronic messages are passed around to conduct the transaction. At every step along the way, security is vital. Systems and processes have been in place for quite some time to handle secure transactions among merchants and banks. This protects the business interests of all the companies involved and instills in customers the confidence they need to feel good about making purchases with credit cards.

To set up a Web site with a sales system, you must create not just a user experience, but also the behind-the-scenes systems, processes, and policies that enable sales, payment, and fulfillment to occur. At every step of the game, security is a key component. You also need a two-part transaction system that works with your shopping cart to allow users to pay using their credit cards. One part logs the transactions into a database, which allows individual transactions to be tracked. The other part handles payment through a secure server. The balance of this chapter describes the issues involved in setting up secure transaction systems.

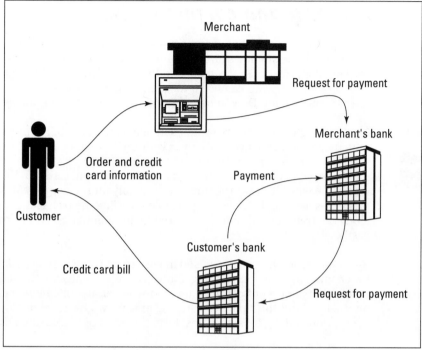

Figure 14-1:
A behind-
the-scenes
view of a
transaction
and
payment
cycle.

Those Not-So-Identical Twins: Security and Commerce

Those twin issues of electronic business — security and commerce — capture a lot of headlines. Security and commerce are closely interrelated, that's for sure. Increased security on the Web encourages Internet commerce, and interest in Internet commerce encourages the development of Web security. However, they aren't quite the identical twins they often seem to be.

Why security counts

To put together a nifty shopping system — to conduct *commerce* — you must provide your users and your partners (for example, your bank) with security. You must give users the knowledge that when they engage in a transaction on your site, they can do so without fear of intrusion or theft. You must assure your bank that you're a reliable business partner. You can create warm fuzzies about the security of your transaction system by using a secure server and trusted payment system. Knowing the underlying technologies involved in electronic security can help you understand and build a secure transaction system.

Security and commerce basics

Many people imagine that someone — some evil person or group — is lurking in the electronic shadows about to pounce. This evil entity wants your credit card number, can get it in a snap, and then can distribute it at will to millions of other evil ones who can use it for unscrupulous means. Are these realistic fears? Probably not. Do you have to take these concerns seriously? You bet.

Oddly enough, the security systems in place for e-commerce are much safer than those used when you fork over your credit card in a store, restaurant, or some other real-world business. When you stroll into a store and charge a purchase, you give your credit card number and signature to a total stranger, who can easily jot down the number or simply lift the carbon. Most bank processes actually involve many people handling the transaction. Anywhere along the transaction's path, your credit card number could be stolen fairly easily.

By comparison, the schemes used in electronic commerce are a lot tougher for an unscrupulous person to get into. These schemes are the basic building blocks that allow confidential data to move over a public network like the Internet without third parties listening in, and two basic technologies, encryption and digital signatures, form the basis of these schemes.

Encryption

Encryption is the process of taking data (for example, the contents of a Web form that includes a credit card number) and using a mathematical formula to scramble it so that you need a *key* (a digital code) to decrypt and read it. Encryption is nothing new: A form of encryption called the *Caesar Cipher* was used in the Roman Empire to protect Roman communications that could fall into enemy hands from being read. Encryption was used extensively during the American Civil War, World War II, and most other conflicts.

Today's uses of encryption have spread beyond the military to all types of commerce, and the combination of advances in *cryptography* (the branch of mathematics that includes encryption) and the rapid growth of inexpensive, powerful computers make encryption important to all of us. One of those advanced forms of encryption that was until recently of interest only to military intelligence units — RSA public key encryption — is now often used to make Web pages that are stored on a secure server remain secure.

Public key encryption is used extensively to protect information on the Web. In public key encryption, everyone gets two keys: a *public key* that is publicly known and a *private key* that is not publicly known. Each of these keys can decipher the data the other encrypted. This method of encryption is based on the idea that some mathematical functions are much easier than their inverse. For example, most people can multiply two numbers fairly quickly but have to think a bit harder when asked to reverse the process and divide those numbers, because division is by nature a tougher calculation. Exploiting this idea allows the possibility that anyone can encrypt data with a *public key,* which is based on something similar to but far more complex than multiplication. Having a two-key system like this solves many problems of cryptography.

A group of people who formed the company RSA Security invented public key encryption. RSA owns patents for public key encryption, and Netscape, Microsoft, and most other major Web-related companies license this technology from RSA. The RSA home page (www.rsasecurity.com) is full of information about public key encryption.

Digital signatures

A related technology, *digital signatures,* is based on the idea that a unique electronic "signature" is like a real signature that you use to sign your checks. Digital signatures are pieces of electronic data that are at the bottom of a document (but you don't actually see them); they guarantee the identity of the author of the document and that no one has modified the document in transit. Digital signatures don't hide the contents of the document; they merely prove the document's legitimacy. But again, public key encryption is working behind the scenes here.

Secure Servers and You

Secure servers are, simply, servers that operate in a secure way. The use of a secure server in conjunction with a secure Web browser allows confidential information to travel over the Internet without the likelihood of outsiders intruding upon the information. Secure servers use technologies such as encryption and digital signatures (described in preceding sections) in a scheme known as *secure socket layer* (SSL) to protect the confidential information as it travels. With SSL, people can securely send information as diverse as credit card numbers, medical records, stock portfolios, and even simple confidential messages over the Internet. SSL manages the security of Web pages that people send from the secure server to a Web browser and back again in the sort of exchange that takes place when a user fills out a Web-page form and submits it.

Advantages and disadvantages of secure servers

For SSL to provide security between the server and the Web browser, both have to support SSL. That's not much of a problem these days: All desktop Web browsers support SSL. If your target audience includes people who are going to be using handheld computers, PDAs, or Internet-enabled cell phones, you will run into the situation where people will not be able to access your secure pages.

SSL offers a way to set up the secure environment that you need to provide for financial transactions on your site. The advantage of using SSL is that it can secure *any* type of data — not just a financial transaction. This becomes important when you're exchanging confidential information with users beyond just payment information — for example, medical records or bank statements.

What you need

To use SSL security on your Web site, you need Web-server software that supports SSL. This is not big a deal: Web-server software, including Internet Information Server (IIS) and Apache, usually supports SSL. You also need to enable SSL security on your server; SSL is disabled by default on most servers. To enable SSL, you must get and install a digital certificate. A digital certificate (described earlier in the section "Security and commerce basics") contains both of the keys used in the public key encryption system that is part of SSL.

You purchase your certificate from a *certificate authority* — a company that is authorized to sell certificates. VeriSign is one such company, which you can reach at `www.verisign.com`. VeriSign offers various grades of certificates; each is designed for different types of transactions. Your certificate will be tied to your domain name. If you ever change your domain name, you'll have to get a new certificate. Also note that if your site is hosted on a shared server, your hosting company may be unwilling to install a certificate for your site. The housekeeping is just too cumbersome. However, it will sometimes offer you the option to share a secure server that has what amounts to a shared certificate.

During the process of purchasing a certificate, you must provide proof of your identity. Your application may have to be stamped by a notary public, or you may have to send in a copy of your business license or a fictitious name statement. It all depends on the type of business you're doing.

What security "looks" like

Typically, not everything on a site is confidential, so SSL does not have to protect an entire site. A home page certainly is not likely to be secure, and informational areas of a site probably don't need to be secure. However, when a user enters a sensitive area of a site — perhaps an area that asks for the person's credit card number or displays medical records — a secure server can kick in and start using SSL to encrypt the data as it travels from the server to the browser.

A number of clues may tell the user whether a Web page is secure:

- ✔ The URL for a page encrypted with SSL starts with `https:` instead of `http:`.

- ✔ A dialog box heralding the fact usually appears as the user enters or exits a secure area. (Although this depends on the browser, the user can often disable the message.)

- ✔ Various browsers offer their own specific visual clues; for example, Internet Explorer shows a lock in the lower-right corner of the screen for secure pages.

Security and online transactions

As the Webmaster, understanding the role of SSL in the world of online transactions is quite important for you. SSL does not do transactions or provide a payment system; it doesn't collect information about payment or the things a user wants to buy. However, here's what you can do with SSL:

- ✔ Address the important issue of securing information as it travels over the Internet.

- ✔ Stop third parties from "eavesdropping" on data moving between the server and the browser and from impersonating you or your user.

- ✔ Create an online shopping environment in conjunction with special server side scripts, such as shopping-cart scripts.

For a secure shopping system, you must not just a have secure server, but also a functional transaction system. And to build a transaction system, you must first establish how your transactions will take place.

Clarifying Your Business Rules

Before you build your e-commerce site, you must address a number of issues that define how business will be conducted on your site. Here's a handy checklist of questions you can ask yourself to come up with your "business rules." First, consider the questions surrounding your products and services:

- ✔ **Presenting products:** What products will you offer? How many? Are they hard deliverables, digital, or a mix? Do you sell intangibles such as services or warranties? How frequently will your catalog change, and how extensive will the changes be?

- ✔ **Pricing:** Does pricing differ for different types of customers, or is it always the same? Will all customers see all prices, or will they see only the prices that apply to them? Do you ever have sales or other price reductions? How does your online pricing differ from your brick-and-mortar or reseller pricing?

- ✔ **Offering discounts and incentives:** What discount structures do you have? Do you offer coupons, memberships, or rebates? Do you bundle products into special packages with special pricing? Do you offer volume discounts?

- ✔ **Selling related items and making substitutions:** Do you offer users who are about to make a purchase an upgrade or any special package or bundle containing the item they're buying? Do you offer users additional items that are related to what they are buying? Do you allow substitutions in a bundle? If an item is out of stock, do you offer a substitution?

- ✔ **Finding products:** How will users search for products? What keywords, terms, or phrases will users associate with your products? Will users search based on size, color, price, availability, vintage, maker, flavor, or what? Will they browse? If so, what categories and subcategories do your products fit into? Can users "spec" the products they want to see? (For example, can they specify a car with four doors, four-wheel drive, a certain price range, a roof rack, and leather seats?)

- ✔ **Choosing or comparing products:** Will your users be able to make their purchase decisions based on information that's as simple as brand, model, price, and description? Will they prefer packaged "solutions" (for example, a small business software suite and a full-featured professional software suite)? Do they need full product specs? Do they need to compare the specs for one product to the specs of another product?

- ✔ **Communicating about products:** How will users get answers to their questions about products? Will you field questions via e-mail, phone, or a visiting sales rep? How can you guide users through a complex purchase decision online? Does the purchase decision for your product require a test drive, taste test, or some other direct experience? How will users who need to experience your product before buying be able to do that?

When to bill a credit card

Keep in mind that ethically, and even legally, you shouldn't bill a customer's credit card until you actually ship the order. This is how mail order works, and it goes a long way toward instilling customer confidence. The downside is that this process requires a two-part transaction, but in the long run, it's really the best way to go.

You'll also have to think about how users will experience your shopping system. Consider these points:

- **Ordering:** How will users "build" an order? Will they place items in a shopping cart and then check out? How many items will be in a typical order? Can they purchase just one, as many as ten, or hundreds? Will they order the same items repeatedly? Will they order similar items, related items, or accessories after the initial purchase? Will a shopping list or wish list be useful to them?

- **Taxing:** What are the tax rules you must follow? Are all items taxable, some, or none? Are there any circumstances where taxes won't be collected? (For example, when your customer is a reseller and they will be collecting taxes, you may not have to collect taxes from them.)

- **Shipping and delivery:** What shipping and delivery options will you offer (postal service, UPS, FedEx, special delivery)? Where will you ship and where won't you ship? How will you calculate shipping costs? What information will you need to calculate shipping costs? Is shipping a profit item?

- **Accepting payment:** Will you accept credit cards? Which ones? Debit cards? Will you accept purchase orders or work orders? In what form? Will some customers set up special accounts? What types?

You must also figure out your own internal processes for tracking the status of products and orders, letting people know where their orders stand, and compiling information about your customers and the trends in their buying. Set policies for:

- **Tracking availability:** How (and at what point in the sales process) will you notify users that an item is out of stock, on back order, or soon to be discontinued? What will you do to get those items to the customer, and how long will that take? How long will you keep back orders in the system? When will you stop selling a "sale" item? When it's sold out or when a certain number have been sold?

- **Processing orders:** How and how often will orders be sent to your processing and fulfillment centers? Daily, hourly, or as received? Do you have a cutoff time for next day delivery?

- **Confirming and tracking orders:** How and when will you let users know that their orders have been received, processed, and shipped? Will order numbers or shipping numbers be included in communications to users? Will users be able to view a Web page that shows the status of their order?

- **Gathering customer data:** What information about customers will you capture as part of the transaction system? Will you use that data to make future offers to specific customers based on past purchases or to view trends among groups of customers? Will you sell aggregated data to third parties? What incentives can you offer users to encourage them to provide you with demographic and other information?

> ✔ **Managing returns:** Under what circumstances will you accept returns? Will you require that the items actually be returned? If a customer returns damaged merchandise, will you pay for shipping the returned item? How will you credit returns? How will you process returns? How will you track the reasons customers return items so you can improve your products and service in the future?

Knowing your business rules sets the stage for making choices about technologies. That's next.

The Deep Skinny on Transaction Systems

A *transaction system* lets users buy something — in this case, online. An online transaction system consists of a secure server, a catalog (a database), a shopping cart (a set of scripts), and a payment system. (We cover databases in Chapter 13.) You can build your own transaction system, you can buy a prepackaged store that includes a transaction system, or you can outsource the whole shebang. In the latter case, hosting is included so you don't need your own secure server. Management and even fulfillment may also be included.

Today, scads of companies are selling and promoting systems for doing secure transactions on the Web. Whether you are building, buying, or outsourcing your transaction system, you must first ask yourself whether any company you're considering as a vendor or partner is reputable. As everyone knows, there's plenty of snake oil on the Web. In the sections that follow, we give you an overview of what's available.

Building your own transaction system

Once upon a time building your own system (or having someone build a system for you) was the only option. Now less labor-intensive (and expensive) options exist (prepackaged stores and outsourced options, for example), so building your own transaction system is not automatically the best route to take.

The advantage of building your own is that you have complete control over the end product. No matter how arcane or Byzantine your business rules, you can implement them. But building your own means creating custom software, which means planning, testing, developing, testing, fixing, and so on. It's a lot of work, and it isn't cheap.

 To minimize the task a bit, programmers can build the system based on an existing foundation — a base of code that they can buy and customize. This route is more labor intensive and expensive than simply customizing a prepackaged solution, but less work than starting from scratch.

Buying customizable prepackaged systems

We want to be clear about this: A prepackaged transaction system is not quite what it seems. You don't pull a freeze-dried storefront from a box, pour on a little steamy water, and — poof! — move in for business. A prepackaged store is a suite of software that contains all the components you need to put your storefront online, but it still requires some customization. A number of companies are putting these conveniences together; the package usually includes components for publishing your catalog (actually the contents of a database), taking orders (via shopping cart scripts), and processing payments (accepting credit cards). Using a prebuilt system like this saves you the time and trouble of setting up all the databases, creating all the scripts, and most importantly, debugging the system. A prepackaged solution may allow you to concentrate on your products and market them, and it can be a real convenience if you aren't a programmer or don't want to hire one.

The drawback in using a prepackaged solution is that it can never be as flexible as something that's custom-built. (Ain't that the way it is in life?) You are stuck with certain assumptions that the suite developer makes about businesses in general, and that may not be right for your business. Generally, these systems follow the "best practices" rules that most businesses follow. But maybe the thing doesn't display information in quite the way you'd prefer, maybe you want to make customers jump through some hoop that isn't there, or maybe (although this is unlikely) the package doesn't support the payment system you'd prefer. And, finally, it may just lock you into using a certain Web server.

Prepackaged solutions do not work "right out of the box." Depending on the one that you choose, you still more or less have to create the HTML pages for your online store, populate the database with your products, and do some connective programming or script writing. These beauties also don't come cheap. But they are typically far less expensive than something custom built for you. If you're prepared to forego complete customization for easier setup with the ability to customize the look and feel to match your own, this may be the way to go. Depending on how elaborate your customization plans are, it may even save you quite a bit of moolah.

Outsourcing the whole thing

Outsourcing any aspect of your site can net you expertise or save you time or both. Outsourcing the running of your transaction system can also relieve you of the burden of running the secure server. (You still need to *understand* secure servers, however, so you can manage the outsourced vendor effectively.)

The sales tax shuffle

Sales tax was in days gone by a relatively simple matter. Merchants used to collect state or local sales tax at the point of purchase and pay the state or local tax board. They didn't have to pay sales tax on merchandise that was purchased by and shipped to customers in other states. Simple enough, eh?

But what's up with that when your business is in the virtual world of online instead of in Connecticut? What if your offices are in San Jose and your servers are in Nevada? The fact is that states consider your place of business to be where your *company* is physically located, not where your Web site is located.

If you plan to sell online, you must, must, must learn your state and local sales tax codes and comply with them. Pay attention to complications. For example, in California, sales tax varies from county to county. If yours is such a situation, to collect the proper tax, you may have to track a purchaser's zip code and cross reference it (electronically, of course) against the tax code for that locale. If you have a business that has physical locations in other multiple states, you may have to collect sales tax on items you sell and ship to those other states.

Our best advice is to consult a professional tax advisor and your state and local tax boards to find out the law where you do business. Best of luck to you, and to us all.

Outsource your transaction system and it will, at least theoretically, be built by experts who can do it quickly. (They should be good at it and fast because they've been doing it a while.) Usually, they'll actually implement something they have on hand to customize it for you rather than building from scratch. In fact, they may use a prepackaged solution — if so, the advantage to you in going to the outsourced company is that they have experience with that product and presumably have tricks up their sleeves that the rest of us don't know.

An outsourced transaction system includes hosting, so it won't be you getting the 3 a.m. calls saying that the server is down. It also won't be you configuring and managing the software. You can concentrate on products and selling instead of technology details.

Outsourcing can be less expensive up front than building or buying your own system. That's because the outsource company can leverage assets (software licenses, development time, equipment) across many clients, minimizing costs to each of them. However, over the long haul, outsourcing can be more expensive, because you pay and pay and pay (monthly, quarterly, or some such), as opposed to paying big time just once (to build or buy).

At the high end, iCat (www.icat.com) and Intershop (www.intershop.com) offer outsourced solutions for large scale sites. Inexpensive, low-end options are available through Yahoo Store! (store.yahoo.com), SmartAge (store.smartage.com), and Microsoft's bCentral (www.bcentral.com).

Selling through others

In some cases, running your own transaction system doesn't make sense. It may not be cost effective, it may not be your core business, it may just not be your cup of tea. It's also possible that if you sell online, you'll irritate the brick-and-mortar retailers who sell the bulk of your products, and you don't want to wreck your relationship with existing retailers, do you? It is quite possible (for smaller or mid-sized operations especially) to ride piggyback or sell through others, and generally thus avoid unwarranted headaches. You can:

✔ Locate a site that sells products like yours (if you are a manufacturer, for example), partner with them to sell your products, and then link to them via a Buy button on your site. Be wary, however, of looking like you're favoring one of your retailers over others.

✔ Sell products by becoming an affiliate or associate; for example, on our own site we sell our books via a link from the site to an online bookseller. The bookseller pays a commission on anything sold via the links from our site.

Do keep in mind that if you sell through others, basically, you're just directing customers to one of your retailers. You don't want to seem like you're favoring one of your retailers over others. The last thing you want is one of your major retailers shaking a fist at you because you partnered with its competition. The best way around this problem is to offer links to *all* the retailers that sell your products.

In another scenario, you may be actually directing your customers to a retailer that also sells products that compete with yours. If you can link directly to a Buy page on the retailer's site that is about only your product, you have no problem. If the retailer's site offers your product on a page with other products that compete with yours, this is a problem with no good solution.

Yet a third option is to sell products in the context of an online mall. An online mall, like a brick-and-mortar mall, is a central location for multiple shops and services. Online malls sometimes act as an Internet presence provider (see Chapter 10) by designing the retail sites of mall stores and providing systems for accepting payments. Online malls aren't very common these days. Shopping portals offer links to many stores but don't act as malls per se. And many smaller sites find the convenience of using services like Yahoo Store and bCentral Site Manager more appealing.

The Myriad Challenges of Fulfillment

People are funny when it comes to shopping: If they buy something, they actually want to receive it. They find that . . . *fulfilling*. Maybe this sounds obvious to you, but when it comes to selling on the Web, this topic is often forgotten until the orders come in. Oddly enough, although the weird and wacky issues of publishing online catalogs and conducting secure financial transactions grab the headlines in articles about online commerce, one of the toughest challenges is actually shipping the merchandise to the customer.

This may seem less of an issue if your product is downloadable, which, to some extent, is true. You don't have to wonder if downloaded software is going to break on the truck, as you would wonder about glass. If you're distributing software, you must track purchases and verify payment, but software distributors usually have software engineers on hand who can set up a nice custom tracking program for you with a nifty database back end.

The issues of fulfillment include

- Attaching an order number to a given order so you can track it
- Checking and maintaining inventory
- Tracking the order so you know it has been paid for (and ultimately delivered)
- Providing the customer with e-mail verification of the order and a method for tracking it, too
- Shipping the order and closing the record

Six steps to setting up a transaction system

By following these basic steps, you can start setting up a transaction system on your site today.

1. **Identify your products and business rules.**

   You need to know what you are selling and how you are selling it. See the section "Clarifying Your Business Rules" earlier in this chapter.

2. **Determine whether you should run your own transaction system or have someone else do the selling for you.**

   Many factors go into making this decision; we introduce them in the section of this chapter titled "The Deep Skinny on Transaction Systems."

3. **Contact your hosting company and determine whether it offers a transaction system.**

   If so, that might be a good route to take. But make sure your decision to use this option is based on clear thinking about your needs. If your hosting company doesn't offer a transaction system that actually fits your needs, host your transaction system with another company.

4. **Contact your bank to open a merchant account for accepting credit card payments.**

   You need a special bank account to receive payments for Internet transactions. Your bank will walk you though the process of setting up the right kind of account.

5. **Build your transaction system.**

   Whether you build, buy, or outsource, you must understand security, the nature of online commerce, and fulfillment. Just as it is your job to mind the budget and manage expectations when you hire a design firm (see Chapter 10), it's your job to manage the development of your transaction system.

6. **Create your product catalog and test the purchase process.**

   Populating the database with product information, add links to your site that will transport visitors to your shopping and transaction system, test, debug, and launch, and — poof! — now you're in business.

Much of what people want is a method for knowing where their order stands. You can set up a simple e-mail system that confirms the order, provides tracking info, notifies the customer of items that are out of stock or on back order, and so on. Use a sequential numbering system to identify orders and make it easy for you and your customers to track them.

If your company has an existing system for fulfilling orders, you may use that system to handle the fulfillment of orders for your Web initiative. Depending on your order system, this may be a simple matter. Surely your fulfillment department is set up to handle phone, fax, and mail orders, for example.

If you're using a shopping system, you can program your online store to interface with your existing inventory system. When a customer submits an order, the inventory can be checked, and if any of the ordered items are not available for immediate shipping, an automatic response can be sent to the customer. The customer can then choose whether he or she wants to place the item on back order or (heaven forbid!) cancel the order. Sounds nice, doesn't it?

Well, connecting your online store to existing back-end systems is no easy task. Some of the prepackaged store software we discuss earlier in this chapter can help smooth the process, but all this software requires some custom database work. This may include writing special database queries or even writing special programs that run on your Web server and query your database to retrieve inventory information and add shipping records. This is not easy stuff, and amateurs shouldn't attempt it. To implement an online shopping system with a sophisticated fulfillment system that provides you with good reports and keeps the customers happy, hire professionals and do it right. Obviously, you don't want to do this unless you have a good reason for it — maybe a big inventory or high-volume sales expectations.

If you've chosen to align yourself with an online mall whose operator says the mall can help you with fulfillment, beware. Look into this carefully — the mall's system may not be able to "talk" to your database back end. In any case, someone is going to have to pack the stuff and ship it out, and an online mall rarely does that for you.

To get the merchandise out the door, you (or your lackeys) can pack it and ship it, or you can contract a distributor or fulfillment house to do this. Amazon.com has a nice deal with various book distributors. The distributors receive really huge shipments from publishers (at least the publishers hope so) and then ship less-huge quantities to book stores everywhere. Instead of keeping a large inventory, Amazon.com relies on the distributors to maintain inventory and simply takes the orders and passes them electronically to the distributor, who actually ships the books. You can use this model in your industry if your sales figures are high enough to interest the distributors.

Of course, distributors and fulfillment houses don't provide their services for free. They usually charge a portion of the purchase price of the item for their cut. For example, if an item sells for $19.99, the distributor or fulfillment house may get as much as $11.99. Be sure to investigate the costs of fulfillment before you launch your super-duper Web site selling millions of Wonderwidgets.

Part III

Winning: Promote Your Site and Assess Its Success

The 5th Wave   By Rich Tennant

NO WEB PAGE

PLEASE

In this part . . .

You can build a work of true genius, but if no one knows it's there . . . well, no one knows it's there. Simply hollering from the Internet rooftops probably won't work. You have to target and reach the right audience with the right marketing techniques to push your site properly and attract the traffic you seek. You have to take the kind of action that's actually going to work. Luckily, these days, information is available to tell you how most people find the Web sites of interest to them. In Part III, you can find out what works in site promotion and how to carry out your promotional efforts. This part describes techniques you can use to better your chances of getting noticed by search engines, portals, and directories. It also describes using banner ads to promote your site, getting recognition in print and other "offline" media, mixing online and offline promotion, leveraging e-mail newsletters to drive traffic your way, and promoting a variety of other techniques you can put into practice.

Finally, in this part, we discuss what winning looks like. That's not such an obvious matter as some might think, and it's tied closely to the goals you originally set for your site. Here, you find out how to recognize, define, and measure the sort of success that you may expect specifically, as well as what changes you can make to your site in response to what you discover.

Chapter 15

Marketing and Promoting Your Web Site

. . . .

In This Chapter

▶ Using permission marketing

▶ Mixing offline and online promotion

▶ Driving traffic with direct e-mail

▶ Establishing backlinks, alliances, and affiliates

▶ Purchasing and trading banner ads

▶ Pitching to the press

. . . .

*Y*ou don't want your site to be a Web wallflower, now, do you? To attract traffic, you have to put substantial energy into marketing the site itself. You have to make it known to the world. Advertising and promoting are crucial. The real questions revolve around what can you do and what's going to work. What are the proven, promising, and even maverick methods of marketing and promoting a Web site? Here, you get a round-up of techniques, from the tried-and-true tactics to the alternative, guerilla ones.

The Foundation of Web Site Marketing

The foundation of any Web site marketing plan is a quality site that's worth visiting regularly. Strong content delivered well is the single most important factor in attracting an audience's attention. It's also crucial to getting good search engine ranking (see Chapter 16). Marketing your site, then, is actually a matter of creating a need that makes users want and actively seek out what your site provides. Marketing includes *positioning* (how the product, service, or company is established in the perception of customers and in relation to other products that fill the same need). You must also attend to *placement* — making your site fully available and getting it noticed.

Know What Works

In the offline, non-Internet world, the usual promotions model has always involved interruption: Advertisements and sponsor messages interrupt television programs, radio broadcasts, and print articles. They even interrupt roadways (ugh!), in the form of billboards and bus signs. However, in the online world, interruption is the surest way to antagonize your target audience. Unsolicited commercial e-mails and commercial postings in discussion groups are considered spam. Given the Internet's early beginnings as a non-commercial arena for publication and communication, users' deep resentment toward commercial messages is not surprising. Marketeers, then, have to come up with new solutions for getting their messages out.

The model is permission, not interruption

The new-media promotion model that works best is one of attraction and permission, rather than interruption. After you build a site that attracts users, invite user participation and leverage what you've gained. Here's how the new model works: The same techniques you use for pulling traffic to your Web site overall also apply to drawing subscribers to your newsletters and participants to your discussion forums. Newsletters and discussion groups, in turn, can play pivotal roles in building your overall site traffic. Word of mouth and write-ups in the press add to the mix. In a best-case scenario, interest in your site spreads like the buzz about the latest Hollywood blockbuster!

Figure 15-1 shows the results of a survey conducted by Forrester Research, which asked a sampling of 8,600 Web-enabled households how they usually find Web pages. (The results don't add up to 100 percent, because participants in the survey often found Web pages by more than one method.)

Mix and match

The Forrester Research statistics, along with reports from numerous other sources, show trends that suggest strongly that you want to use multiple avenues for spreading the word about your site. In general, a mix of offline and online promotion works best. Broadcast, print, and public relations tend to increase public recognition of a brand. E-mail newsletters encourage immediate visits to Web sites. Placing your site in search engines (obviously) helps people find you easily. Rising traffic levels imply better ad revenues and higher sales figures, while e-mail newsletters (again) net you the e-mail addresses of those who subscribe to your newsletter. (Those addresses have value that we describe in upcoming sections.) The question, then, is what's the right mix for you. Your decision about what's best for your site depends partly on your budget. Even on a modest budget you can boost repeat visits to your site, and with abundant financial resources, you still want to achieve the biggest bang for your buck.

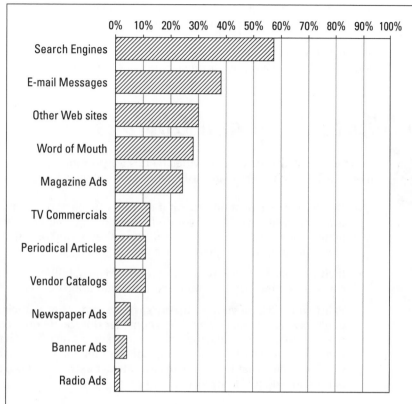

As you form your strategy, stay aware of your overall site goals. Make sure that whatever you do produces measurable results. For example, if your primary goal for your site is sales, then your promotion goal is to get as much promotion as possible at a reasonable cost *per sale*. Print and public relations are expensive and more likely to generate longer-term brand recognition than immediate sales. To encourage online sales, you probably want to focus on marketing and promotion tactics such as search engine placement, an affiliates program, and e-mail newsletters.

Bear in mind that a strategy that has worked for another site may not net the gain you want. Even within any given industry, one promotional strategy doesn't fit all sites. A travel site that wants to boost ad revenue, for example, needs to up its traffic levels in order to raise its ad rates. (Higher traffic makes the site's ad space more valuable.) That site may consider offering a vacation sweepstakes, which can result in a dramatic traffic spike (if it includes yummy prizes that appeal to the target market). But a sweepstakes probably won't benefit a travel site that sells vacation packages as its main revenue stream, because visitors who are attracted to a free vacation may not be interested in paying for one. How you promote your site depends, as all things do, on the goals you set for yourself. (See Chapter 2 for more about setting goals.) Some things, however, are good for everyone.

Do What's Easy and Obvious

Don't overlook the easy and obvious tactics for promoting your site. These methods fall into the tried-and-true, no-brainer category:

- ✓ **Make your URL prominent.** Put it on every piece of paper and every e-mail message that leaves your office, including your company's stationery, business cards, brochures, sales sheets, and product packaging as well as the e-mail signature files of everyone in the company.

- ✓ **Include your URL in any ads.** Put it on taxicabs, billboards, TV, radio, magazines, newspapers, and heck, even matchbook covers.

- ✓ **Paint your URL on your company's trucks and other vehicles.** If you don't have any company vehicles, consider this: Some dot-com companies pay to put their ads, logo, or other branding on other companies' vehicles. Even city buses carry ads for Internet companies. Industry wisdom claims that these moving ads attract extra attention, cover a lot of ground, and make the virtual more real.

One company jacked up its traffic 25 percent by not only showing its URL during an entire TV commercial, but also working the site into the commercial's script. Similarly, if your company sends out a print catalog and your Web site offers content related to the products, note that with the individual catalog items. Inserting *apple pie recipe* and a tiny Web site logo next to the catalog entry for ceramic pie pans costs very little. At the very least, offer a message in your broadcast or print ads that tells people what your site offers. A brief tagline can do the job. The company name The Pinkner Group along with the URL www.pinkner.com doesn't say much. The tagline "Market research for the digital age" clues people in.

- ✓ **Encourage users to spread word about your site.** This can be as simple as adding a Send This Page to a Friend button to your site or offering e-postcards adorned with your company's products.

- ✓ **Offer special benefits.** Offer users who register for your site free newsletters or access to exclusive, sought-after areas of the site. Offer paid members more premium benefits, such as group discounts or frequent-flyer miles.

✔ **Give heavy discounts to first-time buyers, with follow-up marketing of more expensive, "back-end" items.** Think of cellular phone service companies that offer free or cheap cell phones but get your repeat business by selling you a year-long service plan.

✔ **Post Internet-only exclusives that customers can't get anywhere else.** Also offer special online events like live chats, games, contests, or premieres.

✔ **Shell out free goodies.** Offer users tchotchkes such as software, screen savers, games, or Internet postcards.

✔ **Talk, talk, talk.** Scout around for discussion groups, chats, or message boards that are relevant to the topic of your site. There (assuming the culture of the group allows for it) you can offer sterling advice or commentary and pepper your remarks with discreet, wisely placed references to your site and its various features and services. ***Use care:*** Frequent or blatant evangelizing of your own site can disrupt the community spirit and make you seem like some sleazy self promoter. As always in the online world, valuable comments inspire interest and even loyalty.

Send E-Mail Newsletters

E-mail is the most popular application on the Internet. More people want e-mail than want access to the Web. E-mail packs real power, both as a communications medium and a promotional tool. You can prompt users to pop in to your site frequently by delivering to them regular, compelling e-mail newsletters filled with juicy teasers, rich content, and especially links back to the pages on your site.

One e-commerce venture, for example, reports a 25 percent rate of click-through from its e-mail newsletter, along with a 6 to 7 percent rate of conversion to sales. Another produces newsletters containing how-to advice, current tech news, and feature articles. That enterprise reports that it has 70,000 unique users who get their e-mail newsletters weekly. Half of those recipients click through from the newsletter to the site within 16 hours of receiving the newsletter.

Send newsletters on Mondays or Tuesdays, as early in the day as possible, to achieve the best response. Sending newsletters at regular intervals is also a good idea: You risk losing your users' attention if you don't contact them at least once every 21 days, according to some experts. But spamming users with too frequent marketing messages turns them off. Send newsletters no more often than once or twice a week, and make sure your newsletters include some value (not just advertising).

Two basic types of newsletters are in this world:

- ✔ **Announcement newsletters** announce products, specials, features, and
  the like. They often include a quick, snappy promotional blurb with a
  link (in HTML-format newsletters) or a URL (in text-only newsletters)
  that entices users to visit some portion of the Web site for more information or to make a purchase. To get better results with announcement
  newsletters, include added value in them. A tip for using the product, a
  truly bargain price, or some other special angle will make friends and
  win visitors.

- ✔ **A content-driven newsletter** contains content that is a product in its
  own right and isn't promotional in nature. It may include tips, news,
  details about industry trends, or other information that's of interest to
  the user. Although content-driven newsletters sometimes carry ads and
  sponsor messages as a source of revenue, these newsletters do not
  directly promote a product, service, or company per se. Content-driven
  newsletters do often contain links or URLs that take the user to featured
  areas of the site. Dummies Daily, at `www.dummiesdaily.com`, is an example of a content-driven newsletter.

Of course, you can create a hybrid of the two types, if that suits your site's
goals. For example, a content-driven newsletter can include announcements
of your own products or services as well as ads promoting someone else's.

Create and acquire compelling content

To add value to announcement newsletters and make content-driven newsletters appealing, you must offer your newsletter subscribers something of real
interest — tips, specials, intriguing content, and so on. Make the subject line
of the newsletter concise but also intriguing. In the subject line, indicate what
benefit the newsletter has for the user ("Fresh tulips on sale now!" or "Plant
perfect roses"). In general, active verbs work well in the subject lines of
newsletters that contain instructional material, and adjectives are effective
for experience-oriented material (like gardening, travel, or food newsletters).
If you send out several newsletters, differentiate them by topic or some other
system; you don't want users to think they are duplicates and discard them.

Where, oh where can you get real, value-added content for your newsletters?
You can, of course, write it yourself. Information from press releases and
reports from the online newswires can also be a rich source of content. (You
should actually write it up; don't just lift the reports.) Seek out online news
bureaus related to your topic and comb the press releases posted there.
Search for newsworthy stories that relate to your topic and that will interest
your audience. Alternatively, subscribe to the newswire sites' e-mail newsletter services, and get the stories you want delivered to your e-mail in-box.

You can also publish user-submitted content. Ask users to send in tips, "war" stories, recipes, or whatever. You can create a special section of the newsletter that's devoted to user comments and even solicit story ideas. If you do any of these things, credit the source. People generally love seeing their names in (virtual) lights. For many people, posting their names is payment enough. You get unique content; they get recognition.

Use fabulous formatting

Your e-mail newsletters can go out in the usual text-based format, but that doesn't have to mean no-frills ASCII text. Figure 15-2 shows a newsletter that's jazzed up a tad. You can use keyboard characters like plus signs and periods (+.+.+.+), hyphens (- - -), and tildes (~ ~ ~) to make the presentation snappy.

Figure 15-2:
This text-
based
e-mail isn't
plain and
ordinary.

```
==============================
CLIFFS-NOTE-A-DAY: AOL
http://www.cliffsnotes.com
A tip a day to make your day.
==============================

TODAY'S TIP: Follow Your Favorite Sport

Keep current with the happenings in baseball, basketball, hockey, football, and golf. No matter what
sport you like to follow, you'll find great coverage and readable stories in The Sporting News. Use
Keyword: The Sporting News to read it online, and if you like it, subscribing to the print version is
always an option.
```

As always, we caution you not to clutter up things. Visual appeal goes by the wayside when formatting tricks turn into readability speed bumps. To prevent lines of text from breaking in odd places in some e-mail programs, stick to 65 characters per line, at most.

Another alternative is to send newsletters in the more graphically sophisticated HTML format, which is shown in Figure 15-3. HTML-formatted e-newsletters offer more options for page layout creativity than text-based messages. However, HTML-formatted newsletters download more slowly, and only subscribers whose e-mail programs are HTML-enabled can view these beauties. You probably want to offer subscribers the option of choosing either HTML- or text-based formatted e-mail.

Figure 15-3:
Some subscribers enjoy HTML-formatted e-mail.

Treat subscribers well indeed

As you know, permission is the name of the game in Internet marketing. Don't simply bombard an unsuspecting user with your publication: That tactic will blow up in your face when users unsubscribe in droves. For success, you must treat your newsletter recipients with the respect they deserve. Doing so boosts your credibility and lessens the energy you have to expend to manage your newsletter. Follow these tips:

✔ **For best results, let people "opt in."** Research and user response have proven that click-through rates can double and sometimes triple when folks have the option to subscribe willingly to what actually interests them. Don't presume that everyone who visits your site or registers there automatically wants to hear from you. Letting users opt in (elect to receive your messages) gets the nod from them.

✔ **Make unsubscribing a clear option.** Users find having options (such as the option to unsubscribe) comforting, although they frequently don't exercise their options. You risk little and gain a lot by offering an easy exit. Tell folks how to unsubscribe, how to subscribe to other offerings you might have, and how to submit a change-of-e-mail address if need be. A link to your Help page is also handy to users.

✔ **Tread carefully on the privacy of others!** A user who has subscribed to one list doesn't necessarily want more. Fail to respect people's privacy, and you risk alienation and online ruin. Also, if you feel compelled to make your subscriber list available to others (or hit up your list for donations to the noble cause of sending your kid's bagpipe band to march in Scotland next summer), at least make sure you've gained the permission of each and every subscriber on that list. Include a sentence on the original sign-up page notifying people of your intentions and offering them the opportunity to *opt out* of (or exclude themselves from) any lists you sell to others, share, or use in any way other than the way they are expecting.

Create Backlinks and Trade Links

Like real-world gambling casinos, Web sites often work best when they have many entry points, lots for users to do, and as few exit points as possible. (This last item is quite different from providing newsletter subscribers with a way to unsubscribe. In that case, an exit point is comforting to the user and inspires trust.) Getting listed in search engines and sending out e-mail newsletters are both methods for creating Web site entry points. Another set of methods involves getting other Web sites to link to yours.

Boosting your site's popularity can improve your ranking in search engines, as discussed in Chapter 15, and that can provide *entrée* to your site for even more users. So the effort can be worth more than the sum of its parts. It often costs only time and persistence (and perhaps the placement of reciprocal links on your own site).

Check your backlinks

Perhaps you want to check out how many backlinks your site already has. Several online search engines offer ways that you can search for links to your site. To try this out using AltaVista, follow these steps:

1. **Using your favorite browser, open AltaVista (**www.altavista.com**).**

2. **In the text box, where you would usually type the subject of interest to conduct a search of AltaVista's database of Web sites, instead type the following (all in lowercase characters):**

   ```
   www.yourdomainname.com/ -host:yourdomainname.com
   ```

   Note that the - is a minus sign, and be sure to replace "yourdomainname" in both places with your actual domain name. If yours is a dot org (or dot something else) instead of a dot com, replace .com with the correct suffix.

3. **Click the Search button.**

   The list that appears shows the URLs of all the Web pages in the enormous AltaVista database that link to your site. (It doesn't show backlinks to pages within your site, however. To run a search for backlinks to any important internal pages on your site, replace `yourdomainname.com` with the page's entire URL.)

HotBot, Google, and other search sites offer similar check-your-backlinks services, along with instructions for using them.

Get backlinks

Build a wonderful Web site with strong, targeted content or unique, well-delivered services, and you will find that other sites (once they know it exists) link to it. Such links are called *backlinks*. Lots of backlinks means lots of entry points. Lots of backlinks also implies more popularity, which makes your site more attractive to search engines and the press. Getting backlinks can happen magically (as in the case of some sites that are so unusual or intriguing they generate intense word-of-mouth interest). It can also be a process of persuasion, negotiation, and . . . well, swapping.

Trade links

First, if you link to another site, tell the person running that site. Many sites list those that have recognized them, along with links to those sites, and even requesting such a link is no faux pas. Traded links are known as *reciprocal* links.

You can also actively seek out sites related to or complemented by yours (vendors, professional groups, colleagues, your college alumni association) and ask the people running those sites to link to yours. When you approach others about linking to your site, send a polite e-mail, telling them why your site might be of interest and requesting the link. Remember that they are more likely to link to your site if its content or offerings deepen, complement, or add interest to their own. (If your company has some leverage with the big search-engine companies or some other big-time Web sites, you can use that leverage as well to get links, positive reviews of your offerings, and so on.) Phrase your request to underscore what additional value linking to your site will provide to their site, and if possible, offer a reciprocal link. ReciprocalLink (`www.reciprocallink.com`) offers the opportunity to announce your interest in exchanging links along with a matching service that helps you find sites on topics like yours.

Remember, always, to trade links at their actual value. For example, if the page on your site where another company's link appears has more traffic than the page on its site where your link appears, you may want to ask that your link stay on their site longer than theirs or ask for a link to your site on more than one of their pages.

TIP

Earn awards and get recognition

Winning awards looks good and feels terrific. Enter your site into any of the many award, recognition, and listing venues that other sites and organizations offer, and you might just win. Submit your site for consideration only to those awards that actually match the topic of your site, however. Forget design awards if you haven't hired a top-tier designer, and go for Best Craftsman Bungalow Sites only if you have a humdinger of a site *on that topic*. Find niche awards and listings that recognize excellence in your field, or look into how the Webbys (www.webbyawards.com) and Cool Site of the Day, (www.coolsiteoftheday.com) are chosen, then go for the gold. Note that the prestige of the award or listing depends a great deal on the status of the organization offering it. More prestige means more credibility and more visitors, which is definitely better. Of course, you probably don't want an award from Web Sites That Suck (www.websitesthatsuck.com)!

Form Alliances and Partnerships

In the online world as well as the "real" world, two or more parties can form alliances to leverage their assets, making the sum greater than the parts. Internet alliances can be as simple as trading links or ads, or they can be more innovative. Here we concentrate on those alliances and partnerships that further a Web site's marketing goals:

- **Affiliates or associates programs:** A Web site or company provides other Web sites with some compelling incentive (money, for example) to send users, sales leads, or actual sales back to the first site.

- **Sponsorships:** One site pays for representation on another. Usually the sponsoring site gains ad, logo, or backlink placements on selected pages; is allowed to provide pages of about its offerings; or gets some combination of these.

- **Cobranding deals:** Two companies team up to offer a single online product or Web site that carries a merged identity.

For the scoop on how to create and maximize the benefits of alliances and strategic partnerships, read on.

Set up an affiliates program

Here's a great way to encourage other Web sites to link to yours: Offer them a bounty. Or, to put it more delicately, set up an affiliates program. In an affiliates program, you provide other sites with an incentive to send users, leads, or sales to your site. The affiliates' end of the bargain is to place backlinks to you on specified areas of their sites; you, in return, offer them a commission or other reward for results.

Initiating an affiliates program can be easy and inexpensive: Design an affiliates logo or graphic, spread word about your program to potential affiliates, and then provide the logo and program details to interested companies. Of course, if you have a good reputation in your industry or are partnered with a well-reputed company, make that known to potential affiliates. It helps reassure them that they will receive payment as promised. Here are some matters to be aware of:

- ✔ Depending on your agreement, you may define the results you expect as a targeted number of page impressions carrying the link, actual click-throughs on the link, or the number of transactions closed by customers using the link. (*Impressions* and *click-throughs* are discussed later in this chapter and in Chapter 17.)

- ✔ You can reward affiliates who produce results with commission payments (based on gross sales), flat finder's fees, or ad placement of your affiliates' products.

Pony up big rewards, and you get big participation. You may want to offer some reward for carrying a link to your site in the first place, such as a reciprocal link or a listing in an Our Affiliates section. Beyond that, what you pay depends on your product and your industry. Make your program as attractive as possible, but keep the terms realistic. Figure how much a new customer or sale is actually worth to you, and how much reward you can afford. Also, don't forget to take your overhead into account, including those costs associated with your affiliates program and other regular costs of doing business.

In the long term, you have to invest in the management of your affiliates program. You must market it, track its results, and issue checks or other rewards. To keep all this down to a dull roar, you may want to join an affiliate service that can find potential affiliates for you, track what's coming in and what should go out, and take care of accounting and paying commissions. ClickTrade (clicktrade.bcentral.com) is one such service.

Be imaginative about how your affiliates may be able to enhance the effectiveness of the program for your mutual benefit. If your site sells dried figs, a health-oriented affiliate site can include recipes, information, and tips to persuade users to eat more dried figs (and to visit your site for all their dried-fig needs). Also, encourage your affiliates to place linked buttons throughout their sites rather than in one single spot or on a single page several levels into their sites — the better the placement, the greater the return for both the affiliate and you. If one of your affiliates does an outstanding job of incorporating your program into its site, refer other potential affiliates to that site as a showcase to be emulated.

Affiliate programs are highly scalable and can be profitable for all parties. Technically speaking, your program can grow to have many, happy, proliferating affiliates all over the Web. For your efforts, you gain the advantages of extending your reach, increasing awareness of your brand, and closing sales or getting other desired results.

Sponsor someone else's site

You can gain revenue if someone else sponsors your Web site, which we discuss in Chapter 2. Well, what if you're the one doing the sponsoring? Presto! You have yet another way to promote and market your site. As a sponsor, you pay to be represented in some form on some other site. In exchange for your payment, you get special placement within that site, along with links back to your site or any portion of it that you specify. Because you want the audience of the sponsored site to closely align with your target market, sponsor a site with sterling content that complements, deepens, or reflects well on your company, product, or service.

In a sponsorship deal, you can generally expect that users of the sponsored site can view your banners, buttons, and perhaps other sponsor messages a specified number of times. However, sponsorship scenarios are more complex than the simple purchase of ad space; they frequently also contain provisions such as:

- ✔ The sponsor "owns" select pages on the host site. (Content for the sponsored pages comes from the sponsor or the sponsor works with the other company to create content that is mutually acceptable and beneficial to both sites.)
- ✔ The sponsor gets access to marketing data about the users who click through to the sponsored pages or other areas of the host site.
- ✔ The sponsor owns or co-owns specified tools or functions that the host site develops using sponsorship funds.
- ✔ The sponsor distributes some of its existing tools or content through the sponsored site.

Many other sponsorship provisions are also possible; go after the benefits that most suit your overall business and marketing goals. As you size up a potential site to sponsor, do, however, think through some key issues.

- ✔ **Make sure the site's content, design, and functionality enhance the image you want to convey.** If your site sells swimsuits and beachwear, you may sponsor a site that serves content about beach resorts, but you don't want your sponsor messages to appear on pages that describe the risks of skin cancer. Conversely, you may specify that your content appears in targeted places on pages that discuss how to pack for a vacation in Hawaii. (Put all such stipulations into the contract, of course.)

✔ **Verify that the site reaches and pleases the audience you are after.** Ask for user-satisfaction information, site statistics, demographics, or other data. (See Chapter 17.) Remember that the audience you are targeting with your sponsorship doesn't necessarily have to be the exact same as the audience you target for your own site, but you do want them to be the right audience. For example, if your site sells '70s music CDs, you needn't necessarily sponsor a music site, but you do want to go where the boomers are.

✔ **Look for some evidence (such as the number of registered users) that the site has a large enough audience for your message to have an impact.** Again, Chapter 17 discusses site statistics issues and tools.

✔ **Clarify for yourself and the other company what your goals are in sponsoring the site.** Do you want to see a specific number of sales closed? Are you trying to penetrate a new market? Or are you trying to extend your brand awareness overall?

A sponsorship deal gives you the chance to piggyback onto another site's popularity without having to drum up all the buzz and big traffic numbers yourself. Clearly, though, paying for sponsorship is expensive. In addition to money, you also have to devote resources to putting together a sound written agreement, maintaining the relationship, tracking performance, and processing payments. Sponsorship is often the best route only after you have begun promoting your site through less expensive avenues and established a certain amount of recognition or trust in your brand. Then, a few well-placed dollars can help you achieve the next step in your promotional goals.

Extend your reach with cobranding

Cobranding allows multiple companies to bring their core competencies together while presenting their brands and perhaps even their own sites (via linked logos, for example) to an extended audience of users. If you have unique offerings, for example, but not the technological or marketing power to drive real success, you can partner up with another company that offers what you lack. The site that this partnership produces may carry both logos and even blend the look and feel of both companies' brands (your purple and their green?). Cobranding relationships are ideal for companies that offer complementary services or products, but you probably wouldn't enter into a cobranding arrangement with a competitor.

Make the Most of Banner Ads

A banner ad is a graphic advertisement, usually in the form of a GIF image, that appears on a Web site and is linked to a page on the advertiser's site. Most banner ads measure 468 pixels wide by 60 pixels long and appear at the top of a page (though the occasional banner ad is slightly smaller or is relegated to the bottom or the middle of a page). Much smaller versions of banner ads, which are called boxes, buttons, tiles, or thumbnails, sometimes appear on the left- or right-most sides of pages, near the middle or bottom of a page, or perhaps even beside a regular banner ad.

The site selling the ad space determines its own ad rates. The rates are quoted in *cost per thousand* (CPM), meaning the cost for every thousand times the ad is served; each time the ad is served, an *impression* is said to have occurred. An impression is simply a pair of human eyes falling on the ad. CPM rates vary widely.

To determine ad rates, a site's traffic is measured in impressions, which are also known as page views. High-traffic, nationally known sites may seem as though they'd command the higher CPMs, because they deliver more eyeballs falling on the ad. However, all those eyeballs may not belong to people who are interested in whatever the ad is promoting (for example, if you are advertising on a general-interest area of AOL). Smaller, niche sites that attract specialized audiences deliver more interested eyeballs and can justify charging high rates because theirs is a targeted audience. If you want to advertise to a group that is narrowly focused, with interests (golf, diabetes, classic Chevys) or demographic attributes (age, sex, geography) in common, you may go for advertising in a more targeted venue. If you want to reach a broad audience, advertise on a site that gets lots of traffic from a wide variety of people.

Unfortunately, no one has yet developed a precise or standardized way of calculating the number of users who buy a product or service because they saw an ad on a particular site at a particular time. But studies have shown that, although ads may not always prompt click-through, they do serve to establish and reinforce awareness of the identity and message of a company, a product, or a service. And people buy what they readily recognize more often than what they don't recognize. So, friends, it appears that running an eye-catching, creative banner ad campaign can be worthwhile indeed.

Hits aren't the hit they once were

Perhaps you've heard of "hits" as a traffic measurement. People don't like to measure in *hits* these days because the measurement is so imprecise. A hit occurs when a *file* is served by the server, and a single page can be made up of many files. What's more, two seemingly identical pages can be composed in different ways that use fewer or more files, so two pages that look indistinguishable from each other can actually produce widely varying numbers of hits. Given all this, page impressions or page views have become the more standard measurement of traffic. Click-throughs are also counted; a click-through occurs when the user clicks an add or a link and goes zipping off to the associated Web page. See Chapter 17 for details.

Get optimum results

Running a banner ad campaign probably isn't going to send your site's traffic skyrocketing the way a direct e-mail campaign can. But banner ads, along with other, more traditional ads, are a valuable tool for creating and expanding awareness of your product, company, service, or Web site.

To get the best results — maximum awareness and even perhaps a respectable number of click-throughs — at a reasonable rate, you must create snazzy ads and buy the right ad space. You have to keep your campaign fresh, interesting, and appropriately targeted. Like people skimming through a magazine, Web site users often glance past the ads. And just as broadcast ads lose their appeal over time, so do online ads. Your goal is to snatch people's attention while you can, and while you have their attention, insert into their psyches a quick dose of your message.

You have less than one second to do that. According to a study conducted by the Poynter Institute and Stanford University, users do see banner ads, and they focus on them for just about one second — long enough to get a message across. Your goal, then, is to make the most of the moment.

We recently had great success (a click-through rate of over 4 percent!) with an ad for a Linux-related content site. The ad was created with simple clip-art-style images and faded from one panel to another. The first panel showed a dark room with a barely visible lightbulb hanging from the ceiling, and the second showed the lightbulb on, a penguin sitting in the corner, and the text message, "Shed some light on Linux." The ad was placed in highly targeted, Linux-related venues and on other sites with tech themes. It led (when users clicked on the ad) to a subsite that provided Linux tips, tools, and Linux itself.

Create effective ads

To create effective banner ads, first get real about what you expect your ads to accomplish. Click-throughs? Awareness? Hire a professional designer (one with actual experience designing successful banner ads), and tell the designer what your goals are. Let the designer in on how you see whatever you're promoting, any images you want to avoid, and the whole basic drill of information you defined when you decided what your site was all about. You almost certainly want your ad to be clickable. Tell the designer where on your site the click will lead, and make sure that anything the ad's text implies will be there for the user is actually there and is easy to see. If the ad says you offer solutions, for example, the user had better find a solution on the first click from the ad to your site.

A call to action ("buy now") is a fine idea. But forget the overused "click here." Most users know they're supposed to click. Use that teensy ad space and your oh-so-brief opportunity to say something more compelling instead. Here are more tips:

- ✔ **Invoke mystery or leave a question unanswered.** As in our Linux example, this intrigues the user into clicking through to find an answer.

- ✔ **Create ads that are funny, sexy, timely, or topical to appeal to the universal desire to be entertained.** But don't let your advertising goals be overshadowed by the cuteness of the ads.

- ✔ **Have several ads on hand.** This allows you to target one ad to a certain demographic and another ad to a different demographic. Also, rotate the ads so users don't burn out on them.

- ✔ **Bandy about already established brand names.** Whether you use your name or strategic partners' names, brand names can pull in already loyal customers along with curious clickers. But make your own message more prominent than the name of any company or product that's not your own.

One more thing: Keep the file size small. Tell your designer it has to be no more than 10K, whether it's a postage-stamp-size ad or a standard 468x60 pixels. To avoid squandering that one second you have to get your message across, the file has to load very quickly indeed. Until broadband is as common as Starbucks, forget using Flash in your banner ads. Keep 'em lean, keep 'em simple, keep 'em clever.

Understand types of ad buys

Buying ad space is an art unto itself. You can do it yourself or hire a savvy media buyer to do the job for you. Hiring someone else (assuming this person is a real pro) has the advantage that he or she already knows the terrain and can smush together several clients' media purchases to get a better deal for all. Whether you buy the ad space or spring for the services of someone savvy, you ought to understand what's what. Generally, ad buys fall into these types:

- ✔ **Run-of-site:** Your ad appears in rotation with other ads (it is rotated among all other ads that have been sold on a run-of-site basis). These might include ads from other companies as well as in-house ads produced by the site running the ads to promote its own features.

- ✔ **Specific pages:** Your ad appears on selected pages containing content that's of interest to your target users. For example, if you sell hiking boots, you may place ads on a site that deals with outdoor sports, but only on the pages devoted to hiking, climbing, or backpacking.

✔ **Keyword searches:** Your ad appears on pages that are displayed when a user searches for a designated keyword. In this case, you pay for the opportunity to place your ad in front of any user who searches for a keyword. If your site sells bare root roses, for example, you might want to buy keywords such as *gardening, landscaping, flower,* or *floribunda.*

✔ **Targeted to users:** Your ad is served only to those specific users you want to reach. You can target based on the browser or operating system used, the type of domain name (`.org` or `.edu`, for example), or the geographic location of the ISP. You can also target users who have certain preferences or profiles (based on their usage and buying habits, as tracked by cookies; see Chapter 17).

In general, to attract new customers, buy ad space in a broad market, such as run-of-site advertising on a general-interest site, a search engine, or a topic of general interest to your target market. To penetrate more deeply into a targeted market, buy select keywords on big sites or run-of-site ads on specialized niche sites. (The deepest targeting occurs, of course, when you target directly to users.) Sometimes placing your ad on a page immediately *preceding* the page that's directly related to your product or service gets good results. With this head-them-off-at-the-pass strategy, you can divert members of your target audience to your own site and its offerings before they open a page full of content related to your topic. The idea is that people click on the first instance of whatever they seek. If they see your ad before they get to the goodies, that's where they click.

Negotiate good rates

Like used-car prices, online ad rates start high and are almost always negotiable. Don't assume you have to pay the rate that's published or first quoted. Your initial offer can be less than the asking rate: Up to 30 percent less can be reasonable. Also, like most commodities, ad space can be had at a bargain during slow sales periods. Mid-winter is one such slow time, because sales are often sluggish after the end of the year, especially in January. Also, you can often get better rates by making your buy through a media buy service, although you pay for the service itself, which may cancel out your gains.

Centralized services such as bCentral's AdStore (`store.bcentral.com`) can be useful for smaller budgets. These services sell ad space in big sites, such as major search engines, and in targeted niche sites for various industries. They have the collective-pricing power of media buy services but don't make recommendations or do custom buying for you.

Exchange ad space

Another option for extending your reach without laying out a lot of cash is to trade ad space on your site for ad space on another site. You can get even more clever, in fact, and barter your ad space for some other commodity. For example, you may be able to give a specific amount of ad space on your site to another business in exchange for print ads in that business's print directories or newsletters.

The same types of sites that you trade links with make good candidates for ad trades: sister companies, vendors, clients, and sites that offer complementary products or services. Another option is to work with an ad exchange network, such as LinkExchange Banner Network (adnetwork.bcentral.com) or Engage Media (www.engage.com/engagemedia). These networks offer you a wider pool of companies with whom to trade ads, and some are free of charge.

Get Savvy to Good Media

Get press, get good press, and get it often. As any sharp marketeer knows, you want your company and site's name in the media, as favorably and as often as possible. Public relations efforts don't carry the hefty price tag that advertising does, but they do require patience, energy, and ingenuity. Like so many other things in life, professionals are often the best people to handle public relations, though you can achieve some PR yourself. If you do hire the pros, you ought to know enough about what they do to manage them well.

Think of public relations as a matter of creating, sustaining, and leveraging a relationship with the media. People who work in PR know this well. They use their interpersonal skills to get close to and stay on good terms with the editors of key departments at various publications and the producers at radio and TV venues. They know the kinds of stories those people are likely to run and the best ways to pitch stories to them. PR people also use their organizational skills to continually reevaluate priorities, juggle timelines, manage the flow of information, and remain positive and focused when speaking with press contacts. They are skilled at recognizing and publicizing newsworthy successes and at putting the best possible spin on crises. Like human piñatas, good press people attract the media, take the hits, and dispense goodies. To get positive media coverage for your site, you have to either develop these skills or hire someone who has them.

Don't limit your PR efforts to those national media outlets that immediately spring to everyone's mind. Favorable exposure in trade publications related to your topic may be a better fit and easier to obtain. If yours is a site for consumers, consumer publications are also an option. Target business journals, industry magazines, newspapers, other local and regional publications, and, of course, Web sites covering your industry and general news. Choose your venues, however. Put your efforts where they can get the best bang for your PR buck. PR costs time if not money. Yet getting your Web site's URL and name into print or broadcast means not only extra attention; but also extra credibility. Media exposure can put your company on the e-commerce map. So get cracking and get press coverage.

Assemble press materials

First, you must gather a few handy items for your PR tool kit. Start by identifying a couple of brief, precise phrases that describe your company, product, and site. These form the basis of your *elevator pitches* (the phrases you can toss out in a moment to describe what you offer or do). Then, using those phrases, write some prepared descriptions of your company, product, and site: Create one that's no more than a few words, one that's about 15 words, and a longer description that's about 25 words. Use these elevator-pitch descriptions whenever your press releases and other communications call for a brief description that signposts your company's offerings.

Now, assemble the following materials:

- ✔ **A professionally made photograph depicting your product, CEO, store, home page, or whatever seems most appropriate for your business and your particular PR campaign.** This can also be a slide, an 8-x-10-inch glossy print, or a TIFF or JPEG file.

- ✔ **A company backgrounder listing key information about your company and products.** This can include a mission statement (incorporating the descriptions you wrote), important dates, timelines, product specs, graphs, charts, awards, and so on. Take the time to format and print this so it looks good, but don't get gimmicky (unless the image you're conveying *is* gimmicky).

- ✔ **A few testimonials, endorsements, quotes, reviews, or any accolades you can leverage to publicize the site.** (Get permission from the sources of this material.) These should also be nicely formatted and printed, in a style similar to that of the company backgrounder.

Use these materials to assemble your media kit. Keep them on hand, too, for sudden requests for information.

Publicity primers, tips, and pointers

Plenty of sage advice for dealing with the media is available online. Find out more about what to do and what not to do via these resources:

- ✔ "The Care and Feeding of the Press," by Esther Schindler and members of the Internet Press Guild at `www.netpress.org/careandfeeding.html`.

- ✔ "A Publicity Primer," with checklists and tips, by Kirk Hallahan of Colorado State

University at `lamar.colostate.edu/~hallahan/hpubty.htm`.

- ✔ "Press Release Basics," with an extensive list of PR links and advice, compiled by the Voyager Group, at `www.voyagergroup.net/press.htm`.

Create media kits

Media kits, which are also called press kits, are those amalgamations of information in presentation folders that are often emblazoned with company logos. When big budgets are involved, they often come in cute packaging such as miniature briefcases, canisters, lunchboxes, and so forth, depending on the industry and the clever gimmick of the moment. Sometimes they also include disks, fortune cookies, roasted chestnuts, or some other thinly veiled bribe.

Don't worry if you don't have the budget to send out fancy media kits brimming with expensive tchotchkes. A good media kit has to catch the recipient's attention, convey a message about your company that is in line with your overall branding, and contain notable, newsworthy information. It's meant to prompt a journalist to learn about your company or Web site and then cover it in his or her work. Your media kit doesn't have to include Belgian chocolates.

If you have presentation folders personalized with your company logo, use them. Otherwise, you can put stickers with your logo on plain black or white folders or paper-clip your business card on top or inside the folders. Make sure the documents inside the folder are printed on your letterhead. Place the items you assembled above (a photo, a company backgrounder, and a page of testimonials and reviews) into your media kit. You can add other items as well, such as a color print-out of your home page or other important site pages, bios of executive staff, and photocopies of other press coverage you've received (once you get permission to copy it). Note that a media kit is distinct from a sales kit. You're pitching ideas to journalists, not your revenue model to potential sponsors. Typically you won't include information about ad rates and the like, because that's not relevant to the press. Now, roll up your sleeves and get ready to craft a press release.

Write a press release

When you have news to publicize, you can issue a press release. Keep in mind that members of the media pay more attention to press releases that contain really, truly newsworthy information (in fact, press releases are also called news releases). Don't send journalists junk. What exactly is deemed newsworthy depends on the size and focus of the publication you're pitching to, how your news compares to other items received on that day, and general trends in what is considered important in your industry. In general, announcements of the following types can make news:

✔ New products, services, executive personnel, or company locations

✔ New strategic partners, sponsors, or distributors

✔ Sponsored events, awards, or seminars

✔ New programs, such as affiliate programs, incentive programs, and so on

✔ Unusually good sales or a seasonal or time-sensitive special offer

✔ Receiving of awards, grants, or honors or achieving any key industry benchmarks

✔ Offerings of awards, grants, or honors

Keep your press release short and to the point; the ideal is one page. In the text, follow the usual rules of good grammar and style. For example, use active voice ("Insects, Inc., offers the best field guides in the market."), not passive voice ("The best field guides in the market are offered by Insects, Inc."). Keep your text squeaky clean and free of extraneous verbiage, especially corporate or industry jargon. Press releases follow a fairly standard format:

✔ **At the top of the page, provide complete contact information for the person who is the press contact at your end.** This is the person who can answer questions and provide more details.

✔ **Write a concise headline that quickly conveys your message, or the reason you issued the release.**

✔ **Provide a dateline and location.** Your location is usually the city where your company is located. The first paragraph of your release, which summarizes your most important message, directly follows the dateline and location.

✔ **Expand on the news you are announcing.** Use the first and second paragraphs in the main text of the press release to state and clarify what makes your news unique, significant to your industry or consumer, and worth covering in the press.

✔ **Provide a quote from a key member of the company's staff.** Note that quotations are the only place in a press release where you can express an opinion (it should be indicated as such). All the other text in the release should be factual.

✔ **End with a brief statement about your company.** You can mention when it was founded, when your site launched, what your core competency is, what makes you unique, and any major investors and partners. Here, you can also incorporate the 25-word description you created as one of your elevator pitches.

✔ **Include your Web site's URL along with the URLs of pages that contain more information about your company or the news that you are announcing.**

Many books and Web sites show standard formats for press releases. See "Publicity primers, tips, and pointers," in this chapter for some good resources.

Contact the press

With your shining press release tucked into your cleverly informative media kit, you're ready to make first contact with the press. Send your kit (or just your release) to every appropriate person you can identify. That means the actual, individual people who research, write, or otherwise cover news and feature articles for targeted venues in your industry. Appropriate people may include print newspaper, magazine, and business-journal writers and editors; local TV and radio producers and editors; reviewers, reporters, and editors of online business publications; and publishers of e-mailing lists that deal with Internet-oriented news.

Send your press materials to specific, named people, not simply "the Internet editor" or "the news desk." You can find the names you need by looking at the *mastheads* (listings of personnel) in print publications or by checking Web sites and publications that list editors of major media outlets (such as Media Map at `www.mediamap.com`, which lists technology editors).

This little tidbit is crucial: Verify the correct spelling of people's names and then spell those names correctly in all of your communications. People can be incredibly annoyed when their names are misspelled and can quietly but deeply appreciate seeing their names spelled correctly. (Especially if their names are unusual.)

If you are interested in acquiring new customers, target your PR campaign to consumer and general news outlets. To increase penetration into one of your existing markets, pitch your news to more narrowly focused media outlets. For example, if you sell bakeware and are trying to increase your presence among professional chefs, send your press materials to highly targeted restaurant industry magazines.

If you disseminate your press release by e-mail, keep in mind that journalists, like most businesspeople nowadays, get way too much e-mail and toss whatever they can directly into the Delete pile. Follow these tips for maximum impact:

- ✔ **Make your subject line informative and snappy, but not goofy or like a sales pitch, and don't let anyone mistake your e-mail for spam.**

- ✔ **Don't say "Press Release," "News," or some other redundant phrase in your subject line.** Instead, use a brief header that tells what your news is and why it is noteworthy. You might want to use something like the five-word description you wrote earlier.

- ✔ **Include your complete contact information in your signature file.** Your name, phone number, address, e-mail address, and URL make finding you easy.

✓ **Though you may be sending your press release out to a posse of different people, don't list them all in the recipient (To:) list.** Put them in the blind courtesy copy (Bcc:) list, or send the release to people one at a time. Exposing your entire contact list to all the recipients looks plain unprofessional. It also makes each recipient feel less . . . special.

✓ **Don't send your press release as an attachment.** People probably won't open an attachment, because opening it is too much bother and because they may fear that it contains a virus. Paste your press release into the body of your e-mail instead, keep it easy to read, and follow the previous guidelines for keeping it brief and to-the-point.

You or your press contact (who will know from experience which press people like a nudge and which want to be left alone) may want to follow up *gently* on a press release with a brief e-mail to let the journalist know that you are available to answer questions. But a word to the wise: Don't be more aggressive than this. Never annoy the press.

Add a press room to your Web site

These days, having an online press room that contains your press releases and other press information is *de rigeur*. Here are guidelines for creating a welcoming, easy-to-navigate, informative online press room:

✓ **Make PR contact information clear and easy to find.** If you have several people doing PR for you, list each person's name along with his or her e-mail address, phone number, and surface mail address.

✓ **Link to a page listing the company executives' names, titles, and possibly bios and photos.**

✓ **Link to a page describing your products.** If your products are highly technical, you may want to provide another link to product specs.

✓ **Don't overload your press room pages with lots of graphics.** These take time to load, which is going to put off busy journalists with deadline pressures. Offer downloadable photos of your products or whatever you're promoting, but only if the download time is going to be quick as a whip. (You can alternatively indicate what photos are available via surface mail upon request.)

✓ **Don't require media folks to register or log in to access to your press-room.** These people are working under tight deadlines. Don't put obstacles in journalists' way or do anything that might endanger the mutually beneficial but ultimately quite fragile association you intend to build with the press.

Again, PR can be a powerfully effective method of extending public awareness of your company, product, service, or site. It can reel in users, help persuade investors that you mean business, and bump up your credibility quotient. Of course, these benefits don't come without the application of a great deal of patience, effort, and constant hustling. But especially if your site is doing something unique or leading your industry, a dedicated and persuasive PR campaign can ultimately land big rewards.

You naturally want to know how your promotional efforts (and the cleverness of your Web site) are paying off. To find out how to assess the success of your Web endeavor, see Chapter 17.

Chapter 16

Getting in Good with Search Engines

. . . .

In This Chapter

▶ Looking into search engines, directories, and portals

▶ Understanding what gets a better ranking in search result lists

▶ Optimizing your pages for better ranking

▶ Using smart strategies for submitting your site

▶ Excluding parts of your site from searchability

. . . .

*L*et's face it. Even if your whiz-bang beauty of a Web site reveals the one true meaning of life, if no one can find it, no one is going to see it. You want people to visit your site, and you want *lots* of people. As Chapter 15 describes, your site can get attention plenty of ways. The first is to make your site as wonderful as possible. The stronger your content, the punchier your design, and the fresher you keep the thing, the more likely people will tell their associates and the more likely people will return. But the first and foremost way users find Web sites is through searching for the topics that interest them in search engines, directories, and portals.

The bad news is that search sites don't list every site that waves and smiles. And according to the laws of physics, every single site about armadillos or Gumby lunch boxes can't possibly come to the tippy top of the search results list when a user searches for those topics. But when you build your site, you can maximize your chances of getting listed and getting a better ranking. How? Well, first, you need to know how search sites work.

The Truth About Search Engines, Directories, and Portals

Included among the larger grouping of search sites are three types: search engines, directories, and portals. They all compile information about Web sites and make that information searchable by users. How they do it differs.

But in all cases, when a user conducts a search, the results that are returned appear in a list. The list is usually ranked by *relevancy,* with the sites that are the most relevant to the terms of interest to the user at the top of the list. The compiled information exists in a database, where it is stored in no particular order. (Seeming order is "imposed" when a user searches the database and the results appear in a list based on . . . dare we say it? . . . *relevancy.*) Note that in at least one case (Google, at `www.google.com`), the ranking is based on the popularity of the sites listed. The most popular sites are at the top of the list. But for the most part relevancy rules the roost.

Your goal is to create a situation that puts your site at the top of the list whenever a user searches for a site on a topic like yours. To do so, you must take into account how relevancy works. You must also attend to your site's popularity, both because that factor is taken into account by Google (and to some degree by various other search sites) and because it's just plain smart. Making your site popular is a matter of making it good (which we cover throughout this book) and of marketing it well (which we covered in Chapter 15). Here we are going to focus on the issue of relevancy.

The trick here is that relevancy is kind of, well . . . *relative.* You see, relevancy is generally calculated by some simple means — like counting how many times the word or phrase that you searched appears in a given Web page, its URL, its title, and so on. This method of calculating relevancy is both a weakness of the whole search business and something that you can capitalize on. You can make this bug into a feature by including specific tags or repeated word patterns in your page so that a specific search site can catalog your site correctly and give it a truly relevant relevancy ranking. Later in this chapter, we show you how to tweak a Web page to improve its chances of a high ranking. First, though, you need to take a look at search tools in general.

How search engines work

A *search engine,* in the context of this discussion, is a gigantic, automatically built catalog of Web pages. AltaVista is an example of a search engine. So is Google. Typically, a search engine includes a robot, spider, or crawler (software that noses around the Web, investigating sites and sometimes following their links). (*Tip:* When your directory structure is clean, following the link paths is easier for the crawler.) It also includes a database, into which the crawler dumps the URLs and any other related data it picks up from the sites it visits. Then there's the search engine software itself, which is what actually allows users to search the database.

Crawlers take an interest in a given site because its URL was submitted to the search site or because the crawler encountered the site on its own. Crawlers sometimes make return visits to scope out changes, but whether that happens and how often vary from search engine to search engine, so you want to have your house in order the first time the crawler shows up.

What a search engine really is

In actuality, a *search engine* is the software that conducts a search, whether that search occurs in the context of a big database or index of Web sites, in the context of your Web site alone, or even in the context of a database that has nothing to do with the Web. (There is a search engine in Microsoft Access and in other database programs, for example.) Many people call all Web sites that enable searching for stuff on the Internet "search engines." In this chapter, after we define the types of search sites (which we call search engines, directories, and portals), we usually use the term *search site* generically to refer to all three types of Internet search venues, rather than confusing matters by calling them all search engines.

How directories work

A *directory* is a categorized listing of Web sites that are chosen by living, caring human beings who (presumably) keep it intelligently organized and who sometimes add extra value (like site reviews) to the mix. Yahoo!, for example, is a directory. You can submit your site for consideration, but if the folks working at the directory don't think it's terrific or in some way exemplary, it won't be listed. Employees of the directory also sometimes surf around the Web trolling for suitable sites to include. Ask Jeeves is a directory that also provides a "natural language" search engine for searching the directory. A natural language search engine is one that lets you type plain sentences in as your search phrase rather than keywords.

How portals work

A *portal* site provides a doorway to other sites, kind of like an extensive index page, along with feature content and other services (such as free e-mail, discussion groups, and tools such as travel booking or stock quotes). MSN.com is a general interest portal, but portals are often theme- or subject-oriented (listing, say, law sites, as FindLaw.com does, or education, as HungryMinds.com does), or focused on a specific demographic (iVillage.com focuses on information of interest to women). Portals often publish syndicated or licensed content from other sites; they then cite the source, which can be as good as getting a listing with the portal.

The distinctions among search engines, directories, and portals sometimes blur. Some search engines, for example, include browsable categorizations; many directories offer services such as free e-mail, stock quotes, and the like. And as time goes on, they are all likely to shape and reshape their offerings based on what users want, what imagination inspires, and what can be done with new technologies.

For cutting edge information and updates on the workings of search engines, directories, and portals, see Search Engine Watch (`www.searchenginewatch.com`). Its e-mail newsletter distributes news about search engines and is a must-have for serious Web site promoters.

How You Can Get Tip-Top Ranking

Search engines, directories, and portals all include search capabilities in their offerings, and they usually work in more or less the same way — user types topic of interest into text box, user clicks Search button — you know the routine. The search is executed, and the results are returned in a list that's been sorted based on criteria set up by the search-site producers. All clear? Your goal, then, is to manipulate matters to your advantage.

You want your site ranked among the first 20 or 30 sites that appear when a user searches for a topic closely related to your site's topic. Anywhere below the top 30, and your site is not likely to be seen or clicked. The bad news is that everyone else with a site like yours wants the exact same result. More bad news is that search sites, like all businesses, constantly refine and improve their processes, so the techniques that sites use to get a good ranking one month may not work forever.

So just how do you get your site listed among the top 30? Good question. Climbing to the top of these lists may seem as daunting as scaling Everest, and sometimes getting your site listed at all seems to depend on the alignment of the stars or some magic formula. Well . . . formulas are involved, and you can improve your chances of getting a good listing by optimizing your Web pages.

Get popular — it counts

Keep this in mind when trying to get your page listed with a search engine, directory, or portal: Directories and portals are usually interested in listing only the top (home) page of the Web site and maybe a few other selected pages that have knockout content. Search engines, on the other hand, send their Web-crawling robots out to gather *everything*. These 'bots start with a link to your site (which may be a link that you submit to them) and follow all the other links on that page through your site until they've indexed everything they can. Then they follow all the links that leave your site. Although many people find your site by following links on other pages, the corollary is that robots can also find your site more often if other sites have links to your site.

Furthermore, directories and portals are generally more likely to select those sites that have gotten people's attention already (or are likely to). And Google ranks the sites that show up in a list of search results based entirely on popularity. So how popular your site is has an effect on how well it is recognized by search sites. And this, friends, underscores yet again that all of your site promotion efforts affect each other. To enable the best possible ranking of your site in a user's search for your topic, you must promote your site well, make it popular, and optimize it for relevancy rankings.

Optimize your design

As we note earlier, search sites constantly update and change the way they compile data. What's more, different search engines work differently. But most use some mathematical formula based on algorithms to determine the relevancy of a site and, thus, its ranking. The exact formulas used by each search engine are carefully guarded trade secrets, so even if we knew them, we couldn't talk. We do know this: Search engines that rank on relevancy take into consideration how often certain words in some combination appear in the Web page's URL, in the page title (as it appears in the title bar at the top of the browser window), in the page's text (including the title that appears on the page itself), and the page's keyword and description META tags. The frequency and combination these words appear in determines the relevancy of the page to particular searches.

Follow a few simple guidelines, and your site's pages have an improved chance of getting a high ranking in the commonly used search engines. Note, however, that using these techniques doesn't guarantee anything. But ignoring these guidelines does guarantee something — that you will *not* get a high ranking! Start by considering the following points:

✔ Directories are compiled by living, breathing people. They prefer good sites over bad ones. A site with compelling content and easy-as-pie navigation will catch a reviewer's attention and have a leg up on less-appealing sites.

✔ Using *frames* (panes within the window that's a Web page) or *image maps* (large graphics that contain embedded links to other sections of the Web site) in your site's design trips up some search engines The structure of the HTML used in coding such pages just isn't digestible to crawlers and indexes, so they simply skip over such sites. Similarly, search engines have a hard time indexing *dynamically* created pages (pages that retrieve content and images from a database).

✔ You can work around these issues. For example, you can create a straight HTML page as a "jump" page that users must pass through to get to the goodies, and have the jump page listed instead of the actual page; however, the disadvantage in doing this is that it places the stuff people came for one click deeper into the site. Check Search Engine Watch for other techniques, and in general, consider carefully whether your reason for using frames, image maps, and the like is worth the downside.

✔ The structure of HTML tables and JavaScript used to create some Web page's effects can push the tags and content that's of interest to crawlers so far down the page that the page becomes unreadable to the crawler. You need to take this into account as you create the page templates.

Much ballyhoo exists about META tags — special tags that perk up the interest of some search engines. (META tags identify specific pieces of information the search engines will store in their databases.) META tags are no miracle. They provide an opportunity for you to embed defining information in your site's code, which in turn helps search engines identify and index the site's pages correctly. But not all search sites recognize all the usual META tags, and, as we've mentioned, having the right META tags is only part of a bigger picture that can include site popularity and other factors. Nonetheless, to have any chance of getting the good ranking you hope for, you must attend to your META tags as well as other coding tricks.

HEAD tags, TITLE tags, and META tags — what they mean to you

As an Internet pro, you know that the whole web of Web pages hangs on coding. Everything you see on a Web page is the result of HTML tags or some bit of coding. Some tags create text, some create links, some create images — and some convey information about the document as a whole. Knowing how to use these tags well can help you to produce content that the search engines and directories can then correctly catalog.

HEAD tags

The HEAD tag defines a special area of the HTML document that contains information about the document. That information often includes the document's title and perhaps some other coding that describes the document. For example, in the following snippet of HTML, the head section contains the title of the Web page along with a META tag that specifies a description of the page:

```
<HTML>
<HEAD>
<TITLE>Ping-Pong and Table Tennis Champion Strategy </TITLE>
<META NAME="description" CONTENT="ping-pong and table tennis
        champion strategy from a ping-pong and table
        tennis professional">

<META NAME="keywords" CONTENT="ping-pong,table tennis,
        champion,ping
        pong,tournament,tabletennis,professional,pingpong,
        book,ping-pong for dummies,pingpong
        book,tabletennis book  ">
```

```
</HEAD>
<BODY>
Ping-Pong champion reveals professional table tennis
            strategy. You can excel at Ping-Pong and other
            table tennis games.
</BODY>
```

TITLE tags

Every document on the Web has a title. That title appears in the title bar at the top of your browser window (along with the name of your browser) when you're looking at the document. (This is not the title that appears above the text on the page.) So — where did that title come from? The TITLE tag! The following is an example:

```
<TITLE>Ping-Pong and Table Tennis Champion Strategy</TITLE>
```

Remember, the TITLE tag appears within the all-important head section of the page.

"Welcome to XYZ Home Page" is a poor title for a Web page — it's too long, it's full of irrelevant words, and it will appear in alphabetically organized bookmark lists under *W* for *Welcome*. A better title would be short and pithy — it would summarize the page's content and contain specific keywords to help search engines categorize the page. When you're naming your page, keep in mind that the title that appears in the TITLE tag is also the title of the page in a list of hits produced by a search engine. It's also the title that the directory and index people use to refer to your page, not to mention all the random Webmasters who link to you. So if the title is just *Ping-Pong,* it won't stand out from the herd. However, *Ping-Pong and Table Tennis Strategy* would, because it gives some idea about the kind of content you can find on the page (Ping-Pong *strategy,* rather than photographs or table tennis news).

Helping crawlers over the JavaScript hurdle

Placing JavaScript in a Web page can set up yet another speed bump for search engines trying to work their way through "understanding" and cataloging that page. The issues are that JavaScript code has to appear near the top of the page's tags and code, and without special treatment, JavaScript looks to the search engine a little too much like the page's content.

To overcome these problems, surround any JavaScript code with the HTML tags that identify a *comment* (an element that should be visible in the code but not on the page). Placing <!— at the beginning of the JavaScript and —> at the end will signal any search engine crawlers to skip over the code surrounded by those tags as the crawler does its job.

META tags

A META tag is a special tag that contains *meta* information about the page — that is, overview information about the stuff that's contained on the page. For a search engine ranking, the two important META tags are those that describe the site and that provide keywords related to the site. An example of a description META tag is:

```
<META NAME="description" CONTENT="ping-pong and table tennis
            champion strategy from a ping-pong and table
            tennis professional">
```

The overall, agreed-upon specs for HTML allow you to include just about any name and content descriptors in META tags, with a few exceptions. (For example, the name *refresh* is reserved for forcing a browser to reload the document.) Some search engines look specifically for a META tag with the name *keywords,* and then those search engines catalog the page based on the keywords that are included in the META tag. Such a tag looks like this:

```
<META NAME="keywords" CONTENT="ping-pong,table tennis,
            champion,ping
            pong,tournament,tabletennis,professional,pingpong,
            book,ping-pong for dummies,pingpong
            book,tabletennis book">
```

Notice that this list includes *ping-pong, table tennis,* and *ping pong.* Synonyms and common misspellings are important when you're trying to get your page in circulation — whether the intrepid searcher looking for a page like yours types **ping-pong**, **table tennis**, or **ping pong** in the search box, your page ostensibly should show up in the search if you use synonyms carefully. META tags also appear in the head section of an HTML document. Notice, too, that all the keywords are lowercase. Some search engines exclude *Ping-Pong* (the correct name of the game, written with initial caps because the game is trademarked that way) if a user types **ping-pong**.

Now, remembering that search engines focus on the head section of a given Web page, and noting that you can use META tags in a number of ways, the next section explains how to leverage the META tag opportunity.

Use META tags well

The crawlers that many search sites rely on usually factor in how often certain words occur in some combination of a given Web page's URL, its title (which appears in the title bar at the top of the browser window, not in the content of the page), its text (which includes the title that shows up on the page itself, and often at least the first paragraphs on the page), and some META tags (those dealing with keywords and descriptions).

The upshot is that among Web sites devoted to dance shoes, the one that has more iterations of *dance shoe* in its URL, title, text, and META tags is more likely to hit the jackpot by popping to the top of the search results list when a user searches on *dance shoes.* But it's all a bit more complicated than that. Rankings are actually often governed by the frequency and location of these words as compared to all the other words on the page. (This is where the algorithms and the formulas come in.) Search engines snoop through the page's text, uncovering repeated words (assumed to be important because they are repeated) near the top of the page — in the headline and in the first few paragraphs. (Some investigate all the text on the page.) Looking for the same words repeated several times, they waltz right past synonyms. *Footwear, ballet slippers, tap shoes,* and *blue-suede stilettos,* to most search engines, are not the same *dance shoes.*

This provides you with an opportunity. You, armed with all you now know, can massage the content and code for your site to optimize your pages for a better search-engine ranking. To do this for a given Web page, first, figure out what the page is about. What two or three or so words match exactly the topic of that page? Jot them down. Then brainstorm another six or twelve words or brief phrases that also closely relate to the topic.

 If you're stuck, try taking the page's content and crossing out all the irrelevant words until you have a few words left; these are the most important ones. And if you find that these words don't match the topic of the page as you see it, rewrite the content to include the target words.

Next, write a short phrase that describes your page, using some of the most relevant words you listed. (Place the most important, most compelling words at the beginning of the phrase.) This phrase does not have to be an entire sentence, but it should be clear and simple.

Now, with your raw material at the ready, you're poised to make your page search-engine friendly. For best results, make these tweaks *before* you register the page with search engines. (In fact, if you identify the keywords before you write the site's content, you'll have a better shot at fitting them smoothly into the opening paragraphs.) It may be a long time before the search engines come back around to check for any changes, so you want to have all your ducks in a row the first time. Follow these steps:

1. **Open the page's HTML source code in the editor of your choice.**

2. **In the title section of the code, incorporate the three or so words you identified as most important.**

   These need not be the only words in the title section, but they must be there. (The title should still make sense as a title, by the way.) Imagine that your site assists users in finding bed-and-breakfast hotels and making reservations. The title would include *bed-and-breakfast, hotel,* and perhaps more:

```
<TITLE>B&B Escapes: Bed-and-breakfast inns and historic
          hotels; charming weekend getaway vacations, with
          reservations online</TITLE>
```

3. **Repeat the relevant words you've identified in the page's text, somewhere near the top of the page.**

   It also doesn't hurt to scatter them throughout the page so that they appear every few sentences. In our example, the most crucial words are *hotel, bed-and-breakfast, inn,* and *reservations.* We also tossed in the words *getaway, vacation,* and *weekend* from our longer list.

4. **In the head section of your page, insert a META tag listing the three most relevant words you identified along with the other, longer set.**

   Place the most strikingly relevant words at the beginning, and use commas between the words, but no spaces after the commas. For example:

```
<META NAME="keywords" CONTENT="hotel,bed-and-
          breakfast,inn,breakfast,historic hotel,weekend
          getaway,romantic getaway,vacation,romantic
          hotel,united states,online booking,online reser-
          vation,lodging,accommodation,america">
```

All words in the keywords META tag (including titles and proper nouns) should be lowercase. Use only singular nouns (*inn,* not *inns*), except where the plural is formed as a new word (*goose, geese*). Toss in some synonyms (*lodging and accommodations*) here and in the text of the page itself. Also, include a few keywords for the most enticing features or attributes of your site (such as *weekend getaway* and *online booking*); it can only help you to be indexed under multiple attributes. If you can think of any common misspellings for any of your keywords, include them in the META tag as well. But don't make the mistake of simply repeating words (*hotel, hotel, hotel*). The search engines are onto that ploy and penalize for it by dinging ranking or by bouncing the site right out the door.

5. **Add a description META tag.**

   This tag becomes the description of your site that users will see in the search results listings of many search sites. Use the short, simple, clear phrase you wrote to describe the page. Here is an example:

```
<META NAME="description" CONTENT="Hundreds of bed-and-
          breakfast inns and historic hotels, for romantic
          vacations and weekend getaways, all with online
          reservations.">
```

Don't use first-person references (*I*). If necessary, use third-person references (*innkeeper*). Using a third-person reference, which is ultimately more descriptive, also gives you another chance to wedge a keyword (of sorts) into your tags.

Don't start your description (or your title, for that matter) with "Welcome to . . .," an approach that many sites unfortunately continue to use. Your description should focus on keywords; *welcome to* is not a descriptive, specific keyword phrase that will get your site ranked high in the search engines.

These tidbits can give a Web page extra oomph in search engines and can help users who are interested in the site's topic to go straight to it. Remember, though, some additional tips:

- **Establish backlinks from other sites — it's smart business.** Popularity counts. For example, among sites devoted to dance shoes or to B&Bs, the sites with the highest number of *backlinks* (links to it from other sites, discussed in Chapter 15) may get priority in ranking.

- **Get your site listed in specialized directories devoted to your particular topic or industry (such as travel, health, personal finance, and so on).** This can be easier than going for the biggies and can get you a quick boost in traffic and popularity, which may do the trick in getting you listed in the majors.

- **View the source code of other sites that have that top ranking you covet to discover what they did to get there.** Perform a search on the keywords you use for your own site and then go to the sites that appear near the top of the results list. On each site, use your browser's view page source feature to see the META tag keywords, description, and other tricks the site used to achieve its ranking. (***Remember:*** You can't copy the code of other sites, but you can get a gander at their technique.)

- **Nip quickly any thought you may have of fetching traffic to your site by popping the names of competitors or their products into your META tags.** Doing so may be grounds for a lawsuit. Instead, take the high road. Attract users through the merits of your own whiz-bang genius of a site and your brilliant promotion of it.

- **Stay on the ball.** Say you've achieved the top spot in search engine rankings. Good for you! If you want to keep it, your job isn't done. New sites will be added to the game every day, and the search sites constantly refine and update their processes, including those mysterious ranking formulas. To stay on top when you get on top is challenging. Monitor your standing regularly and update your techniques to reflect what's developing. Tools are available for testing and tracking your ranking and for submitting your site to multiple search engines quickly and easily; they range from the inexpensive (bCentral's SubmitIt! — `submitit.bcentral.com`) to expensive, licensed products that dig deeply into your site and offer suggestions for improvement as well as an analysis of your ranking prospects.

Feeling frisky with a little extra cash? Some search sites may accept payment for better placement in the search results. As of this writing, one does. Most search sites position themselves as objective services, so maybe others will start to charge, and maybe they won't. But if you've got the bucks and want placement badly enough, you can look around for a paid ranking opportunity.

Also, some site stat software, such as Webtrends (www.webtrends.com), reports on which search sites are sending folks your way and which keywords are being used to find you. You want to know what results your site is getting anyway, so site stat software isn't a bad idea in general. See Chapter 17 for more on tools for finding out about the results your site is producing.

Preventing Selected Pages from Being Searched

Maybe you don't want every blasted search engine in the universe beating a path to your door and listing every page on your site so that others can drop in just anywhere. Transaction pages, pages that have to be entered through others to make sense to the user, and dynamically created pages (database-driven pages whose content is dependent on the user's actions or other variable circumstances), for example, probably shouldn't be indexed on their own.

You can communicate to crawlers your intent to exclude a specific page from indexing by placing a META tag within the page's document head. (This doesn't actually prevent the indexing, it just tells the crawlers that you'd prefer to be excluded.) The name of the META tag in this case is *robots,* and the possible instructions are index (or noindex) and follow (or nofollow). *Index* means that robots record the page's contents for use in a database or search engine. *Follow* means that the robot follows all the links on that page to collect more data.

To invite a robot to index and follow this page, the tag would look like this:

```
<META NAME="robots" CONTENT="index,follow">
```

To instruct a robot not to index or follow the links on a page, the tag would look like this:

```
<META NAME="robots" CONTENT="noindex,nofollow">
```

You can use any combination of these tags (index,nofollow or noindex, follow), but be sure not to use conflicting instructions (such as noindex, index).

An alternative to placing tags in every file of the many you may want excluded is to place a special file — called robots.txt — in your Web server's document root directory (which is discussed in Chapter 11). In the robots.txt file, place a list of the pages to be included or excluded. To find out more, see SearchEngineWatch.

Submitting with Savvy

With your site all spiffy and optimized for the best possible ranking, you're ready to submit it. You can, if you like, visit each search site's submissions page and enter your site or a bunch of its important pages into the handy form that's provided. Or, you can take advantage of any of the automated services (such as bCentral's SubmitIt! at submitit.bcentral.com) that let you fill out just one form, where you enter your site info, select which search sites you want to target, and then click to zip off your submission to (if you like) the entire universe of search sites. Yahoo! lists hundreds of such sites, some of which are free and some of which offer premium services at premium prices.

Automated submission services are admittedly convenient. They're also not as effective as submitting manually to each search site. Why? Because by submitting your entry manually, you can tailor your entry to the venue. No more than a half dozen premiere search sites exist. If you feel ready for them, why not max your chances by providing them with exactly the info they need?

Before you even get to that, though, some folks say you ought to submit your two or three most important pages to selected second- and third-tier search sites and to specialized directories that focus on your topic. The wisdom goes that you can establish backlinks this way, get a head start on site popularity, and perk up the interest of first-tier search sites. Other wisdom suggests that automated mass submission services are good for getting into second- and third-tier search sites that may not be as picky (or as strategically crucial) as the top search sites.

Your site should be optimized for ranking before you submit it anywhere. If you are listed, it's going to be a while before the crawlers come back or the diligent directory employees check you out again. So have your ducks in a row first and then submit.

Then . . . wait calmly. It takes time — perhaps a month or two — for submissions to be processed. Don't get impatient and start pumping repeated submissions out; that simply clogs up the works. It can also damage your chances. Getting listed can be a months-long effort, and then investigating your ranking, monitoring it, tweaking your code, and requesting and getting a fresh check can take even longer. However, if you do your homework (read the tips on SearchEngineWatch at www.searchenginewatch.com), and manage to climb into the top 30, the traffic payoff will be well worth your effort.

Checking Your Ranking

You can use any of several services to check your site's ranking across a variety of search sites. Some of these services are free; others charge fees. The Informant (informant.dartmouth.edu), Microsoft bCentral's PositionAgent (www.positionagent.com), and ScoreCheck (www.scorecheck.com), among others, allow you to specify your URL and a set of keywords. Then they check with a number of search sites and report back the ranking of the specified site in the search results based on the specified keywords. Typically, the free services offer a single use at a time, while the fee-based services will check ranking repeatedly over some interval of time and will e-mail the results to you.

Finally, bear in mind that getting listed in search engines should be only one part of your overall promotions strategy. Okay, so it's important, but there are so many sites on the Web that no single search site can now index more than 16 percent of all public Web sites (according to data released by the NEC Research Institute). You simply must explore other creative strategies for keeping your site visible, to support and augment your search site listing efforts (see Chapter 15).

You must also monitor the success of your site's areas and pages, so you can fine-tune and refresh the site appropriately. This will lead to greater popularity, and that, presumably, can lead to better ranking. Monitoring success is the subject of the next chapter.

Chapter 17

Measuring and Monitoring Success

*T*raffic is traffic, and you definitely want to know how much traffic your Web site is getting. But if your site is intended to sell, sell, sell, and all that traffic isn't resulting in revenue, are you actually succeeding? What if your site is supposed to be focused on community, generating media attention, saving costs, or facilitating workgroup collaboration? Is it traffic that counts, or is there a better measure of your site's true success?

This chapter addresses how you can measure success specifically for your Web site. First and foremost, your benchmarks for success depend deeply on the goals set for the site (see Chapter 2) and on your company's values. After you know what you want to measure, you can glean the information you need from some combination of hard data and user feedback. Then, you can use this information to assess what you've done and improve your site. As a Webmaster, you have the coolest job in the world. Part of doing that job is to stay clear about where your site is headed, how to get there, and what success is going to look like to you and others.

What Success Looks Like

As you surely know by now, you may intend for your Web site to promote, inform, educate, distribute, sell, research and report, provide support, foster or serve community, facilitate workflow, or something else. It's probably also intended to generate revenue (and eventually profit), save on costs, achieve acceptance or attain a presence, build and retain a customer base, or accomplish some other business-related goal.

Basing measurements on goals

For any endeavor, the stated goals, the definition of success, and what can be measured are all interrelated. (That's why, in Chapter 2, we advise you to read *this* chapter before you settle on your goals.) Don't fall victim to inappropriate goals. It's all too easy for the naïve to hear about the millions of pages visitors to Yahoo! or CNN Interactive view daily and decide that their sites should get just as much traffic. That may not be the correct goal for your site, and it may not be an accurate measure of your success. You must set your goals early and realistically, and then consider how you plan to measure success within the context of those goals. Your success benchmarks must also be within reasonable expectations. *Remember:* As Webmaster, part of your role (see Chapter 1) is to manage expectations.

Do remember that the success of one area of your site may differ from that of another area. For example, you measure the success of your online press room differently from the success of your customer service area. Track the success of each area or feature of your site as well as the whole site. Table 17-1 offers some ideas for metrics that may apply to your site or to areas within it.

Table 17-1	Metrics of Success for Specific Goals
For This Goal	*Consider These Metrics*
Promote	Media presence as shown by the number and quality of references to the site in print, broadcast, and online media
	Registrations at the site
	Traffic measured in impressions, users, and length of user sessions
	Backlinks to the site
Inform	Media presence, especially when references to the information cite it as credible
	Similar references from audience members
	Subscriptions and traffic going up
	Ad sales increasing and at higher rates

For This Goal	*Consider These Metrics*
Educate	Enrollments of students and repeat enrollments Graduations and successful completions of courses Higher scores on tests and evaluations Indications of recognition, credibility, and acceptance
Distribute	Number of downloads of the product or file Comparison of number of unique users to number of downloads Lower number of support events
Sell	Number of buyers and repeat buyers Sales generated Revenue generated, profit produced Lower number of returns Fewer customer service events
Research	Higher quality data gathered More credibility, more media presence More site users participating in online surveys Users participating more completely
Customer Service or Tech Support	Lower service or support costs Faster resolution of issues Lower number of events that require staff intervention

Community	Number of unique users and registrations
	Traffic, as measured in impressions and length
	  of user sessions
	Posting ratio: How many posts as compared to
	  number of impressions
	Penetration: How much of the potential audience has
	  been reached and is participating

Workflow	Increase in productivity Better frequency of meeting deadlines Higher morale among team members

Choosing the right traffic measurements

Measuring traffic and having rising traffic levels are urgent matters regardless of your site's main mission. It's the very rare Web site that can fulfill its purpose with only scant traffic, so traffic always matters. You can measure traffic in a number of ways. The most obvious ways are through hits, impressions, visitors, unique users, and clickpaths.

Hits refer to the number of files that are served by the server when a user accesses a page on your Web site. But describing traffic according to the number of hits a site gets is a poor way to talk about traffic. Why? Well, a hit is generated for each file that makes up a page. Two pages that look identical can be constructed so that one is made up of, say, 5 files and the other is made up of 25 files. When one is loaded on a user's computer, it will generate five hits. The other will generate 25 hits. Yet in each case only one access of the page has occurred. Counting hits doesn't describe the number of visitors to the site, nor the number of pages they've viewed. Measuring hits is, in fact, really quite meaningless. A site with lots of graphics may get 100,000 hits per week, for example, even though it gets only a few dozen actual visitors. Still, some people find yacking on about the number of hits they receive an expedient way to describe their site's traffic. Hit counts at least sound huge (even if they're actually insignificant) and because each file that's served generates one hit to the server, they're definitely easy to measure. (See the later section titled "How Traffic Measurements Are Calculated" for more detail.)

One *impression* (also known as a *page view*) occurs each time a single page on your site is loaded into a user's Web browser. In theory, one pair of eyes falling on a page equals one impression (or page view). This is a far better measure of traffic than hits, because the number of images and other items appearing on the page doesn't affect the count. What's more, *everyone* cares how many people are viewing a site or a page. When sites sell ad space, they often base their rates on a guaranteed number of impressions. (See "Setting ad rates based on impressions," later in this chapter.)

Unique users are widely thought by the uninitiated to be the number of individual visitors who've stopped by a site. But that just isn't so. It's easy, you see, to count how many individual *computers* are stopping by, but it's tough to know (without hidden cameras) exactly how many people are sitting at any one computer in any given timeframe. Knowing whether one person uses a computer or four people do is tricky, so a count of unique users actually refers to the number of unique computers using the site.

Visitors are, all too simply, actual users who visit your site. This is a number everyone wants to know. Note that in a single visit, a visitor may view one page (causing one impression) or many pages (causing many impressions).

Everyone also wants to know which way, when a user clicks around the site, he or she is going. This is known as a *clickpath*. Tracking clickpaths is handy for determining which of your navigational gizmos are working and which are not. It also indicates which content is appealing and which content is duddier.

The *clickthrough rate* is the number of times someone clicks a linked item (like a banner ad or a link). Lots of folks talk about clickthrough rates in regards to banner ads, assuming that the number of times users clicked through an ad to the linked site is a nice, hard number that indicates the ad's success. But focusing on ad impressions may actually be a truer measure of an ad's value than the clickthrough rate. A joint study by the Poynter Institute (`www.poynter.org`) and Stanford University showed that users focus on banner ads for perhaps one full second, which is enough time to get a marketing message across, even if the users do not click on the ad.

Again, for the technical lowdown on all these ways of measuring traffic, see "How Traffic Measurements Are Calculated," later in this chapter. You can also find more on specific traffic-measuring tools and techniques in upcoming sections.

Measuring media presence

If the goal of your site is promotion or brand recognition, you may find that *media attention* is the best measure of success. Media attention takes many forms, ranging from notices in *Forbes* or features in *The New York Times* to (for smaller sites) blurbs in the local alternative newspaper. Of course, getting attention is easier after you've *had* attention, so big companies are generally more likely to get press attention than smaller ones. But here is where the Web can indeed become the great leveler. Media attention flocks to what's hot, so creating a buzz and then becoming famous for being famous is quite possible. If this media attention is how you're going to measure success, make your site outstandingly different, shiningly charismatic, and really useful.

Remember, too, that measuring media attention is both a matter of quantity and quality. You can get clips of all the media mentions you get, which is a way of counting results. But track the *quality* of the media's comments as well.

Measuring sales, distribution, revenue, or savings

If the overriding purpose of your site is to sell (or even just distribute) a product, you probably measure your success in sales (or units delivered) rather than traffic. Just how many wonderwidgets you need to sell or distribute (and how quickly or with how little fuss and muss) is another matter. The specifics are up to you.

As a cautionary note, you should not start with absurdly high expectations and base your revenue model on this alone. We know of one case where an online shopping system for a *hard-deliverable product* (a product that is tangible, like wine, books, or car parts) was installed. Four units sold on the first day, and the system was considered a success! In that case, the expectation was that sales would build and that slow sales in the beginning would allow time to refine the shopping system and test *fulfillment* (the shipping of the items). Because the company was not relying on this shopping system as its primary method of distribution — at least not yet — it had the luxury of considering opening sales of four units a success.

We also know of a Web enterprise that launched its sales system on a Monday, and within one week the units sold exceeded projections by 500 percent. Unfortunately, the fulfillment system wasn't quite ready to rock. Build your business plan or project plan on a foundation of market research that allows you to project realistic numbers and plan accordingly.

Assessing the success of a sales or distribution site can include

- ✔ **Market penetration:** A measure of how many people you could be reaching that you actually are reaching.

- ✔ **Conversion rate:** The number of visitors to the site who are becoming buyers, as shown in Figure 3-2 in Chapter 3. (You also want to know the number of first-time buyers who come back for more.)

- ✔ **Service:** A measure of your customer care program, which can be quantified according to the number of returns you get, the number of support events you experience, and the quickness with which events are resolved. (Remember to make sure that when those events were resolved quickly the customers also went away happy.)

If your site's goal is to produce revenue through ad sales, subscriptions, sponsorship, or paid placement, the amount of revenue that's produced can certainly be a benchmark of success. To drive interest in the purchase of ads, subscriptions, sponsorships, or paid placements, however, you've got to have incredibly compelling content pulling forth an audience that's big, targeted, or both. (See Chapters 2 and 3 for more on how content can drive revenue.)

Keep in mind what you already know: *Revenue is not profit.* To produce profit, you must minimize costs and maximize revenue. Profit is the result of high revenue and low costs. If your site sells, your ultimate goal is, presumably profit. As of this writing, many of the highly trafficked search-engines, directories, and portal sites are not producing a reliable profit through ad sales, sponsorship, or licensing — despite the hundreds of millions of visitors that they receive *per day*. It simply costs a mint to produce those sites. And yet, we know of two smallish sites that are content-driven and quite profitable. They keep costs down and with minimal investment they still manage to produce content that draws traffic.

Savings also is not profit (nor is it revenue). Cost savings is an especially appropriate measure of success for intranets and for sites that focus on distribution (where the costs of manufacturing, packaging, and getting the goods physically into stores are saved). However, consider for a moment the following case.

We once worked with a team whose company Web site cost a relatively usual $5 million per year to maintain. The site's main goal was to market its products, which were sold mainly in brick-and-mortar stores. The company shipped out its packaged products with a user response card — a survey printed on heavy paper — in every package. When the survey was placed on the Web site instead (and a URL leading to it was simply printed on the packaging), the company saved (coincidentally) $5 million per year. Voilà! But was this savings credited to the Web site budget? No. The expense was a line item in the *marketing* budget, and the Web site was not in the marketing department's portfolio. After this seeming success, the company still wanted the Web site to produce actual revenue. The moral: Your online endeavors may well benefit the company as a whole, but the company must clarify its expectations and values and you must have top-management buy-in on the specific measures of the Web site's success.

Measuring information gathered and reported

When the goal of the site is to research, conduct a survey, or gather information, you can generally see the success of the venture in the number of respondents and the quality of the report that came from the study. However, *who* participates also affects the quality of the gathered information. You want qualified participants. For example, a survey looking into whether people will vote for candidate A or candidate B in an election is much more useful if the survey participants are registered voters.

Other interesting measurements are the number of visitors to the Web site who took the time to complete a questionnaire (this may comment on the quality or format of the questions) as well as the number who complete the *entire* survey. Market penetration (the number of people qualified to answer the survey who did answer) may also be of interest.

If you are compiling reports that are based on an online survey or study and either selling or distributing the reports, measures such as those for sales and distribution may be best. Recognition (which would be measured according to the standards of media presence) could also be considered.

Where Measuring Is Going to Get You

The benefits of measuring your success appropriately and accurately are many. With the right numbers in hand, for example, you can maximize ad revenue by quantifying and verifying traffic to advertisers and time promotions to leverage what you know about traffic and your audience's habits. These numbers can also help you increase response rates for promotions, surveys, registrations, and other ventures. They can help you demonstrate return on investment to yourself, investors, company executives, and others. They can help you find peace of joy (of a sort).

You can use what you learn to make your Web site an even better Web site than it already is. For example, you can:

✔ Monitor and forecast trends, and then use that information to improve service.

✔ Fine-tune your site's features and performance and make better technology decisions.

✔ Modify and optimize your site's content, navigation, and usability.

✔ Allocate resources more appropriately to benefit those areas or features of the site that warrant upgrades or improvements.

The ultimate benefits of measurement stem from knowing how measurement enables you, the intrepid Webmaster, to better meet the needs of your site's users. Using what you learn from data, you can expand and focus your site's offerings, and extend your reach to meet the target audience you intend.

What You Can Know

You can know quite a lot about who's visiting your site and what they're up to when they stop by. To know anything as specific as exact demographics and psychographics, you have to get users to fill out surveys or track their preferences via *cookies* (special files that insert themselves on the user's computer; see the "Gotta Cookie?" sidebar of this chapter for details). But from hard data and user feedback that's readily available, you can get well acquainted with your site's visitors. Hard data sources include:

✔ Server, network, and OS log files, which are generated automatically by the computers involved

✔ User registration databases, which contain the accumulation of data that's gleaned when you ask users to register on your site

✔ Third-party services that provide reports, which are usually based on data from your log files

Even without complicated, state-of-the-science tools and techniques, you can infer some information. For example, from a simple reading of (admittedly boring and seemingly obtuse) log files, you can know how many users are visiting the site or one area of it, how many are returning users as opposed to new users, and so on. And from this simple basis, you can judge what users want and need. Then you can determine how to address those needs. All of the data shown in Table 17-2 can be obtained, interpreted, or inferred from log files.

Table 17-2	What You Can Find Out from Log Files
To Find Out About	*Look At*
What's Accessed	Pages most requested Files frequently downloaded Entry and exit pages most often used Activity levels by the day and hour Number of pages viewed in an average session
Demographics	Number of new users Where users live (based on location of computers 　　and ISPs used) Which browsers and platforms are used 　　(name and version)
Technology Failures	Pages not accessed when requested Scripts not running correctly Server errors that affect site performance
Sources of Referrals	Sites, URLs, and search engines that are referring 　　traffic to your site or specific pages Which keywords are most effective in guiding 　　searchers to your site

Reading Log Files

To measure traffic, you can simply read the log files that your server generates, you can rely on reports put out by any of a number of site-statistic packages, or you can hand the whole matter to an external service or auditor. Each of these options presents different advantages; for most sites, some combination is best. In all cases the reports that are generated are usually based on your servers' log files, so an understanding of log files is in order.

Your Web server generates log files that record everything that happens while the server is running. Log files exist so that system administrators (like tech-type Webmasters) can track and resolve issues. Most Web servers generate a variety of log files, including an *access log* and an *error log*. The access log file contains a record for every hit that the site gets. Remember, a hit is a request for a file, and a single document can be constructed of many small and large files. The error log file contains information about every error that occurs while the server is running. Peeking into both of these files is a routine part of doing server maintenance. To find out more about error log files, refer to server administration books. The access log file is our focus here, because it reveals how much traffic your site is getting, and what users are up to on your site.

Most Web servers produce log files in a standard format, which is called (sensibly enough) the *common log file format.* You can read a definition of the common log file format at the URL `www.w3.org/pub/WWW/Daemon/User/Config/Logging.html`.

A typical access log file entry looks like this:

```
www.dnai.com aneth-12.execpc.com - - [30/Aug/2001:18:56:15 -
      0700] "GET /~vox/news/welcome2.html HTTP/1.0" 200
      1253
```

Like a database record, an access log file record appears in *fields,* or chunks, of data. The data in the first field in our sample log file, `www.dnai.com`, contains the name of the Web server that served the specific Web file that this entry discusses. While this information may seem repetitive when you first start looking at log files — of course it's *your* Web server that served your document — it can be very useful to those who run multiple Web servers and have piles of log files from different servers to read.

The data in the second field of our sample, `aneth-12.execpc.com`, is from the machine that requested that this document be served. If the actual name of that machine is not available, its *IP address* appears instead. (Every computer with an Internet connection has a unique number assigned to it as an identifier; that's the IP address.)

In the third field of our sample, a single dash appears. This shows that the field is empty, as this particular field usually is. Some Web servers place a username — the username of whomever is requesting the document from the server — in this field. But this data is usually available only if the Web server has been configured to retrieve that information *and* the person running the Web browser is using a UNIX-based computer running a special server (called an *identd* server). The combination of these two events is quite rare, so for the most part, don't expect to see any information in this field.

The fourth field in our example is also blank. It would contain the user's authenticated username if it were filled in. If you were to set up your Web server to require a username and password to access particular parts of your site, the username of the person requesting and accessing the file would appear here. (Note that this is different from the username that may have appeared just before it — *that* username is described in the preceding paragraph.)

The fifth field shows the date and time the file was served. In our case, this is `30/Aug/2001:18:56:15 -0700`, meaning that the requested item was served on August 30, 2001, at 18:56:15 GMT (Greenwich mean time). Servers log time in Greenwich-mean-time format, the international standard of expressing time that disregards the time zone that you are in. The last part of the time notation in the field, –0700, indicates that the local time (where the server is located) is seven hours behind GMT. Therefore, the local time when this file was served was 11:56:15 a.m.

The sixth field shows the request that the Web browser made. This indicates what the server was asked to serve. The request usually appears in the form of a command followed by a directory and filename. In a log file, you usually see the `get` command, which is the one that Web browsers send to fetch files from Web servers. The `get` command is followed by the full path and filename for the file that the server is expected to return. In this case, the Web browser is getting the file `/~vox/news/welcome2.html` from the Web server. Other commands that you may see in your log file are the `put` and `post` commands; these are used by Web browsers to send the contents of a form.

The seventh field contains a status code. This code indicates whether the command resulted in success (serving of the file) or failure (and if so, why that failure occurred). Your Web server can generate many status codes (a list of them should appear in your server's documentation). Table 17-3 shows the common ones.

Table 17-3	Common Status Codes
Code	**Description**
200	Success
201	File not found
202	Permission to access file denied
401	Unauthorized: The file requested is protected by a password that was not correctly supplied
500	Internal server error: A problem may have occurred with a script on the server

The eighth and final field in our sample log file record shows the number of bytes of data that was sent to the Web browser when the requested item was served.

A single Web page is usually made up of many files, including graphics, HTML files, and so on. Note that the access log file includes a record for each hit (each file that's requested). Therefore, a seemingly simple request to the server for a document can generate dozens of records in the access log file.

Log files are really the only statistics that the server records; any other statistics (such as how many impressions you get) are based on them. Understanding log files, then, gives you a leg up on understanding how measurements are calculated as well as how site statistics packages and services accomplish their tasks.

How Traffic Measurements Are Calculated

Hits, impressions, visitors, unique users, and clickpaths are the building blocks of measuring traffic. ("Choosing the right traffic measurements," earlier in this chapter, introduced these measurements.) Each measures something different; understanding those differences can help you judge your site's success and choose methods of assessing it more accurately.

Hits

A hit is generated for each file that makes up a Web page. Each graphic, each scrap of animation, and each other bit of stuff that makes up the page generates a hit. Every hit that occurs is recorded in the server's access log file (which we describe in an earlier section), and any server can easily spit out a number that indicates how many files the server has dished out in a given time frame. However, knowing exactly how many files make up each Web page on your site is actually pretty tricky. Two Web pages that look exactly the same can be constructed so that one is made up of, say, 10 files and the other is made up of 30 files. When one is loaded on a user's computer, it will generate 10 hits. The other will generate 30 hits. Yet in each case, only one access of the page has occurred.

When a hit is not a hit

Noodle on this: Not every viewing of a page on your site results in a hit being produced. That's because cache systems, like the ones that Web browsers and "proxy servers" use, throw the whole thing off. Caching exists to facilitate fast loading of pages, but it does so by loading saved copies of the pages rather than by loading fresh copies. Depending on how an individual user's Web browser is set up to use the cache, that user's view of a particular page at a particular moment may or may not be a fresh view. The browser may sometimes be caching the pages (or elements of the pages). And a cached view doesn't produce hits in your log files. Meantime, at the server end, many corporations and most commercial online services (such as America Online) use *proxy servers* (servers that "stand in" for other servers) to cache Web pages, again so that users can access them more quickly. In this case, many users may access the same cached Web page, which has been stored on the caching proxy server. You as the Webmaster or as a user can't and shouldn't do a dang thing about this — just keep it in mind when you consider the relative accuracy and wisdom of counting hits.

Impressions

An *impression* is the serving of an entire Web page, no matter how many hits make up that page. While a user loading a single page from your Web server may generate many hits, that user loading that page generates only one impression. Figuring out the number of impressions that occurs is more complicated than figuring out the number of hits because, while Web servers automatically track hits in an access log file, they don't have an easy way to track impressions. However, calculating the number of impressions that occur based on the hit data that's stored in the access log file is possible, and a number of handy software packages can do this for you.

Visitors

Visitors are harder to track than impressions. Some software packages try to determine the number of visitors from analyzing the access log file. This file does not include specific information about visitors, but it does contain some information that, in conjunction with some basic assumptions, can be used to *guess* the number of visitors. Here's how it works: Using the access log file, the software assumes that a single visit lasts for a certain amount of time — 15 minutes is common — and that any two impressions that the server sends to the same Web browser during that time are part of the same visit. Simple enough, but that's obviously not the most accurate way to go. Counting visitors, if it were more precise, would be a highly desirable way to measure traffic.

Unique users

Special software you run on your server can track unique users. This handy-dandy software typically uses cookie technology to assign a unique identification number to each user who visits your site. (See the sidebar "Gotta cookie?") When a user visits the site, the software checks the cookies to see whether the ID number is there, assigns one if it isn't, and thereafter logs in the user and tracks the pages that the user views. Again, remember that these are unique users only in theory. This method of calculating traffic is close enough for many purposes but is not an exact science.

Counting backlinks

Counting *backlinks* — links on other sites that go to your site — measures your site's popularity. What's more, each backlink provides users with a doorway to your site, so counting your backlinks and beefing up those numbers are good ways to build traffic. Chapter 15 describes how you can easily count the backlinks to your site using well known search engines.

Gotta cookie?

When a user visits a Web site that uses cookies, the site's Web server creates a *cookie*, which is a kind of a note to itself, and passes the cookie to the user's browser. The cookie is then stored among the browser's files. Forever after, when that user visits the same site, the site's server checks (just as it did the first time) to see if a cookie is there. On finding the cookie, the server can automatically identify the user and pick up any information (a password, online shopping preferences, or whatever) that's been stored in the cookie.

Marketing people and many Web developers love cookies; some users, however, have been suspicious of them. To the marketing people, cookies offer a terrific method of counting users and even tracking what they like and don't like. To the Web developers, cookies are a good way to track passwords and what's in a shopping cart. To some users, however, cookies are all too akin to an invasion of privacy. Some users even go so far as to disable cookies, which most Web browsers allow them to do. If a cookie-hating user visits your site with cookies disabled, all bets are off in terms of counting that user as a visitor to your site through cookie technology.

Clickpaths

Clickpaths — the order in which various users click through a set of pages — are tough to track. A simple example of the complicating factors that are involved is when a user clicks on the browser's Back button to return to pages that were previously viewed. Usually no record for this is generated in the access log file, so the clickpath trail is lost.

Some software packages attempt to extract clickpath information from the server's access log file, while other packages include special software that you can run on your Web server to track clickpaths. Again, this is no exact science, and determining clickpaths is a matter of sorting all the records in the access log file and trying to work through where a person went at a given time.

Finding the right tools to use for tracking and reporting on the numbers you want makes a world of difference. Read on.

Choosing Tools to Make Measuring Traffic Easier

Various software packages are available for your use in tracking traffic as a measure of the success of your Web site. Which package is right for you depends, as usual, on a number of factors. You need only a fairly simple tool if yours is a small company site but a more sophisticated setup if you plan to sell ad space on your site. As you sift through the options available to you, consider these criteria:

- ✔ **Price:** What you pay ranges from free or cheap (for the most basic software) to $300,000 and up for more customizable options.

- ✔ **Capacity:** Consider the software's ability to crunch numbers and digest large files, and compare that to how much traffic you anticipate and how complex your site is.

- ✔ **Customization:** Determine up front whether you can live with predefined reports or need to write your own queries and get more elaborate custom reports.

- ✔ **Platform:** Find out whether the software runs on your desktop computer (it often does); if so, you have to choose software that's appropriate for your desktop operating system as well as your server's operating system.

- ✔ **Service:** Get the best service you can, and make sure the company that provides your sites statistics tool is going to stick around for a while and support it; refer to Chapters 10 and 11 for information about choosing vendors and assessing service agreements.

As you're shopping around, consider the vendor's reliability and stability. You probably want support not just for getting started, but for the length of time that you are using the product. Look into the company's past stability and its growth potential, and choose software from a known and reputable source. Check references and ask the same sort of "due diligence" questions you'd ask of designers and other vendors.

Counting on Third-Party Audits

As the Web has taken its place as the most important communications medium since the advent of television (or perhaps even the telephone), advertisers have looked at it more seriously as a medium for their message. Big-name advertisers pay big ad rates for big traffic, but they also want results. They want to know how many people they're reaching, and they want credible, third-party verification that a Web site actually has the traffic it claims to have. This is nothing new; in the worlds of print and television, established auditors exist and provide reliable, trusted information that boosts credibility in the industry. Similarly, in the magazine and newspaper world, well known third-party auditors verify a publication's circulation at least annually, and advertisers see that verified number as being credible enough to warrant paying the publication for ad space.

In the online world, the same logic prevails: If you want to sell ad space, the ad space buyers (especially the big-name ones) are going to want to know what they're getting for their dollar. They want to know how many people are going to see the ad at what frequency, and they want a disinterested but respected third party to verify that number.

Third-party auditors offer exactly these objective reports. The information they gather and the reports they produce are sometimes similar to those you can generate or have generated using site-statistic tools and services. (Some third-party auditors even use the same software you can use!) However, their reports about your site's traffic carry more weight with potential advertisers than yours (or your ISP or hosting company's), because an auditor does not have the conflict of interest you may have. You do, after all, have a stake in having higher numbers. And your ISP works for you, so it isn't seen as objective, either. Third-party auditors have a specific kind of professional reputation based on a kind of objectivity that others believe.

The procedures used for audits vary. Generally speaking, third-party auditors may require you to run special software on your Web server or to make some minor change to your Web pages to enable their tracking system to work. In some cases, they may conduct their audits based solely on copies of your access log file. Some auditors want to come to your site — your physical site, not your Web site — and kick the tires by examining how you run your server and how log files are generated. They may want to investigate for signs of tampering or odd procedures. (Which they won't find, will they now? But that's not the point.)

Setting ad rates based on impressions

In the nonvirtual, print world, ad rates are based on circulation. Basically, one pays an ad rate per CPM, which stands for cost per thousand (*M* is the Roman numeral for 1,000). In the online world, the phrase CPM is also tossed around. However, the thousand generally refers to impressions rather than copies, and the rates per CPM for advertising vary widely.

Sites with highly targeted usership sometimes charge higher rates than sites with broader usership because they can offer those who advertise a direct line to an exact type of customer. For example, a golf equipment advertiser, who may advertise on a search-engine site like Excite (www.excite.com), would get a great deal of impressions for its advertising dollar. But if the purchase of ad space was for the run of the site (rather than a golf page or the keyword "golf"), only a small percentage of those reached would likely be golfers. The same golf equipment advertiser, advertising on iGolf (www.igolf.com), would get fewer impressions for its dollar. But the advertiser could assume that most, if not all, of those impressions would be placed before the shining eyes of golf enthusiasts.

Thus, the ability to set a high CPM for ad space on your site and actually get that rate is a sign of success in the sense of the traffic you get and the number of users you reach who are interested in the topic of your site.

Unlike print and broadcast media, where certain auditors are industry leaders, one leading third-party auditor of Web sites hasn't yet emerged. Nor has a standard system for measuring and reporting. As time goes on, this is sure to settle down; as of this writing, these basic techniques are in use:

- ✔ **Consumer sampling:** Tracking software is installed on the computers of selected groups of users, and the software simply tracks the users' activities as they go about their online business. Media Metrix (`www.mediametrix.com`) and ACNielsen Media Research (`www.acnielsen.com`) currently use this method to establish traffic numbers for Web sites.

- ✔ **Server-side software:** The audit company installs software on your Web server to track frequently accessed directories and pages, the geographic distribution of the audience, the organizations from which site visitors are coming, and so on. ABC Interactive (`www.abcinteractiveaudits.com`) and Engage (`www.engage.com`) both now use server-side software.

Based on these techniques, in the end, all third-party auditors produce verified, signed off reports. They do not, unfortunately, all produce identically organized reports that show the same categories of data. Although all of their reports contain information that's of interest to media buyers, the format and selection of data that's best for the online industry has not yet been standardized. As of this writing, organizations representing those who buy ad space on Web sites want standardization, for the sake of easy comparison. Surely a standard will emerge soon.

A word on awards

Awards can be, well, rewarding. They boost egos, and to many audience members (as well as investors, advertisers, and others), they look like external validation of success. (Bravo! You won an award!) There has been, however, a tendency among Web sites to fabricate awards and offer them to others as a means for getting backlinks to the award-giver's site. Awards can be so ego-gratifying they're hard to resist, and this was for a while a notoriously successful tactic.

Having too many award-like logos on your home page heralding your success is a bit like having touristy bumper stickers pasted all over your car. The first issue is: No one can see the site for the stickers. The second: Who cares?

Awards are a sign of success only if they have been given by a respected entity for a specific accomplishment. If someone offers you an award, you may want to look that gift horse in the mouth. If it seems truly prestigious, by all means, let others know about it. (The Webbys seem poised to become the Oscars or Grammies of the Internet; getting a Webby means something.) Issue a press release, tell your advertisers, and plaster that award wherever you like. Just remember how many times you've heard the phrase "award-winning" in marketing hype and not really known what that "award" really meant.

You can probably imagine that the services of third-party auditors are not cheap. Prices vary tremendously and how rates are set depends on the type of relationship you establish with the company providing the audit. Checking various auditors' Web sites and then contacting the companies to get up-to-date information is a good idea.

Getting Cozy with User Input

Everyone has an opinion. Some are smart, objective, and even informed; some are based on personal preference, guesswork, and something heard while standing in line at the grocery store. Before the advent of the Internet, market researchers had to spend beaucoup bucks to conduct *focus groups;* the researchers gathered people in a room to give them feedback about the company's product or services. Sometimes they conducted surveys, too. The point is that they had to work hard to get that information. You can get immediate feedback via your Web site through any of several methods.

Soliciting user input via e-mail

You can offer users a link to an easy-to-use e-mail form. This is a very powerful tool in that it lets your users talk to you whenever they have an opinion or request, but don't let that incoming e-mail languish. Answering user e-mail is crucial. An automated response will do for acknowledgment that you've received the message, but users who take the trouble to contact you want real answers. Get back to them quickly.

Also, note that some users are going to express opinions that are articulate and respectful, and some are going to write e-mails filled with rants and gobbledygook. You *must* treat each of these users with respect. These are people, they are your audience, and they are key to your success.

You may want to establish a set of polite responses to commonly received feedback. These responses can act as a knowledge base that your staff members can quickly choose and customize as necessary as they respond to users. Also, be sure to track what users are saying in their messages about what is and is not working on your site. When you redesign your navigational bar, revamp your content areas, or overhaul your whole look, you can refer that information.

Getting input via online surveys

Use surveys as another method of getting user feedback, but get hip to the fact that creating surveys is an art in itself. Not everyone wants to participate, so your first hurdle is rounding up a good sampling of people and persuading them to give you information. To encourage participation, you can offer an incentive — a prize, a bonus, or even access to the information gathered in the survey, if it's going to be of interest to your audience. But keep in mind that the participation of some folks who simply want what you're giving away may skew the results. To get a more random sampling, you can use an automated interception technique; basically, you can have a dialog box pop up asking people to fill out your survey (which is linked from the dialog box). Gently interrupting every tenth or twentieth visitor to your site is a good general rule.

Whatever methods you use to encourage participation, your survey should be short, with brief, specific questions. Offering multiple choice responses (between two and five options from which to choose) forces users to select a response and actually makes answering the questions easier. It's also a lot easier to convert multiple-choice answers into a measurable set of data. Offering open-ended, essay-style questions, on the other hand, makes quantifying the responses harder. Keep your survey simple, and ask the most personal questions last. People don't like telling others their income levels, for example, but if those questions come up only after several less intrusive ones, survey participants will have warmed up to the process of giving you information.

Remember that security is as much an issue for users participating in surveys as anyone else. They'll be more inclined to join in if you assure them that the survey is taking place on a secure server, that you aren't planning to give their individual responses to any third parties, and that you won't take advantage of their confidences to push your products on them.

What to Do About What You Learn

Having gathered an enormous pile of hard data and user feedback, you're probably wondering what to do with all this handy-dandy information. We can't offer you blanket rules because everyone's situation is different. What you will do probably depends on the same variety of factors that led to your first decisions about your site's strategic focus, offerings, and so on. We can offer a few pointers based (as usual) on the primary goals a Web site can generally accomplish.

✔ If the purpose of your site is *to promote*, (a company, product, service, person, or viewpoint, for example), you can, as you know, monitor its media presence to measure the site's success. You may use a service that monitors the press and broadcast media and sends you clippings for a fee. You may also look at how many registrations your site has and how many impressions you're serving. With this information, you can determine to what extent you need to modify the branding message, the price, methods of promotion, and how the site's offerings, content, and design fulfill the branding promise.

✔ If the goal of your site is *to inform*, monitor the number of subscribers to your content as well as the number of impressions served and, again, the media presence (which is another indicator of people listening to your message). Based on what you learn, you can modify your content, your site's navigation (which may affect the paths users are or are not finding to the content), and the site's usability (which again may affect user experience of the content).

✔ When your site is meant to *educate*, monitor the number of registrants into classes or programs, how many graduate, how many return for more learning, scores on tests, and so on. You may have to adjust the course content, its pricing, the promotional methods you use, your branding message, or your site's content, navigation, or usability.

✔ For a site that *distributes*, monitor the number of visitors the site gets, the number of downloads, and how the two numbers compare. Also, watch the number of support events required. As a result of what you discover, you may modify the placement of the downloads on the site or the page, the descriptions of the product, the site's navigation, the speed of the download, or even the quality or usability of your customer care area.

✔ If your site's intent is *to sell*, monitor how many customers and repeat customers you're getting, the number of sales or leads generated, how much revenue is generated, and ultimately how much profit is produced. Also, take note of how much market penetration you've achieved and how few customer service events you're experiencing. Based on your data, you may have to adjust the call to action that's supposed to be inspiring customers to buy now; the value proposition that's intended to communicate to them why what you offer is such a splendid choice; the methods of promotion you're using; the pricing; the product descriptions; or the ease of use of your site, its navigation, or its transaction system.

✔ When a site's purpose is to conduct *research* (and perhaps report it), measure your success according to the quality of data gathered, the number and appropriateness of participants in the site's surveys, and the credibility and media presence that are achieved. You may find that you need to change the call to action that urges participation, the relative ease of participating, or the method of generating either a random or a targeted sampling.

✔ If the site provides *customer service* or *technical support*, monitor the cost per event, the time that achieving a resolution takes, the number of events that wind up requiring staff response, and the general satisfaction of customers. You may then have to modify the customer self-service tools (the FAQ, for example), or you may have to refocus the writing on the site to more closely target the audience.

✔ For a site that *fosters or serves a community*, keep an eye on the number of participants, the quality and frequency of their participation, and the loyalty to the group or sponsor that's apparent. When necessary, make improvements to the level of on-topic interaction (as compared to off-topic digressions) and the moderation. Also give recognition to community leaders, and keep the community lively and growing by allowing spin-off topics to become their own discussions.

✔ When the site's reason for being is *to facilitate workflow*, focus on productivity and how well the team is meeting deadlines. Also consider whether the morale of the workgroup is perky. High morale is an indicator that people feel supported in accomplishing their jobs, and a Web site that is intended to facilitate workflow ought to be enabling people to work well and feel good about it. As needed, you can make adjustments to the selection of tools on the site, to how the site enables communication among the workgroup, and, as always, to the speed of downloads and the site's overall usability.

Take a Look at Yourself

Remaining objective is as important as listening and responding to your audience. When you listen to feedback e-mail, for example, don't take everything that everyone says as gospel. That can drive you nuts, and more importantly, you simply can't make every living person happy.

Similarly, you must not fall prey to your own preferences. You may love that fluorescent fuchsia on your navigational bar, but does the color suit your high-finance audience? In writing classes, wise teachers often tell their students that to write well, one must be willing to "murder your precious darlings." This is as true in creating and maintaining a Web site as it is in writing a novel. If something you absolutely adore does not serve the user's interests and the site's mission, you simply must ax it.

In the end, remember who you are and what you do (Chapter 1), and stay conscious of your site's overall mission and specific goals (Chapter 2). You are the Webmaster. This is your site, your responsibility, and we hope, your pleasure. The site's success depends on your vision. And your skill (or your team's) in technical development, design, content creation, marketing, and management can make that vision a reality.

Active archiving and true purging

So you're ready to kill off that tired, old Web page. You seek and destroy every link that leads to it, and — poof! — you're done. Nope. Guess what? If you kill the links and leave the page, it's still there. Search engines continue indexing that tired, old, out-of-date content, and the links to your Web site still lead to it. What's more, when users search your site, it often shows up in the search results like some weird ghost of content past.

Old Web pages don't die unless you kill them off completely. You have to actively remove not just the links, but also the page itself. You can place the file, if you simply must store it, in some section of the server reserved for old stuff. But that section of the server must be inaccessible to the public and search engine crawlers or you're going to find that moldy old content rearing its ugly head again, like the monster that never dies in horror flicks.

Part IV
Working: Get Credentials, Get Hired, Hire Others

The 5th Wave   By Rich Tennant

"You're the Webblasters? Oh, sorry fellas the ad asked for Webmasters."

In this part . . .

Hiring and getting hired are the topics du jour here. Where Webmasters get credentials, where they hang out with each other (and network), and where to find or place job postings are all covered in Chapter 18. Hiring managers and job candidates alike may find the information here illuminating.

But wait! You've got that interview with a seemingly swell start-up and you want to know what to ask them to find out whether they know what they're doing? You aren't sure how to assess them or what to think about before you take that alluring but possibly risky job? (Maybe it'll turn out to be a blast, and maybe it will be a bust.) Chapter 19 clues you in to some things to look into and think about before you say yes to what may be the biggest adventure of your life.

Chapter 18

Hiring and Getting Hired

*L*ittle Webmasters can be found in cabbage patches under the leafy purple stuff — too bad this isn't true. As of this writing, certification programs are sprouting up all over the United States (and presumably other countries, too). But still, hiring Internet professionals or focusing your career path as a Net pro can be challenging. This chapter is for both those doing the hiring and those hoping to be hired. Here, we discuss what makes a Webmaster a real Internet pro, where Internet pros get qualified, how to benchmark staffing requirements, and a few hiring (and getting hired) tricks and tactics.

Assessing and Getting Credentials

In an industry that has yet to mature, it's tough to know where to find the best place to get credentials and what credentials or experience you'll need. A wide variety of freshly minted (but not yet truly standardized) job titles appear on the resumes of people who have acquired Web site experience. Knowing what actual skills and potential paths those job titles represent is enough to drive a hiring manager batty.

Universities and technical seminars have been training programmers and system administrators for years, so for those jobs, the confusion is less than for the other types of Internet pros. Still, it's tough for a hiring manager to know how to assess the skills and abilities of a job candidate for a Web site team. And taking the short route of simply hiring someone with years of

Java experience is a big mistake. As we discuss in Chapter 1, *Webmaster* is a catchall title that can describe a wide variety of charters and tasks. Although it may be reassuring to the corporate hiring manager to think that a certificate in Microsoft technologies, for example, assures someone's legitimate skill level, the Webmaster community argues that it's really tough to test technical skills that change at the speed of light, let alone more abstract skills like the ability to imagine this design and that functionality working together smoothly.

The perfect one-person-band Webmaster may be someone with an MBA in marketing, two bachelor's degrees (one in computer science and one in design), and a minor in English or journalism. Of course, this person should also probably have five years of project management experience as well! But expecting a single person to have all these skills is hardly reasonable. The bottom line is this: Don't bother looking for degrees or certification in all those areas when you try to hire a Webmaster; instead, look for shining accomplishments and demonstrated skills in the areas you need most.

The good news is that as time goes on, more and more colleges, extension programs, and training centers are training people in the specialized skills involved in creating and managing a Web site. But the entire field is still quite new, and although the Internet may exist in fast-forward mode, the educational system certainly does not. The best programs are those that avoid this year's degree becoming next year's birdcage liner. Intensives (those programs that crunch a year-and-a-half's training into four months or so) are good. So are programs that ground themselves in the fundamentals and best practices of online business, intellectual property, marketing, and so on, without focusing on this week's buzz phrases.

Ultimately, it's vision, accomplishment, drive, and demonstrated skills that count. Completing coursework or a certificate program that addresses running, designing, or promoting Web sites is certainly desirable, but a clear understanding of a Web site's objectives and an ability to carry them out counts most.

Finding Talented, Smart People

Everyone wants to hire the best and brightest. Where are those people? In the face of low unemployment, high demand for Internet pros, and fierce competition for skilled and experienced people, industry analysts say, "Hire for potential." Okay, fine. Just what does that mean, though? And where are all the job candidates with "potential"? They may be right under your nose.

In-house staff with transferable skills

Don't overlook the folks you already have. Think about it — they know your business, they know the company values, and they know their current fields. A small Web team may consist of someone from marketing, someone from the technical side, and someone from corporate communications (or, for a content-driven site, editorial). If your company creates its own marketing collateral, someone from your in-house design department might join in.

These people must get specific training in the unique issues associated with Web sites, however. And it's tough to have these people work on the Web initiative in their spare time. The problem is that the company's core business — which is presumably generating revenue — is usually thought of as a first priority, with the Web work slipping to a much lower spot on the priority scale. If you decide to create a Web team from existing staff, place those individuals in a separate team so that they can gel, work toward a focused goal, and put their best effort into the Web initiative.

Avoid the inclination to believe no one in-house is qualified to be Webmaster. The job is too broad for any one person to be fully qualified, what *Webmaster* means (and who is best qualified to fill the job or jobs) depends on your site's goals, and no universally reliable certification standards exist at this time. In the face of low unemployment and other pressures that make hiring Web site staff challenging, research giant Jupiter Communications has suggested "hiring for potential." ***Remember:*** An in-house Webmaster's primary responsibility is to fulfill the mission of the company's Web initiative, and who knows your company's mission better than in-house people? Finding talented, smart in-house staff and providing those folks with the training they need to make the move to online may pay off in netting you a qualified Webmaster who also knows your business.

Other fields

If you go outside to seek a Webmaster, first determine the purpose of your site and where your in-house staff is strongest. If you have a solid IS department but no one in marketing who knows the Web, you may find that a producer is a better choice than a hands-on techie. If your site will deliver a great deal of text as its content, you may look for someone with an editorial background to act as content manager. You may have to get creative about where you look for a Webmaster. But do try to get someone who has a fundamental understanding of your business as well as the right mix of skills to be a good Webmaster for the sort of site you're creating.

Universities, colleges, and training programs

As e-commerce has burst forth and more and more people are drawn to the flame, more and more colleges and universities have taken notice. Many now offer Webmaster courses or certification programs; these programs are sometimes cobbled together out of existing courses in various departments, sometimes deeply focused on the area of technical Webmastering, and sometimes focused on specialized aspects of building and running a Web site. Additionally, online coursework is available from the distance learning programs of many universities and colleges as well as through such venues as DigitalThink (www. digitalthink.com) and others. (Take a look at HungryMinds.com, an education portal, for listings of courses and programs.)

If you are thinking about becoming a Webmaster, can't find a specific program near you, and are looking for where to start, you may be able to put together your own quick-study program that pulls together coursework in network and system administration, graphic production, interactive marketing, writing for Web sites, and programming. Many colleges and universities grant independent study degrees if you have a well-thought-out course plan that you can present. Alternatively, just having the right mix of coursework on your resume can, in combination with some measure of demonstrated skill, get you a job in this field.

Getting Experience

If you're a Webmastering newbie, it is important to get some experience in the field. Just a couple of years ago, anyone who knew HTML could get some kind of Web work, but these days, the best jobs go (understandably) to seasoned pros. To make yourself at least semi-seasoned, start building a portfolio by creating your own site. Get experience working as a volunteer or intern on a good, working Web site. And as you seek your first job, think as much about finding a mentor as you do about getting top dollar. A mentor may further your career more quickly than you could have imagined by offering you pointers and insight that can come only from real experience.

Who's Who on the Web Site Team

How a Web site team will be specifically configured depends on many factors. The size of the endeavor and where the financing comes from will have an effect. Another factor is whether the company's commitment is short term (suggesting the assembling of a virtual team of freelancers or even outsourcing to vendors) or long term (suggesting actual hiring).

FIELD NOTES

Take some classes and build a good portfolio

According to Web developer Ann Marie Michaels, "If you have a good portfolio, that says much more about your ability than a degree. In fact, some of the best graphic designers and programmers I have worked with had no college education. They taught themselves. Then there are others, just as talented, who went to a two-year trade school. Still others went to a university. The point is, what you do to get the skills doesn't matter. It's what you do with your skills that is important. I think it's smart to take some classes (even part-time) to ramp up your skills — this is much faster than trying to learn on your own. Don't worry about completing a degree."

A small operation might consist of

- ✔ A producer, who manages the site, gets content from marketing or communications, does coding and page layout, and oversees the review and approval process

- ✔ A Webmaster, who does technical administration and back-end programming, monitors the log files, and oversees security

A mid-sized operation might include

- ✔ A producer, who again manages the site and its content as well as pitches in with coding as needed

- ✔ A designer, who creates graphics, banners, page design, and layout

- ✔ A developer, who is a programmer with Web site specialties

- ✔ A Webmaster or system administrator, who handles the basic tasks of keeping the site's technologies (and perhaps its servers) running

A larger operation adds more people to the mix. How many of which sort depends on the site's purpose, but in general, layers of management-level people will be in place. Here is a general rundown:

- ✔ Senior producers and producers

- ✔ An art director or creative director as well as designers

- ✔ A content director, content manager, content editors, and perhaps specialized copy editors

- ✔ A director of technology along with developers, database administrators, and programmers

- ✔ A network or systems administrator

As you can see, larger teams allow for more differentiation. Larger groups also often support several Web sites, sometimes including both public Web sites and intranets or extranets. All the staff members might work on all the sites or some might be assigned to work on each site.

Determining Staffing Levels

Figuring how much staffing you'll need depends on so many factors (the scope of your endeavor, its goals, the timeline, the technologies used, and so on) that providing a one-size-fits-all formula is not possible. According to surveys of organizations running large-scale Web sites, however, it is possible to benchmark staff requirements based very generally on how much traffic you anticipate:

- ✓ **Under 100,000 daily page views:** You may need a staff of 1 to 10 people.

- ✓ **Between 100,000 and 1 million daily page views:** You need to ramp up.

- ✓ **More than 1 million page views per day:** You may need more than 100 people.

Note that these are page views we're discussing, not hits or unique users. Note, too, that whether the ten employees needed to support 100,000 daily page views are weighted toward content, technology, or design depends entirely on whether the site is driven more by content, technology, or design. And whether you need one, five, or ten depends on how labor-intensive your processes are, as well as how much original content or creative technology will be required. How the content is shaped — whether it's more evergreen or requires more updating, as discussed in Chapter 3 — is also a factor. And finally, note that if yours is a stand-alone venture (rather than part of an existing company), human resources, administrative, and other staff will be needed as well.

Your online enterprise will not be comparable in staffing to your brick-and-mortar operation. One company found that its online store, with 9 or 10 employees, produced revenue equal to one of its brick-and-mortar stores with 25 employees. You have to determine staffing levels based on the realities of your Web site. But how can you do this if the site's not yet built? Some companies find it advantageous to build and launch with outsourced talent or by building a virtual team. For the short-term, this strategy can net you expertise without having to make commitments to staffing levels and organizational structures that may change quickly. After the long-term needs are clear, then you can actually hire permanent staff.

Remember, too, to plan for project management. Planning, needs assessment, brainstorming, research, meetings, preparation of executive summaries, and presentations all take time. So does hands-on management of the schedule, the staff, and the budget. When you budget time for any project, add approximately 20 percent onto the overall time allotted for the project to account for project management. In-house teams can build this into the schedule. If you're outsourcing, watch the bids and contracts for mention of project management. This cost may be included in the rates, or it may be broken out as a separate item.

Turnover in the world of Web work is very, very common. As much as 20 or 25 percent per year is all too typical. As a Web site manager or team leader, to ease the pain of turnover, remember that job-hopping is typical. Plan for it. Make sure that your systems are documented (see Chapter 22) and you aren't relying on verbal lore as a training method. Build depth into your team, always looking at who can be promoted and who can pinch hit in an emergency. Remember when you're hiring that company culture is as important to many employees as benefits and what appeals to many does not appeal to all.

Dot coms have the seeming hiring advantages of being able to offer stock options as well as a faster growth path. They also often offer the opportunity to "play" with cooler toys and, frequently, more high-profile projects. But not all start-ups succeed. And working at a start-up can be an especially demanding, stressful experience; the standard start-up workweek is often six days of terribly long hours. The Web site teams that run company Web sites, intranets, or extranets at more established, brick-and-mortar companies can compete in the hiring arena by offering stability, a less stressful culture, and even a standard 40- or 50-hour workweek — all of which can be appealing to the right people.

Placing and Finding Job Listings

As manager of a Web team or as a hiring manager, you may have to think creatively about hiring. Placing an ad in the newspaper or even trade publications may not pan out — people who work online look online for news, industry info, and job listings. Online is where these people (especially the experienced, qualified ones) hang out. Here are some national venues that post job listings, including Webmaster listings:

✔ The Monster Board (www.monster.com) is a huge site with listings for all sorts of jobs.

✔ Dice.com (www.dice.com) specializes in listing jobs in the tech industry.

✔ CraigsList (www.craigslist.com) has localized listings of jobs (and many other things) for major metropolitan areas of the United States.

Don't forget, too, to look into professional organizations and guilds, such as those listed in the next section, and to post ads to discussion groups or mailing lists that accept ads (such as the Webgrrls list noted in the next section). Not all discussion groups and mailing lists accept ads, but hey, if you can find one that's populated by Webmaster types and accepts ads, too, where better to look for qualified people? If you aren't sure whether a given group or list does accept ads, ask who's moderating the thing and inquire with that person. Even if you can't place the ad there, you may get word of mouth going.

Where Webmasters Meet, Greet, and Network

So you want to be a Webmaster — or maybe you already are one — and you're looking around for other Webmasters to network with. Where are your colleagues trading tips and strategies? They probably aren't gathering around the water cooler at your job. Even if your job is at a Web shop or a search-engine company, they're probably yakking it up online. To find communities of Internet pros, go where they are. Many sites devoted to Web site topics now offer discussion groups related to those topics. For tips about using Macromedia tools, for example, go to the Macromedia site and log on. Builder.com offers Builder Buzz discussions. Many sites offer e-mail newsletters (some of which we mention throughout this book).

Professional groups are also springing up. Here are some that have been around for a while and have strong credibility:

- ✔ **The Association of Internet Professionals** (www.association.org) is a premier professional association of the Internet industry. Its mission is "to unify, support and represent the global community of Internet professionals. The organization also serves as a forum for the ideas, people and issues shaping the future of the Internet industry."

- ✔ **Webgrrls** (www.webgrrls.com) "provides a forum for women in or interested in new media and technology to network, exchange job and business leads, form strategic alliances, mentor and teach, intern and learn the skills to help women succeed in an increasingly technical workplace and world."

- ✔ **The International Webmasters Association** (www.iwanet.org) has over 100 official chapters in 106 countries. It establishes guidelines for the field as well as professional standards and certification and education programs. It also offers specialized employment resources and technical assistance to individuals and businesses.

You can also look for local groups. Here in San Francisco, we've found the SFWoW mailing list (see `www.sfwow.org`) to be a constant source of good information. Additionally, the Software Development Forum (`www.sdforum.org`) sponsors many meetings monthly with speakers on business and Internet topics.

And for more segmented areas of Web work, don't overlook groups that dedicate themselves to the special aspects of design, editing, writing, and marketing for online endeavors. Throughout this book, we highlight online resources of special interest to the well-rounded Internet professional. Any of these resources could be a starting place for finding out what's au courant. Some will also accept job postings for their e-mail newsletters or in their discussion groups.

Chapter 19

What to Ask Before You Take That Start-Up Job

In This Chapter

▶ Will the company succeed?

▶ Are the terms good?

▶ Will you enjoy working with the company?

▶ How will this job further your professional goals?

*H*ave you heard about the Silicon Valley secretary who cashed out her dot com stock options, started a foundation, and is living happily ever after in a million-dollar beach house? Or the many Internet pros driving company-issued Porsches? How about the hundreds of programming hot-shots, content whizzes, and biz dev go-getters who were laid off moments before their options vested, or the thousands who slaved night and day for a start-up that burned through so much cash it flopped before its IPO? Not every Web work story has a happy ending.

Before you take that juicy offer from an Internet start-up, remember that chasing stock options doesn't always pan out. You need to know that the company you're joining is as smart, able, and willing as you are. Go beyond the usual "what will my typical day look like" inquiry and find out if the company has real potential by posing to yourself and others the questions noted in this chapter. To find answers, start by looking at the company's Web site.

Who's Who Here?

In the About Us section of your prospective employer's Web site, find out about the members of the executive team and their credentials. Do the top people in the company have appropriate business and Internet experience? Do they have degrees from high-ranking universities? What achievements are under their belts? Does the total picture of their backgrounds suggest to you the business acumen, drive, vision, and determination necessary for real success?

A balanced board whose members can advise the company well is also a good sign. Indicators of a good board are similar to indicators of a solid executive team. But on the executive team, you can make allowances for a few promising newcomers with a hot business plan but not years of experience. On the board, you want people with sterling credentials and substantial experience.

Where's the Cash Coming From?

Here's a hot question: Who's funding the company? (You can find this out either via the company's Web site or in an interview.) Companies that are backed by known parent companies or venture capitalist firms tend to have refined their business plans. Those backed by *angel-funding* (individual investors) may be less mature or based on less closely scrutinized strategies. If the company is angel-funded, you'll also want to know what its level of funding is and its *burn rate* (the speed at which it is using up capital). Some start-ups are as busy looking for the next round of funding as they are building a company. Similarly, some executive teams aren't as frugal as they probably should be. A company that's well positioned for success is one that balances the need to grow quickly in this industry against the company's funding levels.

What's the Plan?

What are the company's business and revenue models? Are the revenue streams tried and true, or at least based on sound logic? Are multiple revenue streams at work so that if one possibly more experimental source of revenue is less successful, another can carry the day? Again, knowing this information tells you how well poised the company is. Find out, too, whether the company has big-name, marquee customers, investors, or strategic partners. This can be a sign of credibility, stability, and potential for going the distance. It certainly says that people with business savvy have looked over this company and found it worth betting on.

Are the Goals Defined and Achievable?

What is the company's long-term vision, and what are its shorter-term goals? Will achieving these goals lead to fulfilling the vision? Are the vision and goals clearly articulated and sensible? Search the sites of major industry publications to see what analysts may have said about the company, but also look at what's posted in the company's own online press room. Press releases can reveal the company's strategic vision, timeline, achievements, people, and partners, and the information in press releases doesn't always actually make it into the press.

What's the Competition?

Who are the company's competitors, and how does the company differentiate itself from them? Again, you can find out a lot on this topic via the press or a company's online press releases. You may also consider checking into the competitors' executive teams, boards, revenue models, press, funding, and so on. Ultimately, you want to know how this company stacks up against its competitors — who's more likely to make it to the big time and what makes that so?

Does This Company Have What It Takes?

To dig more deeply into whether the company is on the ball, you may want to look into some nitty-gritty details. If the company is business-to-consumer, what is the current cost of customer acquisition? If the company is business-to-business, how long has it been in partnership with key partners? And here's an interview question that, if it is posed tactfully, will sound savvy rather than intrusive: What keeps the company's executives up at night? What are management's current concerns, and how are they addressing them? (You can follow up with a question about how you, in your position, can help, or a suggestion about how you'll be able to contribute to solutions.)

What Are the Terms?

Of course you'll ask the terms — what salary, benefits, and other compensation are being offered. In a start-up scenario, you'll also want to know about the stock options and vesting schedule. But also, find out how many shares have been issued and how many are yet to be issued. (Your options may be well under 1 percent of the total; it would be unusual even at the executive level to be offered 5 percent or more.) Investigate on your own how the offering compares to what other companies might offer or what might be offered to other job candidates. You can do this, for example, by asking trusted peers.

What's your work worth?

Wondering what you should be earning in your new job? Or what you'd make doing the same job in Tuscaloosa, Buffalo, Fargo, or Stockton? Or how Silicon Valley, NYC, and LA salaries compare? Find out at Salary.com (www. salary.com). Also see Aquent (www. aquent.com) for more job descriptions and for freelance rates.

What Is the Company's Culture?

Two questions that are often asked in interviews to get an idea of the company's culture are

- ✔ What will a typical day be like?
- ✔ Who will I be working closely with?

Follow up these questions with a few more. Can you talk with the people you'd be working with most closely? If so, ask those people what they did today. With whom did they interact, what went well (and not so well), and how was their most recent success recognized? What time did these people leave work for home each night this week? What inspired them to join this company? Were their expectations realized? What do they anticipate doing after leaving their current jobs?

Will This Job Further Your Goals?

Finally, ask yourself these questions. Will I thrive in this company? Will I enjoy being here, in this building, with these people? Will coming to work be a pleasure? Do my future colleagues appear energized (or just frantic)? At the end of the day, will I feel I've made a contribution, that the work I've done is satisfying? A job in a company with a "fun" culture can be a blast, but where will it lead?

Even if the job looks intriguing to you and the company looks promising, ask for a day or so to think over the offer. (Remember — a company that hires easily is often a company that will fire easily, and a company that demands an on-the-spot response is likely to behave that way in general.) Go back through what you've learned in the course of asking all these questions. Look at the overall picture. Getting in on things is great, but you want to feel good about staying onboard long enough for those terrific stock options to start vesting! You also want to know that this job is going to contribute as much to your life as you will to your work.

Part V
The Part of Tens

The 5th Wave   By Rich Tennant

THE MODERN JAMES BOND

The name is bond.com,
JAMES bond.com.

In this part . . .

In the world famous The Part of Tens, we offer you life-saving treats and quick tricks. You may want to book-mark this part. It includes ten techniques to help you manage complex projects with true aplomb and ten indications (get a clue!) that the time has come to redesign your site. It also describes ten things you can do to manage your content, keep it fresh, and assure yourself that it's as Web-savvy and user-friendly as you are.

Chapter 20

Ten Techniques for Hyper-Effective Project Management

In This Chapter

▶ Making big projects more manageable

▶ Defining who you need and how long you need them

▶ Using good tools and monitoring progress

▶ Assessing the project's upside and trouble spots

*B*uilding even a smallish Web site involves addressing a complex series of interconnected tasks, which are often tackled by a posse of people with differing skills and agendas. These project management techniques should help you stay on track as you barrel toward your launch date.

Break It Down

To make projects more manageable, break them into stages, steps, or phases. Specify milestones to allow people to see progress. Assess your success at key points and make adjustments to the plan to account for reality rearing its ugly head along the way. Classic big-picture phases for a Web site project include defining the project, analyzing and strategizing, designing, developing, testing, implementing, launching, and reviewing the project. (That last item is also called the *post mortem*.) Within each of these larger categories, break down tasks even further, until you have a clear picture of the activities and tasks necessary to get you and your team from defining to launch and beyond.

Decide Who's Accountable for What

Assign the right jobs to the right people, and half your challenge will actually be met. Roles and responsibilities should be clearly defined and communicated; giving specific people "ownership" of specific deliverables makes them accountable. You can delegate planning and execution of phases to the individual team member or expert specialist responsible for that aspect of the project. After you've assigned accountability, let people do their jobs. Someone (presumably you, the project manager) must be accountable for the overview, however. Keep tabs on the milestones you've set and be available for consultation, but don't micromanage. If you have the right people and they know what they're accountable for, managing their every move shouldn't be necessary.

Determine Who Needs Who

Whose work depends on who else's work is a question that uncovers potential breakdowns in the path ahead of you. Know ahead of time who's going to pass what baton, and you can make sure the team's on track at each crucial juncture. If Gloria needs the specs from John on a certain date so she can meet her database development deadlines, missing that date will affect later deadlines. Know where these touch points are in your schedule, and keep your eye on them as things roll along.

Tasks can be related to each other in various ways:

- In a *finish-start* relationship, one task must be completed before another, successive task can be started. (For example, the project must be defined before bids can be solicited.)

- In a *start-start* relationship, one task has to start before another can start. (This doesn't necessarily mean that both tasks must start at once. For example, meetings with potential vendors have to be arranged before the meetings can take place.)

- In a *finish-finish* relationship, one task must be completed before another can be completed (as when coding has to be done before testing can be done).

Identify the relationships among various tasks with these concepts in mind. Clarify how team members will rely on each other to make the process of finishing interdependent tasks smooth.

Assess Task Lengths and Create Deadlines

Consider both the *elapsed time* it will take for a task to be completed ("I can do it within a week") and the *actual number of hours* necessary to do the task ("it's going to take ten hours"). This information lets you consider applying more resources to the task so that it can be completed sooner.

Allow enough lead time so that tasks can be completed well and won't have to be done over. For example, writing often requires a few drafts. Ask writers to turn in their material on time even if it's going to be a first draft, and you'll risk getting rough copy that has to be more heavily massaged by content editors, which will eat up more time in the schedule anyway. Give people like writers and designers the time they need to be creative when creativity is called for. When you find slack time in the schedule, apply it as lead time to tasks that will benefit from it.

Assign deadlines, but also drop-deadlines. In other words, back your true deadline (the date on which someone will have to "drop dead" to complete the task *now*) up a bit, and assign a deadline earlier than that, to allow for slippage. After you've set deadlines, stick to them. Life will throw its own barriers in the way, don't fritter away your slack time.

Assign Resources

Resources include people, equipment, budgets, outsourced solutions, and so on. Obviously, assigning equipment resources to people as needed allows them to get their jobs done. Perhaps the trickier part of assigning resources is determining which tasks will require what personnel and how long those people will be needed. Maintaining a consistent workload (so that people aren't working 20 hours one day and sitting in their chairs knitting the next day) involves allocating resources wisely. You can either adjust the schedule to level things out or apply more people at key times. This is perhaps the most highly dynamic area of project management. Knowing how to move people from one task smoothly to another and back again takes keen managerial skill and is often crucial to keeping a project on track.

Refine Your Plan; Have Contingency Plans

Having set forth a big-picture plan, you'll probably see bumps and twists in the road before you. Level them out by considering what actually has to be scheduled for completion ASAP (as soon as possible) and what should be scheduled ALAP (as late as possible). Scheduling some items ALAP helps you keep resources spread appropriately across the schedule. When scheduling ALAP, though, remember that anything that slips may affect the overall schedule. You want to provide some slack here and there, and making too many tasks ALAP can create its own area of risk.

After your plan is in place, look through it again for problem areas. If a certain aspect of the project relies on one individual's expertise, consider what you're going to do if that person quits the job or (banish the thought!) is hit by a truck. What if a vendor who's new to you doesn't deliver on time? You needn't think up every possible gotcha and solve it now, but identifying a few and considering alternate routes to your intended result will provide you with options if and when the touchiest points in your plan give way.

Use the Right Tools

The right tools can make any job easier. Use project management software to make and track schedules, allocate resources, and monitor budgets. At the very least, create a central location for your Gantt chart (the floating bar chart showing the duration and overlap of task paths), contact lists, the files that team members are working on, and your style guide. You'll almost certainly use e-mail to communicate and send files to each other. You can also set up e-mail discussion groups or message boards for group communication. Even if your project is very low budget, you can use services such as those offered by Visto.com or Intranets.com for file sharing, calendaring, and to set up discussion groups.

Communicate, Revise, Update

Management means monitoring. You can keep your project on track and within your budget only by having a plan, telling people about it, revising it, and eyeballing it as it moves forward. Watch critical paths; monitor dates, hours, costs; and look ahead for potholes you can fill before you reach them. (Don't forget to communicate to team members that you've moved to Plan B, C, or D.)

Recognize and Reward Achievement

We simply cannot stress enough the importance of having set clearly defined, measurable goals. That theme has been woven through this book, but here it has individual meaning. As your team or team members reach goals, applaud them appropriately. Recognition in front of the group will do for interim achievements; bigger rewards should occur when bigger objectives are met.

Conduct Post-Mortems (Really)

The best time to reflect on what worked and didn't work (so you can refine processes and improve tool sets, for example) is while the project is still fresh in everyone's minds. Before you move on to the next project, get the entire team's perspective on how it went and what might work better next time. Ask what didn't work *and* what went splendidly. You'll not only gain valuable information, but also allow the team to get things off their chests and prime their enthusiasm for working together again.

Chapter 21

Ten Tip-Offs That It's Time to Redesign

In This Chapter

▶ Redesigning to take advantage of new options, technologies, or techniques

▶ Redesigning to better serve the site's users

▶ Redesigning to reposition the company, product, or site

▶ Redesigning to get attention

*I*n a perfect world, you'll be making incremental changes to your site. Your site will have been designed so well by such a brilliant designer that those changes will seamlessly integrate with what was there before. But once in a while, you'll have to make more drastic changes. Do you know when a real revamping is called for? Here are some indicators that it's time to redesign.

Technology Is Marching Forward

Every new generation of browsers offers new options in Web site design and inspires new design techniques. To keep up with the Joneses (your competition, in other words), you'll probably redesign in tandem with each generation of browsers. Similarly, advances in wireless access, broadband, and new capabilities in HTML, XML, programming, and other technologies will open doors. Beware, though, the temptation to slap new gadgets on your site just because you can. Way too many people thought blinking text was cool a few years ago (without realizing it was annoying), and it came as a surprise to some that while frames may have solved some navigation problems, they weren't well received by search engines.

You Have Tantalizing New Features

Offering something new? This may call for redesign because the nifty new stuff uses different technology, because it is so wild and wonderful it ought to be in the forefront or because its introduction actually changes the way you do business, for example.

Audience Feedback Suggests Modification

Okay, so you're getting the message from your site's users requesting or suggesting changes. Perhaps you ran a survey, or maybe you've simply been tracking e-mail. Hey, maybe you're using technology to track actual user patterns — great! If you find out that 80 percent of your audience hates your purple and yellow palette (why didn't you know this before launch?) or that 92 percent are using 10 percent of your site, you'll want to make changes. (Chapter 15 discusses all this in detail.)

Current Fashion Is Evolving

Society has a kind of group aesthetic, which is often called fashion. For a while people wear back-to-nature clothes and avoid haircuts, kitchen appliances appear in earth colors, and sitcoms feature salt-of-the-earth dialogue. Then neon colors, hairspray, and sharp repartee make an appearance. On Web sites, first there was the utilitarian look, then the online-can-do-anything-print-can-do image-map look, then the CNET-invented leftside-vertical nav-bar with a color-GIF behind-it, and then the every-site-is-a-portal look. Although we generally encourage more originality and less following-the-leader, we also recognize that fashion plays a part in Web design as in all things.

Your Business Model Has Changed

Say you launched your site as a publication, planning to offer pure editorial content, and somewhere along the way you concluded that advertising sales weren't going to pay all the bills. Your executive team, in casting about for a better way to do business, decided that now you'd be a portal, with product reviews contributed by users instead of articles written by journalists, and with sales of those products as a key component of the business strategy. Your site, then, is definitely ripe for redesign.

Whoa! Part of Your Site Is Profitable

One part of your site may actually be profitable, while the rest is a cost center. If and when you decide to spin off the profitable part of your venture or cut loose the money-sucking loss venture, you may have to redesign or revamp entirely.

You're Repositioning

When you have a new logo, a repositioned branding message, or a powerful new spin on your branding, you may want to redesign the site to bring it more in line with the fresh image.

You've Merged, Partnered, Been Acquired, or Spun Off

When two companies merge, one acquires another, or, at the opposite end, a company spins off a division, a new company may be formed. Or, the new entity may simply feel it's a good time for repositioning. In any case, a new name, look, or branding message is likely, and that, in turn, is likely to require big changes on the Web site. (Similarly, some strategic partnerships are so powerful they suggest an opportunity for either creating a new site or freshening up an existing one.)

Redesigning Will Create Hullabaloo

Psst! Redesign your site, and you can generate fresh interest (New! Improved! Better than ever!). You can, for example, send out a press release announcing your new launch. You can send an e-mail announcement to those who've signed up for your mailing list, telling them you listened to their feedback and did something about it. You can do everything you did to publicize and generate excitement for your first launch. Of course, relaunching is expensive, so you don't want to do this too often, and you're best off doing it at a key moment — for example, to coincide with an important trade show or investor meeting — to leverage as much marketing muscle as possible.

You Inherited a Site with (Ahem) Problems

And finally, inevitably, it sometimes happens that a sadly neglected or mismanaged Web site gets new management — management that realizes the sad state of the site. In the face of your inherited site's mysterious directory structure, labyrinthine navigational paths, sorry editorial standards, and unfortunate overuse of animation (three moving pictures on one page?!), your best alternative may be a clean sweep. Reorganize, tidy up that mess, get to know the site, organize the directories, and slap a fresh new face on things. You'll feel a lot better and so will your site's users.

Chapter 22

Ten Pointers Toward Content Management Mastery

In This Chapter

▶ Laying the groundwork for easier maintenance

▶ Choosing content management tools

▶ Making quality a top priority

▶ Establishing quality standards and processes

▶ Tracking feedback and acting on it

*F*or many people, creating content is one thing, and keeping it lined up in those ducky little rows you put it in when you built the site is quite another matter. Things change, you modify your focus, and areas of the site come and go. How can the intrepid Internet professional keep the Web site in order? Read on.

Think Strategically

First, and foremost, don't take the spaghetti-against-the-wall approach. When you create your site plan, define your audience and business goals, and determine what content is most likely to achieve your intended results. Don't assume that having to have *content, community, and commerce* on your site means *articles, chat, and product sales*. Instead, choose what you want to offer and how you position it based on a clear strategic plan. Consider your audience, what they want or need, and what will reach them. Then organize your offerings for excellent usability and easy maintenance. Think of the future; for example, name files so you and your team can find them easily. And in those areas of your site that don't really require daily maintenance, make your content evergreen. Chapters 2 through 8 discuss thinking strategically about your site's offerings and organization.

Automate Processes

You can automate processes for small or mid-sized sites using basic file-sharing and communication techniques as well as site management software. Visto.com and Intranets.com offer some tools; others are built into software products like FrontPage, or in a more high-powered, professional setting, Dreamweaver. Very large sites often use content management software. Content management software can work with the database where your content is stored (see Chapter 13). It usually provides tools for team workflow and version control as well as for facilitating syndication or sharing content with strategic partners and licensees.

Select the Right Software

Content management software is expensive but provides large-scale sites with the tools they need to transcend very big challenges. Good content management tools help you track who has done what in the course of creating, editing, reviewing, and posting the content. The software may offer distinct "work areas" for each content team member, a staging area for testing changes, the opportunity to test using multiple browsers, easy posting to the live server, and so on.

The most important issues are how the software sets up and enforces processes. When you compare the various software packages, look at how each one allows content creators, editors, managers, and others to work on the type of content you have. Some offer more or less automation for scheduling the content workflow, creating relevant links to and from the content, and so on. Check into how the software ensures that content goes through the right channels and gets the right reviews and approvals before it's actually published on the site. You also want to consider whether the product

- ✔ Is a proven solution that other sites or companies like yours are using.
- ✔ Meets technical standards for reliability, robustness, security, scalability, customization, and caching.
- ✔ Is compatible with your back-end systems as well as your projections for growth.
- ✔ Allows you to include your existing content and handle any new content.
- ✔ Has an acceptable level of technical support and training available for your team.

For a checklist showing the specifics of business, technical, version control, workflow, ease of use, and other criteria to consider, visit the E-Commerce Management Center at www.tauberkienan.com.

Make Quality a Priority

You are your Web site. First impressions last, and poor impressions fade slowly. You may have heard the line about airline passengers seeing a coffee pot not working on the plane and extending that into a concern about whether the engine is well maintained. You've almost certainly had the experience of reading along in a print publication, running across a typo, misspelled word, or misplaced phrase, and — blip! — having the reverie of your reading interrupted. On Web sites, errors in the language, broken links or graphics, and mistakes in implementing navigational paths can trip up a smooth user experience. Errors and inconsistencies create a poor impression, distract users from the purpose of your site, and undermine credibility and trustworthiness.

We've seen such disregard for professionalism among some Internet start-ups that one company misspelled its own name four different ways on its own Web site. This could easily have been avoided with a simple process that's familiar to any editor in the print publication world. (And freelance editors are easy enough to hire; see the Bay Area Editors' Forum at `www.editorsforum.org` to find out more.)

Some all too common rationales for skipping over early testing, editorial processes, and final reviews of details by a qualified team have to do with the speed at which most sites are built. Some say they haven't the time for quality checks, the documentation to check against, the personnel, or the budget.

Keep this in mind: Putting your site in order later is more expensive than doing it as you build. Testing late in your building process can leave you painted into corners you can't get out of; if you find that users aren't responding well to key elements in the site, you may not have the budget to scrap the site and start over. Although you may think you don't have the wiggle room in your overall project budget to pay for documentation, remember that reverse-engineering the site and creating documentation later may cost *five times more* than doing it during the process of building the site.

Quality assurance is a two-part process. First, you create (and maintain) a *style guide* (documentation that lists or explains decisions you've made about editorial, design, legal, and other issues that may arise). Then, you use standard quality assurance procedures (a review process) to compare your pages to the policies. Without a style guide, though, you're sunk. In the long run, the hours that you spend creating a style guide equal days shaved off the testing and quality review process. And putting in place a good review process assures everyone who works on and uses the site that the surprises or "gotchas" that often pop up after launch are minimized.

Create a Style Guide

A style guide can be as simple as a list of agreed-upon conventions (in alphabetical order) or as sophisticated as an intranet with sections of the style guide linked to each other. Your style guide may be limited to your specialty in working on the site (a design group or a content group may have its own style guide, for example), or the entire Web site team may use one big, comprehensive style guide.

A comprehensive style guide can cover editorial, branding, design, production, marketing, and legal issues. It should clarify cross-departmental information; for example, how to use logos cuts across marketing, editorial, production, and legal. In general, a style guide may cover:

- ✔ The site's architecture, format, structure, and logic
- ✔ The visual style, or "look and feel" of the site
- ✔ Page layout and coding conventions
- ✔ Graphics and multimedia specs
- ✔ Editorial style standards, content specs, and linking guidelines
- ✔ Legal matters, including guidelines for protecting intellectual property, getting permissions, and using logos and other assets
- ✔ Procedures for creating, testing, reviewing, and approving content

Specifics about which tools to use (HTML editors, validators, image editors, content managers, compression tools) and which not to use also go in the guide. Noting who designs or develops various elements of the site is a great idea. That way, you can go back for more of the same style later. Similarly, note who approves various items (so, for example, you don't have to have the same old tired argument with the CEO that your predecessor had). For a complete checklist, describing what to cover in a style guide see the E-Commerce Management Center at www.tauberkienan.com. For sample style guides, see the Yale C/AIM Style Guide (info.med.yale.edu/caim/manual/) or the Dreamlnk Web Design Guide (www.dreamink.com/).

Make Your Style Guide a Living Document

Generally, we suggest that everyone on a team work from the same style guide, for which we like to create an intranet that everyone can access. To build the guide, you can make one person on the team responsible for documenting key decisions. That person can simply pop the info into folders at first, and then the larger effort of building a style guide can come when some key information is compiled. Remember, though, that the team needs to be able to access the style guide as you build the Web site it documents.

Using agreed-upon conventions as you build your site is going to save a lot of effort in tracking down errors and fixing them in the always-tense days just before the site launches. Make sure that updating the style guide is not a low priority. To be really useful, it has to be a living document everyone can turn to for answers. Link sections of the style guide to each other, and instead of just referring people to online tools (like a Web-safe palette or an HTML reference), actually link to them.

Establish a Workable Review Process

So you've taken an idea and made it a reality. You're just about ready to launch. But hang on a minute; you need to take one more detour before you move forward. The time has come to ask reviewers to take a look before you leap.

One important group of reviewers may be representatives of various departments in your company. Typically, this review occurs before a *soft launch*, which is a launch of the site onto the live server but in a very late beta stage; a soft launch is not announced to the public. Sometimes, another round of this sort of review occurs before the official launch.

Assembling a group of in-house people to bang away at your beta site to test it is also wise. What may seem like an obvious clickpath to you may never cross someone else's mind. Likewise, having a representative sample of your expected users test the site can help you identify problems that arise from the use of different browsers, operating systems, and connection speeds. A testing group that is diverse and that represents your final user base is good for your site and for you.

Clarify the Review Team's Roles

Depending on the policies of your company, you may simply want a single person in the marketing department (or whichever department is ultimately responsible for the site) to review individual pages or whole sections of your site, or you may want to get a number of people involved. A review squad of this type often includes representatives of the editorial, marketing, finance, and legal departments. Even if your company isn't large enough to have an in-house attorney, you may want a qualified legal mind or trained reviewer to examine your content for potential libel and copyright infringement problems. The review process is a good time to clear up issues that are potential legal land mines. Especially if you publish news stories, reviews, or feature pieces (or if you cater to minors or face other liability issues), you may want to consult a qualified professional who's trained in issues of Internet law before sending out your proverbial message in a bottle.

The review team must understand the scope of the feedback that you expect from them. You want the marketing people, for example, to look at marketing-related issues and the legal people to look at legal issues. You don't want the legal people waxing on about their impressions of the colors chosen, and you don't want the marketing people rewriting the legalese to make it warmer and fuzzier (at least not without the legal group's participation and approval). Typically, members of a review team have these roles:

- Web developers or technology people test for usability and functionality.

- Marketing people look at the use of logos, slogans, colors, and overall compliance with branding guidelines.

- Members of the legal group review for issues of liability, protection of assets, and so on.

- The content, editorial, and production people look at layout, usage, style, and details of usability.

- A selected group of "typical" users or a focus group test for its responses to usability and overall appeal.

You can outsource testing to a professional testing lab; if so, the internal review by key management or their representatives is still likely to be crucial. Large companies may also have specialized internal testing groups. In any case, clarify the roles of testing teams, and make sure they know when you need feedback from them and in what form.

Before you approach the review team, decide on the most efficient way to conduct the review. You may want to simply send each person a copy of the documents and have him or her respond by e-mail. Or, you may choose to put your pride and joy on a staging server and have everyone you've chosen take a look. If you use content management software, it undoubtedly provides methods for showing material to the review team.

Whatever your approach, give everyone a deadline for sending in feedback. Make that date a tad before you actually need the comments and well before you must post the corrected material. You don't want any delays. Besides, some office joker has probably set up a pool to predict the date you'll finally launch. Surprise them all by meeting your own deadlines.

Put Your Style Guide through the Review Process

To test your review processes and your style guide, and to rehearse your overall quality assurance procedures, run your style guide through the review process. This, of course, assumes the style guide has been created as an intranet; testing your style guide isn't necessary if it exists only in the form of a list in a Word document.

Track Feedback and Act on It

Getting feedback is one thing. Tracking it and doing something about it is another. If you use content management software, it probably provides you with tools for tracking feedback and the fixes that usually must follow hot on the heels of feedback. If you're working sans content management software, create a matrix that tracks the review team feedback, user feedback, and what fixes are implemented. You can set up a simple spreadsheet that does the job of tracking both content fixes and bug fixes. (Alternatively, special bug-fix-tracking software is also available.) Remember to list the filenames of the pages that your team reviews to make implementing the fixes easier for your team, and set up a system for communicating to everyone involved that specific fixes have occurred.

Managing content well, setting professional standards, creating a style guide, and conducting a review and approval process goes a long way toward providing your site's users with an excellent experience at your Web site. Having a good style guide shortens your quality assurance cycle. It also provides the opportunity for consistency on your site despite staff turnover. (If you don't have a style guide, information has to be passed on as verbal lore, and everyone knows that even the clearest messages change as they're whispered down the line.)

Nothing marks a pro like professional standards. And you are an Internet professional, aren't you?

Index

• D •

Notes

FOR DUMMIES
BOOK REGISTRATION

Register This Book and Win!

We want to hear from you!

Visit **dummies.com** to register this book and tell us how you liked it!

- Get entered in our monthly prize giveaway.

- Give us feedback about this book — tell us what you like best, what you like least, or maybe what you'd like to ask the author and us to change!

- Let us know any other *For Dummies* topics that interest you.

Your feedback helps us determine what books to publish, tells us what coverage to add as we revise our books, and lets us know whether we're meeting your needs as a *For Dummies* reader. You're our most valuable resource, and what you have to say is important to us!

Not on the Web yet? It's easy to get started with *Dummies 101: The Internet For Windows 98* or *The Internet For Dummies* at local retailers everywhere.

Or let us know what you think by sending us a letter at the following address:

For Dummies Book Registration
Dummies Press
10475 Crosspoint Blvd.
Indianapolis, IN 46256

BESTSELLING BOOK SERIES